I0754922

SIR JOHN FRANKLIN, CAPT R N

John Franklin

THE

United States Grinnell Expedition

IN SEARCH OF

SIR JOHN FRANKLIN.

A Personal Narrative.

BY

ELISHA KENT KANE, M.D., U. S. N.

NEW EDITION.

NEW YORK:
SHELDON, BLAKEMAN & CO., 115 NASSAU ST.
PHILADELPHIA:
CHILDS & PETERSON, 124 ARCH ST.
1857.

PRINTED BY DEACON & PETERSON.
PHILADELPHIA.

Sold only by Subscription.

TO

HENRY GRINNELL,

THE AUTHOR, AND ADVOCATE, AND PATRON OF THE UNITED STATES' EXPEDITION IN SEARCH OF SIR JOHN FRANKLIN,

This Volume is Inscribed.

NOTE.

It may apologize, perhaps, for some imperfections in this book, to mention, that the greater portion of it has gone through the press without the author's revisal. While he was engaged in preparing it, the liberality of Mr. Grinnell, of New York, and Mr. Peabody, of London, enabled him to set on foot a second Polar Expedition, which sailed under his command on the 31st of May last. It was his purpose to remodel some of the chapters, and to add one or two on collateral topics, if his time had not been engrossed by the preparations for his departure.

July, 1853.

A SKETCH

OF THE

LIFE OF SIR JOHN FRANKLIN.

From "Allibone's Dictionary of Literature and Authors."

SIR JOHN FRANKLIN, an eminent navigator, born 1786, at Spilsby, Lincolnshire, entered the Royal Navy as a midshipman in 1800, was present at the battle of Trafalgar in 1806 and the battle of New Orleans in 1814, and was selected in 1819 to head an expedition overland from Hudson's Bay to the Arctic Ocean. After encountering great hardships, and very frequently at the point of death from hunger and fatigue, he reached home in October, 1822. In the next year he was married to Miss Porden. In 1825 he submitted to Lord Bathurst "a plan for an expedition overland, to the mouth of the Mackenzie River, and thence by sea, to the northwest extremity of America, with the combined object also of surveying the coast between the Mackenzie and Copper Mine Rivers."

This proposition was accepted; and, to superintend the expedition, he embarked at Liverpool, February 16, 1825, after the "severe struggle of taking leave of his wife, whose death, then hourly expected, took place six days after his departure."

After encountering great hardships, the moving masses of ice forced the heroic sailors to retrace their steps. September 1, 1827, Captain Franklin arrived at Liverpool, married a second time in November of the following year, and in 1829 received the honor of knighthood. The persevering zeal of Lady Franklin in stimulating the search for

Sir John, for ten years past, is well known to the world. He was greatly disappointed at his unsuccessful attempts to accomplish the object of his voyages; remarking, with reference to his compulsory return in 1827 :—

"It was with no ordinary pain that I could now bring myself even to think of relinquishing the great object of my ambition, [the discovery of a northwest passage from the Atlantic to the Pacific Ocean,] and of disappointing the flattering hopes which had been reposed in my exertions. But I had higher duties to perform than the gratification of my own feelings; and a mature consideration of all things forced me to the conclusion that we had reached that point beyond which perseverance would be rashness and the best efforts would be fruitless."

The Montreal Gazette of September 11, 1822, remarks:—

"It appears that the toils and sufferings of the expedition have been of the most trying description, and that, if they do not exceed belief, they were at least of such a nature as almost to overcome the stoutest heart, and deter all future attempts of a similar tendency."

But this writer little knew the iron stuff of which Sir John Franklin was made.

On the 26th of May, 1845, Sir John started upon a third expedition, in two ships, the Erebus and Terror; he was heard from on the 26th of July of the same year, and passed his first winter in a cove between Cape Riley and Beechy Island. Since that period, many expeditions from England and America have been despatched in search of the adventurer; but it was not until November, 1854, that news reached England, which leaves little doubt that the whole party perished in the winter of 1850–51. See London Gentleman's Magazine, November, 1854, 749; December, 1854, 594–95. Since the above was written, we have further intelligence,—by the return of Mr. James G. Stuart's expedition, despatched by the British Hudson's Bay Company, 18th November, 1854; arrived at St. Paul, Minnesota, 10th December, 1855,—which places beyond all doubt the loss of Sir John Franklin and his party. Some of their shoes, cooking-utensils, &c. were found among the Esquimaux, who declared that they had died of starvation

By a curious coincidence, on the day that we are penning this article, (October 11, 1855,) the last expedition—sent specially in search of Dr. Kane and his party—which sailed from New York in June, 1855, has arrived at home. The explorers bring with them Dr. Kane and all of his company save three,—a carpenter, a cook, and a seaman, lost by death. The remainder of the party are more or less frost-bitten. Of the last expedition—the steamer (propeller) Arctic, Lieutenant Simms, and the barque Release, Lieutenant Hartstene—the Arctic (Lieutenant Hartstene was on board) made its way north to latitude 78° 32′, when it was stopped by the ice. The Advance, Dr. Kane's vessel, had been pushed as far north as possible, when she was frozen in, and of course had to be abandoned. The ship's company were found by the Arctic and Release on the island of Disco. They have been absent from home since May 31, 1853, and are received with great rejoicings. They have made several important discoveries, and added largely to our knowledge of the inhospitable region the perils and discomforts of which they have so bravely encountered.

* * * * * *

The reader who desires to pursue this interesting topic must refer to the following publications:—1. Captain John Franklin's Narrative of a Journey to the Shores of the Polar Sea, 1819–22, with an Appendix on various Subjects relating to Science and Natural History, London, 1823, 4to, pp. 784; 34 Plates and four Maps, £4 4*s*. The Appendix on Natural History is by Sir John Richardson, Sabine, Lieutenant Hood, &c. The plates are beautifully engraved by Finden (some of them colored) after drawings by Lieutenants Hood and Back. A second and third edition were published in 1824, both in 2 vols. 8vo, without the plates.

Also an edition in Philadelphia, 8vo, same year.

"The unstudied and seamanlike simplicity of the style is not the least of its merits; and the illustrations and embellishments, from the drawings of the late unfortunate Mr. Hood, and Mr. Back, are of a very superior kind."—*London Quarterly Review.*

"A work of intense and indeed painful interest, from the sufferings of those who performed this journey: of value to geography by no means proportional to these sufferings; but instructive in meteorology and natural history."—*Stevenson's Voyages and Travels.*

2. Captain John Franklin's Narrative of a Second Expedition to the Shores of the Polar Sea, 1825–27; including an Account of the Progress of a Detachment to the Eastward, by John Richardson, M.D., F.R.S., &c., Surgeon and Naturalist to the Expedition. Illustrated by numerous Maps and Plates, 1828, 4to, pp. 447, £4 4*s*. The Second Expedition has not in England been published in 8vo, but see below.

"The views of Arctic Scenery with which this volume is both illustrated and embellished are of extreme beauty. They supply, in a great measure, the absence of picturesque description, and delineate, with singular truth, the striking peculiarities which distinguish the aspect of these regions from that of the temperate climates."—*Edin. Review.*

"It is difficult to do sufficient justice either to the skill and intelligence displayed in its conduct, or the information to be derived from it."—*American Quarterly Review.*

There is an edition published in 1829, London, 4 vols. 18mo, of Sir John Franklin's Two Journeys to the Shores of the Polar Sea, in 1819–27, with engravings by Finden, £1. An edition of the second expedition was published in Philadelphia, 1828, 8vo.

The reader must also peruse—1. Mr. P. L. Simmonds's account of Sir John Franklin and the Arctic Regions, 1851, 12mo; 2d ed., 1852, 12mo; 3d ed., 1853, 12mo. 2. Papers and Correspondence relative to the Arctic Expedition under Sir John Franklin. Ordered by the House of Commons to be printed, March 5, 1850–52, fol. 3. The Franklin Expedition, or Considerations on Measures for the Discovery and Relief of our Absent Adventurers in the Arctic Regions; with Maps, by the Rev. W. Scoresby, D.D., 1850. 4. Arctic Searching Expedition: a Journal of a Boat Voyage through Rupert's Land and the Arctic Sea, in Search of the Discovery Ships under Command of Sir John Franklin; with an Appendix on the Physical Geography of North America. By Sir John Richardson, M.D., F.R.S., &c., Inspector of Hospitals and Fleets. Published by Authority of the Admiralty. With a colored Map, several Plates printed in Colors, and Woodcuts, 2 vols. 8vo.

"Valuable alike to the scientific student or the future wanderer over these wild plains, and the lonely settler whom European enterprise may locate among these far-distant tribes. It is a book to study rather than to read; and yet so attractive in its style, and so instructive in its collation of facts, that many will be led to its study as a work of science whilst merely engaged in its perusal as a book of travels."—*Brittania.*

5. A Lecture on Arctic Expeditions, delivered at the London Institution, by C. R. Weld, Esq. Second edition, Map, post 8vo.

"An intelligent general view of the subject of Arctic Discovery from early times, a rapid but well-informed sketch of its heroes and its vicissitudes in modern days, a hopeful view of the chances of Franklin's return, and an account of the circumstances of the original expedition and of the voyages in search, which will be read with considerable interest just now."—*London Examiner.*

6. Article entitled Attempts to find a Northwest Passage, in North American Review, lxix. 1; and the following articles on Sir John Franklin and the Arctic Regions: 7. North American Review, lxxi. 168. 8. New York Eclectic Magazine, xx. 60. 9, 10. Boston Living Age, (from the London Examiner,) xxiv. 275 and 279. Search for Sir John Franklin. 11. Fraser's Magazine, xliii. 198; same article, New York Eclectic Magazine, xxii. 420. 12. Fraser's Magazine, xliv. 502. 13. Boston Living Age, (from the London New Monthly Magazine,) xxxi. 291. Second Expedition of Sir John Franklin. 14. London Quarterly Review, xxxviii. 335. 15, 16. London Monthly Review, cii. 1, 156; 17. South Review, iii. 261. Track of Sir John Franklin. 18. New York Eclectic Magazine, xxii. 112. Also, 19. Meares, J., Voyages made in 1788–89 from China to the Northwest Coast of America; with Observations on the Existence of a Northwest Passage, &c., maps and plates, 1790, 4to.

To the above must be added—20. Dr. Elisha Kent Kane's Narrative of the Expedition in search of Sir John Franklin, New York, 1854, 8vo, the Voyages of Beechy, Parry and Ross, Back's Arctic Expedition, Sabine's North Georgia Gazette, 1821, 4to, and A Souvenir of the late Polar Search, by the Officers and Seamen of the Expedition, 1852, 8vo. Nor must the Historical Accounts and numerous essays of Sir

John Barrow upon this subject be overlooked by the reader. We are promised another work from Dr. Kane, who, as mentioned above, has returned this day from a fruitless search after Sir John Franklin. Upon the subject of a Northwest Passage we append an interesting paper:—

"THE EFFORTS MADE TO DISCOVER A NORTHWEST PASSAGE.

"The attempt to discover a northwest passage was made by a Portuguese named Cortereal, about A.D. 1500. It was attempted by the English in 1553; and the project was greatly encouraged by Queen Elizabeth in 1585, in which year a company was associated in London, and was called the 'Fellowship for the Discovery of the Northwest Passage.' The following voyages with this design were undertaken, under British and American navigators, in the years respectively stated:—

Sir Hugh Willoughby's expedition to find a northwest passage to China sailed from the Thames........................May 20, 1553
Sir Martin Frobisher's attempt to find a northwest passage to China....... 1576
Captain Davis's expedition to find a northwest passage........................ 1585
Barentz's expedition.. 1594
Weymouth and Knight's.. 1602
Hudson's voyages; the last undertaken.. 1610
Sir Thomas Button's.. 1612
Baffin's.. 1616
Foxe's expedition.. 1631
(A number of enterprises, undertaken by various countries, followed.)
Middleton's expedition.. 1742
Moore and Smith's.. 1746
Hearne's land expedition.. 1769
Captain Phipps, afterwards Lord Mulgrave, his expedition.................. 1773
Captain Cook, in the Resolution and Discovery............................July, 1776
Mackenzie's expedition.. 1789
Captain Duncan's voyage.. 1790
The Discovery, Captain Vancouver, returned from a voyage of survey and discovery on the northwest coast of America........................Sept. 24, 1795
Lieutenant Kotzebue's expedition...Oct. 1815
Captain Buchan and Lieutenant Franklin's expedition in the Dorothea and Trent.. 1818
Captain Ross and Lieutenant Parry, in the Isabella and Alexander.......... 1818
Lieutenants Parry and Liddon, in the Hecla and Griper.. ....May 4, 1819
They return to Leith..Nov. 3, 1820
Captains Parry and Lyon, in the Fury and Hecla.......................May 8, 1821
Captain Parry's third expedition with the Hecla........................May 8, 1824
Captains Franklin and Lyon, after having attempted a land expedition, again sail from Liverpool..Feb. 16, 1825
Captain Parry, again in the Hecla, sails from Deptford...........March 25, 1827
And returns..Oct. 6, 1827

Captain John Ross arrived at Hull, on his return from his Arctic expedi tion, after an absence of four years, and when all hope of his return had been nearly abandoned ....Oct. 18, 1833

Captain Back and his companions arrived at Liverpool from their perilous Arctic land expedition, after having visited the Great Fish River, and examined its course to the Polar Seas............Sept. 8, 1835

Captain Back sailed from Chatham in command of His Majesty's ship Terror, on an exploring adventure to Wager River. Captain Back, in the month of December, 1835, was awarded, by the Geographical Society, the King's annual premium for his polar discoveries and enterprise............June 21, 1836

Dease and Simpson traverse the intervening space between the discoveries of Ross and the Castor and Pollux River............Oct. 1839

Sir John Franklin and Captain Crozier, in the Erebus and Terror, leave England............May 24, 1845

Captain James Ross returned from an unsuccessful expedition in search of Franklin............ 1849

Another expedition (one sent out by Lady Franklin) in search of Sir John Franklin, consisting of two vessels, sailed from England.....April–May, 1850

Another, under Captain M'Clure, who succeeded in effecting a transit over ice from ocean to ocean; and another under Sir Edward Belcher......... 1851

Another, consisting of two vessels, the Advance and Rescue, liberally purchased for the purpose by Henry Grinnell, a New York merchant, and manned at government cost from the United States navy, under command of Lieutenant De Haven, sailed from New York..........May, 1850

The expedition of Dr. Kane, in the Advance. Kane discovered the open Polar Sea, in latitude 82° 30′ N............May 31, 1853

The last expedition, consisting of the Release and Arctic, under Lieutenant Hartstene, sailed............June, 1855

He reached the highest north latitude next to Kane, and returns...Oct. 11, 1855

"There may be some omissions in the above, but it will be found generally correct."

CONTENTS.

CHAPTER XI.

CHAPTER XII.

CHAPTER XIII.

CHAPTER XIV.

CHAPTER XV.

CHAPTER XVI.

CHAPTER XVII.

CHAPTER XVIII.

CHAPTER XIX.

CHAPTER XX.

CHAPTER XXI.

CHAPTER XXII.

CHAPTER XXIII.

CHAPTER XXIV.

CHAPTER XXV.

CHAPTER XXVI.

CHAPTER XXVII.

CHAPTER XXVIII.

CHAPTER XXIX.

CHAPTER XXX.

CHAPTER XXXI.

CHAPTER XXXII.

CHAPTER XXXIII.

CHAPTER XXXIV.

CHAPTER XXXV.

CHAPTER XXXVI.

CHAPTER XXXVII.

CHAPTER XXXVIII.

CHAPTER XXXIX.

CHAPTER XL.

CHAPTER XLI.

CHAPTER XLII.

CHAPTER XLIII.

CHAPTER XLIV.

CHAPTER XLV.

CHAPTER XLVI.

CHAPTER XLVII.

CHAPTER XLVIII.

CHAPTER XLIX.

CHAPTER L.

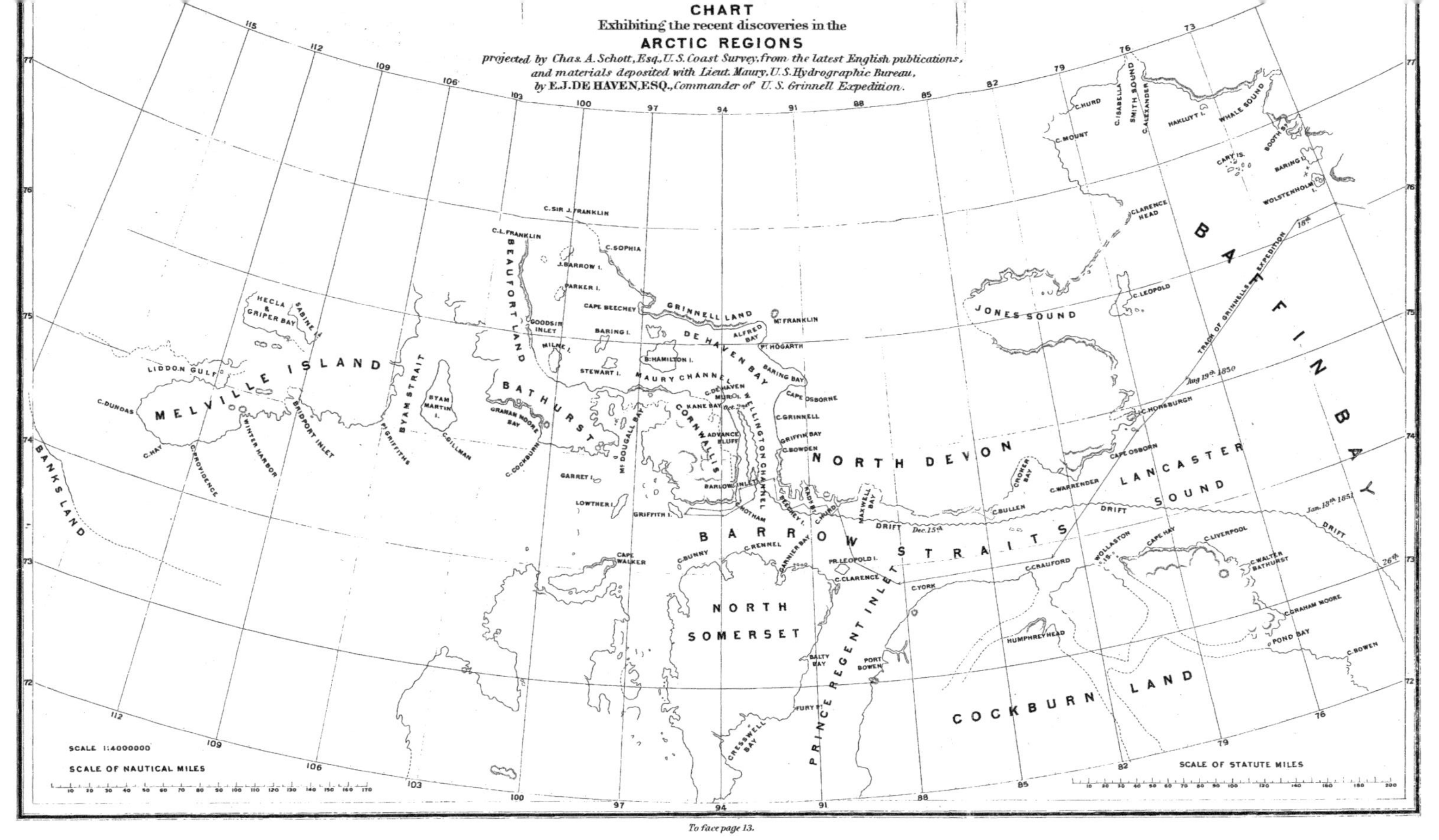

To face page 13.

United States Grinnell Expedition.

CHAPTER I.

INTRODUCTORY.

THE region which is known on our maps as the Arctic Ocean is inclosed between the northern shores of Asia, Europe, and America. It has an area of about four and a half millions of square miles: its tributary waters exceed those of the Western Atlantic from Hudson's Bay to the Caribbean; and it girds the Pole with an ice-locked coast of nearly three thousand marine leagues: it is a mysterious sea, that has baffled for centuries the research of navigators. One of the more recent attempts to penetrate its recesses will form the subject of this volume.

About the year 1816, the notion of a northwestern passage, which had fallen for a time into the same category with the El Dorado and the Cathay of a less practical era, began to find favor with the British government. The spirit of private enterprise took the same direction. Year after year expedition followed expedition, under commanders of tried gallantry and intelligence. But they all came back without traversing the forbidden channel; bearing contributions, indeed, to our knowledge of its character and aspects, but accumulating proofs also of the hazards of exploring even its barrier.

It was in 1844 that Sir John Franklin was appointed to the charge of his latest Polar expedition. His first visit to the Arctic regions had been in 1818, as a captain in Commodore Buchan's squadron; and after this had returned unsuccessful, he had headed that most fearful of all the overland journeys of our period, the descent to the mouth of the Coppermine River. Still later, in 1825, he had gone back to the same field of toil, and had delineated, in conjunction with Sir John Richardson, the more western portions of Arctic America.

No officer could have been found in the marine of any country who combined more admirable qualifications for the duties of an explorer. To the resolute enterprise and powers of endurance, which his former expeditions had tested so severely, Sir John Franklin united many delightful traits of character. With an enthusiasm almost boyish, he had a spirit of large but fearless forecast, and a sensitive kindness of heart that commiserated every one but himself. He is remembered to this day among the Indians of North America, as "the great chief who would not kill a mosquito."

His vessels, the Erebus and Terror, were soon fitted for sea; and on the 25th of May, 1845, he weighed anchor, with a picked crew, and as noble a band of officers as ever volunteered for a service of peril. They were met by a whaler on the 26th of July following, in the upper waters of Baffin's Bay, moored to an iceberg, and waiting for an opening in "the pack." They have not been seen since.

When the year 1848 had arrived without any tidings of this gallant party, Great Britain dispatched three separate expeditions to reclaim them. These were well devised; but peculiar drawbacks seemed to attend their efforts, and before the beginning of 1850 they had all abandoned the search, almost without attaining the first threshold of inquiry.

Their failure aroused every where the generous sympathies of men. Science felt for its votaries, humanity mourned its fellows, and an impulse, holier and more energetic than either, invoked a crusade of rescue. That admirable woman, the wife of Sir John Franklin, not content with stimulating the renewed efforts of her own countrymen, claimed the co-operation of the world. In letters to the President of the United States, full of the eloquence of feeling, she called on us, as a "kindred people, to join heart and hand in the enterprise of snatching the lost navigators from a dreary grave."

The delays incident to much of our national legislation menaced the defeat of her appeal. The bill making appropriations for the outfit of an expedition lingered on its passage, and the season for commencing operations had nearly gone by. At this juncture, a noble-spirited merchant of New York, of whom as an American and a man I can hardly trust myself to speak, fitted out two of his own vessels, and proffered them gratuitously to the government. Thus prompted by the munificent liberality of Mr. Grinnell, Congress hastened to take the expedition under its charge, and authorized the president to detail from the navy such necessary officers and seamen as might be willing to engage in it.

Though I accompanied this expedition as its senior medical officer, I had no claim to be considered as its historian. Such a province belonged strictly to our commander; but he having declined making any other than an official report, I have been invited to prepare a history of the cruise, under the form of a personal narrative. I had promised my brother at parting, that I would keep a journal, to furnish topics, perhaps, for a fireside conversation; and I have chosen to draw most of my materials from this record. I might have done more wisely, if I had been content to substitute sometimes the educated opinions of others for those which impressed me at the moment. My apology must be, that I do not profess to be accurate, but truthful.

CHAPTER II.

On the 12th of May, while bathing in the tepid waters of the Gulf of Mexico, I received one of those courteous little epistles from Washington which the electric telegraph has made so familiar to naval officers. It detached me from the coast survey, and ordered me to "proceed forthwith to New York, for duty upon the Arctic Expedition."

Seven and a half days later, I had accomplished my overland journey of thirteen hundred miles, and in forty hours more our squadron was beyond the limits of the United States: the Department had calculated my traveling time to a nicety.

During the fraction of a day that was left me at New York, I strove assiduously to secure a few implements for scientific observation, as well as to get together the elements of an Arctic wardrobe. I had, of course, the zealous aid of Mr. Grinnell in these hurried arrangements; but I could not help being struck with the universal sympathy displayed toward our expedition. From the ladies who busied themselves in sealing up air-tight packages of fruit-cakes, to the managers of the Astor House, who insisted that their hotel should be the free head-quarters of our party, it was one continued round of proffered services. I should have a long list of citizens to thank if I were allowed to name them on these pages.

It was not, perhaps, to be expected that an expedition equipped so hastily as ours, and with one engrossing object, should have facilities for observing very accurately, or go out of its way to find matters for curious research. But even the routine of a national ship might, I was confident, allow us to gather something for the stock of general knowledge. With the assistance of Professor Loomis, I collected as I could some simple instruments for thermal and magnetic registration, which would have been of use if they had found their way on board. A very few books for the dark hours of winter, and a stock of coarse woolen clothing, re-enforced by a magnificent robe of wolf-skins, that had wandered down to me from the snow-drifts of Utah, constituted my entire outfit; and with these I made my report to Commodore Salter at the Brooklyn Navy Yard.

Almost within the shadow of the line-of-battle ship North Carolina, their hulls completely hidden beneath a projecting wharf, were two little hermaphrodite brigs. Their spars had no man-of-war trigness; their decks were choked with half-stowed cargo; and for size, I felt as if I could straddle from the main hatch to the bulwarks.

At this first sight of the Grinnell Expedition, I confess that the fastidious experience of naval life on board frigates and corvettes made me look down on these humble vessels. They seemed to me more like a couple of coasting schooners than a national squadron bound for a perilous and distant sea. Many a time afterward I recalled the short-sighted ignorance of these first impressions, when some rude encounter with the ice made comfort and dignity very secondary thoughts.

The "Advance," my immediate home, had been originally intended for the transport of machinery. Her timbers were heavily moulded, and her fastenings of the most careful sort. She was fifty-three tons larger than her consort, the "Rescue;" yet both together barely equaled two hundred and thirty-five tons.

To navigate an ice-bound sea, speed, though important, is much less so than strength. Extreme power of resistance to pressure must be combined with facility of handling, adequate stowage, and a solidity of frame that may encounter sudden concussions fearlessly; and it seemed to both Mr. Grinnell and Lieutenant De Haven that these qualities might be best embodied in such small vessels as the Advance and Rescue. It was, indeed, something like a return to the dimensions of our predecessors of the olden time; for the three vessels of Frobisher summed up only seventy-five tons, and Baffin's largest was ten tons less in burden than the Rescue. As the vessels of our expedition were more thoroughly adapted, perhaps, for this dangerous service than any that had been fitted out before for the Arctic Seas, I will describe them in detail.

Commencing with the outside: the hull was literally double, a brig within a brig. An outer sheathing of two and a half inch oak was covered with a second of the same material; and strips of heavy sheet-iron extended from the bows to the beam, as a shield against the cutting action of the new ice. The decks were double, made water-tight by a packing of tarred felt between them. The entire interior was lined, *ceiled*, with cork; which, independently of its low conducting power, was a valuable protection against the condensing moisture, one of the greatest evils of the polar climate.

The strengthening of her skeleton, her wooden frame-work, was admirable. Forward, from kelson to deck, was a mass of solid timber, clamped and dove-tailed with nautical wisdom, for seven feet from the cutwater; so that we could spare a foot or two of our bows without springing a leak. To prevent the ice from forcing in her sides, she was built with an extra set of beams running athwart her length at intervals of four feet, and so arranged as to ship and unship at pleasure. From the Samson-posts, strong radiating timbers, called shores, diverged in every direction; and oaken knees, hanging and oblique, were added wherever space permitted.

Looking forward to the hampering ice fields, our rudder was so constructed that it could be taken on board and replaced again in less than four minutes. Our winch, capstan, and patent windlass were of the best and newest construction.

A little hurricane-house amidships contained the one galley that cooked for all hands, and a large funnel of galvanized iron was connected with the chimney, in such a way that the heat circulating round it might supply us with melted snow. An armorer's forge, a full set of ice anchors, a couple of well-built whale-boats, and three anthracite stoves, made part of the outfit.

In a word, every thing about the two vessels bore the marks of intelligent foresight and unsparing expenditure.

With the governmental arrangements we were not so fortunate. It seems to be inseparable from national as well as corporate administration, that it is less effective than the action of individuals. Neither our own navy nor that of Great Britain attains results so cheaply, promptly, or well, as the commercial marine; and it is a fact, only expressed from a sad conviction of its truth, that, in spite of the disciplined intelligence of many of our officers, the naval service of the public is regarded among our merchant brethren, and by the community they belong to, as non-progressive and old-fashioned in all that admits of comparison between the two. They excel us in equipment, and speed, and substantial economy.

I can not, then, say much in praise of either the dispatch or excellence of our strictly naval equipment. There were other things, besides the diminutive size of our brigs, to remind one of the days of the ancient mariners. Some that were matters of serious vexation at the moment may be forgotten now, or remembered with a smile. Our heterogeneous collection of obsolete old carbines, with the impracticable ball-cartridges that accompanied them, gave us many a laugh before we got home. Thanks to the incessant labors of our commander, and the exhaustless liberality of Mr. Grinnell, most of our deficiencies were made up, and we effected our departure in time for the navigation of Baffin's Bay.

Our crews consisted of man-of-war's-men of various

climes and habitudes, with constitutions most of them impaired by disease, or temporarily broken by the excesses of shore life. But this original defect of material was in a great degree counteracted by the strict and judicious discipline of our executive officers. The crews proved in the end willing and reliable; and, in the midst of trials which would have tested men of more pretension, were never found to waver. I record, in the commencement of this narrative, how much respect and kindly feeling I, as one of their little body, entertain for their essential contribution to the ends of the expedition.

Of my brother officers I can not say a word. I am so intimately bound to them by the kindly and unbroken associations of friend and mess-mate, that I shrink from any other mention of them than such as my narrative requires. All told, our little corps of officers numbered four for each ship, including that non-effective limb, the doctor. Our two crews, with the aid of a cook and steward, counted twelve and thirteen; giving a total of but thirty-three, whose distribution and positions will be seen in the accompanying list.

ADVANCE.

Officers.

Lieutenant Commanding—Edwin J. De Haven, commanding the expedition.
Passed Midshipman—William H. Murdaugh, acting master and first officer.
Midshipman—William I. Lovell, second officer.
E. K. Kane, M.D., passed assistant surgeon.

Crew.

William Morton, Henry De Roque, John Blinn, Gibson Caruthers, Thomas Dunning, William West, Charles Berry, Louis Costa, William Holmes, Edward Wilson, William Benson, Edward C. Delano, James Smith.

RESCUE.

Officers.

Acting Master—Samuel P. Griffin, commanding the Rescue.
Passed Midshipman—Robert R. Carter, acting master and first officer.
Boatswain—Henry Brooks, second officer.
Benjamin Vreeland, M.D., assistant surgeon.

Crew.

William J Kurner, Auguste Canot, John Williams, Robert Bruce, William Lincoln, Smith Benjamin, Rufus C. Baggs, David Davis, James Johnson, James Stewart, Alexander Daly, H. J. White.—Total, 33.

CHAPTER III.

About one o'clock on the 22d of May, the asthmatic old steam-tug that was to be our escort to the sea moved slowly off. Our adieux from the Navy Yard were silent enough. We cost our country no complimentary gunpowder; and it was not until we got abreast of the city that the crowded wharves and shipping showed how much that bigger community sympathized with our undertaking. Cheers and hurras followed us till we had passed the Battery, and the ferry-boats and steamers came out of their track to salute us in the bay.

The sky was overcast before we lost sight of the spire of old Trinity; and by evening it had clouded over so rapidly, that it was evident we had to look for a dirty night outside. Off Sandy Hook the wind freshened, and the sea grew so rough, that we were forced to part abruptly from the friends who had kept us company. We were eating and drinking in our little cabin, when the summons came for them to hurry up instantly and leap aboard the boat. The same heavy squall which made us cast loose so suddenly the cable of the steamer gathered upon us the night and the storm together; and in a few minutes our transition was complete, from harbor life and home associations to the discomforts and hardships of our career.

The difference struck me, and not quite pleasantly, as I climbed over straw and rubbish into the little peculium which was to be my resting-place for so long a time. The cabin, which made the homestead of four human beings, was somewhat less in dimensions than a penitentiary cell. There was just room enough for two berths of six feet each on a side; and the area between, which is known to naval men as "the country," seemed completely filled up with the hinged table, the four camp-stools, and the lockers. A hanging lamp, that creaked uneasily on its "gimbals," illustrated through the mist some long rows of crockery shelves and the dripping step-ladder that led directly from the wet deck above. Every thing spoke of cheerless discomfort and narrow restraint.

By the next day the storm had abated. We were out of sight of land, but had not yet parted with the last of our well-wishers. A beautiful pilot-boat, the Washington, with Mr. Grinnell and his sons on board, continued to bear us company. But on the 25th we saw the white flag hoisted as the signal of farewell. We closed up our letters and took them aboard, drank healths, shook hands—and the wind being fair, were out of sight of the schooner before evening.

I now began, with an instinct of future exigencies, to fortify my retreat. The only spot I could call my own was the berth I have spoken of before. It was a sort of *bunk*—a right-angled excavation, of six feet by two feet eight in horizontal dimensions, let into the side of the vessel, with a height of something less than a yard. My first care was to keep water out, my second to make it warm. A bundle of tacks, and a few yards of India-rubber cloth, soon made me an impenetrable casing over the entire wood-work. Upon this were laid my Mormon wolf-skin and a somewhat ostentatious Astracan fur cloak, a relic of former travel. Two little wooden shelves held my scanty library; a third supported a reading lamp, or, upon occasion, a Berzelius' argand, to be lighted when the dampness made an increase of heat necessary. My watch ticked from its particular nail, and a more noiseless monitor, my thermometer, occupied another. My ink-bottle was suspended, pendulum fashion, from a hook, and to one long string was fastened, like the ladle of a street-pump, my entire toilet, a tooth-brush, a comb, and a hair-brush.

Now, when all these distributions had been happily accomplished, and I crawled in from the wet, and cold, and disorder of without, through a slit in the India-rubber cloth, to the very centre of my complicated resources, it would be hard for any one to realize the quantity of comfort which I felt I had manufactured. My lamp burned brightly; little or no water distilled from the roof; my furs warmed me into satisfaction; and I realized that I was sweating myself out of my preliminary cold, and could temper down at pleasure the abruptness of my acclimation.

From this time I began my journal. At first its entries were little else than a selfish record of personal discomforts. It was less than a fortnight since I was under the sky of Florida, looking out on the live oak with its bearded moss, and breathing the magnolia. Comfortable as my bunk was, compared with the deck, I was conscious that, on the whole, I had not bettered my quarters.

But with the 7th of June came fine, bright, bracing weather. We were off Newfoundland, getting along well over a smooth sea. We had been looking at the low hills near Cape Race, when, about noon, a great mass of whiteness was seen floating in the sunshine. It was our first iceberg. It was in shape an oblong cube, and about twice as large as Girard College. Its color was an unmixed, but not dazzling white: indeed, it seemed entirely coated with snow of such unsullied, unreflecting purity, that, as we passed within a hundred yards of it, not a glitter reached us. It reminded me of a great marble monolith, only awaiting the chisel to stand out in peristyle and pediment a floating Parthenon. There was something very imposing in the impassive tranquillity with which it received the lashings of the sea.

The next day we were off St. John's, surrounded by bergs, which nearly blockaded the harbor. A boat's crew of six brawny Saxon men rowed out nine miles to meet us, and offer their services as pilots. They were disappointed when we told them we were "bound for Greenland;" but their hearty countenances brightened into a glow when we added, "in search of Sir John Franklin."

We ran into an iceberg the night after, and carried away our jib-boom and martingale: it was our first adventure with these mountains of the sea. We thumped against it for a few seconds, but slid off smoothly enough into open water afterward. Two days later, we met a *school* of fin-backed whales, great, crude, wallowing sea-hogs, snorting out fountains of white spray, and tumbling, porpoise fashion, one over another about the vessel. My journal compares them to a huge old-fashioned India-rubber shoe.

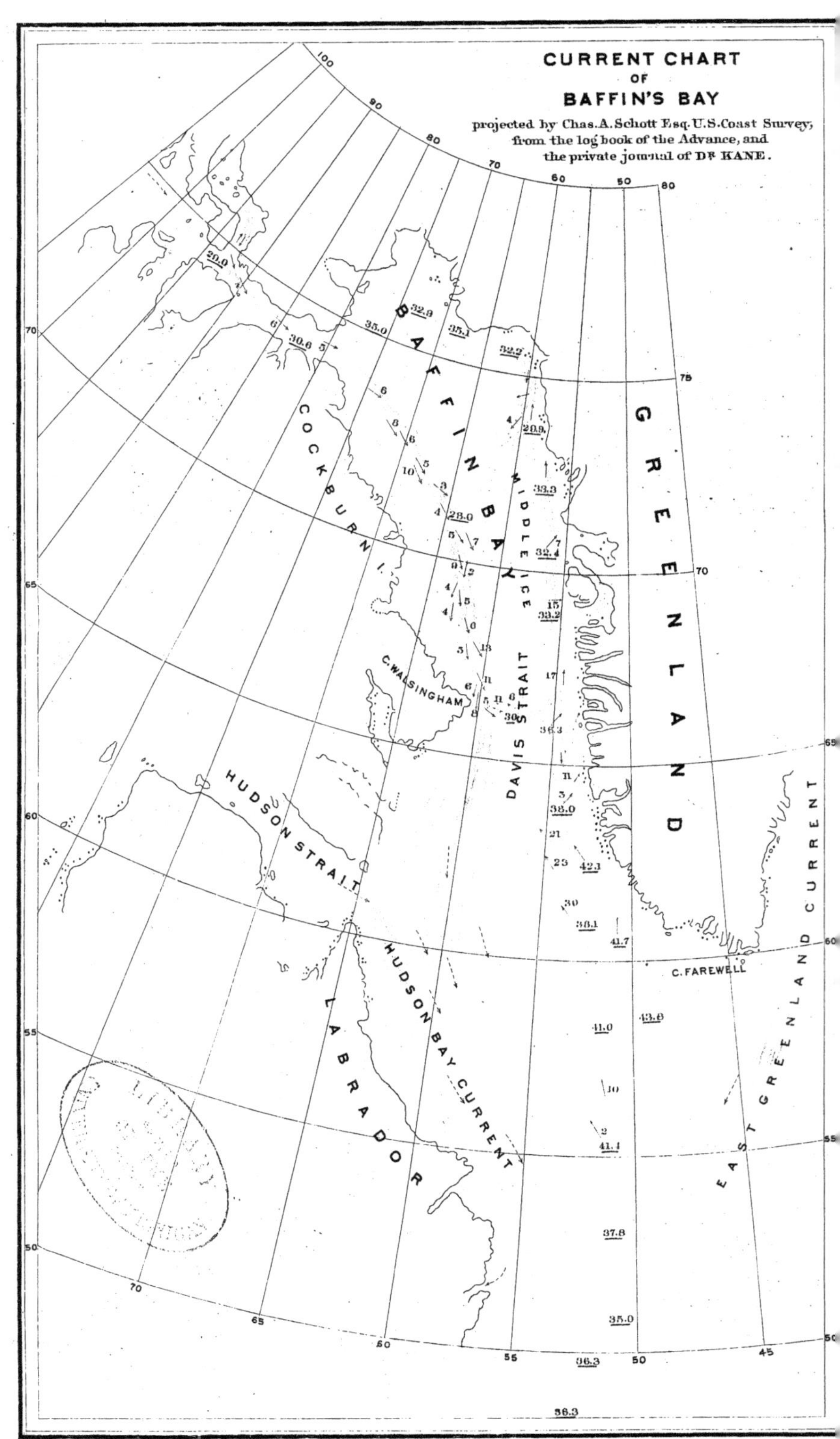

CURRENT CHART
OF
BAFFIN'S BAY
projected by Chas. A. Schott Esq. U.S. Coast Survey, from the log book of the Advance, and the private journal of Dr. KANE.
BAFFIN BAY
COCKBURN I.
MIDDLE ICE
GREENLAND
C. WALSINGHAM
DAVIS STRAIT
HUDSON STRAIT
HUDSON BAY CURRENT
LABRADOR
C. FAREWELL
EAST GREENLAND CURRENT

THE SUKKERTOPPEN.

CHAPTER IV.

We were now drawing near to Davis's Straits, and the names which recorded our progress upon the charts were full of Arctic associations. The *Meta Incognita* of Frobisher and the Cape of God's Mercy greeted us from the American coast: Cape Farewell was on our starboard quarter, and the "Land of Desolation" nearly abeam.

A piece of drift-wood, a wanderer from the region of trees, passed us on its northward journey. The course of this drift-wood illustrates remarkably the beneficent adaptation of ocean currents to the wants of man. It is found abundantly on the lower coasts of Greenland, and, passing round them from the Atlantic, floats along the eastern shore of Baffin's Bay to the north, in opposition to the general tendency of its waters.

The great counter-current, which in the North Atlantic borders the Gulf Stream, flowing from the northeast to the southwest, is deflected at Cape Farewell, and carried abruptly along the west coast of Greenland toward the north. Such is the observation of all the Danish settlers, strikingly confirmed by the accumulations of ice on the southeastern shores of the Peninsula. This ice is evidently from the Spitzbergen Seas; and at seasons of the year when the upper waters of Greenland are comparatively unobstructed, it completely fills up the fiords of the southeastern coast. Thus the settlements of Baal's River and Julianshaab are for months of the summer in a state of blockade, owing to the inroads of the ice-fields from the south; while at Holsteinberg and to the north the land is perfectly accessible.

The drift-wood is at first entangled with these frozen masses; but there is every reason to believe it continues its way onward long after the ice has left it. At Egedesminde, for instance, it is almost a staple commodity; though in the Bay of Disco, where the current is controlled by local causes, it is found only in some places. Our expedition met it as high as Storoë Island, in latitude 71°.

When it is remembered that this wood, coming from the Atlantic quarter, is the offcast of the great Siberian and American rivers, and that the distant bay to which it travels has its great discharge of water *from* the north, we can appreciate the importance of the reflex current in supplying these destitute shores with fuel and timber.

Our enemies, the icebergs—for we had not yet learned to regard them as friends—made their appearance again on the 16th. One of them was an irregular quadrangle, at least a quarter of a mile long in its presenting face. Its summit reminded me of the crevasses seen in the Alpine glaciers. It was completely cut up with jagged ridges and intervening hollows, through some of which the water of the surface drainage fell in little cascades.

The night had now left us: we were in the continuous sunlight of the Arctic summer. I copy the entries from my journal of the 17th.

"We are just 'turning in,' that is, seeking our den for sleep. It has been a long day, but to me a Godsend, so clear and fogless. My time-piece points to half past nine, and yet the sunshine is streaming down the little hatchway.

"Our Arctic day has commenced. Last night we read the thermometer without a lantern, and the binnacle was not lighted up. To-day the sun sets after ten, to rise again before two; and during the bright twilight interval he will dip but a few degrees below the horizon. We have followed him for some time past in one scarcely varying track of brightness. The words night and day begin to puzzle me, as I recognize the arbitrary character of the hour cycles that have borne these names. Indeed, I miss that soothing tranquillizer, the dear old darkness, and can hardly, as I give way to sleep, bid the mental good-night which travelers like to send from their darkened pillows to friends at home.

"Only one iceberg was seen to-day. The sun was behind it, his low rays lighting up the sea with crimson, and defining the black shadow of the berg like a silhouette. While we were watching it, one of those changes of equilibrium, so frequent in partially submerged ice, caused it first to tremble, and then to roll in long oscillating curves. At the same moment, myriads of birds, which had roosted unseen in its inhospitable clefts, rose into the line of sunshine, and flew in circles round their unstable resting-place."

Our little vessel pursued her way without drawback, heading, as nearly as the wind permitted, for our appointed rendezvous with the Rescue. The zones of discolored sea, which we met upon entering Baffin's Bay, still continued, though less frequent than further to the south. Their color varied from a chocolate to a muddy green, and it seemed as if their general direction was governed by some uniform cause not directly connected with superficial currents. Of eight belts which I noted, five had a marked trend from the northeast to the southwest. It struck me as remarkable, too, that the movements of the acalephæ beneath the surface were seldom in the axis of the stream. They crossed it obliquely. May it not be that such belts of discoloration as are visible at the surface are merely protruding ridges of great, submerged areas?

My meteorological abstract shows for this period a comfortless alternation of fogs, scanty sunshine, and drizzling rain. These fogs extended generally over a considerable surface, and, though not accompanied by such changes of wind or temperature as to attract notice, had no doubt some relation to the fishing shoals over which we were passing. Sometimes, however, we entered continuous streams of mist, not extending higher than our cross trees, and emerged from them again so suddenly as to make me ascribe them to local refrigeration induced by the neighborhood of ice. The effect of these fogs upon the diffusion of light was far from pleasant. Our now nominal twilight reminded me of a bright glare, subdued by a ground glass screen: our eyes suffered more than during the unobstructed sunshine.

On the 20th an unknown schooner came within the same dome of mist with ourselves. We had not seen a sail since leaving Newfoundland, and the sight pleased us. We showed our colors, but the little craft declined a reciprocation.

On the same day, jutting up above the misty horizon, we sighted the mountainous coast of Greenland. It was a bold antiphrasis that gave such a vernal title to this birth-place of icebergs. Old Crantz, the quaintest, and, in many things, the most exact of the missionary authorities, says that it got the name from the Norsemen, because it was greener than Iceland—a poor compliment, certainly, to the land of the Geysers!

We first made the coast near Sukkertoppen, a remarkable peak, called so, perhaps, because its form is not unlike that of a sugar-loaf, perhaps because its top is whitened with the snow. Mountains that mark their unbroken profile on the distant sky are very apt to suggest these fanciful remembrances to the navigator; and it is probably this which makes their names so frequently characteristic.

This peak is a noted landmark, and gives its name to the entire district it overlooks. Our own observations confirm those of Graah and Ross, which place it in latitude 65° 22′ north, longitude 53° 05′ west. It may be seen under ordinary circumstances many miles out to sea.

We were favored in our view of the Sukkertoppen. We had approached it through an atmosphere of fog; and when the morning of the 23d gave us a clear sky, we found ourselves close upon the beach, so close that we could see the white surf mingling with the snow streaks. A more rugged and inhospitable region never met my eye. Its unyielding expression differed from any that belongs to the recognized desert, the Sahara, or the South American Arridas; for in these tropical wastes there is rarely wanting some group of Euphorbia or stunted Gum Arabic trees, to qualify by their contrast the general barrenness. It was startling to see, beneath a smiling sun and upon the level of the all-fertilizing sea, an entire country without an apparent trace of vegetable life.

The hills had the peculiar configuration that belongs to the metamorphic rocks. Their summits were gnarled and torn; and in the immediate foreground, some gneissoid spurs of lesser elevation were so rounded as to resemble gigantic bowlders. The axis of the chain seemed to incline rudely from the N.N.W. to the S.S.E. Its sides were nearly destitute of those minor valleys that characterize the more recent deposits. Yet, even at fifteen miles distance, I could remark the clean abrupt edge of the fractures, which creased their otherwise symmetrical outline.

Over these hills the snow lay in patches, occupying principally the protected and dependent grooves. But, with the exception of a few escarped faces, too precipitous to retain it, the various inclinations of the surface appeared to be covered equally, without regard to their exposure toward different points of the compass.

Far off to the south and east, the glacier showed its characteristic pinnacle.

ENTERING DISCO.

CHAPTER V.

On the 24th, the sun did not pass below the horizon. We had already begun to realize that power of adaptation to a new state of things, which seems to be a distinguishing characteristic of man. We marked our day by its routine. Though the temptation to avoid a regular bed-hour was sometimes irresistible, yet seven bells always found us washing by turns at our one tin wash-basin: at eight bells we breakfasted; at eight again we called to grog; two hours afterward we met at dinner; and at six o'clock in the afternoon we came with laudable regularity to our salt junk and coffee.

Our daily reckoning kept us advised of the recurring noonday, the meridian starting-point of sea-life; and our indefatigable master had his unvarying hour for winding up and comparing the chronometers. It is hard not to mark the regulated steps of time, where such a man-of-war routine prevails; and I can scarcely understand the necessity for the twenty-four hours' registering dial-plate, which Parry and others carried with them, to avert the disastrous consequences of a twelve hours' skip in their polar reckonings.

We had now been a month and a day out from New York. Our immediate destination was the Crown Prince Islands, more generally known by the misnomer of the Whale Fish. This little group is situated in the Bay of Disco, thirty miles south of the island of that name. It is the largest of three similar groups, and seems to be part of a ledge extending from the southern cape of Disco to the Bunkë Islands. Sir Edward Parry surveyed the entrance to them in 1821, and determined their position very carefully; since which time, from the facilities which they offer for rating chronometers, they have become an established resort for whalers and expedition ships. Knowing nothing of their character or resources, we had looked forward to them with that sort of expectation which sea-tossed men attach to port. We were not sorry then, when, on the 24th of June, in the midst of the usual combination of cold rain and fogs, we sighted some low hilly rocks, about which the sea-swallow and kittiwake were whirling in endless rounds.

As we entered the narrow passage which formed our anchorage, we looked in vain for indications of life. Water-worn gneiss, intersected by huge injections of feldspar, made up the entire prospect. To the eye every thing was inorganic ruggedness. In one or two places, water distilled in drops over the rocks, and found its way to the sea; but there was no vegetation to define its course, not even the green conferva, that obscure vitality which follows water at home. It was only after landing that I became aware that these apparently destitute islands contributed their part to the varied and peculiar flora of the Arctic regions.

The entrance to the anchorage from the southwest is between two islands, and the harbor, which is completely sheltered from ice, is formed, as will be seen from the sketch, by the conjunction of a third. On turning the corner, we suddenly came upon a wooden store-house for oil and skins; and opposite to it, a clumsy-looking collier, moored stem and stern by hawsers leading to rocks on either side of the channel. Soon after, we were boarded by Lieutenant Power, of the British navy, and from him we learned that the clumsy craft was the Emma Eugenia, a provision transport chartered by the Admiralty, and that in less than a week she would take our letters to England.

We learned, too, that the British relief squadron under Commodore Austin had sailed the day before for the regions of search. They had left England on the 6th of May, or seventeen days before our own departure from New York.

While we were standing upon deck, waiting for the boat to be manned which was to take us to the shore, something like a large Newfoundland dog was seen moving rapidly through the water. As it approached, we could see a horn-like prolongation bulging from its chest, and every now and then a queer movement, as of two flapping wings, which, acting alternately on either side, seemed to urge it through the water. Almost immediately it was alongside of us, and then we realized what was the much talked-of kayack of the Greenlanders.

It was a canoe-shaped frame-work, carefully and *entirely* covered with tensely-stretched seal-skins, beautiful in model, and graceful as the nautilus, to which it has been compared. With the exception of an elliptical hole, nearly in its centre, to receive its occupant, it was both air and water tight. Into this hole was wedged its human freight, a black-locked Esquimaux, enveloped in an undressed seal-skin, drawn tightly around the head and wrists, and fastened, where it met the kayack, about an elevated rim made for the purpose, over which it slipped like a bladder over the lip of a jar.

The length of the kayack was about eighteen feet, tapering fore and aft to an absolute point. The beam was but twenty-one inches. When laden, as we saw it, the top or deck was at its centre but two inches by measurement above the water-line. The waves often broke completely over it. A double-bladed oar, grasped in the middle, was the sole propeller. It was wonderful to see how rapidly the will of the kayacker communicated itself to his little bark. One impulse seemed to control both. Indeed, even for a careful observer, it was hard to say where the boat ended or the man commenced; the rider seemed one with his frail craft, an amphibious realization of the centaur, or a practical improvement upon the merman.

These boats, not only as specimens of beautiful naval architecture, but from their controlling influence upon the fortunes of their owners, became to me subjects of careful study. I will revert to them at another time. As we rowed to the shore, crowds of them followed us, hanging like Mother Carey's chickens in our wake, and just outside the sweep of our oars.

We landed at a small cove formed by two protruding masses of coarsely granular feldspar. Some forty odd souls, the men, women, and children of the entire settlement, received us. The men were in the front rank; the women, with their infants on their backs, came next: and behind them, in yelling phalanx, the children. Still further back were crowds of dogs, seated on their haunches, and howling in unison with their masters.

The one feeling which, I venture to say, pervaded us all, to the momentary exclusion of every thing else, was disgust. Offal was strewn around without regard to position; scabs of drying seal-meat were spread over the rocks; oil and blubber smeared every thing, from the dogs' coats to their masters'; animal refuse tainted all we saw; and we afterward found, while botanizing among the snow valleys, bones of the seal, walrus, and whale, buried in the mosses.

But if filth characterized the open air, what was it in the habitations! One poor family had escaped to their summer tent, pitched upon an adjacent rock that overlooked the sea. Within a little area of six feet by eight, I counted a father, mother, grandfather, and four children, a tea-kettle, a rude box, two rifles, and a litter of puppies.

This island is used by the Danes as a sort of fishing station, where one European, generally a carpenter or cooper, presides over a few families of Esquimaux, who live by the chase of the seal. This functionary had a hut built of timber, which we visited. Except the oil-house, which we had observed before, it was the only wooden edifice.

The natives, if the amalgamation of Dane and Esquimaux can be called such, spend their summer in the reindeer tent, their winters in the semi-subterranean hut. These last have not been materially improved since the days of Egedé and Fabricius. A square inclosure of stone or turf is raftered over with drift-wood or whalebones, and then roofed in with earth, skins, mosses, and broken-up kayack frames. One small aperture of eighteen inches square, covered with the scraped intestines of the seal, forms the window; and a long, tunnel-like entry, opening to the south, and not exceeding three feet in height, leads to a skin-covered door. Inside, perched upon an elevated dais or stall, with an earthen lamp to establish the "focus," several families reside together. I have seen as many as four in an apartment of sixteen feet square.

Some of these huts were garnished with little tinseled pictures, and looked as if their inmates were not insensible to the decorative vanities of other lands. Others were a very caricature of discomfort—mouldy, dank, and fetid; their rude ceilings distilling filthy water, and sometimes covered with introverted grasses (*poa Danica*), which had originally formed part of the outer thatching, but now intruded upon the greater warmth of the interior.

I had but a few hours to examine this group. It evidently belongs to that class of rocky islets known to the Danes as "skerries," *skiers*, which are the not unfrequent appendages of a primary coast ridge. Well-defined gneiss, with intersecting veins of coarse red feldspar, was the basis material, the quartzine element greatly predominating. From several rude sections, I made the dip of the strata to the northeast to be at an angle of 25° or 30°. .

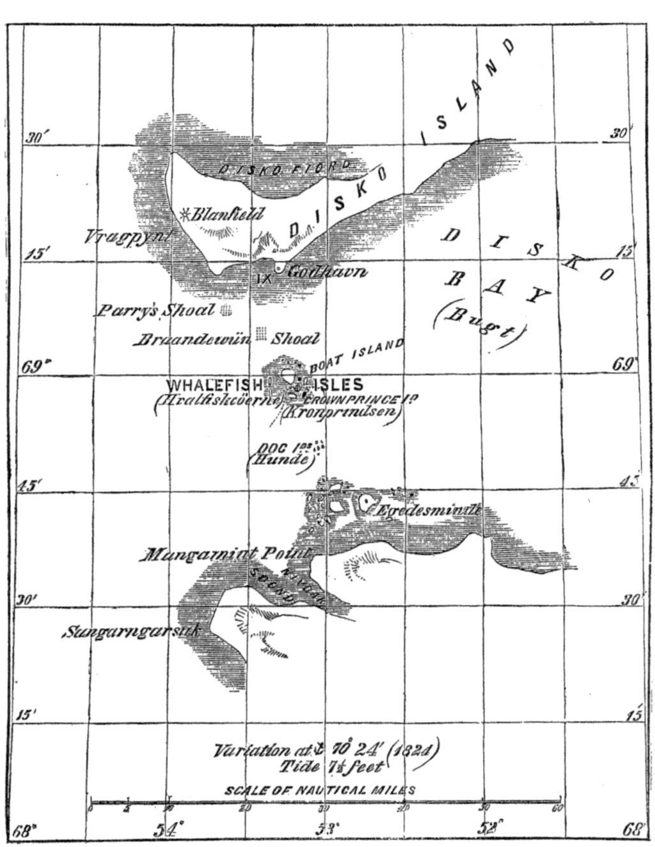

CHART OF THE WHALE-FISH ISLANDS.

INSPECTOR'S HOUSE, LIEVELY.

CHAPTER VI.

Our commander intended to remain at the Crown Prince Islands no longer than was absolutely necessary for our consort, the Rescue, to rejoin us; but, upon reviewing our hurried preparation for the hardships of the winter, he determined, with characteristic forethought, to send a boat party to the settlement of Lievely, on the neighboring island of Disco, for the double purpose of collecting information and purchasing a stock of furs. The execution of this duty he devolved upon me.

We started on the 27th, Mr. Lovell, myself, an Esquimaux pilot, and a crew of five men. As we rowed along the narrow channels before we emerged from this rocky group, I observed for the first time that extreme transparency of the water which has so often been alluded to by authors as characteristic of the Polar Seas. At the depth of ten fathoms every feature of the bottom was distinctly visible.

Even for one who has seen the crimson dulses and coral groves of the equatorial zones, this arctic growth had its rival beauties. Enormous bottle-green fronds were waving their ungainly lengths above a labyrinthine jungle of snake-like stems; and far down, where the claws of the fucus had grappled the round gneisses, great glaring lime patches shone like upset whitewash upon a home grassplot.

It was a rough sail outside. The bergs were numerous; and the heavy sea way and eddying current, sweeping like a mill-race along the southern face of the island, made us barely able to double the entrance to the little harbor. We did double it, however, and by a sudden transition found ourselves in a quiet landlocked basin, shadowed by wall-like hills.

Snow, as usual, covered the lower slopes; but, cheerful in spite of its cold envelope, rose a group of rude houses, mottling the sky with the comfortable smoke of their huge chimneys. Among the most conspicuous of these was one antique and gable fronted, with timbers so heavy and besmeared with tar, that it seemed as if built from the stranded wreck of a vessel. Little man-of-war port-holes, recessed into its wooden sides, and a flag-staff, as tall as the mast of a jolly-boat, gave it dignity. This was the house of the "Royal Inspector of the Northern portions of Davis's Straits;" whose occupant—well and kindly remembered by all of us—no less than the royal inspector himself, stood awaiting our landing.

There are but two inspectorates for the Danish coast of Greenland: one termed the Southern, whose centre is Holsteinberg; the other the Northern, whose seat is Lievely. The representatives of these are educated men, hard-working and responsible, ruling dictatorially the entire affairs of that somewhat singular monopoly, the Royal Greenland Company. The official labor of these exiled servants is very heavy They boat or sledge it from post to post; and not only settle all the squabbles, white, half-breed, and Esquimaux, but audit all the accounts, and keep up between the little settlements writing enough to rule a realm. Except that every where forlorn peripatetic, the doctor, no one has a more toilsome office.

The incumbent, Mr. Olrik, was an accomplished and hospitable gentleman, well read in the natural sciences, and an acute observer. In a few minutes we were seated by a ponderous stove, and in a few more discussing a hot Eider duck and a bottle of Latour.

Upon commencing my negotiations as to furs, the object of my journey, I learned that the reindeer do not abound on the island of Disco as in the days of Crantz and Egedé; though to the south, about Bunkë Land, and the fiords around Holsteinberg, and to the north of the Waigat, they are still very numerous. Nevertheless, by drumming up the resources of the settlement, we obtained a supply of second-hand *late summer* skins; and with these, aided by the seal, soon fitted out a wardrobe.

The most popular article of attire was the *karah*, a "jumper" or close jacket, slipping on like a shirt, and hooded like the cowl of a Franciscan monk; but the seal-skin boot, a water-tight buskin, ingeniously crimped, so as to do away with a seam, was in great request. Thanks to Mr. Olrik, who actually robbed himself to supply our wants, we were eminently successful. We felt that we could now look forward to the winter with comparative trust.

ESQUIMAUX HUT.

Of Disco, save its Esquimaux huts, its oil-house, its smith-shop, its little school, and its gubernatorial mansion, I can say but little. Its statistics, vital, political, or economic, would have little interest for the readers of this narrative. But my limited florula, gathered as I made a few hasty walks under the guidance of our hospitable and intelligent friend, the governor, may be worth a notice.

In a ravine, back of the settlement, the washings of the melted snows had accumulated, in little escalades or terraces, a scanty mould, rich with Arctic growths.

The mosses, which met the lichens at a sort of neutral ground between rock and soil, were particularly rich. So sodden were they with the percolating waters, that you sank up to your ankles. Nestling curiously under their protecting tufts rose a complete parterre of tinted flowers, consisting of Gentians, Ranunculus, Ledum, Draba, Potentilla, Saxifrages, Poppy, and Sedums.

The Arctic turf is unequaled: nothing in the tropics approaches it for specific variety, and in density it far exceeds its Alpine congener. Two birches (*Betula alba* and *B. nana*), three willows (*Salix lanata*, *S. glauca*, and *S. herbacea*), that noble heath, the Andromeda (*A. tetragona*), the whortle-berry (*Vaccinium vitis-idæa* and *V. uliginosum*), the crow-berry (*Empetrum nigrum*), and a Potentilla, were, in one instance, all wreathed together in a matted sod, from whose intricate net-work, rising within an area of a single foot, I counted no less than six species of flowering plants.

The appearance of such turf, where the tree growths of more favored regions have become pronate and vine-like, and crowding individuals of non-opposing families of flowering plants fill up the intervals with a carpet pattern of rich colors, might puzzle a painter. It reminded me of Humboldt's covering with his cloak the vegetation of four continents.

This little port of Lievely or Godhavn is on a gneissoid spur, offsetting from the larger mass of Disco. I subjoin the few observations which I was able to make on the physical characters of this island.

Disco is the largest circumnavigable island on the coast of Greenland. Its long diameter is from the northwest to southeast, and its eastern edge is in a continuous line with the coast to the north and south. It is rendered insular by a large strait, called the Waigat, which inosculates with the bay.

Its general geognostical structure is determined by a great green-stone dike which crosses its entire length, and is continued conformably across the Waigat. As nearly as I could arrive at it, the general trend of this injection was to the E.N.E., which, when afterward compared with the northern Labrador and Greenland coast, seemed to indicate a correspondence with the line of uplift of the Lake Superior traps. To the southeast, it cuts a ledge of syenitic gneiss, leaving a knobbed peninsula, abounding in low islands and harbors, on one of which is the little settlement of Lievely.

I had not many hours to devote to this rude reconnoissance, much of which was aided by bird's-eye views from the adjacent peaks. Commencing at the southeastern end of the island, and walking to the N.N.W., I met abundant schistose material, inclining to the northeast at an angle of 25°. Against this the dike cut cleanly, with little adjacent alteration, rising up from its long, conoidal slopes of detritus into escarped terraces nearly 1400 feet high. These were like the Hindoo Ghauts, as I had seen them about Kandalah; they had the same monumental structure, the same *plateau*-formed summit, the same sublime ravines. How strangely this crust we wander over asserts its identity through all the disguises of climate!

Some five miles further to the east, the injection had caused more disturbance. My walk upon this line was soon varied with chloritic and slaty indications; and, where these met the traps, they were interfused with sandstones, and abounding with coarsely vesicular amygdaloids. In this transitional belt I picked up some fine zeolites. I noticed, too, nodular epidotes in profusion.

So much for Disco. Paul Zachareus, long-haired, swarthy, Christian Paul, said that the wind was fair: Lovell, like a good sailor, exercised his authority over the doctor: the furs were packed, my sketches and *wet* hortus siccus properly combined, and we started again for our little brig.

We left the Whale-fish Islands on the 29th, in company with the Rescue. On the 30th we doubled the southwest cape of Disco, and stood to the northward, through a crowd of noble icebergs. On the first of July, early in the morning, we encountered our first field-ice. From this date really commenced the characteristic voyaging of a Polar cruise.

LIEVELY.

OMENAK'S FIORD.

CHAPTER VII.

It will be readily seen, that of the voyages to Lancaster Sound, or indeed any of the northwestern seas of Baffin's Bay, the transit of the middle ice is the essential feature. Its several "crossings" have been divided into the South, the Middle, and the Northern passages. By the first of these, vessels reach the American side south of 68°. Any passage between this parallel and 74° is called a "Middle" passage; while the "Northern," which, early in the season, is the almost universal track, skirts the coast of Greenland, and, passing the accumulated shore ices of Melville Bay, bears to the westward through a comparatively iceless area, known as the North Water.

The Southern passage is not unfrequently resorted to for the fisheries of the American coast. It is the alternative of the whalers late in the season, when they have failed to reach their western cruising grounds by the North Water.

Instances of the Middle passage are rare. Old legends, preserved at Uppernavik, speak vaguely of a period when a direct communication existed between that settlement and Pond's Bay; but Parry was the first modern navigator to attempt it successfully. In his voyage of 1819, he entered the Middle Ice on the 21st of July, and emerged from it on the 28th. He tried the experiment again in the July of 1824; but, after many weeks' delay, was forced to turn his head to the northward, and did not reach the open water of the west till the 9th of September.

Other instances have since occurred of like success; but among the whalers, who possess an admirable tact in ice navigation, it is looked upon with distrust. Later in the season, when the disintegration of the middle barrier has advanced, and the predominant winds have opened it into transverse "leads," the passage, though far from easy or certain, is more practicable.

It is by the "North Water," however, that vessels have generally approached the highway of Arctic search; and, in order to reach this, a mysterious region of terrors must be traversed—Melville Bay—notorious in the annals of the whalers for its many disasters.

After the voyage of Sir John Ross in 1818, the fishing fleet, which had even then nearly driven the whale beyond the coasts of Greenland, began to follow him to the more western waters of the bay. Vessels reaching the other side were at that time almost sure of a cargo; and it was not uncommon to see more than thirty sail, of many nations, English, French, and Baltic, awaiting at one time a favoring opportunity for this dreaded transit. It was called running the gauntlet, and the opening scene of the exploits was generally known as the "Devil's Nip."

It was for this region, then, we were making when

we first fell in with the ice. It was off Haröe Island, and consisted probably of a tongue or process from the main pack I have just described. Such interruptions are not uncommon earlier in the season, and the whalers sometimes avoid them by passing to the inner or inshore side of the island. We learned afterward to regard such ice as hardly worthy of note; but as this was the first time we had met it, I have thought it best to quote literally from my journal.

"*July* 1. This morning was called on deck at 4 A.M. by our commander.

"About two hundred yards to the windward, forming a lee-shore, was a vast plane of undulating ice, in nowise differing from that which we see in the Delaware when mid-winter is contending with the ice-boats. There was the same crackling, and grinding, and splashing, but the indefinite extent—an ocean instead of a river—multiplied it to a din unspeakable; and with it came a strange undertone accompaniment, a not discordant drone. This was the floe ice; perhaps a tongue from the 'Great Pack,' through which we are now every day expecting to force our way. A great number of bergs, of shapes the most simple and most complicated, of colors blue, white, and earth-stained, were tangled in this floating field. Such, however, was the inertia of the huge masses, that the sheet ice piled itself up about them as on fixed rocks.

"The sea immediately around, saving the ground-swell, was smooth as a mill-pond; but it was studded over with dark, protruding little globules, about the size of hens' eggs, producing an effect like the dimples of so many overgrown rain-drops fallen on the water. These, as I afterward found, were rounded fragments of transparent and fresh-water ice, the debris and detritus of the bergs. We sailed along this field about ten miles.

"At 9 P.M. the fogs settled around us, and we entered again upon an area full of floating masses of berg. As it was impossible to avoid them, they gave us some heavy thumps. Taking our main-mast for a guide, we estimated the height of the larger bergs at about two hundred feet.

"At 11 we cleared the floes, and, favored with a free wind, found ourselves nearly opposite Omenak's Fiord, a noted seat of iceberg growth and distribution."

There is a something in the atmosphere of these latitudes that makes the estimate of distance fallacious. How far we were from land I could not tell; but we saw distinctly the configuration of the hills and the deep recesses of the fiord. The sun, although nearing midnight, was five degrees above the horizon, and threw its rich coloring over the snow. Many large bergs were moving in procession from the fiord, those in the foreground in full sunshine, those in the distance obscured by the shadow of their parent hills.

Omenak's Fiord, known as Jacob's Bight, is one of the largest of those strange clefts, which, penetrating the mountain range at right angles to its long axis, form so majestic a feature of Greenland scenery. Its inland termination has never been reached; and it is supposed by Scoresby to be continuous with the large sounds, which on a corresponding parallel (70° 40′) enter from the eastern coast.*

This idea of an inosculation, or even more direct connection between the waters of Baffin's Bay and the

* Although Graah expresses a doubt whether this sound, which, it seems, was discovered by Boon as far back as 1761, is any thing more than a large bay, I incline strongly to the view, just expressed, of that excellent observer, Scoresby

Atlantic, is entertained by many of the more intelligent Danish and Esquimaux residents. It is certain that on the Atlantic coast a deep sea current drives the icebergs seaward; and strong tidal currents on the Greenland side are spoken of by the Danes. The Esquimaux, too, whose information, however, must be received with caution, assert the existence of a well-marked indraft. All this points vaguely to an interior water connection between the two coasts.

Both Ovinde Oerme and Omenak's Fiord, the two largest indentations of the bay, form at their mouths a complicated archipelago; a fact that lends, at least, a certain support to Sir Charles Geiseke's opinion, that the so-called peninsula of Greenland is a congeries of islands, cemented by interior ice. I will mention at another portion of my narrative the exceptions which I take to a full acceptation of this view. But a stronger indication of the direct connection between this strait and the Atlantic may be derived from the geognostical characters of the two coasts.

The southern side of the large opening before us rose in a green-stone escalade, a series of true trachytic terraces, losing themselves in the distance; while on the northern side the formation was evidently primary and schistose. This corresponds with the arrangement described by Scoresby on the Atlantic coast.

I had observed the green-stone extending in unbroken continuity from the southern cape of Disco (C Kearsak) across the Waigat; and though my sources of information were limited, I had little doubt but that it passed along the promontory of Rittenbank to the so-called main, abutting throughout upon waters of the sound. A similar range is described by Scoresby, nearly opposite on the Atlantic side, as two thousand six hundred feet high, "forming ledges not unlike steps, on a gigantic scale," evidently a continuation of the same dioritic series; while the syenites and stratified gneisses to the north have their corresponding relative positions on both coasts.

It is up this fiord, probably in the chasms of the trap, that those enormous glaciers accumulate which have made Jacob's Bight, perhaps, the most remarkable locality in the *genesis* of icebergs on the face of the globe. It is not uncommon to have the shore here completely blocked in by these gigantic monsters: I myself counted in one evening, the 3d of July, no less than two hundred and forty of primary magnitude, from the decks of our vessel. The inquiries I was enabled to make may perhaps throw some light on the causes of this excessive accumulation.

CHAPTER VIII.

THE glaciers which abut upon this sound are probably offsets from an interior *mer de glace*. The valleys or canals which conduct these offsets were described to me as singularly rectilinear and uniform in diameter, a fact which derives ready confirmation from the known configuration of a dioritic country. Now the protrusion of these abutting faces into the waters of the sound has been a subject of observation among both Danes and Esquimaux. Places about Jacob's Harbor, remembered as the former seats of habitation, are now overrun by glaciers; and Mr. Olrik told me of a naked escarpment of ice, twelve hundred feet high, which he had seen protruding nearly half a mile into the sea.

Crantz and Graah describe similar protrusions to the south. In the conditions which I have just described, of a rectilinear duct of unvarying diameter, and a parent source of great elevation and extent, we have an explanation of the excessive advance of these glaciers. But the existence of an interior reservoir or fountain head, as the source from which this protruding supply is furnished, has an interesting bearing upon Forbes' beautifully simple views of a viscous movement.

That such a movement takes place in the Greenland glaciers, I have, as I hope to show hereafter, ample reasons for believing; and, although the absolute rate of this advance has never been a subject of educated observation, it would not surprise me if the gelid flow of these glacial rivers exceeded during the summer season that of the Alps.

The materials thus afforded in redundant profusion are rapidly converted into icebergs. The water at the bases of these cliffs is very deep—I have in my note-book well-established instances of three hundred fathoms; and the pyramidal structure of the trap is such as to favor a precipitous coast line. The glacier, thus exposed to a saline water base of a temperature above the freezing point, and to an undermining wave action, aided by tides and winds, is of course speedily detached by its own gravitation. I am enabled to give a perfectly reliable account of this rarely witnessed sight, the creation of an iceberg by *debacle* or *avalanche.*

Up this fiord, at an island known in the Esquimaux tongue as Ekarasak, there lived a deputy assistant of the Royal Greenland Company, a worthy man by the name of Grundëitz. It seems that the deep water of Omenak's Fiord is resorted to for halibut fishing, an operation which is carried on at the base of the cliffs with very long lines of whalebone. While Mr. Grundëitz, in a jolly-boat belonging to the company, was fishing up the fiord, his attention was called to a large number of bearded seals, who were sporting about beneath one of the glaciers that protruded into the bay. While approaching for the purpose of a shot, he heard a strange sound, repeated at intervals like the ticking of a clock, and apparently proceeding from the body of the ice. At the same time the seal, which the moment before had been perfectly unconcerned, disappeared entirely, and his Esquimaux attendants, probably admonished by previous experience, insisted upon removing the boat to a greater distance. It was well they did so; for, while gazing at the white face of the glacier at a distance of about a mile, a loud explosive detonation, like the crack of a whip vastly exaggerated, reached their ears, and at the same instant, with reverberations like near thunder, a great mass fell into the sea, obscuring every thing in a cloud of foam and mist.

The undulations which radiated from this great centre of displacement were fearful. Fortunately for Mr. Grundëitz, floating bodies do not change their position very readily under the action of propagated waves, and the boat, in consequence, remained outside the grinding fragments; but the commotion was intense, and the rapid succession of huge swells such as to make the preservation of the little party almost miraculous.

The detached mass slowly adjusted itself after some minutes, but it was nearly an hour before it attained its equilibrium. It then floated on the sea, an iceberg.*

* This title is applied by many authors to ice masses either on shore or at sea. I restrict it to detached ice, in contradistinction to the glacier or ice *in situ*

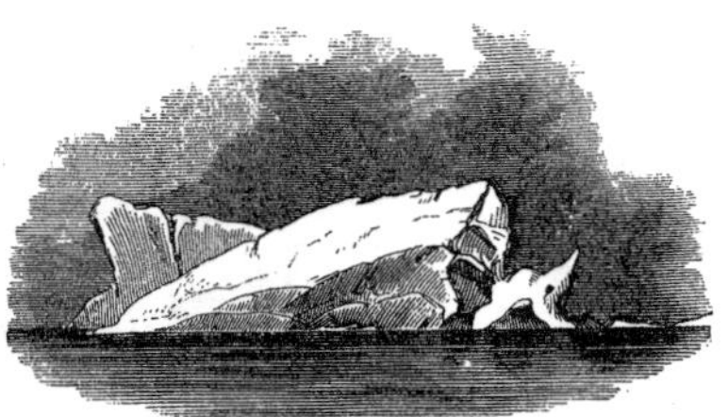

The mass thus detached appeared, from the description of my informant, to be a nearly complete parallelopipedon. It measured, by rude estimate, three hundred yards on its exposed face, by about one hundred and fifty in breadth; its height above the sea "greater than that of our main-mast."

The leading circumstances of this narrative were confirmed in our own after experience in Melville Bay. Disruptions are witnessed not unfrequently in icebergs after they are afloat, and sometimes on a majestic scale. Instances of the *debacle* are more rare.

July 2. The next day we passed this fiord and stood on our course beyond an imposing headland, known on the charts as Cape Cranstown, through a sea unobstructed by floe ice, but abounding in bergs.

In the afternoon the wind subsided into a mere cat's-paw, and we were enabled to visit several of the icebergs. I am amused with the embarrassments which my journal exhibits in the effort to describe them. Certain it is that no objects ever impressed me more. There was something about them so slumberous and so pure, so massive yet so evanescent, so majestic in their cheerless beauty, without, after all, any of the salient points which give character to description, that they almost seemed to me the material for a dream, rather than things to be definitely painted in words.

The first that we approached was entirely inaccessible. Our commander, in whose estimates of distance and magnitude I have great confidence, made it nearly a mile in circumference. With the exception of one rugged corner, it was in shape a truncated wedge, and its surface a nearly horizontal plateau. The next presented a well-marked characteristic, which, as I observed it afterward in other examples, enabled me to follow the history of the berg throughout all its changes of equilibrium: it was a rectilinear groove at the water-line, hollowed out by the action of the waves.

These "grooves" were seen in all the bergs which had remained long in one position. They were sometimes crested with fantastic serratures, and their tunnel-like roofs were often pendant with icicles. On a grounded berg the tides may be accurately guaged by these lines, and, in the berg before me, a number of them, converging to a point not unlike the rays of a fan, pointed clearly to those changes of equilibrium which had depressed one end and elevated the other.

A third was a monster ice mountain, at least two hundred feet high, irregularly polyhedral in shape, and its surface diversified with hill and dale. Upon this one we landed. I had never appreciated before the glorious variety of iceberg scenery. The sea at the base of this berg was dashing into hollow caves of pure and intense ultramarine; and to leeward the quiet water lit the eye down to a long, spindle-shaped root of milky whiteness, which seemed to dye the sea as it descended, until the blue and white were mixed in a pale turkois. Above, and high enough to give an expression akin to sublimity, were bristling crags.

This was the first berg that I had visited. I was struck with its peculiar opacity, the result of its granulated structure. I had incidentally met with the remark of Professor Forbes, that "the floating icebergs of the Polar Seas are for the most part of the nature of nevé;" and, while I was at a distance, had looked upon the substance of the mass before me as identical with the "firn," or consolidated snow of the Alpine glaciers. I now found cause, for the first time, to change this opinion. The ice of this berg, although opaque and vesicular, was true glacier ice, having the fracture, lustre, and other external characters of a nearly homogeneous growth. The same authority, in speaking of these bergs, declares that "the occurrence of true ice is comparatively rare, and is justly dreaded by ships." From this impression, which was undoubtedly derived from the appearance of a berg at a distance, I am also compelled to dissent. The iceberg is true ice, and is always dreaded by ships. Indeed, though modified by climate, and especially by the alternation of day and night, the Polar glacier must be regarded as strictly atmospheric in its increments, and not essentially differing from the glacier of the Alps.

The general color of a berg I have before compared to frosted silver. But when its fractures are very extensive, the exposed faces have a very brilliant lustre. Nothing can be more exquisite than a fresh, cleanly-fractured berg surface. It reminded me of the recent cleavage of sulphate of strontian—a resemblance more striking from the slightly lazulitic tinge of each.

CHAPTER IX.

We pursued our way, flapping lazily along side of the "pack," and sometimes forcing an opening through its projecting tongues. On the morning of the 3d, while beating between the ice and the shore, we stood close in to a lofty headland, known as Svartehuk, or Black Head. This dark promontory deserves its name. It is of the usual metamorphic structure, owing its color to the hornblende it contains. The retreating character of the coast to the north and south of it, makes it a noted landmark among the whalers. At the distance of three miles, I sketched an escarped

section of it, discolored by iron-clay conglomerates, and exhibiting a gnarled and irregular structure.

Our American birth-day, the 4th of July, could not pass us without at least a festive effort; so we tapped a bottle of Heidsieck in the cabin, and all hands spliced the main-brace. But the day was nevertheless a busy one. What little wind we had was nearly dead ahead, though we managed to work along the open water, making "the pack" and the shore by alternate "tacks." At 8 A.M. it fell calm, leaving us entangled among fragments of heavy floe. We got the brig's head to the eastward with difficulty, and, in the midst of a dense fog, fired our blunderbuss and hove to for the "Rescue," no objects being visible more than a half ship's length from the decks.

The fog left us about mid-day, and the atmosphere was so clear in the afternoon, that the land, although thirty miles off, was seen distinctly. The water and the sky, in somewhat anomalous contrast with this extremely pellucid state of air, had a pearly or ash-colored tinting, and the floe ice, of which large quantities were around us, varied like the shadows of a daguerreotype.

Toward 11 P.M. the temperature of the water fell to 30°, while that of the air rose to 36° and 37°. Looking toward the shore, I observed a sort of shimmering, as of the heated air above a stove, and, at the same time, the base of the hills assumed a columnar character, as marked as in the basalts of Staffa. Soon afterward, the entire land came up to us through a highly refractive medium, and the vertical arrangement which had displayed itself before in columns was broken into waving curves, the parallelism of their lines remaining unchanged. As the sun reached his greatest meridional depression, this was accompanied by an extreme distortion. The homogeneous character of the atmosphere was singularly disturbed. It was like gazing at a panorama through badly blown and uneven glass.

The little islands about the shore were elevated into Champagne bottles and mushrooms, and some headlands, which I had sketched before the distortion, now sent out lateral prolongations which almost bridged the contiguous hills.

Although I have since seen many beautiful displays of this phenomenon, I have never known it more strikingly varied within such limited compass. My sketch shows in the upper line the true profile of the coast; the two lower lines give a very imperfect idea of its successive phases as refracted. It was, indeed, impossible to embody them in a drawing. A thousand forms, inverted, looming, and distorted most extravagantly, were shifting about within an arc of ten degrees of coast. At the same time, we had out among the icebergs, toward the southwest, the repetition on an enlarged scale of the complicated modifications of refraction seen off Ramsgate, and described by Professor Vince. I allude to those in which the object has a three-fold representation. The single repetition was visible all around us; the secondary or inverted image sometimes above and sometimes below the primary. But it was not uncommon to see, also, the uplifted iceberg, with its accompanying or false horizon, joined at its summit by its inverted image, and then, above a second horizon, a *third* berg in its natural position. Professor Agassiz has described a similar class of repeated images upon Lake Superior, limited, however, to two—one inverted, and above that the same erect. He suggests that it may be simply the reflection of the landscape inverted upon the surface of the lake, and reproduced with the actual landscape. The calm, reflecting surface of the *ice lakes* of Baffin's Bay would favor such an explanation. The extension to a third and fourth image is very interesting. I am afraid to attempt delineating it.

July 5. Although the next day was nearly calm, the water was so smooth, from the protection of the "floes," that, with hardly any perceptible motion, we managed to fan along at a rate of two knots an hour, our sails flapping all the time lazily against the masts. The sailing of these ice-environed waters is incomparable in its way. The sea swell, arrested by successive break-waters, does not reach them. We sailed as though upon a placid lake, towed by invisible hands, and were only made conscious of motion by the changes of the icy pack whose margin we were skirting.

Toward the close of the day, refraction came back to us. I see by my journal that I spent four hours upon deck, taking sextant observations with Mr. Lovell. No fata morgana nor tropical mirage ever surpassed the extraordinary scene of this night.

Voyagers speak of the effects of Arctic refraction in language as exact and mathematical as their own correction tables. It almost seems as if their minute observations of dip-sectors and repeating-circles had left them no scope for picturesque sublimity. This may excuse a literal transcript from my diary, which runs perhaps into the other extreme.

"*Friday*, 11 P.M. A strip of horizon, commencing about 8° to the east of the sun, and between it and the land, resembled an extended plain, covered with the debris of ruined cities. No effort of imagination was necessary for me to travel from the true watery horizon to the false one of refraction above it, and there to see huge structures lining an aerial ocean-margin. Some of rusty, Egyptian, rubbish-clogged propyla, and hypæthral courts — some tapering and columnar, like Palmyra and Baalbec — some with architrave and portico, like Telmessus or Athens, or else vague and grotto-like, such as dreamy memories recalled of Ellora and Carli.

"I can hardly realize it as I write; but it was no trick of fancy. The things were there half an hour ago. I saw them, capricious, versatile, full of forms, but bright and definite as the phases of sober life. And as my eyes ran round upon the marvelous and varying scene, every one of these well-remembered cities rose before me, built up by some suggestive feature of the ice.

"An iceberg is one of God's own buildings, preaching its lessons of humility to the miniature structures of man. Its material, one colossal Pentelicus; its mass, the representative of power in repose; its distribution, simulating every architectural type. It makes one smile at those classical remnants which our own period reproduces in its Madeleines, Walhallas, and Girard colleges, like university poems in the dead languages. Still, we can compare them with the iceberg; for the same standard measures both, as it does Chimborazo and the Hill of Howth. But this thing of refraction is supernatural throughout. The wildest frolic of an opium-eater's revery is nothing to the phantasmagoria of the sky to-night. Karnaks of ice, turned upside down, were resting upon rainbow-colored pedestals: great needles, obelisks of pure whiteness, shot up above their false horizons, and, after an hour-glass-like contraction at their point of union with their duplicated images, lost themselves in the blue of the upper sky.

"While I was looking—the sextant useless in my hand, for I could not think of angles—a blurred and wavy change came over the fantastic picture. Prismatic tintings, too vague to admit of dioptric analysis, began to margin my architectural marbles, and the scene faded like one of Fresnel's dissolving views. Suddenly, by a flash, they reappeared in full beauty; and, just as I was beginning to note in my memorandum-book the changes which this brief interval had produced, they went out entirely, and left a nearly clear horizon."

Abrupt and versatile as were these changes in the refracting medium, those in the temperature about us were no less so. The relation between them was apparent, even within the limited range to which we could extend our observations. At 3 A.M., while the phenomena I have described were in full brilliancy, my thermometers on deck and in the main-top stood respectively at 36° and 39°, while the surface water indicated 32°. Ten minutes afterward, there were no evidences of refraction visible, except some slight loomings of the more distant bergs. The same thermometers now gave, both below and aloft, 36°, and the water had risen to 38°. The surface of the sea at this time was *cat's-pawed* as far as could be seen. A barely perceptible breeze, which set in suddenly from the northeast, had undoubtedly contributed to restore the homogeneity of the atmosphere.

My sketches of the coast, which had now been visible for nearly three days without interruption, show what strange diversities of outline may be induced by refraction. The illusions are so perfect that it is hardly possible to arrive at the normal aspect of the shore. Such changes, especially of altitude, must be a source of serious embarrassment in the recognition of landmarks.

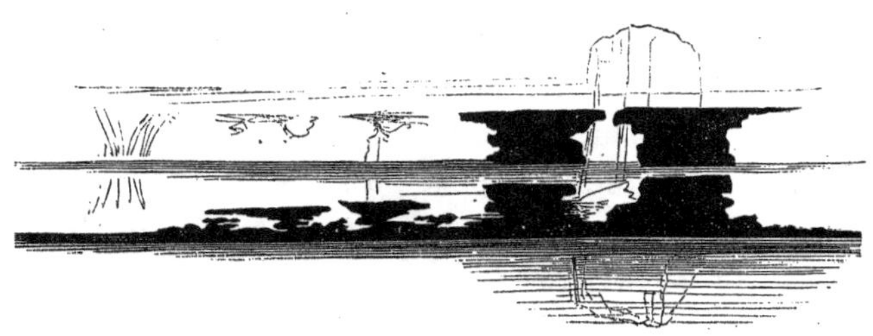

OOMIAK AND KAYACK.

CHAPTER X.

July 6. The 6th found us in latitude 72° 54′, beating to windward, as usual, between "the pack" and the land. This land was of some interest to us, for we were now in the neighborhood of the Danish settlement of Uppernavik.

With the exception of one subordinate station, eighteen miles further to the north, this is the last of the Danish settlements. It is the jumping-off place of Arctic navigators—our last point of communication with the outside world. Here the British explorers put the date to their official reports, and send home their last letters of good-by We sent ours without the delay of seeking the little port; for a couple of kayacks boarded us twenty miles out to sea, and for a few biscuits gladly took charge of our dispatches. The honesty of these poor Esquimaux is proverbial. Letters committed to their care are delivered with unerring safety to the superintendent of the port or station.

We were boarded, too, by an oomiak, or woman's boat, returning from a successful seal hunt. From the crew, consisting of three women and four men, we purchased a goodly stock of eider eggs and three young seals.

July 7. We had now passed the seventy-third degree of latitude without being materially retarded by ice. The weather was one unbroken sunshine, and worthier of the Bay of Naples than Baffin's. The coast on our right hand consisted of low islands, so grouped as to resemble continuous land. They were a part of the archipelago at the mouth of the large fiord of Ovinde Oerme, and varied in size from mere knobs to lofty headlands not less than fifteen hundred feet high. To our left was a coast of a different character—the ice. This we had now skirted since the 3d. We knew it, therefore, to be a part of that great barrier, the "middle pack," around whose dangerous circuit we had to pass before reaching the western waters. By standing in and out, we made the distance of the pack from shore to be about thirty miles. The space between was clear, and it was along this, as upon a great river, we had thus far pushed our way uninterrupted.

July 7. On the morning of the 7th, a large vacant sheet of water showed itself to the westward, penetrating the ice as far as the eye could reach; and from the top-mast-head we could see the southern margin of this ice losing itself in a clear, watery horizon. It was a strong temptation. Our commander determined to try for a passage through.

As this day exercised a somewhat controlling influence upon our future progress, I will give its occurrences as they stand in my journal.

"It commenced," says the log-book, with "the pack ahead, a four-knot breeze from the E.N.E., and our course to the southwest." By ten we fastened in the ice; but, by cutting and boring, succeeded in penetrating it, and sailed on through loose streams until noon.

"We now entered fairly the so-thought open water, keeping the shore on our starboard beam, and steering for the northeast and north, at a rate of six knots, through an apparently unobstructed sea. But the sanguine anticipations of our commander were soon to be moderated. By four in the afternoon, after placing at least fifty miles between us and the coast, the leads began to close around us. Fearing a separation from the Rescue, we took her in tow and continued our efforts; but from 5 P.M. until the termination of the day, our progress was absolutely nothing. The morning of the 8th opened upon us fast in summer ice.

"*July* 8. Fast! Around us a circle of snow-covered ice, streaked with puddles of dark water, and varied (alas for the variety!) by the very distant looming of some icebergs. In the centre of this dreariness are the two vessels—'Advance' and 'Rescue.'

"Our commander, loth to relinquish his hopes, determined to 'bore.' This operation, which consists in forcing a passage through the ice, continued throughout the night—'all hands' jumping upon the floes, and working away with crow-bar, boat-hook, ice-anchor, and warping-lines. The result of all this labor was, that the two vessels made about three quarters of a mile into deeper entanglement; and now, at 11 P.M., we are fast in the apparent centre of a solid sea.

"All the men are asleep except Dunning, our watchman; and but for his tramp on the deck overhead, and the scraping of my pen over the paper, the silence is complete. My mess-mates, thoroughly tired out, are breathing heavily from their bunks.

"*July* 9. Although we commenced bright and early

to warp our way through the impacted ice, we found, after much labor, that the entire day's reward was about three miles. We are now again fast, completely 'beset,' and only waiting to rest the crew before we renew our efforts."

What these efforts were it may be as well to explain, for the benefit of fireside navigators, and perhaps some others. Those who go down to the sea in ships know that it is easy enough to drive along in a clear sea on a free wind, or to haul into dock, or to warp up a quiet river, butting aside the lazy vessels as they swing at anchor. How do we sail, and haul, and warp in these Arctic Seas! It is a long story, and, to understand it, we must begin at the beginning.

HUMMOCKS.

I have already described that enormous winter growth which, under the name of the "great pack," blocks up the entire waters of this region from the unknown North to the marginal influences of the Gulf Stream. What is this "middle" pack, into whose eastern margin we had now thrust ourselves?

The short but ardent summer of the Arctic zone, with its continuous sun, aided by a rapid drift toward the Atlantic Ocean, and by compensating currents

6

from the warm regions of the equator, soon reduces the winter pack into straggling fields of diminished thickness and integrity. These, uniting again by their cohesive tendencies, form an irregularly lenticular raft, which occupies the central portions of the bay, and is called the "middle" ice, to distinguish it from the great pack of winter.

This, then, is the summer remnant of the winter growth—a patch-work composed of all sorts of ice, diversified in pattern, age, and condition, and varying in size from small fragments, called "skreed," to "floes" or fields, so limited that the eye defines their extent. The floes may be said to form the basis of the pack. Their thickness ranges from a few inches to many feet, and their diameter is often many miles. I can not attempt to describe the uniform dreariness of their water-sodden marshes and long snow-covered platforms, without a point to mark "the level waste, the rounding gray." This sameness, however, is not always so absolute; for, at the margins of the floes, where their ragged edges have come into grinding contact, the ice is piled up into ridges, that streak the surface like the mounds of a recently-ditched meadow. These are the "hummocks."

The near effect of the ice and water, where they come together is not without beauty of its own. The water is itself of an inky darkness, a quality seemingly independent of mere contrast. It is rarely even ruffled by the wind; and its placid surface reflects the marginal ice, with its submerged tongues, in mirror-like accuracy.

This ice is the great bugbear of Baffin's Bay navigation: yet I can not help thinking that somewhat too much stress is laid by the English navigators upon its character of a central barrier. Not only its condition, but its general extent, varies with the season. It is well known to the most observant of the whalers that the winds of the early spring, or "breaking-up" period, almost enable them to determine its position in advance. A preponderance of northwest winds will drive it from the American coast; or the northeasters of the spring and summer will often distribute it into long straggling bands, that intrude upon certain portions of the upper coast, as at Haröe, Svartehuk, and the Duck Islands.

The axis of Baffin's Bay, according to our own observations, which add nearly thirty miles to the width of Davis' Straits at Cape Walsingham, is from the north by east. The great bodies of ice, which enter this bay from Lancaster Sound and the northern estuaries of Jones and Smith, are undoubtedly impressed by the earth's rotation as they proceed to the south, thus causing an accumulation on the coasts of North America, which augments with the increasing radius of rotation, while the Greenland side is left completely open.

As we advance to the north, this passage becomes more circumscribed and uncertain, so that the ice is generally encountered by the whalers before they reach the 70th parallel. When, however, they pass to the north of latitude 73° 50′ they enter upon a region of nearly perpetual ice. Here the middle pack intrudes upon the shores, and fills that large horse-shoe indentation which is known as Melville Bay. This term is vaguely applied by the whalers to a sweep of coast extending from the Devil's Thumb, or Wilcox Point, to Capes Dudley Diggs and York. It comprises on the charts the several bays of Prince Regent, Melville, Duneira, and Allison.

The causes of this accumulation, so disastrous to the navigation of the western and northern waters of the bay, may be attributed in some measure to the high latitudes leaving the ice as yet unaffected by the southerly and westerly influences to which I have alluded, and therefore more open to local causes of deviation, such as currents and winds. The neighborhood of this region to the sources of ice supply, the sounds of Jones, Lancaster, and Wolstenholme, may be referred to as another cause; for the ice, after changing its original axis of drift, has not yet attained its free rate of motion in a new direction. Then, too, there are some peculiarities in the current action of the bay, as yet imperfectly studied, which can not be without their influence. It is altogether probable that a portion of the interval between the eastern and western coasts is the seat of a partial slackwater, or even rotating eddy. And, in addition to all these, there is the direct agency of that great body of water which issues from Lancaster Sound. This passes from west to east, in latitude 74° 30′; and my notes indicate the axis of its course as the line at which the Melville Bay accumulation begins.

All of these causes are undoubtedly aided by the numerous bergs discharged from the glaciers of this portion of the Greenland coast, which have often movements counter to those of the surface ice, and retard its descent and progress very considerably.

It is through this ice-clogged bay that the great fleets of Baffin whale ships have, for the last thirty-two years, made an annual attempt to pass. The mysticete, driven from their feeding grounds on the coast of Greenland, have sought a refuge on the western side; and their seats of favorite resort, in the early part of the season, are now in the waters of Lancaster, Prince Regent, and Wellington Sounds, and the indentations of the northwestern coast of Baffin's Bay. The vessels which have succeeded in penetrating this intervening ice-barrier before August are sure of a full cargo; but after this time all efforts are useless. The "fleet" is spoken of as "baffled," and is obliged to seek other "grounds" to the south and west. It is, in fact, a great lottery, the caprices of the ice controlling the efforts of the most daring; and, for the last two years or "seasons" before our arrival, the whalers had completely failed in effecting a passage.

I have been surprised that this region has been so little attended to by the very able English hydrographers who have visited these seas. The valuable "wind and current" generalizations of Lieutenant Maury would be especially applicable to ice navigation, and their application to the fishing grounds of Baffin's Bay would be a matter of large utilitarian interest. The commanders of the whaling ships are an intelligent set of men, and they have acquired, by dint of long and sometimes dearly bought experience, a valuable tact in the navigation of this intricate region. It is surely to be regretted that the materials which they could furnish have not yet been made a subject of scientific record and comparison. Since the year 1819, from which we may date the opening of Melville Bay, no less than 210 vessels have been destroyed in attempting its passage!

MIDDLE PACK.

CHAPTER XI.

We left the American expedition on the threshold of the ice of Melville Bay, immovably fixed, to all appearance, in the middle pack. I promised at that time to describe the sort of efforts that were making for its release; but I shall do better, perhaps, by giving a general view of what one of the figures of speech allows us to call ice navigation. To those who prefer a more specific form of narrative, I give the choice of dates from the 8th to the 29th of July, and permit them to be assured that they are reading the story of our progress for the day they have chosen.

Let us begin by imagining a vessel, or, for variety, two of them, speeding along at eight knots an hour, and heading directly for a long, low margin of ice about two miles off. "D'ye see any opening?" cries the captain, hailing an officer on the foretopsail-yard. "Something like 'a lead' a little to leeward of that iceberg on our port-bow." In a little while we near the ice; our light sails are got in, our commander taking the place of the officer, who has resumed his station on the deck.

Before you, in a plain of solid ice, is a huge iceberg, and near it a black, zigzag canal, checkered with recent fragments.

Now commences the process of "conning." Such work with the helm is not often seen in ordinary seas. The brig's head is pointed for the open gap; the watch

MELVILLE BAY.

are stationed at the braces; a sort of silence prevails. Presently comes down the stentorian voice of our commander, "Hard-a-starboard," and at the same moment the yards yield to the ready haul at the braces. The brig turns her nose into a sudden indentation, and bangs her quarter against a big lump of "swashing" ice. "Steady there!" For half a minute not a sound, until a second yell—"Down, down! hard down!" and then we rub, and scrape, and jam, and thrust aside, and are thrust aside; but somehow or other find ourselves in an open canal, losing itself in the distance. This is "a lead."

As we move on, congratulating ourselves—if we think about the thing at all—that we are "good" for a few hundred yards more, a sudden exclamation, addressed to nobody, but sufficiently distinctive, comes from the yard-arm (we'll call it "pshaw!"), and, looking ahead, we see that our "lead" is getting narrower, its sides edging toward each other—it is losing its straightness. At the same moment comes a complicated succession of orders: "Helm-a-starboard!" "Port!" "Easy!" "So!" "Stead*ie-ee-ee!*" "Hard-a-port!" "Hard, hard, hard!" (scrape, scratch, thump!) "Eugh!" an anomalous grunt, and we are jammed fast between two great ice-fields of unknown extent. The captain comes down, and we all go quietly to supper.

Next come some processes unconnected with the sails, our wings. These will explain, after Arctic fashion, the terms "heave," and "warp," and "track," and "haul," for we are now beset in ice, and what little wind we have is dead ahead. A couple of hands, under orders, of course, seize an iron hook or "ice-anchor," of which we have two sizes, one of forty, and another of about a hundred pounds. With this they jump from the bows, and "plant it" in the ice ahead, close to the edge of the crack, along which we wish to force our way. To plant an ice-anchor, a hole is cut obliquely to the surface of the floe, either with an ice-chisel, or with the anchor itself used pickaxe fashion, and into this hole the larger curve of the anchor is hooked. Once fast, you slip a hawser

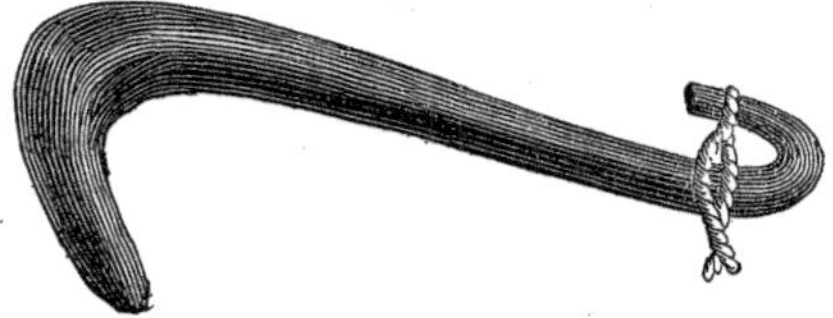

ICE-CHISEL

around its smaller end, and secure it from slips by a "mousing" of rope-yarn. The slack of the hawser is passed around the shaft of our patent winch—an apparatus of cogs and levers standing in our bows—and every thing, in far less time than it has taken me to describe it, is ready for "heaving."

Then comes the hard work. The hawser is hauled *taut;* the strain is increased; every body, captain, cook, steward, and doctor, is taking a *spell* at the "pump handles" or overhauling the warping gear; for dignity does not take care of its hands in the middle pack; until at last, if the floes be not too obdurate, they separate by the wedge action of our bows, and we force our way into a little cleft, which is kept open on either side by the vessel's beam. But the quiescence, the equilibrium of the ice, which allows it to be thus severed at its line of junction, is rare enough. Oftentimes we heave, and haul, and sweat, and, after parting a ten-inch hawser, go to bed wet, and tired, and discontented, with nothing but experience to pay for our toil. This is "warping."

But let us suppose that, after many hours of this sort of unprofitable labor, the floes release their pressure, or the ice becomes frail and light. "Get ready the lines!" Out jumps an unfortunate with a forty-pound "hook" upon his shoulder, and, after one or two duckings, tumbles over the ice and plants his anchor on a distant cape, in line with our wished-for direction. The poor fellow has done more than carry his anchor; for a long white cord has been securely fastened to it, which they "pay out" from aboard ship as occasion requires. This is a whale-line—cordage thin, light, strong, and of the best material. It passes inboard through a block, and then, with a few artistic turns, around the capstan. Its "slack" or loose end is carried to a little windlass at our main-mast. Now comes the warping again. The first or heavy warping we called "heaving:" this last is a civilized performance; "all hands" walking round with the capstan-bars to the click of its iron pauls, or else, if the watch be fresh, to a jolly chorus of sailors' songs.

We have made a few hundred yards of this light warping, when the floes, never at rest, open into a tortuous canal again. We can dispense with the slow traction of the capstan. The same whale-line is passed out ahead, and a party of human horses take us in tow. Each man—or horse, if you please—has a canvas strap passing over his shoulder and fastened to the tow-line; or, nautically, as this is a chapter explanatory of terms, "toggled to the warp." This harnessing is no slight comfort to hands wet with water at the freezing point; and with its aid they tug along, sometimes at a weary walk, and sometimes at a dog-trot. This is "tracking."

When we could neither "heave," nor "warp," nor "track," nor sail, we resorted to all sorts of useless expedients, such as sawing, cutting, and vainly striving to force our way into a more hopeful neighborhood. It was long before experience taught us to spare ourselves this useless labor, and even after we had become convinced that the periods for effective effort of this sort were so few and far between, it was hard for men of our temperaments to await idly a change for better things.

We were twenty-one days thus imprisoned, never leaving a little circle of some six miles radius, and measuring our progress by yards and feet rather than by miles. For the rest, my journal must give its own picture of this season of "besetment."

DEVIL'S THUMB.

CHAPTER XII.

"*July* 10. For the past twenty-four hours helplessly fast, unable to move in any direction more than twenty yards. The wind, which had been from the northeast, hauled yesterday afternoon to the westward, since when, blowing at times quite freshly, it has acquired more and more southing, till it has got round to southwest by west. From the commencement of this change to this moment, the pack has been steadily closing, becoming more and more impenetrable.

"Now I begin to realize some of the scenes described in polar travel. Go up to the foretop, a height of eighty-five feet, and the entire horizon is snow-covered ice. Here and there a very distant berg breaks the uniformity, but the hummocks and the water-pools are softened down by the distance into one plane surface of cold white, and, except to landward, there is nothing to arrest the eye.

"This shore, however, although fifty miles off, is visible enough, showing throughout all the hours of our now perpetual day a tall peak, rising like a lighthouse from a group of hills. This striking landmark is called the 'Devil's Thumb.'

"*July* 11. The wind changed at 8 A.M., coming from the northward and eastward; but the pack seems as yet uninfluenced. We are hemmed in as closely as ever.

"Last night Lieutenant De Haven, who had been fixedly examining an object between us and the shore, passed the glass to me, with the question, 'What do you make of that?' Without any hesitation, I answered, 'A mast, with gaff and main-sail partially clewed up.' It seemed to me that one of the Danish fore-and-aft schooners had anchored at the edge of the pack, or just within it. Our commander thought so too; but a glance through a Fraunhofer telescope showed it to be a mere freak of refraction.

"Several seals were seen upon the more distant floes, but, in spite of all my efforts, I could not approach near enough for a shot. They are always on the alert, and at the slightest suspicion betake themselves to their holes. The Esquimaux use a canvas frame or screen, which they move before their persons, and, by a patient process of stalking, succeed in getting within rifle shot. The Danish company supply them with arms, and they seldom miss their aim. I managed to get sufficiently close to recognize two species—the Greenland Saddle-back and the Vituline (*Phoca Groenlandica* and *P. vitulina*); but strange to say, the Rough seal, the *Phoca fœtida* of the Greenland fau na, of which we had seen so many, was not with them.

"With a good glass, you may study these animals in their natural habitudes undisturbed by suspicion. As thus seen, in the centre of a large floe, and within retreating distance of his hole, the seal is a perfect picture of solitary enjoyment, rolling not unlike a horse stretching his hide, awkwardly spreading out his flippers, and twisting his rump toward his head. Again he will wriggle about in the most grotesque manner —the sailors call it 'squirming'—every now and then rubbing his head against the snow. The shapes of a seal, or rather his aspects, are full of strange variety. At a side view, with his caudal end *slued* round to the side from you, and his head lifted suspiciously in the air, he is the exact image of a dog—*Chien de mer*. During his wriggles, he resembles a great snail: a little while after, he turns his back to you, and rises up on his side flippers like a couching hunter preparing for a shot, the very image of an Esquimaux.

"It is said by the systematic writers that the ice-hole of the Vituline seal is often used by several of them in common. This was not confirmed by our observations while in the pack. Each animal seemed to have its separate hole, though two of them would occasionally be close to one another.

"The Bearded seal (*P. barbata*) attains a greater size than any of these. Two overgrown obese monsters were seen at a distance. They are regarded by the Danes as differing only in age from the Greenland seal (*P. Groenlandica*), the lighter color and greater fineness of the fur being a universal accompaniment of youth.

"I shot to-day several specimens of the white gull

of Baffin's Bay, well called the Ivory (*Larus eburneus*). It is a singularly beautiful bird, so faultless in its purity of white as to be descried with difficulty on the surface of the snow. The legs, which are deep black, are all that you see at a little distance. A specimen shot a few days afterward had numerous ash-colored spots on the wings and shoulders, perhaps immature markings.

"In addition to the Ivory, I have noticed, since our entry into the pack, the Silvery and Burgomaster gulls (*L. argentatus* and *L. glaucus*), but the kittiwakes (*L. tridactylus*) have disappeared. The mollemokes are still abundant. Two terns, one the *Sterna arctica*, the other unrecognized, with a solitary Lestris (*L. parasitica*), complete our catalogue of birds.

"The Aneroid index now stands at 29° 05′, corrected—lower than it has been since leaving New York.

"*July* 12. The changes in the ice since dinner have been such as to invite us to renewed exertion. They were indeed protean; the pack was not the same for ten minutes together. Go below, congratulating yourself on the headway you are making, and when you come back you are hopelessly 'fast.' Go down again to chronicle your vexation, and you are surrounded by open leads before you have put away your journal. Stranger still is the uncertain influence of warping. A single whale-line will sometimes force the brig into a barely perceptible crevice, enlarging it into a 'trackable' canal, while in another attempt a four-inch hawser will be stranded without producing the slightest effect.

"This afternoon before we began our work, except that the water-pools had become larger and more frequent, you would not at first glance have detected any change; but by fixing the eye carefully and continuously upon a line in advance of us, where an old lead had closed two days before, you could perceive a very slight separation. The closed line had become a crack at least three or four inches wide. On our sending out a hawser to a solid floe ahead, and heaving in with the patent windlass, a distinct movement was seen in the floe. The aperture, at first a mere crack, widened to a couple of feet, dividing, as it did so, two fields of at least twenty acres area. The traction continuing, our wedge-shaped bows insinuated themselves into a self-made channel, and, acquiring new momentum, we forced a barrier ahead, dragging the Rescue after us. Such instances illustrate strikingly the effects of a constant force upon large masses in equilibrium. To the eye it would seem impossible to influence by such means fields of ice weighing hundreds of thousands of tons. Yet, in the nicely poised condition of the floes, they invariably yield to continued traction.

"While working with the rest of the crew upon the ice, I was startled by a cry of 'bear.' Sure enough it was that menagerie wonder. Not, however, the sleepy thing which, with begrimed hair, and subdued, dirty face, appeals to your sympathies as he walks the endless rounds of a wet cage. Our first polar bear moved past us on the floes, a short half mile off, with the leisurely march of fearless freedom. He was a bear of the first magnitude, about nine feet long, as we afterward found by measuring his tracks. His length appeared to us still greater than this, for he carried his head and neck on a line with the long axis of his body. His color, as defined upon the white snow, was a delicate yellow—not tawny, but a true ochre or gamboge—and his black, blue-black, nose looked abrupt and accidental. His haunches were regularly arched, and, supported as they were on ponderous legs, gave him an almost elephantine look. The movements of the animal were peculiar. A sort of drawling dignity seemed to oppress him, and to forbid his lifting his august legs higher than was absolutely necessary. It might have been an instinctive philosophy that led him to avoid the impact of his toes upon ice of uncertain strength; but whatever it was, he reminded me of a colossal puss in boots.

"I will not dwell upon our adventures, as, on murderous thoughts intent, we chased this bear. We were an absurd party of zealots, rushing pell-mell upon the floes with vastly more energy than discretion. While walking in the lightest manner over suspicious ice, my companion next in line behind me disappeared, gun and all; yet, after getting him out, we insanely continued our chase with the aid of boats. After laboring very hard for about three hours, repeated duckings in water at 30° cooled down our enthusiasm. The bear, meantime, never varied from his unconcerned walk. We saw him last in a labyrinth of hummock ice.

"In the evening it blew a gale from the southward and eastward, holding on until midnight. Strange to say, it produced no marked effects on the pack. At first we feared a nip, for, judging from the wind which swept our floes, it must have been severe in the open sea. But we rode it out in our icy harbor without any trouble, although the undulations of both ice and water told of the commotion outside.

"Our day's progress was one mile and a half.

"*July* 13. Fast again! for, except that mile and a

half of yesterday, we are nearly where we started from. The prevalent winds have been from the southward. Is it to them that we owe our exemption from the southeasterly drift, which otherwise we had been taught to expect?

"The drift of the surface acalephæ, as seen in the leads, is to the northward.

"Day delightful, crew playing foot-ball and running races on the ice.

"*July* 14–15. The American expedition advances half a ship's length.

"*July* 16. How very strange! can it be midsummer? The ice through which we yesterday attempted to work our way was from two to four feet thick, and, as the broken fragments closed around the vessels, they froze into a solid mass. For sixteen hours the thermometer stood below the freezing point, and the mean temperature of the entire day was but 34° 4′.

"The sun shines always, and, except when in his low curve, about the northern meridian, his glare is so bright that we go about in owl-like goggles, that buckle over the nose. Yet, with all this light, we are fortunate if our noonday thermometers give us 40°.

"On the 13th two vessels were entered in the log-book as seen to the southward and eastward, on the margin of the pack. On the 15th they were observed to have changed their bearings, thus proving that it was not a freak of refraction. On the 16th five were reported; as nearly as we could make out, one ship, a brig, and three barques. They proved to be whalers, returning from their unsuccessful attempt to penetrate Melville Bay to the North Water.

"*July* 17. New ice forming constantly in the little pool which holds our vessels. This morning it was half an inch thick. This process of cementing going on in the month of July looks discouraging. We have now been ten days beset; and, with the exception of the 12th, when an unusual wind slightly affected our ice, we have advanced but little more than a couple of ship's lengths. Indeed, for the past five days, our progress has been absolutely nothing; for, although our daily observations prove that the great pack is in motion, our relative position remains unchanged. In four days we have made about four miles of southerly drift, and to-day our chronometers indicate another four to the west. How very sad it would be to remain prison-bound in this icy prairie until the season of search has passed by! Certain it is that some great commotion must influence this ice, if it is ever to liberate us, for upon thaws we can place no reliance.

"To-day we organized foot-races, and our friends of the Rescue had a regular *divertissement* of single-stick, foot-ball, and fancy matches against time. Our best runner made his mile in seven minutes eleven seconds.

"*July* 18. To-day is our eleventh day since entering the ice, our sixth of nearly absolute immobility. We made, however, two ship's lengths by alternate warping and cutting through ice three feet thick. Our incessant exertions have fatigued us: we have already parted four cables by heaving; fortunately nobody injured.

"I took to-day a long gun-walk, bringing back a couple of tern and some gulls. Our commander counted from aloft nearly a hundred seals, distributed listlessly over the ice. I have tried in vain to stalk them.

"*July* 19. The men turned in at midnight, to awake again at six. All hands are pretty well used up.

"Ahead of us a hundred and fifty yards is a sheet of water, which some of us have called 'the lake.' During the processes by which the various floes of the great pack have been condensed into one unbroken level, some peculiarity in the shape of the floes has rescued here and there a little of the mother element, leaving it in the form of open pools or lakes. These form the radiating centres of the leads, which are now our only avenues of escape. It is toward one of them that our efforts of progress are directed. If we reach it to-night, we may make a good mile on our dreary course. Such is our immovable besetment, that we look to 'a mile' as a marked progress.

"Our men are now 'all hands' at the windlass, singing and heaving, 'rousing her home.' The strain is sometimes enormous, but there is no remedy: it is tug or stick. We have parted two hawsers already, and, although some half dozen strong men take charge of the slack, the great cable sometimes surges from the snatch with such force and speed that clouds of smoke arise from the friction.

"Sending out or 'planting' these cables is an operation of no little danger. The ice is very varying in its thickness and tenacity, and long detours are necessary before the anchor can be placed in the desired position. On such parties a ducking is an expected consummation; and more than once I have seen both man and anchor suddenly disappear together. It is often necessary, also, to clear or straighten the hawser after its attachment, for the hummocks and other projections catch the rope, and, unless released, would divert the line of traction from the required direction. On such occasions the men must crawl, jump, wade, or swim to clear the 'slack.' Operations like this are severe trials, both of energy and health ; more severe, I sometimes think, than any which are encountered in the systematic explorations of the British voyagers.

"*July* 20. We failed to reach the 'lake' yesterday, gaining it to-day. We cast off from the Rescue and made three minutes and twenty seconds of sail, measured by a Parkinson and Frodsham chronometer! That over, we are again wedged in ice.

"Our commander, who had heretofore miraculously escaped his ducking, while standing upon a miniature South America of ice, punching with a boat-hook at a little Cape Horn, went down suddenly this morning, leaving a Terra del Fuego of slush and water to mark the place where he had been. He had some trouble in scrambling out.

"A short time after this, while we were joking about his adventure over a quiet little noggin of whisky-punch, Mr. Boatswain Brooks, a capital seaman, who did watch duties on board the Rescue, whispered down the hatchway, 'A bear along side!' This time the rascal was right aboard of us, and we kept below the bulwarks, so that his wanderings were rather matters of caprice than of fear.

"He was a young animal, not more than six or seven feet in length, with a color even more delicately tinted than the other, for the yellow was only apparent at the armpits, haunches, and spinal ridge; his muzzle, lips, and dew-laps were of dark purple.

"When first seen he rose upon his hind palms, and, lifting his neck in the direction of our brig, snuffed the air inspectingly. Satisfied with our appearance, he walked well within shot; but just as we were about to reward his confidence with a bullet, he gamboled off to a neighboring hummock. The poor fellow had such a look of life enjoyment that I felt glad that I had not fired, although my hand was upon the trigger.

"Once upon this little hill of ice, he was at home again, favoring us with some bear play, snapping at the inoffending icicles, rubbing his mouth sideways against the snow, and rolling over and over from top to bottom. I mention all these as characteristics of the animal. Of course we chased him, and of course we failed. We had not yet acquired our experience as bear hunters.

"*July* 21. It rained yesterday, and the ice is perceptibly affected. These rains, of which we have now had several, exercise a very rapid influence upon the weaker floes.

"Heaving, boring, sailing, but no progress worth noting!

"*July* 22. As we were in the act of warping into a narrow chasm, the capricious ice closed in upon us, nipping us on our counter, and heaping up some two feet.

"We filled our water casks from a pool in a glued-up iceberg, and saw another bear! We were too wise this time to chase him.

"Our progress—not to be measured by yards."

CHAPTER XIII.

I HAVE continued my journal long enough to prove the wearying sameness of our days. I wish now to say a few words about the local characters of the seat of our imprisonment.

The ice was of several kinds. One was the true material of the winter floe, varying in thickness from seven feet to as many inches. This was snow-covered, patched by fresh water-pools, and sufficiently unaltered to retain its crystalline structure in full integrity. When it was over two feet in thickness, portions taken from its surface gave no evidence of salt under the test of nitrate of silver.

A second ice I have called water-sodden. It seldom exceeded a foot in thickness, but was irregularly thawed in patches and striated lines. It was thoroughly infiltrated with salt water, and broke readily under a blow, displaying at the lines of fracture the

vertical prisms of its crystalline structure. This ice formed the basis of the pack; and although, by selecting our pathway, it could be traversed on foot, it was irregular and unsafe. It cracked readily before the wedge-action of our bows.

A third variety of ice was the honey-combed or cellular, seen beneath the surface in crude, olive-green masses. This ice, though generally very tenacious, was sometimes so soft that you could plunge a boat-hook through it. It resembled a grossly-cellular Parmesan cheese.

A fourth was as finely granulated as loaf-sugar, yet as tough as whitleather. Although thoroughly permeated with water, it was as unyielding as asphalt. We were often helplessly impacted in its insidious rottenness. It would neither fracture nor give. A cutting instrument pierced it like a cork, leaving a merely local puncture, and it differed so little in specific gravity from the water as to remain almost suspended.

But the surface of all this diversity was mantled over by the leading feature of our prospect, snow; not snow as at home, with rounded hill slope and gesticulating tree, but a surface deprived of all variety save such as resides in itself. This is not so scanty as one might at first suppose, for it rises into hummocks, which impress their shadows on the ice; it thaws, and black pools eat themselves into its level wastes; it freezes again, and bright silver streaks run like metal rivers along the leads. The winds, too, which drive into one this great mass of floating fields, leave here and there little areas protected by icy edges. These lake-like pools are haunts of the seal and the diver. I have often observed the white lip of the snow at the margin of them reflected in the water of a marked claret color, the shades varying from a rose-pink to a decided red. For a long time I supposed these reflected images to be real, till one day the captain, calling my attention to this "red ice," thrust a boat-hook at it, and cried out that it was a reflection. This reflected image is generally very well defined, and beneath it there is sometimes a second image of a bluish tinge. The explanation is at once suggested by the fact.

The movements of this aggregated plain upon itself are even more incapable of analysis than the great general laws of its drift.

I spent many days in trying to determine the surface currents by the movements of the acalephæ, especially the clios, in the leads; but the disturbing influences of the floes moving upon each other prevented any reliable deductions. Camphor floats were equally deceptive, probably from the same cause.

I found, however, that there existed in nearly every case a second current, some one or two fathoms below the first, and that the upper of them generally followed the direction of the wind; so that I regarded it at last as a tolerable index of the surface drift. The second or inferior current is more difficult to explain by rule. It is influenced, of course, by the shape of the floes, their various deflecting angles, the degrees of resistance they exert, as determined by their weight and mass, and no doubt by other causes of which we are ignorant.

Taken in connection with the great general movement of the pack, these currents form a complicated problem of high practical interest to those who navigate in the ice. But its solution must be reserved for scientific men. Much as I respect the ice-masters, the Greenland pilots as they are termed, who have devoted their lives to its practical study, I confess that I am altogether skeptical as to their ability to generalize in an area like this. Even the general axis of motion, the trend of the pack, can seldom be ascertained. I have seen the ice open into parallel and transverse canals from horizon to horizon; and a few moments afterward, without any observed changes of current, wind, or temperature, these canals would rapidly become curvilinear, and we seemed as if in the centre of a great system of rotation.

Since our entry into the ice, we were comparatively without visits from birds. The ducks had deserted us; but the red-throated diver (*Colymbus septentrionalis*, Temm.) abounded in the larger openings. The black guillemots (*Uria grylle*, Temm.) sometimes passed us in groups, or were started up in the leads. We missed the kittiwake. The Laridæ were represented only by the Glaucous and Ivory gulls. These last were in company with tern, and flew over the floes seeking the refuse of our vessels. The strong and graceful flight which distinguishes the gulls is especially evident in the Ivory variety—without exception, the most attractive bird I ever saw. The Fulmar petrel, a solitary jager (*Lestris parasitica*), the Stunt jager of Marten, one "boatswain," a bird which I had not previously seen, except in company with the Tridactyl gull—these complete the list.

The only fish we met with at this time was the *Merlangus polaris* of Parry's first voyage. We caught it often in the surface pools that adjoined the leads. It never exceeded six inches in length. From these I obtained some specimens of lernians. Strange to say, no less than three individuals were noticed with these parasites, and in one the dorsal ridge was completely covered with them.

ENTERING MELVILLE BAY.

CHAPTER XIV.

Our position, on entering this pack twenty-one days ago, was latitude 74° 08′, longitude 59° 04′. Our observations now gave us a latitude of 73° 54′, longitude 60° 06′—an average progress of about a mile a day. We had therefore been three weeks completely imprisoned, and the season for useful search was rapidly flitting by, when, on the 27th of July, came the dawning promise of escape.

A steady breeze had been blowing for several days from the northward and westward, and under its influence the ice had so relaxed, that, had not the wind been dead ahead, we should have attempted sails. Our floe surface, disturbed by these new influences, gave us a constantly-shifting topography. It was curious to see the rapidity of the transformations. At one moment we were closed in by ice three feet thick, with a worn-down berg fifty feet deep on our beam; our bows buried in hummocky masses, and our stern-post clogged with frozen sludge: in ten minutes open lanes were radiating from us in every direction, cracks becoming rivers, and puddles lakes: warping ahead for five minutes, every thing around us was ice again.

But changes were going on. The sky had become lowering, the gulls had left us, and the barometer had fallen eight tenths since the day before.

Late on the afternoon of the 28th, after another long day of unprofitable warping, the wind shifted to the eastward. The floes opened still wider, something like water was visible to the north and east, and at 9h. 30m. P.M. we "cast off," set our main-sail, and, with feelings of joyous relief, began to bore the ice. This wind soon freshened to a southeaster, and we dashed along to the northeast in a sea studded with icebergs. Broken floes running out into "streams" were on all sides of us; but, only too glad to be once more free, we bored through them for the inshore circuit of Melville Bay.

After a little while the horizon thickened; and although our wind, surrounded as we were by ice, could hardly be called a gale, heavy undulations began to set in, making an uncomfortable sea, rendered dangerous indeed by the swashing ice and a growing fog.

The ice, too, after a little while, was no longer the rotten, half-thawed material of the middle pack, but heavy floes eight or ten feet of solid thickness, which seemed to stand out from the shore.

Presently we found ourselves, urged by wind and sea, on a lee ridge of undulating fragments. There was no help for it: with grinding crash we entered its tumultuous margin. Before we had bored into it more than ten yards, we were on the edge of a nearly submerged iceberg, which, not being large enough to resist the swell, rolled fearfully. The sea dashed in an angry surf over its inclined sides, rattling the icy fragments or "brash" against its irregular surface. Our position reminded me of the scenes so well described by Beechy in the voyage of the Dorothea and Trent. For a time we were awkwardly placed, but we bored through; and the Rescue, after skirting the same obstruction, managed also to get through without damage.

We continued to run along with our top-sail yard on the cap, but the growing fog made it impossible to keep on our course very long. After several encounters with the floating hummocks, we succeeded in tying fast to a heavy floe, which seemed to be connected with the land, and were thus moored within that mysterious circuit known as Melville Bay.

It is during the transit of this bay that most of the catastrophes occur which have made the statistics of the whalers so fearful. It was here, about twenty miles to the south of us, that in one year more than one thousand human beings were cast shelterless upon the ice, their ships ground up before their eyes. It is rarely that a season goes by in which the passage is attempted without disaster.

The inshore side of the indentation is lined by a sweep of glacier, through which here and there the dark headlands of the coast force themselves with severe contrast. Outside of this, the shore, if we can call it such, is again lined with a heavy ledge of ground ice, thicker and more permanent than that in motion. This extends out for miles, forming an icy margin or beach, known technically as the "land ice," or "the fast." Against this margin, the great "drift" through which we had been passing exerts a remitting action, receding sometimes under the influence of wind and currents so as to open a tortuous and uncertain canal along its edge, at others closing against it in a barrier of contending floes and bergs.

Our initiation into the mysteries of this region was ominous enough. It blew a gale. The offing was a scene of noisy contention, obscured by a dense fog, through which rose the tops of the icebergs as they drifted by us. Twice in the night we were called up to escape these bergs by warping out of their path. Imagine a mass as large as the Parthenon bearing down upon you before a storm-wind!

The immediate site of our anchorage was about eighteen miles from the Black Hills, which rose above the glacier. It was truly an iron-bound coast, bergs, floes, and hummock ridges, in all the disarray of wintery conflict, cemented in a basis of ice ten feet thick, and lashed by an angry sea. It was the first time I had witnessed the stupendous results of ice action. I went out with Captain De Haven to observe them more closely. The hummocks had piled themselves at the edges of the floes in a set of rugged walls, sometimes twenty feet high; and here and there were icebergs firmly incorporated in the vast plain. Our attention was of course directed more anxiously to those which were drifting at large upon the open water; but we could not help being impressed by the solid majesty of these stationary mountains. The height of one of them, measured by the sextant, was two hundred and forty feet.

It was the motion of the floating bergs that surrounded us at this time, which first gave me the idea of a great under-current to the northward. Their drift followed some system of advance entirely independent of the wind, and not apparently at variance with the received views of a great southern current. On the night of the 30th, while the surface ice or floe was drifting to the southward with the wind, the bergs were making a northern progress, crushing through the floes in the very eye of the breeze at a measured rate of a mile and a half an hour. The disproportion that uniformly subsists between the submerged and upper masses of a floating berg makes it a good index of the deep sea current, especially when its movement is against the wind. I noticed very many ice-mountains traveling to the north in opposition to both wind and surface ice. One of them we recognized five days afterward, nearly a hundred miles on its northern journey.

In the so-called night, "all hands" were turned to, and the old system of warping was renewed. The unyielding ice made it a slow process, but enough was gained to give us an entrance to some clear water about a mile in apparent length. While we were warping, one of these current-driven bergs kept us constant company, and at one time it was a regular race between us, for the narrow passage we were striving to reach would have been completely barricaded if our icy opponent had got ahead.

This exciting race, against wind and drift, and with the Rescue in tow, was at its height when we reached a point where, by warping around our opponent, we might be able to make sail. Three active men were instantly dispatched to prepare the warps. One took charge of the hawser, and another of the iron crow or chisel which is used to cut the hole; the third, a brawny seaman, named Costa, was in the act of lift ing the anchor and driving it by main force into the solid ice, when, with a roar like near thunder, a crack ran across the berg, and almost instantly a segment about twice the size of our ship was severed from the rest. One man remained oscillating on the principal mass, a second escaped by jumping to the back ropes and chain shrouds of the bowsprit; but poor Costa! anchor and all, disappeared in the chasm! By a merciful Godsend, the sunken fragment had broken off so cleanly that, when it rose, it scraped against the fractured surface, and brought up its living freight along with it. Scared half to death, he was caught by the captain as he passed the jib-boom, and brought safe on board. This incident, coming thus early in our cruise, was a useful warning.

In spite of all our efforts, we had effected little since anchoring to this ice; but our position, as determined by observation and chronometer, was latitude 75° 02 27″, longitude 59° 50′ 42″, showing an advance of 40 miles to the northward since leaving the pack on the 29th.

"*August* 1. The last month of summer was upon us. July, the mid-summer of highest mean temperature and greatest ice dissolution, had done little for us. Our prospects were far from cheery. The season of complete consolidation, when winter closes the navigation of these seas, could not be postponed beyond fifty days longer, and we had yet to double the ice of Melville. Our mean daily temperature for the past week had been 37° 1′, and ice had formed during the hours of low sun three quarters of an inch thick. What an idea it gives one of the Arctic winter, to think that this short summer is nature's only compensation for the eight months of constant freezing that fill up the year. Our thermometers to-day fell to 28°; our mean for the entire twenty-four hours was but 32° 9′, not quite a degree above the freezing point.

"*August* 2. 'Warping!' Tired of the very word! About 2 P.M. a lead, less obstructed than its fellows, enabled us to crowd on the canvas, and sail with gentle airs for about two miles to the eastward, and then, losing what little wind we had, we tied up again to our friend the land ice; the little Rescue, as usual, a few yards astern.

"We have learned to love the sunshine, though we have lost the night that gives it value to others. It comes back to us this evening, after the gale, with a circuit of sparkling and imaginative beauty, like the spangled petticoat of a ballet-dancer in full twirl to a boy on his first visit to the opera. I borrow the comparison from one of my mess-mates; but, in truth, all this about sunshine and warmth is only comparative at the best, for, though writing on deck, 'out of doors,' as they say at home, the thermometers give us but 43°."

REMAINS OF A BERG.

IN A FOG.

CHAPTER XV.

WE were now opposite the line of coast between Allison's and Duneira Bays, immediately north of 75°. Here, with the new sunshine, the Greenland shore broke upon us. It was covered with extended glaciers, filling up the intervals between protruding masses of gneiss and other metamorphic rocks. The configuration of their surface, as seen from a distance of eighteen miles, had an apparent relation to that of the basis of country on which they were erected.

My first feeling was one of disappointment, for I had expected a more palpable resemblance to the glaciers of the Alps. But this feeling soon gave place to amazement. It is true that they were neither suspended upon the flanks of lofty mountains nor inclosed in valley hills; but these regions of eternal snow needed no mountain altitudes to furnish forth the increments of ice growth. Before us was an extended area of ice, rising by a regular talus till it cut against the sky, at the height of perhaps nine hundred feet. Its area, visible to the eye, measured rudely from two projecting headlands, was about forty miles by ten in one unbroken sweep; and its edges, where it entered the sea, were abrupt precipices, resembling the terrace-work of trap-rocks.

The icebergs were very numerous: I counted two hundred and eight within the horizon; and the in-shore or glacier face was quite choked with grounded masses, the more recent product of this great manufactory. Mr. Griffin, who visited one of those impacted in the floe, estimated its height by the fall of a bullet and a seconds' watch at three hundred and eighty feet. This was, of course, only an approximation; but the characteristic accuracy of the gentleman whose estimate it was, makes it certain that the altitude of this berg exceeded three hundred feet, a height which our subsequent observations proved to be of rare occurrence.

Baffin's Bay is not only the most abundant source of icebergs known, but their magnitude here is greater, probably, than any where else. The greatest altitude of antarctic ice mountains reported by Forster was "100 feet and upward." Graah's highest, on the east coast of Greenland, did not exceed 120 feet; Scoresby's, in the Spitzbergen seas, 200 feet; and Beechey's, in Magdalena Bay, not exceeding the same height; while Sir John Ross measured one in this very bay of 325 feet in height by 1200 long. Our own greatest sextant measurement, with a floe serving for a base line, gave us 260 feet; but we met others much higher. One of these bergs presented a long inclined talus, which was evidently part of an original slope, unaltered by after changes in equilibrium. I here noticed some interesting changes in the granular condition of its surface snows, establishing the same gradual increase of diameter which has been observed in the grains of the Alpine Neve.

August 3. On the 3d, while we were engaged in the eternal warping, a large Polar bear walked leisurely toward us. The floes were so separated that he had to take to the water, when a party from the Rescue pursued him in boats. Several times he attempted to gain the ice; but it crumbled under him, and he was forced to continue his swim. The boat gained on him rapidly; and at last, just as he had succeeded in effecting a foothold, gave him a ball at sixty yards. But, although wounded, he gained the ice, and, continuing his march, was soon lost among the icebergs.

Our progress to-day was by alternate warping and sailing; but in this latter resort we met a new impediment, the "young," or, as it is called by the whalers, the "bay ice." This formed a brittle pellicle nearly an inch thick, which, besides retarding our way, cut into our sides like glass. We combated it till 2 P. M., but then a thick fog obliged us to tie up to the floe.

In an atmosphere close upon the point of saturation, the fog vesicle is precipitated by a very slight difference in the temperatures of the atmospheric strata. I had observed these fogs before, when the surface water was a few degrees warmer than the atmosphere, which was generally near the freezing point. Now, however, the converse was the case; the temperature of the air was about 39°, and the water as low as 30°. The belt of condensation was singularly well defined Although we could not distinguish objects thirty paces off on the level of the decks, every thing was clearly discernible at an elevation of forty feet. I saw distinctly the surrounding bergs rising above a sea of mist.

One phenomenon, however, struck me as novel: at least I have never seen it described. It was this: Though the bergs were thus obscured at their bases by a dense plain of vapor, the Rescue, at an equal distance, was visible throughout her entire extent, encircled as by an *oriole* in a clear atmosphere. Repeated observations have suggested to me this explanation of this phenomenon.

These fogs, due to local refrigeration, are merely exceptional breaks-in upon our pervading sunshine. They are generally temporary, and the stratum of precipitation is so narrow that the sun is hardly intercepted. Evaporation continues as before; the decks are dry and heated; and the radiating influences of the vessel while stationary invest it with a sort of dome or halo of transparency. I have noticed this effect when looking at one of our brigs from on board the other, and have found that, if the sun was obscured for any length of time, the hull disappeared, and the upper rigging only protruded from a sea of mist. My sketch at the head of this chapter will show some of the curious phases of this phenomenon.

The effects of fogs upon our estimation of dimension and distance are well known: men are magnified to giants, and brigs "loom up," as the sailors term it, into ships of the line. They are especially interesting among the icebergs of this region. Two bergs were measured trigonometrically on the 4th, with a carefully ascertained base-line of four hundred yards. One of these, which I had estimated by eye as nearly three hundred feet high, gave but eighty-four. A second, measured by Captain Griffin, gave but forty: I had confidently assumed it to be over two hundred feet in height. In fact, our very hummocks were enlarged to icebergs, and every berg we looked at flared up into a colossal mountain. Scoresby, the most practical and observant of all who have written upon these seas, attributes this effect to an increase in the apparent distance. It seems to me that this false estimate of distance itself falls under an interesting class of deceptions almost convertible with the other, and, like it, dependent on the educated habitudes of the eye. Our ideas of distance determine our appreciation of magnitude, and a mistake of the one makes an error of the other. In the words of Professor Henry, who has ingeniously applied this view to our apprehension of relative motion, "The mind draws wrong conclusions from the evidence of the senses."

We remained with our anchors in the field ice for several days. The weather was clear and still, and gave us a favorable opportunity for observing the formation of the young ice on a large scale. When the thermometer is ranging between 33° and 28°, irregular polyhedral disks are seen forming over the whole open surface of the sea with a rapidity unknown under more southern skies, and covering it with a mosaic of pellicles about the size of a common saucer. From these, acicular rays shoot out in every direction, and in a very little while interlock themselves in a net-work of crystals. The ice film is now complete. In a few minutes more it has thickened to sheet ice, and becomes dangerous to navigators. One of our boats, which had been employed in passing from the brig to the field, was nearly cut through in a few hours. The

Advance herself, though plated with iron as perhaps no other vessel has been, showed unequivocal marks of damage upon her sheathing. She was heeled over, and fortified with three additional strips of boiler iron, extending back from her cut-water to her beam.

Our position was immediately opposite Duneira Bay, or, more exactly speaking, within it, at the distance of perhaps twelve miles from the shore. The scenery was peculiar, wanting the sameness which generally characterizes an Arctic landscape, and the atmosphere so bright that we could see every wrinkle on the face of the hills. An immense glacier formed a parapet wall of white masonry at their feet. On the other side of us was what had been the sea, a ragged surface of ice, unbroken except by the black rivers which wound themselves among its ridges, and here and there by the pinnacle of a projecting iceberg. Beyond came the varying horizon of icebergs; and still further on, shaded towers and sunlit pyramids of ice penciled their fantastic outlines against the sky. The sun, at its midnight elevation of three degrees, bathed the whole hemisphere in the purple light of our American sunset.

The bergs were an interesting subject of study. I counted one morning no less than two hundred and ten of them from our decks, forming a beaded line from the N.N.W. to the S.S.E. It was, in fact, an investing chain of ice mountains, for the offsets from the glaciers completed an apparent circle.

As we warped slowly along, I had an opportunity of partially measuring some of them. One, a magnificent specimen of ice architecture, was 195 feet high; another was, on its longest face, 310 fathoms, or 1860 feet: its height was 140 feet; and, reducing its mass

ENGRAVED BY J. SARTAIN FROM AN ORIGINAL SKETCH BY Dr KANE.

Under the lee of a berg.

STRIATED BY CHANGES OF EQUILIBRIUM.

to a parallelopipedon, its remaining side could not have been less than 1000 feet.

The symmetrical character of this great body of ice allowed me to estimate its magnitude and weight. Applying the recognized proportion of 8.2 below water for 1 above, and assuming, as Scoresby's experiments seem to justify, that thirty-five cubic feet of water in the Greenland seas have a weight of one ton, we have more than 2135 millions of cubic feet as the solid contents of the berg, and 61 millions of tons for its weight. It was therefore at least one third larger than the one which Scoresby measured on the eastern coast (Scoresby's Jour., p. 233). But great as it was, we saw others afterward still more stupendous, one of which I measured topographically.

Many of the bergs were covered with detritus. From one which had thawed down to the water's edge, I obtained some specimens of different rocks, which were found adhering to its upper face. They all belonged to the primary series—quartz, gneiss, syenite, augitic green-stone and clay slate. Some of them were marked with well-defined striæ, without angular crossings, smooth, and occasionally polished even highly; others were cut in facets of more or less regularity. They varied in size from large blocks to mere pebbles, conglomerated in the ice with finely-powdered gneissoid material. The berg had evidently changed its equilibrium; and it seemed as if these rocks had been cemented in its former base, and had there been subjected to attrition during its rotary oscillations against the bottom of the sea.

Others of them bore unmistakable marks of the moraines through which they had passed. The deposited material had a linear arrangement, as if dropped in series during the progress of the original glacier. In one instance an escarped face of berg was impressed in intaglio with the mould of the cliff from which it had been severed, and the upper marginal line was studded with angular and attrited fragments, evidently deposited during the movement of the glacier. This interesting fact, which I have not found noticed in any of the books, admitted of no deception. We could not stop to collect specimens, but I had time to make an accurate sketch of the section, and was near enough to recognize the schistose character of the adhering detritus.

The glacier, although too distant for nice observation, showed how very readily such a debacle might carry with it not only the impression of its valley side, but rudimentary moraine traces, deposited from the ridges adjacent and above. With a Fraünhofer glass, I could see that the dark knob-like protrusions, which rose here and there above the surface of the glacier, were the presenting faces of hills that went back in winding ridges, on both sides of which a discolored line indicated the accumulation of detritus.

The forms of these bergs were constantly varying under the action of the waves and the consequent changes in their equilibrium. Many of them were interesting, some fantastic, and some occasionally beautiful for their symmetry; but I do not think they impressed us as vividly as they seem to have done other voyagers with their resemblance to more familiar objects. Except when they came to us embellished by refraction, we had few of these imaginative pictures. Yet there was about the forms, and the coloring also, of the berg ice, a harmonious variety and grace, that needed no prototype to commend them.

The general shapes were those of the symmetrical solids, cubes, rhombs, and wedges, with surfaces presenting all the varieties of terrene configuration; but these were of the recently disrupted ice. In the older structures, where the degrading actions of the sea and air were aided by constantly recurring fractures, and with these constantly shifting centres of flotation, the changes had a more picturesque character; archways, natural bridges, terraces, and spiral ledges, from which the long icicles hung in grotesque and sparkling variety.

Sometimes, while I was studying the escarped faces of these bergs, we would enter little caves with shelving bottoms of pure blue, and, strange to say, teeming with crustacean life. I see by my journal that on one occasion, while trying, in company with my friend, Mr. Murdaugh, to net some of these misplaced entomostraca, I brought up a couple of forms of beroë, both with ciliate margins, apparently quite at home upon the pure surface of this icy basin.

In the course of our observations upon the different forms of ice that surrounded us, we realized some additional proofs of the deceptive character of Arctic distances. That aerial perspective, which is with us so palpable an element in the composition of a landscape, was scarcely to be noticed, except as tinting the background with a deeper transparency of blue. In the estimate of both altitude and horizontal distance, the iceberg was a complete puzzle. I have often started for a berg fast in the land floe, seemingly within musket-shot, and, after walking for nearly an hour, found its apparent position unchanged.

On one occasion, when engaged with our commander in an attempt to inspect a low mass of ice covered with detritus, which we expected to reach in a few minutes, a hard hour's pull left us the meagre satisfaction of finding the object perched on the summit of a lofty berg, whose base was even then below the horizon. That isolated projection upon an expanded level, and destitution of points of comparison, which make the pyramids so deceptive to the Egyptian traveler as he approaches them over the desert, have an equally marked application to the icebergs of the Polar Seas.

We had been struck, as I have mentioned already, by the absence of birds since our approach to the middle ice. Now, however, our stay had been so prolonged, that the absentees began to meet us on their return. Among the first and most welcome was the little Auk, the Rotgé of the whalers, coming down from its breeding-places in the still further north.

This bird, the *Uria alle* of Temminck, occupies, according to the ornithologists, an intermediate position between the Auk and the Guillemot. It is of the size of a partridge, fat, and delicately flavored; and it came to us in such immense flocks as to form a highly important addition to our diet list.

Indeed, no other bird migrates in such numbers, or contributes so largely to the pleasures of the Arctic table. Sir James Ross, in the Investigator, killed four thousand; and Mr. Martin, of the whale-ship Enterprise, who received the parting farewell of Sir John Franklin in this region, assures us that this far-sighted commander had killed and salted down so many of these birds as to augment his resources by nearly a two years' supply of food. For ourselves, without any special organization for the pursuit, we shot enough of them, from the time of their arrival till we entered

Lancaster Sound, to furnish the tables of all our messes abundantly.

They were first seen on the 6th, flying in detached parties to the southeast, and descending during the hours of low sun to the floes. As they became more numerous, they would cover the sea in detached patches, so crowding the margins of the floes and the detached pieces of ice as to streak the surrounding area with black figures. On such occasions, while feeding on the ciliogrades and entomostraca, they can be approached near enough to be knocked down with poles and boat-hooks. The whalers even shoot them with dried peas. The slaughter of these poor birds fell in large share to me; it was not uncommon to kill more than a hundred in a couple of hours.

CHAPTER XVI.

August 7. This morning our friends of the Rescue killed a bear. His curiosity cost him his life. When first seen, he was swimming toward the brig, breaking the newly-formed ice with his fore paws. Finding his progress by this method unsatisfactory, he made a succession of dives, coming up each time nearer his assailants, who were advancing to meet him in a boat. He had a strange look as he rose after one of these submersions, breaking the ice with his upward momentum, panting, and shaking his head like a dog to free it from the water. Captain Griffin, who was one of our best shots, lodged a ball under his left shoulder without effect. Several other bullets struck him before he turned to get away; and even when one of them had severed the lumbar vertebræ, the hardy animal regained the floe, dragging after him his paralyzed extremity. In this condition he was brought to bay, and received the *coup-de-grace* from a bayonet.

This bear had a coating of fat round the back and abdomen, which measured nearly three inches. When the animal is in good condition, this investing envelope of blubber pervades the entire cellular tissue, communicating to the flesh a strong and fishy taste. He is therefore, contrary to our butchers' rules at home, most palatable when lean. In the present case, we ate liberally of his steaks, although they savored somewhat of lamp oil.

The liver of the Polar bear is avoided by the Esquimaux. The whalers say that it produces a cutaneous eruption; and Scoresby, who observes upon this as a "curious fact," speaks also of sailors having died from its poisonous effects. Knowing that the seal, upon which the bear chiefly feeds, is palatable and nutritious throughout, I determined to test the somewhat anomalous fact of a poisonous viscus in a quadruped, and therefore ate of it freely. I found no ill effect from it. On the contrary, it was accepted afterward as a frequent dish upon our breakfast table; and during the trials of our long winter, it was never rejected by the crew. This idea, which has crept very generally into our systematic books, Fabricius, Richardson, and Parry among the rest, is probably based on some accidental cases of a diseased organ: it is as much at variance with sound analogies as with the experience of our party.

Three days after this we had another hunt. Three bears were seen stalking over the floes to our left, and almost at the same moment three more were reported on the land ice. While we were hesitating which party to attack, those on the land side took to the water ahead of us, and, with a sort of infatuation, swam toward the brig. The lead in which we were was not wider than the Schuylkill at Gray's Ferry, some three hundred yards perhaps, and a couple of minutes therefore brought our boat within shot.

The animals showed no signs of fear; instead of retreating, they bore directly down upon us. Imagine three huge beasts, of the largest size seen in our menageries, in white contrast with the dark water; their mouths open, as is their custom in swimming; and so close, that you could see their teeth shining over their dew-laps.

I do not think that we distinguished ourselves. The captain's gun missed fire; and I reserved mine for an occasion that never came. Mr. Lovell deposited his bullet in the base of the brain, killing his animal at first shot; but, while we were securing him, the rest turned tail, gained the floe, and escaped.

August 9. The day, although warm and delightful, with a temperature at noon of 38°, became toward its close suddenly obscured by fog. Our sensations of cold attendant upon this change were singularly disproportioned to the thermometrical indications. At 8 P.M., the temperature of the surface water, which had previously been 31°, suddenly rose to 36°; the air falling to 29°. This, while it had a direct connection with the fog, was interesting, as it marked the presence of a belt of warm water, surrounded by the same ice influences which depressed it before. I have had repeated occasion, while passing through this bay, to remark these sudden elevations of temperature in the surface water: the large areas of ice in their immediate neighborhood make the fact worth noting.

During this fog, we made fast to a permanent floe, awaiting our consort, the Rescue. The ice meanwhile drifted rapidly to the northward and westward while the wind was from the opposite quarter.

We sighted to-day a second spire of trap, resembling

Drawn by J. Hamilton, after a Sketch by Dr. E. K. Kane, U.S.N. — Engraved by J. Sartain.

The "Rescue" nipped in Melville Bay, August 1850.

the Devil's Thumb. It was Lord Melville's Monument; so named by Sir John Ross. The islands which are marked on the chart as "Brown's" we did not see, though we passed near their assumed position.

"*August* 10. Another day of sunshine. Were we in the Mediterranean, there could not be a warmer sky. It ends with the sky though; for our thermometers fell at four A.M. to 24°. A careful set of observations with Green's standard thermometers gave 18° as the difference between the sunshine and shade at noonday. The young ice was nearly an inch thick. Myriads of Auks were seen, and the usual supply duly slaughtered.

"Melville's Monument appeared to-day under a new phase, rising out from the surrounding floe ice, either a salient peninsula or an isolated rock.

"The land ice measured but five feet seven inches, the reduced growth, probably, of a single season. The open leads multiply, for we made under sail about fifteen miles N.N.W."

As the next day glided in, the skies became overcast, and the wind rose. Mist gathered about the horizon, shutting out the icebergs. The floes, which had opened before with a slender wind from the northward, now shed off dusty wreaths of snow, and began to close rapidly.

Moving along in our little river passage, we observed it growing almost too narrow for navigation, and every now and then, where a projecting cape stretched out toward this advancing ice, we had to run the gauntlet between the opposing margins.

It is under these circumstances, with a gale probably outside, and a fog gathering around, that the whalers, less strengthened than ourselves, and taught by a fearful experience, seek protecting bights among the floes or cut harbors in the ice. For us, the word delay did not enter into our commander's thoughts. We had not purchased caution by disaster; and it was essential to success that we should make the most of this Godsend, a "slant" from the southeast.

We pushed on; but the Rescue, less fortunate than ourselves, could not follow. She was jammed in between two closing surfaces. We were looking out for a temporary niche in which to secure ourselves, when we were challenged to the bear hunt I have spoken of a few pages back.

Upon regaining the deck with Mr. Lovell's prize, we were struck with the indications of a brooding wind outside. The ice was closing in every direction; and our master, Mr. Murdaugh, had no alternative but to tie up and await events. The Rescue did the same, some three hundred yards to the southward.

By five A.M., a projecting edge of the outside floe came into contact with our own, at a point midway between the two vessels. This assailing floe was three feet eight inches thick, perhaps a mile in diameter, and moving at a rate of a knot an hour. Its weight was some two or three millions of tons. So irresistible was its momentum, that, as it impinged against the solid margin of the land ice, there was no recoil, no interruption to its progress. The elastic material corrugated before the enormous pressure; then cracked, then crumbled, and at last rose, the lesser over the greater, sliding up in great inclined planes: and these, again, breaking by their weight and their continued impulse, toppled over in long lines of fragmentary ice.

This imposing process of dynamics is called "Hummocking." Its most striking feature was its unswerving, unchecked continuousness. The mere commotion was hardly proportioned either to the intensity of the force or the tremendous effects which it produced. Tables of white marble were thrust into the air, as if by invisible machinery.

First, an inclined face would rise, say ten feet; then you would hear a grinding, tooth-pulling *crunch:* it has cracked at its base, and a second is sliding up upon it. Over this, again, comes a third; and hereupon the first breaks down, carrying with it the second; and just as you are expecting to see the whole pile disappear, up comes a fourth, larger than any of the rest, and converts all its predecessors into a chaotic mass of crushed marble. Now the fragments thus comminuted are about the size of an old-fashioned Conestoga wagon, and the line thus eating its way is several hundred yards long.

The action soon began to near our brig, which now, fast by a heavy cable, stood bows on awaiting the onset. It was an uncomfortable time for us, as we momentarily expected it to "nip" her sides, or bear her down with the pressure. But, thanks to the inverted wedge action of her bows, she shot out like a squeezed water-melon seed, snapping her hawser like pack-thread, and backing into wider quarters. The Rescue was borne almost to her beam ends, but eventually rose upon the ice. The rudders of both brigs were unshipped.

This closure of the seaward ice upon the land floe was evidently connected with a change of winds. On the day before, the 10th, the ice had relaxed all around us, under a gentle air from the northward; but a gradually increasing breeze from the E.S.E., commencing about nine in the evening, had tightened the floes and this morning bore them down upon us. As the wind hauled to the S.S.E., the ice opened again; and on the early morning of the twelfth we warped ahead into a safer berth.

We cast off again about 7 A.M.; and after a wearisome day of warping, tracking, towing, and sailing, advanced some six or eight miles, along a coast-line of hills to the northeast, edged with glaciers.

The currents were such as to entirely destroy our steerage way. Our rudder was for a time useless; and the surface water was covered by ripple marks, which flowed in strangely looping curves. On the 13th the sea abounded with life. Cetochili, as well as other entomostracan forms which I had not seen before, lined, and, in fact, tinted the margins of the floe ice; and for the first time I noticed among them some of those higher orders of crustacean life, which had heretofore been only found adhering to our warping lines. Among these were asellus and idotea, and that jerking little amphipod, the gammarus. Acalephæ and limacinæ abounded in the quiet leads. The birds, too, were back with us, the mollemoke, the Ivory gull, the Burgomaster, and the tern; and while the little Auks crowded the floes below, feeding eagerly upon the abundant harvest of the ice, the air above us was filled with swooping crowds, equally intent on their marine pasture grounds. I can not think that the powerful mandible of the Fulmar petrels ever condescends to the surface forms of acalephæ. It is true that they follow in the stormy wake of vessels, like the Mother Carey's chickens, but their food is of a higher grade. It was a curious spectacle to see them fighting for the garbage of our vessel, and gormandizing on the blubber of our game.

We saw to-day two Rorqual whales (*Rorqualis Borealis*), apparently feeding upon these living waters. They were the first that we had seen since leaving Disco. We hailed them as an earnest of an open sea. As the day grew older, a breeze carried us along gloriously. We made at least twenty miles upon our course; and although we were forced to cut through some intercepting ice, it became evident that we had passed the trials of the bay, and were hourly approaching the North Water.

The shore, which we had been so long skirting, again rose into mountains; on whose southern flanks, as they receded, we could still see the great glacier. We had traced it all the way from the Devil's Thumb in a nearly continuous circuit; now we were about to lose it. The icebergs had sensibly diminished already.

CHAPTER XVII.

As the afternoon advanced, we had another visit of the phenomena of refraction This time they passed before us in all the costumes and mutations of a carnival frolic. I am afraid to paint them from recollection, and would make an apology, if I could, for the seeming extravagance with which they reflect themselves in my journal.

"6 P.M Refraction again! There is a black globe floating in the air, about 3° north of the sun. What it is you can not tell. Is it a bird or a balloon? Presently comes a sort of shimmering about its circumference, and on a sudden it changes its shape. Now you see plainly what it is. It is a grand piano, and nothing else. Too quick this time! You had hardly named it, before it was an anvil—an anvil large enough for Mulciber and his Cyclops to beat out the loadstone of the poles. You have not got it quite adjusted to your satisfaction, before your anvil itself is changing; it contracts itself centrewise, and rounds itself endwise, and, *presto*, it has made itself duplicate—a pair of colossal dumb-bells. A moment! and it is the black globe again."

About an hour after this necromantic juggle, the whole horizon became distorted: great bergs lifted themselves above it, and a pearly sky and pearly water blended with each other in such a way, that you could not determine where the one began or the other ended. Your ship was in the concave of a vast sphere; ice shapes of indescribable variety around you, floating, like yourself, on nothingness; the flight of a bird as apparent in the deeps of the sea as in the continuous element above. Nothing could be more curiously beautiful than our consort the Rescue, as she lay in mid-space, duplicated by her secondary image.

This unequally refractive condition continued on into the next day; diminishing as the sun approached his meridian altitude, but again coming back in the afternoon with augmented intensity. The appearance at night was more wonderful than it had been on the 12th. I am desirous to give the impressions it made on me at the moment, and I therefore copy again from my journal, without erasing or modifying a single line.

"*August* 13. To-night, at ten o'clock, we were opposite a striking cliff, supposed to be Cape Melville, when, attracted by the irregular radiation from the sun, then about two hours from the lowest point of his curve, I saw suddenly flaring up all around him the signs of active combustion. Great volumes of black smoke rose above the horizon, narrowing and expanding as it rolled away. Black specks, to which the eye, by its compensation for distance, gave the size of masses, mingled with it, rising and falling, appearing and disappearing; and above all this was the peculiar waving movement of air, rarefied by an adjacent heat. The whole intervening atmosphere was disturbed and flickering.

"Upon looking at this curious spectacle through our best Fraünhofer glass, the clearly defined edges of a number of large icebergs could be seen, borne by refraction into the air, duplicated by inversion, and preserving that vertical parallelism of sides before alluded to as characteristic of the refracted berg. From the lower face of their inverted images were exhaling—if I may use the word—those wonderful clouds of apparent smoke. Here, too, at an altitude which, judging by the bases of the bergs, corresponded to the refracted or secondary horizon, a lateral distortion sent out huge tongues, like projecting rafters, which, when not obscured by the 'smoke,' contrasted black against the sky. All this was so combined with architectural forms, that it was hard to avoid the impression of some mighty city in conflagration."

During all these phenomena, the position of the sun with reference to the elevated object had a marked influence. Immediately below his disk, the excessive illumination prevented my taking altitudes by the sextant; but on either side of it, to a distance of twenty degrees, I could note that the false horizon, which I had selected as an index of the uplift, rose as it receded from the sun. A similarly progressive elevation of the refracted bergs was observable by the unassisted eye. The range thus noted was from .06′ to 1° 40′.

The entire sea at this time was studded with fragments of floating ice. Heretofore the more striking manifestations of this sort of refraction had occurred on warm sunny days, when the area immediately adjacent to us was entirely ice-bound; and we had remarked, on several occasions, that the presence of open water between us and the sun had the effect of depressing the refracted images. I have prepared some curious tables, indicating the relation of the surface temperature of the water to the temperature of the air on board ship. They would be out of place here.

Another extract from my journal of the next morning has less of imaginative interest:

"*August* 14. I have just returned from a couple of hours' shooting. With two sailors to row, and as many ships' muskets to slay with, I brought back seventy birds. They are more scattered than they were, not flocking along the floes, but covering the sea. I notice them, with their crops full of shrimps, the ungrateful little gluttons, winging their way off to shoreward.

"We are living luxuriously. Yesterday our French cook, Henri, gave us a salmi of Auks, worthy of the *Trois Frères;* and to-day I enjoyed an Arctic imitation of a trussed partridge. Bear is strong, very strong, and withal most capricious meat; you can not tell where to find him. One day he is quite beefy and bearable; another, hircine, hippuric, and damnable. As a part of my Polar practice, I make it a point—albeit I esteem a discriminating palate—to eat of every thing; and, in the course of my culinary experience, I have already managed to convert several outcast eatables to good palatable food. Seal is not fishy, but *sealy;* and with a little patience and a good deal of *sauce piquante,* is very excellent diet. The mollemoke is the hardest to manage; the infiltration of fatty matter is rather alarming. But I give my method, for future *maitres d'hotel* who may task themselves in these regions. Cut off his breast; fling every thing else to his fellows, who are waiting for him outside;

rub with soda; wash out the soap thus freely made; parboil and pickle. The bird is, after all, not so detestable, early in the season. At the Hudson Bay's settlements they preserve him in salt. Sea-gull is worthy of all honorable mention. The *filet* of a large Ivory one is a morceau between a spring chicken and our own unsurpassed canvas back. As to these little Guillemots or Auks (*Uria alle*, or *alke*), *quocunque nomine gaudent*, like all birds feeding on crustaceal life, they are very red in meat, juicy, fat, delicate, and flavorsome, something between a blue-wing and a Delaware rail; in a word, the perfection of good eating.

"We ran along the coast to-day with gentle airs, and near enough to keep me busy with my pencil. Glacier after glacier met us, and the background of rounding snow-covered mountains contrasted finely with the square blocking of the rugged precipices at the water-line. These glaciers, however, were detached, not running in continuous curves along the coast, but abutting from opening valleys. The structure of the shore was evidently metamorphic. It reminded me of some portions of our Alleghany ridge, and I even thought that I could distinguish in the arrangement of these valley indentations our own familiar form of anticlinal rupture.

"Although icebergs still crowd the horizon, and some two hundred of them can be counted within the eye circle, we are evidently fast getting rid of the ice. It is true that the shore pack still stretches out close upon our left—a barrier apparently as permanent as the glaciered hills with which it is united; but to seaward, open water-leads gladden us in every direction. We forced to-day through but one floe tongue, using the hawser and windlass about an hour. With this exception, we have had no drawback but that capricious and feeble motive power, upon which, under the most favorable circumstances, our little craft is dependent. How often, when retarded by baffling winds or unfavoring leads, have I wished for a few hours of steam!"

The arguments in favor of a towing steamer to promote the transit of this tedious bay seem to me very simple and conclusive. The linear distance, including tortuosities, is but three hundred miles, or two days' run. It had cost us already, including our besetment off the Thumb, five weeks.

The causes of this delay were either closed ice, calms and adverse surface currents, contrary winds, or baffling leads. None of these, except the first, would have arrested a steamer. The predominant winds of July and August are, to use the expression of the whalers, "closing winds;" and, except easters and southeasters (true), which are comparatively rare and of short continuance, all the "opening winds" are contrary, and impracticable for sailing vessels.

I have observed that in calm weather, especially if it continues for some time, the ice becomes less tenacious, and opens gradually in leads; but sails are powerless in a calm. Slight airs from the north always relaxed the ice, and these were frequent; yet here, too, we were hampered, for the north wind was dead ahead; and, while it lasted, we had nothing to do but tie up and await a change.

Even in that rare conjunction of an opening wind and a favoring wind, the tortuous leads may utterly check the navigator's advance. When a "slant" from the southward and eastward did come, as my wind tables will show that it sometimes did, a single tongue of ice or a zigzag lead would delay us until the favoring opportunity had gone by. In all of these cases a steamer would have been of incalculable advantage.

"*August* 15. The Rescue, which has proved herself a dull sailer, had lagged astern of us, when our master, Mr. Murdaugh, observed the signal of 'men ashore' flying from her peak. We were now as far north as latitude 75° 58′, and the idea of human life somehow or other involuntarily connected itself with disaster. A boat was hastily stocked with provisions and dispatched for the shore. Two men were there upon the land ice, gesticulating in grotesque and not very decent pantomime—genuine, unmitigated Esquimaux. Verging on 76° is a far northern limit for human life; yet these poor animals were as fat as the bears which we killed a few days ago. Their hair, mane-like, flowed over their oily cheeks, and their countenances had the true prognathous character seen so rarely among the adulterated breeds of the Danish settlements. They were jolly, laughing fellows, full of social feeling. Their dress consisted of a bear-skin pair of breeches, considerably the worse for wear; a seal-skin jacket, hooded, but not pointed at its skirt; and a pair of coarsely-stitched seal-hide boots. They were armed with a lance, harpoon, and air-bladder, for spearing seals upon the land floe. The kaiack, with its host of resources, they seemed unacquainted with.

"When questioned by Mr. Murdaugh, to whom I owe these details, they indicated five huts, or families, or individuals, toward a sort of valley between two hills. They were ignorant of the use of bread, and rejected salt beef; but they appeared familiar with ships, and would have gladly invited themselves to visit us, if the officer had not inhospitably declined the honor."

It was not very far from Cape York that we met these men. They belonged, probably, to the same detached parties of seal and fish catching coast nomads, that were met by Sir John Ross in his voyage of 1819, and whom he designated, fancifully enough, as the "Arctic Highlanders."

Eleven years after his visit, some boat-crews, from a whaler which had escaped the ice disasters of 1830, landed at nearly the same spot, and made for a group of huts. They were struck as they approached them to find no beaten snow-tracks about the entrance, nor any of the more unsavory indications of an Esquimaux homestead. The riddle was read when they lifted up the skin curtain, that served to cover at once doorway and window. Grouped around an oilless lamp, in the attitudes of life, were four or five human corpses, with darkened lip and sunken eyeball; but all else preserved in perennial ice. The frozen dog lay beside his frozen master, and the child, stark and stiff, in the reindeer hood which enveloped the frozen mother. The cause was a mystery, for the hunting apparatus was near them, and the bay abounds with seals, the habitual food, and light, and fire of the Esquimaux. Perhaps the excessive cold had shut off their supplies for a time by closing the ice-holes—perhaps an epidemic had stricken them. Some three or four huts that were near had the same melancholy furniture of extinct life.

ESQUIMAUX ON SNOW-SHOES.

BESSIE'S COVE.

CHAPTER XVIII.

We sailed along the coast quietly, but with the comfortable excitement of expectation. We had not yet seen such open water, and were momentarily expecting the change, of course, which was to lead us through the North Water to Lancaster Sound. The glaciers were no longer near the water-line; but an escarped shore, of the usual primary structure, gave us a pleasing substitute.

In a short time we reached the "Crimson Cliffs of Beverley," the seat of the often-described "red snow." The coast was high and rugged, the sea-line broken by precipitous sections and choked by detritus. Sailing slowly along, at a distance of about ten miles, we could distinctly see outcropping faces of red feldspathic rock, while in depending positions, between the cones of detritus, the scanty patches of snow were tinged with a brick-dust or brown stain. As yet indeed we could not see the "Crimson" of Sir John Ross, who gave to this spot its somewhat euphonious title; but the locality was not without indications which should excuse this gallant navigator from imputations against his veracity of narrative. The bright red outcroppings of the feldspar, the scarlet patches of a lichen (*Lepraria*) which was in extreme abundance, and, finally, the excretions of the numerous birds that resort to these cliffs, might, in favoring seasons, combine with the snow in such a manner as to give at a distance the tint which he has described.

But it fell calm, and I had an opportunity of visiting the shore. The place where we landed was in latitude 76° 04′ N., nearly. It was a little cove, bordered on one side by a glacier; on the other, watered by distillations from it, and green with luxuriant mosses. It was, indeed, a fairy little spot, brightened, perhaps, by its contrast with the icy element, on which I had been floating for a month and a half before; yet even now, as it comes back to me in beautiful companionship with many sweet places of the earth, I am sure that its charms were real.

The glacier came down by a twisted circuit from a deep valley, which it nearly filled. As it approached the sea, it seemed unable to spread itself over the horseshoe-like expansion in which we stood; but, retaining still the impress marks of its own little valley birthplace, it rose up in a huge dome-like escarpment, one side frozen to the cliffs, the other a wall beside us, and the end a rounded mass protruding into the sea.

Close by the foot of its precipitous face, in a furrowed water-course, was a mountain torrent, which, emerging from the point at which the glacier met the hill, came dashing wildly over the rocks, green with the mosses and carices of Arctic vegetation; while from the dome-like summit a stream, that had tunneled its way through the ice from the valley still higher above, burst out like a fountain, and fell in a cascade of foam-whitened water into the sea.

The glacier itself was of the class which Saussure has designated as the second order. It was a small but elegant type of glacial structure, and was to me conclusive as to the identity in all essential features of the Polar and Alpine ice-growths. Its material was hard but vesicular ice, and seemed marked by stratified bands rudely parallel with its rocky base. These bands commenced with bluish-green compact ice, nearly transparent, and then gradually shaded off as they rose into a more vesicular structure, which ended in an almost granular whiteness.

These markings, which I had an opportunity afterward of studying in the bergs, were seemingly independent of veined or ribboned structure. I look upon them as indices of the annual growth; made up by the snows and atmospheric deposits of the non-thawing season, gradually melted, compressed, and refrozen during the alternating temperatures of the summer months. This view will explain the compact, transparent character of the lower portions of the band, and also its gradual transition into a nearly granular material; for the surface thaws and rains which follow the long winter growth, percolating to the bottom, would impress the mass throughout its extent with these different changes.

The direction of these lines was thus nearly in the long axis of the glacier. As they descended to the surface of its trough, a gradually deepening earth-stain made the stratification for a time more apparent; but near its base its substance was so incorporated with detritus and pasty silt, that it was hard to distinguish it from soil.

The shape of the mass which protruded into the cove was that of a horse-shoe, its curve pointing to the west upon the waters of the bay. Its northern side was flanked by the walls of the valley; but its entire southern sweep was completely clear and unobstructed. On this I made the observations which I have just detailed.

It is with mortification that I confess that I had not then made myself familiar with the views detailed by Professor Forbes in his work on the Pennine Alps; for it has since occurred to me that this so-called dome was of a true scallop-shell shape, and might, perhaps, have illustrated the conoidal structure, which forms so beautiful a feature of the viscous theory. But I have thought it best to adhere to my original remarks, lest I should impair the value of my facts by connecting them with views not directly imparted by the occasion.

Four of these bands I succeeded, with some trouble, in measuring. They ranged from sixteen to nineteen inches in width. The height of the glacier where it entered the sea was eighty-four feet. Sixty paces back from its face, measured rudely by stepping a corresponding line of ground, its height was but seventy; and it there spread itself out so as to cover a greater area, and its sides were less precipitous. Its protrusion into the sea beyond the water-line was but eight feet, passing over a bottom of rounded pebbles, none of which presented facettes of attrition. The depth of the portion thus immersed could be sounded with a boat-hook; and through the clear liquid I could see that a sort of beveling prevented the ice-mass from actual contact with the bottom.

Our very limited time prevented me from tracing this glacier up to its trough, my entire attention being occupied with its presenting face. Captain De Haven, who walked for a mile and a half up the valley, described it to me as rapidly diminishing in size, and deriving contributions from the ice-streams of several minor valleys.

I made a careful sketch of the configuration of this cove. Sandstones and coarse conglomerates, rounded porphyritic quartzes and altered slates, with greenstone and amygdaloids, chlorites and actinolites, &c., were found freely among the loose material spread out over the shore. The detritus from the cliffs was excessive, and the effect of frost as a degrading agent strikingly manifest.

But the object which seemed to usurp the undivided attention of our party was the red snow. It abounded in the depressions between the slopes of deposited detritus, and wherever a protected or dependant hollow gave protection from excessive wind or thaw. It was never seen unless in association with foreign matter, such as the fronds of lichens or filaments of moss. Its surface was always contaminated by these accumulations, and I observed that the color of the Protococcus was most decided when they were in greatest abundance. This I mention, not for its bearing upon the question whether unmixed snow can act as a vegetative matrix, but as indicating, for the locality in question, an adventitious source for the supply of ammonia. I may say, while upon the subject of this interesting production, that I subsequently collected it at Barlow's Inlet and Point Innes, on both sides of Wellington Sound and in Baffin's Bay, at various points, as high as latitude 76° 15′; but in no instance, throughout this extended range, from snow un sullied by extraneous vegetable matter.

This growth, however, under a modified and less luxuriant form, may take place upon an apparently unsullied and isolated surface; for, in addition to its high mountain localities, as described by Saussure, Bier, and others, Parry found it upon the Spitzbergen ice-fields; and I myself, in the May of 1851, met with it on the floe ice of Baffin's Bay fifty miles from any land.

But I would suggest that, even in these far-removed situations, we can not positively assert the exemption of the atmosphere from organic matter. By this I do not mean merely effluvia, acetic and hippuric acids, &c., &c., as detected by Fresenius and others, but a direct transportation of visibly organized material. The highly-polished and dry surface of the Arctic winter-ice admits of such transportation to an almost indefinite extent. I have exhibited to the American Philosophical Society filaments of mosses sufficiently large to be recognized as such by the unassisted eye, which I collected on the ice off Cape Adair in the month of February, 1851, some seventy odd miles from the shore.

The atmospheric transfer of volcanic ash, or the still more remarkable infusorial (*Polythalamia*, etc.) dust on the coast of Africa, has struck me as not superior in interest to this diffusion of organic sporules over the Arctic snows.

To return to the "Crimson Cliffs." We found the red snow in greatest abundance upon a talus fronting to the southwest, which stretched obliquely across the glacier at the seat of its emergence from the valley. It was here in great abundance, staining the surface in patches six or eight yards in diameter. Similar patches were to be seen at short intervals extending up the valley.

Its color was a deep but not bright red. It resembled, with its accompanying impurities, crushed preserved cranberries, with the seed and capsule strewn over the snow. It imparted to paper drawn over it a nearly cherry-red, or perhaps crimson stain, which became brown with exposure; and a handful thawed in a glass tumbler resembled muddy claret.

Its coloring matter was evidently soluble; for, on scraping away the surface, we found that it had dyed the snow beneath with a pure and beautiful rose color, which penetrated, with a gradually softening tint, some eight inches below the surface.

CHAPTER XIX.

At 4 P.M. we left this interesting spot, for which some pleasant associations had suggested to me the name of "Bessie's Cove," and commenced beating to the northward. The sea was crowded with entomostraca and clios, on which myriads of Auks were feeding. The prospects of open water were most cheering. One mile from the shore, we got soundings in rocky bottom, at twenty-three fathoms, and then, wishing to "fill up" with water before attempting our passage to the west, we stood close in, seeking a favorable spot.

About eleven o'clock we were attracted by a bight, midway between Capes York and Dudley Diggs. Its foreground was of rugged syenitic rocks, and over these we could distinctly see the water rushing down in a foaming torrent. Here was a watering-place.

By means of our old friends the warps, we hauled in so close that the sides of our vessels touched the rocks. A few inches only intervened between our keel and the shining pebbles. We could jump on shore as from a wharf. The sun was so low at this midnight hour as to bathe every thing in an atmosphere of Italian pink, deliciously unlike the Arctic regions. The recess was in blackest shadow, but the cliffs which formed the walls of the cove rose up into full sunshine. The Auks crowded these rocks in myriads. So, with gun and sextant, I started on a tramp.

This range, called by Sir John Ross the "Arctic Highlands," is not simply a continuation of the Duneira chain, but a part of a great coast ridge, observed on either side of the so-called Peninsula of Greenland. The culminating peak of the northern abutment of this indentation gave me, trigonometrically, 1383 feet; and others, more distant, were at least one third higher.

The cove itself measured but six hundred yards from bluff to bluff. It was recessed in a regular ellipse, or rather horseshoe, around which the strongly-featured gneisses, relieved, as usual, with the outcroppings of feldspar, formed lofty mural precipices. I estimated their mean elevation at twelve hundred feet. At their bases a mass of schistose rubbish had accumulated.

I have described this recess as a perfect horseshoe: it was not exactly such, for at its northeast end a rugged little water-feeder, formed by the melting snows, sent down a stream of foam which buried itself under the frozen surface of a lake. Yet to the eye it was a nearly absolute theatre, this little cove, and its arena a moss-covered succession of terraces, each of indescribable richness.

Strange as it seemed, on the immediate level of snow and ice, the constant infiltrations, aided by solar reverberation, had made an Arctic garden-spot. The surface of the moss, owing, probably, to the extreme alternations of heat and cold, was divided into regular hexagons and other polyhedral figures, and scattered over these, nestling between the tufts, and forming little groups on their southern faces, was a quiet, unobtrusive community of Alpine flowering plants. The weakness of individual growth allowed no ambitious species to overpower its neighbor, so that many families were crowded together in a rich flower-bed. In a little space that I could cover with my pea-jacket, the veined leaves of the Pyrola were peeping out among chickweeds and saxifrages, the sorrel and Ranunculus. I even found a poor gentian, stunted and reduced, but still, like every thing around it, in all the perfection of miniature proportions.

As this mossy parterre approached the rocky walls that hemmed it in, tussocks of sedges and coarse grass began to show themselves, mixed with heaths and birches; and still further on, at the margin of the horseshoe, and fringing its union with the stupendous piles of debris, came an annulus of Arctic shrubs and trees.

Shrubs and trees! the words recall a smile, for they only typed those natives of another zone. The poor things had lost their uprightness, and learned to escape the elements by trailing along the rocks. Few rose above my shoes, and none above my ankles; yet shady alleys and heaven-pointing avenues could not be more impressive examples of creative adaptation. Here I saw the bleaberry (*Vaccinium uliginosum*) in flower and in fruit—I could cover it with a wine-glass; the wild honeysuckle (*Azalea procumbens*) of our Pennsylvania woods—I could stick the entire plant in my button-hole; the *Andromeda tetragona*, like a green marabou feather.

Strangest among these transformations came the willows. One, the *Salix herbacea*, hardly larger than a trefoil clover; another, the *S. glauca*, like a young althea, just bursting from its seed. A third, the *S. lanata*, a triton among these boreal minnows, looked like an unfortunate garter-snake, bound here and there by claw-like radicles, which, unable to penetrate the inhospitable soil, had spread themselves out upon the surface—traps for the broken lichens and fostering moss which formed its scanty mould.

I had several opportunities, while taking sextant elevations of the headlands, to measure the moss-beds of this cove, both by sections where streams from the lake had left denuded faces, and by piercing through them with a pointed staff. These mosses formed an investing mould, built up layer upon layer, until it had attained a mean depth of five feet. At one place, near the sea line, it was seven feet; and even here the slow processes of Arctic decomposition had not entirely destroyed the delicate radicles and stems. The fronds of the pioneering lichens were still recognizable, entangled among the rest.

Yet these little layers represented, in their diminutive stratification, the deposits of vegetable periods. I counted sixty-eight in the greatest section.* Those chemical processes by which nature converts our autumnal leaves into pabulum for future growths work slowly here.

My companions were already firing away at the Auks, which covered in great numbers the debris of fallen rock. This was deposited at an excessive inclination, sometimes as great as 47°; its talus, some three hundred feet in height, cutting in cone-like processes against the mural faces of the cliff.

There was something about this great inclined plane, with its enormous fragments, their wild distribution, and steep angle of deposit, almost fearfully characteristic of the destructive agencies of Arctic congelation. I had never seen, not even at the bases of the mural traps of India and South America—or better, perhaps, than either, our own Connecticut—such evidences of active degradation. It is not to the geologist alone

* I copy the number of these layers as I find it marked in my journal; yet I do so, not without some fear that I may be misled by the chirography of a very hurried note. My recollections are of a very large number, yet not so large as that which my respect for the *littera scripta* induces me to retain in the text.

Drawn by J. Hamilton from a Sketch by D^r. E. K. Kane U.S.N.

Engraved by J. Sartain.

that these talus and debris are impressive. They tell of changes which have begun and been going on since the existence of the earth in its present state by the friction of time against its surface; and they carry us on with solemn force to the period when the dehiscent edges and mountain ravines of this same earth shall have been worn down into rounded hill and gentle valley. Well may they be called "geological chronometers."* They point with impressive finger to the rotation of years. The dial-plate and the index are both there, and human wisdom almost deciphers the notation!

On the steeper flanks of these rocky cones the little Auks had built their nests. The season of incubation, though far advanced, had not gone by, for the young fledglings were looking down upon me in thousands; and the mothers, with crops full of provender, were constantly arriving from the sea. Urged by a wish to study the domestic habits of these little Arctic emigrants at their homestead, I foolishly clambered up to one of their most popular colonies, without thinking of my descent.

The angle of deposit was already very great, not much less than 50°; and as I moved on, with a walking-pole substituted for my gun, I was not surprised to find the fragments receding under my feet, and rolling, with a resounding crash, to the plain below. Stopping, however, to regain my breath, I found that above, beneath, around me, every thing was in motion. The entire surface seemed to be sliding down. Ridiculous as it may seem to dwell upon a matter apparently so trivial, my position became one of danger. The accelerated velocity of the masses caused them to leap off

* Mantell's "Wonders of Geology."

in deflected lines. Several uncomfortable fragments had already passed by me, some even over my head, and my walking-pole was jerked from my hands and buried in the ruins. Thus helpless, I commenced my own half-involuntary descent, expecting momentarily to follow my pole, when my eye caught a projecting outcrop of feldspar, against which the strong current split into two minor streams. This, with some hard jumps, I succeeded in reaching.

As I sat upon the temporary security of this little rock, surrounded by falling fragments, and awaiting their slow adjustment to a new equilibrium before I ventured to descend, I was struck with the Arctic originality of every thing around. It was midnight, and the sun, now to the north, was hidden by the rocks; but the whole atmosphere was pink with light. Over head and around me whirled innumerable crowds of Auks and Ivory gulls, screeching with execrable clamor, almost in contact with my person. On the frozen lake below, contrasting with its snowy covering, were a couple of ravens, fighting zealously for a morsel of garbage; and high up, on the crags above me, sat some unmoved, phlegmatic burgomasters.

I missed my opportunity of inspecting the nests of the Auks. They issued from the crevices between the detached fragments, and, it is probable, deposited their eggs, like other Uria, upon the naked rock. Some of the men succeeded in reaching their squabs by introducing their arms. It is said that the Esquimaux trap them by spreading out their clothing opposite these apertures, so that the birds, when disturbed, pass into and fill the sleeves and legs.

While at this cove, I saw at a distance a black animal, which, but for its apparently lesser size, I would have taken for a fox. One of our officers fired at another, and I saw a third fifteen miles further north, both of which were undoubtedly of the same species.

They were probably the "black fox" of Sir John Ross, about which there has been much discussion. Throwing aside less obvious marks of distinction, this fox was dark sooty brown or black, not blue, nor, as I am disposed to think, of the shed summer-coat-color of the white fox (*Canis lagopus*). Its pinched expression of head and diminished size might be explained by the absence of its winter covering.

The rest of the day was beautifully clear. We spent it in working to windward, and at 4 P.M. again landed to get observations. This spot, the most northern that we reached in Baffin's Bay, was in latitude 76° 25′. I here saw and collected in the protected nooks, among the grasses and saxifrages, a large number of the Cochlearia (*C. Danica*) and Ranunculus. Emberiza and Plectrophanes were seen also.

The calm which had given us these two days of shore rambles left us suddenly on the 18th. We stood towards Wolstenholme Sound, and bore across to the west in more open water than we had seen for several weeks. It was now beyond doubt that we were to winter somewhere among the scenes of Arctic trial. We were past the barrier, heading direct for Lancaster Sound, with the motion of waves once more under us, and a breeze aloft. As I refer to my journal, I see how the tone of feeling rose among our little party. We began again with something of confidence to connect the probable results with the objects of the expedition. We had lost three weeks off the Devil's Tongue, the British steamers were far ahead of us in point of time, and their superior ability and practice would still keep them in the advance; and we were ignorant of their course and intended scheme of search. We had dreamed before this, and pleasantly enough, of fellowship with them in our efforts, dividing between us the hazards of the way, and perhaps in the long winter holding with them the cheery intercourse of kindred sympathies. We waked now to the probabilities of passing the dark days alone. Yet fairly on the way, an energetic commander, a united ship's company, the wind freshening, our well-tried little ice-boat now groping her way like a blind man through fog and bergs, and now dashing on as if reckless of all but success—it was impossible to repress a sentiment almost akin to the so-called joyous excitement of conflict.

We were bidding good-by to "ye goode baye of old William Baffin;" and as we looked round with a farewell remembrance upon the still water, the diminished icebergs, and the constant sun which had served us so long and faithfully, we felt that the bay had used us kindly.

Though I had read a good deal in the voyagers' books about Baffin's Bay, I had strangely and entirely misconceived the prominent features of its summer scenery. There is a combination of warmth and cold in the tone of its landscapes, a daring, eccentric variety of forms, an intense clearness, almost energy of expression, which might tax Turner and Stanfield together to reproduce them with an approach to truth. How could they trace the features of the iceberg, melting into shapes so boldly marked, yet so undefined; or body forth its cold varieties of unshaded white, or the azure clare-obscure of the ice-chasm! There are the black hills, blots upon rolling snow; the ice-plain, margined with glaciers, and jutting out in capes from the cliffed shore: there is the still blue water. Or, if you want action instead of repose, here is the crashing floe, the grinding hummock, and the monumental berg rising above both! itself, though perishable, a seeming permanency compared with the ephemeral ruins that beat against its sides.

All this is attempered by the warm glazing of a tinted atmosphere. The sky of Baffin's Bay, though but eight hundred miles from the Polar limit of all northernness, is as warm as the Bay of Naples after a June rain. What artist, then, could give this mysterious union of warm atmosphere and cold landscape?

The perpetual daylight had continued up to this moment with unabated glare. The sun had reached his north meridian altitude some days before, but the eye was hardly aware of change. Midnight had a softened character, like the low summer's sun at home, but there was no twilight.

At first the novelty of this great unvarying day made it pleasing. It was curious to see the "midnight Arctic sun set into sunrise," and pleasant to find that, whether you ate or slept, or idled or toiled, the same daylight was always there. No irksome night forced upon you its system of compulsory alternations. I could dine at midnight, sup at breakfast-time, and go to bed at noonday; and but for an apparatus of coils and cogs, called a watch, would have been no wiser and no worse.

My feeling was at first an extravagant sense of undefined relief, of some vague restraint removed. I seemed to have thrown off the slavery of hours. In fact, I could hardly realize its entirety. The astral lamps, standing, dust-covered, on our lockers—I am quoting the words of my journal—puzzled me, as things obsolete and fanciful.

This was instinctive, perhaps; but by-and-by came other feelings. The perpetual light, garish and unfluctuating, disturbed me. I became gradually aware of an unknown excitant, a stimulus, acting constantly, like the diminutive of a cup of strong coffee. My sleep was curtailed and irregular; my meal hours trod upon each other's heels; and but for stringent regulations of my own imposing, my routine would have been completely broken up.

My lot had been cast in the zone of liriodendrons and sugar-maples, in the nearly midway latitude of 40°. I had been habituated to day and night; and every portion of these two great divisions had for me its periods of peculiar association. Even in the tropics, I had mourned the lost twilight. How much more did I miss the soothing darkness, of which twilight should have been the precursor! I began to feel, with more of emotion than a man writing for others likes to confess to, how admirable, as a systematic law, is the alternation of day and night—words that type the two great conditions of living nature, action and repose. To those who with daily labor earn the daily bread, how kindly the season of sleep! To the drone who, urged by the waning daylight, hastens the deferred task, how fortunate that his procrastination has not a six months' morrow! To the brain-workers among men, the enthusiasts, who bear irksomely the dark screen which falls upon their day-dreams, how benignant the dear night blessing, which enforces reluctant rest!

BEECHY, FROM POINT INNES.

CHAPTER XX.

"*August* 19. The wind continued freshening, the Aneroid falling two tenths in the night. About eight I was called by our master, with the news that a couple of vessels were following in our wake. We were shortening sail for our consort; and by half past twelve, the larger stranger, the Lady Franklin, came up along side of us. A cordial greeting, such as those only know who have been pelted for weeks in the solitudes of Arctic ice—and we learned that this was Captain Penny's squadron, bound on the same pursuit as ourselves. A hurried interchange of news followed. The ice in Melville Bay had bothered both parties alike; Commodore Austin, with his steamer tenders, was three days ago at Carey's Islands, a group nearly as high as 77° north latitude; the North Star, the missing provision transport of last summer, was safe somewhere in Lancaster Sound, probably at Leopold Island. For the rest, God speed!

"As she slowly forged ahead, there came over the rough sea that good old English hurra, which we inherit on our side the water. 'Three cheers, hearty, with a will!' indicating as much of brotherhood as sympathy. 'Stand aloft, boys!' and we gave back the greeting. One cheer more of acknowledgment on each side, and the sister flags separated, each on its errand of mercy.

"8 P.M. The breeze has freshened to a gale. Fogs have closed round us, and we are driving ahead again, with look-outs on every side. We have no observation; but by estimate we must have got into Lancaster Sound.

"The sea is short and excessive. Every thing on deck, even anchors and quarter-boats, have 'fetched away,' and the little cabin is half afloat. The Rescue is staggering under heavy sail astern of us. We are making six or seven knots an hour. Murdaugh is ahead, looking out for ice and rocks; De Haven conning the ship.

"All at once a high mountain shore rises before us, and a couple of isolated rocks show themselves, not more than a quarter of a mile ahead, white with breakers. Both vessels are laid to."

The storm reminded me of a Mexican "norther." It was not till the afternoon of the next day that we were able to resume our track, under a double-reefed top-sail, stay-sail, and spencer. We were, of course, without observation still, and could only reckon that we had passed the Cunningham Mountains and Cape Warrender.

About three o'clock in the morning of the 21st, another sail was reported ahead, a top-sail schooner, towing after her what appeared to be a launch, decked over.

"When I reached the deck, we were nearly up to her, for we had shaken out our reefs, and were driving before the wind, shipping seas at every roll. The little schooner was under a single close-reefed top-sail, and seemed fluttering over the waves like a crippled bird. Presently an old fellow, with a cloak tossed over his night gear, appeared in the lee gangway, and saluted with a voice that rose above the winds.

"It was the Felix, commanded by that practical Arctic veteran, Sir John Ross. I shall never forget the heartiness with which the hailing officer sang out, in the midst of our dialogue, 'You and I are ahead of them all.' It was so indeed. Austin, with two vessels, was at Pond's Bay; Penny was somewhere in the gale; and others of Austin's squadron were exploring the north side of the Sound. The Felix and the Advance were on the lead.

"Before we separated, Sir John Ross came on deck, and stood at the side of his officer. He was a square-built man, apparently very little stricken in years, and well able to bear his part in the toils and hazards of life. He has been wounded in four several engagements—twice desperately—and is scarred from head to foot. He has conducted two Polar expeditions already, and performed in one of them the unparalleled feat of wintering four years in Arctic snows. And here he is again, in a flimsy cockle-shell, after contributing his purse and his influence, embarked himself in the crusade of search for a lost comrade. We met him off Admiralty Inlet, just about the spot at which he was picked up seventeen years before."

Soon after midnight, the land became visible on the north side of the Sound. We had passed Cape Charles Yorke and Cape Crawfurd, and were fanning along sluggishly with all the sail we could crowd for Port Leopold.

It was the next day, however, before we came in sight of the island, and it was nearly spent when we found ourselves slowly approaching Whaler Point, the seat of the harbor. Our way had been remarkably clear of ice for some days, and we were vexed to find, therefore, that a firm and rugged barrier extended along the western shore of the inlet, and apparently across the entrance we were seeking.

It was a great relief to us to see, at half past six in the evening, a top-sail schooner working toward us through the ice. She boarded us at ten, and proved to be Lady Franklin's own search-vessel, the Prince Albert.

This was a very pleasant meeting. Captain Forsyth, who commanded the Albert, and Mr. Snow, who acted as a sort of adjutant under him, were very agreeable gentlemen. They spent some hours with us, which Mr. Snow has remembered kindly in the journal he has published since his return to England. Their little vessel was much less perfectly fitted than ours to encounter the perils of the ice; but in one respect at least their expedition resembled our own. They had to rough it: to use a Western phrase, they had no fancy fixings—nothing but what a hasty outfit and a limited purse could supply. They were now bound for Cape Rennell, after which they proposed making a sledge excursion over the lower Boothian and Cockburne lands.

The North Star, they told us, had been caught by

the ice last season in the neighborhood of our own first imprisonment, off the Devil's Thumb. After a perilous drift, she had succeeded in entering Wolstenholme Sound, whence, after a tedious winter, she had only recently arrived at Port Bowen.

They followed in our wake the next day as we pushed through many streams of ice across the strait. We sighted the shore about five miles to the west of Cape Hurd very closely; a miserable wilderness, rising in terraces of broken-down limestone, arranged between the hills like a vast theatre.

On the 25th, still beating through the ice off Radstock Bay, we discovered on Cape Riley two cairns, one of them, the most conspicuous, with a flag-staff and ball. A couple of hours after, we were near enough to land. The cape itself is a low projecting tongue of limestone, but at a short distance behind it the cliff rises to the height of some eight hundred feet. We found a tin canister within the larger cairn, containing the information that Captain Ommanney had been there two days before us, with the Assistance and Intrepid, belonging to Captain Austin's squadron, and had discovered traces of an encampment, and other indications "that some party belonging to her Britannic majesty's service had been detained at this spot." Similar traces, it was added, had been found also on Beechy Island, a projection on the channel side some ten miles from Cape Riley.

Our consort, the Rescue, as we afterward learned, had shared in this discovery, though the British commander's inscription in the cairn, as well as his official reports, might lead perhaps to a different conclusion. Captain Griffin, in fact, landed with Captain Ommanney, and the traces were registered while the two officers were in company.

I inspected these different traces very carefully, and noted what I observed at the moment. The appearances which connect them with the story of Sir John Franklin have been described by others; but there may still be interest in a description of them made while they were under my eye. I transcribe it word for word from my journal.

"On a tongue of fossiliferous limestone, fronting toward the west on a little indentation of the water, and shielded from the north by the precipitous cliffs, are five distinct remnants of habitation.

"Nearest the cliffs, four circular mounds or heapings-up of the crumbled limestone, aided by larger stones placed at the outer edge, as if to protect the leash of a tent. Two larger stones, with an interval of two feet, fronting the west, mark the places of entrance.

"Several large square stones, so arranged as to serve probably for a fire-place. These have been tumbled over by parties before us.

"More distant from the cliffs, yet in line with the four already described, is a larger inclosure; the door facing south, and looking toward the strait: this so-called door is simply an entrance made of large stones placed one above the other. The inclosure itself triangular; its northern side about eighteen inches high, built up of flat stones. Some bird bones and one rib of a seal were found exactly in the centre of this triangle, as if a party had sat round it eating; and the top of a preserved meat case, much rusted, was found in the same place. I picked up a piece of canvas or duck on the cliff side, well worn by the weather: the sailors recognized it at once as the gore of a pair of trowsers.

"A fifth circle is discernible nearer the cliffs, which may have belonged to the same party. It was less perfect than the others, and seemed of an older date.

"On the beach, some twenty or thirty yards from the triangular inclosure, were several pieces of pine wood about four inches long, painted green, and white, and black, and, in one instance, puttied; evidently parts of a boat, and apparently collected as kindling wood."

The indications were meagre, but the conclusion they led to was irresistible. They could not be the work of Esquimaux: the whole character of them contradicted it: and the only European who could have visited Cape Riley was Parry, twenty-eight years before; and we knew from his journal that he had not encamped here. Then, again, Ommanney's discovery of like vestiges on Beechy Island, just on the track of a party moving in either direction between it and the channel: all these speak of a land party from Franklin's squadron.

Our commander resolved to press onward along the eastern shore of Wellington Channel. We were under weigh in the early morning of the 26th, and working along with our consort toward Beechy—I drop the "Island," for it is more strictly a peninsula or a promontory of limestone, as high and abrupt as that at Cape Riley, connected with what we call the main by a low isthmus. Still further on we passed Cape Spencer; then a fine bluff point, called by Parry Point Innes; and further on again, the trend being to the east of north, we saw the low tongue, Cape Bowden. Parry merely sighted these points from a distance, so that the shore line has never been traced. I sketched it myself with some care; but the running survey of this celebrated explorer had left nothing to alter. To the north of Cape Innes, though the coast retains the same geognostical character, the bluff promontories subside into low hills, between which the beach, composed of coarse silicious limestone, sweeps in long curvilinear terraces. Measuring some of these rudely afterward, I found that the elevation of the highest plateau did not exceed forty feet.

Our way northward was along an ice channel close under the eastern shore, and bounded on the other side by the ice-pack, at a distance varying from a quarter of a mile to a mile and three quarters. Off Cape Spencer the way seemed more open, widening perhaps to two miles, and showing something like continued free water to the north and west. Here we met Captain Penny, with the Lady Franklin and Sophia. He told us that the channel was completely shut in ahead by a compact ice barrier, which connected itself with that to the west, describing a horseshoe bend. He thought a southwester was coming on, and counseled us to prepare for the chances of an impactment. The go-ahead determination which characterized our commander made us test the correctness of his advice. We pushed on, tracked the horseshoe circuit of the ice without finding an outlet, and were glad to labor back again almost in the teeth of a gale.

Captain Penny had occupied the time more profitably. In company with Dr. Goodsir, an enthusiastic explorer and highly educated gentleman, whose brother was an assistant surgeon on board the missing vessels, he had been examining the shore. On the ridge of limestone, between Cape Spencer and Point Innes, they had come across additional proofs that Sir John's party had been here—very important these proofs as extending the line along the shore over which the party must have moved from Cape Riley.

Among the articles they had found were tin canisters, with the London maker's label; scraps of newspaper, bearing the date 1844; a paper fragment, with the words "until called" on it, seemingly part of a watch order; and two other fragments, each with the name of one of Franklin's officers written on it in pencil. I annex a fac-simile of one of these, the assistant surgeon of the Terror. They told us, too, that among the articles found by Captain Penny's men was a dredge, rudely fashioned of iron hoops beat round, with spikes inserted in them, and arranged for a long handle, as if to fish up missing articles; besides some footless stockings, tied up at the lower end to serve as socks, an officer's pocket, velvet-lined, torn off from the dress, &c., &c.; all of which, they thought, spoke of a party that had suffered wreck, and were moving eastward. Acting on this impression, Captain Penny was about to proceed toward Baffin's Bay, along the north shore of Lancaster Sound, in the hope of encountering them, or, more probably, their bleached remains.

For myself, looking only at the facts, and carefully discarding every deduction that might be prompted by sympathy rather than reason, my journal reminds me that I did not see in these signs the evidence of a lost party. The party was evidently in motion; but it might be that it was a detachment, engaged in making observations, or in exploring with a view to the operations of the spring, while the ships were locked in winter quarters at Cape Riley or Beechy, which had returned on board before the opening of the ice.

I may add, as not without some bearing on the fortunes of this party, whatever may have been its condi tion or purposes, that the vacant water-spaces around us at this time were teeming with animal life. After passing Beechy, we saw seal disporting in great flocks, rising out of the water as high as their middle, like boys in swimming; the white whale, the first we had seen, to the extent of thirty-eight separate shoals; the narwhal, or sea-unicorn; and, finally, that marine pachyderm, the tusky walrus. These last were always crowded on small tongues of ice, whose purity they marred not a little—grim-looking monsters, reminding me of the stage hobgoblins, something venerable and semi-Egyptian withal. We passed so close as to have several shots at them. They invariably rose after plunging, and looked snortingly around, as if to make fight. Polar bears were numerous beyond our previous experience, and the Arctic fox and hare abounded. If we add to these the crowding tenants of the air, the Brent goose, which now came in great cunoid flocks from the north and north by east, the loons, the mollemokes, and the divers, we may form an estimate of the means of human subsistence in these seas.

Mc. Donald.

CHAPTER XXI.

On the 27th, the chances of this narrow and capricious navigation had gathered five of the searching vessels, under three different commands, within the same quarter of a mile—Sir John Ross', Penny's, and our own. Both Ross and Penny had made the effort to push through the sound to the west, but found a great belt of ice, reaching in an almost regular crescent from Leopold's Island across to the northern shore, about half a mile from the entrance of the channel. Captain Ommanney, with the Intrepid and Assistance, had been less fortunate. He had attempted to break his way through the barrier, but it had closed on him, and he was now fast, within fifteen miles of us, to the west.

After breakfast, our commander and myself took a boat to visit the traces discovered yesterday by Captain Penny. Taking the Lady Franklin in our way, we met Sir John Ross and Commander Phillips, and a conference naturally took place upon the best plans for concerted operations. I was very much struck with the gallant disinterestedness of spirit which was shown by all the officers in this discussion. Penny, an energetic, practical fellow, sketched out at once a plan of action for each vessel of the party. He himself would take the western search; Ross should run over to Prince Regent's Sound, communicate the news to the Prince Albert, and so relieve that little vessel from the now unnecessary perils of her intended expedition; and we were *to press through* the first openings in the ice by Wellington Channel, to the north and east.

It was wisely determined by brave old Sir John that he would leave the Mary, his tender of twelve tons, at a little inlet near the point, to serve as a fall-back in case we should lose our vessels or become sealed up in permanent ice, and De Haven and Penny engaged their respective shares of her outfit, in the snape of some barrels of beef and flour. Sir John Ross, I think, had just left us to go on board his little craft, and I was still talking over our projects with Captain Penny, when a messenger was reported, making all speed to us over the ice.

The news he brought was thrilling. "Graves, Captain Penny! graves! Franklin's winter quarters!" We were instantly in motion. Captain De Haven, Captain Penny, Commander Phillips, and myself, joined by a party from the Rescue, hurried on over the ice, and, scrambling along the loose and rugged slope that extends from Beechy to the shore, came, after a weary walk, to the crest of the isthmus. Here, amid the sterile uniformity of snow and slate, were the head-boards of three graves, made after the old orthodox fashion of gravestones at home. The mounds which adjoined them were arranged with some pretensions to symmetry, coped and defended with limestone slabs. They occupied a line facing toward Cape Riley, which was distinctly visible across a little cove at the distance of some four hundred yards.

The first, or that most to the southward, is nearest to

Drawn by J. Hamilton, after a Sketch by Dr. E. K. Kane, U.S.N. Engraved by Sartain.

Beechey Island — Franklin's first Winter Quarters

the front in the accompanying sketch. Its inscrip tion, cut in by a chisel, ran thus:

"Sacred
to the
memory
of
W. BRAINE, R. M.,
H. M. S. Erebus.
Died April 3d, 1846,
aged 32 years.
'Choose ye this day whom ye will serve.'
Joshua, ch. xxiv., 15."

The second was:

"Sacred to the memory of
JOHN HARTNELL, A. B. of H. M. S.
Erebus,
aged 23 years.
'Thus saith the Lord, consider your ways.'
Haggai, i., 7."

The third and last of these memorials was not quite so well finished as the others. The mound was not of stone-work, but its general appearance was more grave-like, more like the sleeping-place of Christians in happier lands. It was inscribed:

"Sacred
to
the memory
of
JOHN TORRINGTON,
who departed this life
January 1st, A.D. 1846,
on board of
H. M. ship Terror,
aged 20 years."

"Departed this life *on board* the Terror, 1st January, 1846!" Franklin's ships, then, had not been wrecked when he occupied the encampment at Beechy!

Two large stones were imbedded in the friable lime-stone a little to the left of these sad records, and near them was a piece of wood, more than a foot in diam eter, and two feet eight inches high, which had evidently served for an anvil-block: the marks were unmistakable. Near it again, but still more to the east, and therefore nearer the beach, was a large blackened space, covered with coal cinders, iron nails, spikes, hinges, rings, clearly the remains of the armorer's forge. Still nearer the beach, but more to the south, was the carpenter's shop, its marks equally distinctive.

Leaving "the graves," and walking toward Wellington Straits, about four hundred yards, or perhaps less, we came to a mound, or rather a series of mounds, which, considering the Arctic character of the surface at this spot, must have been a work of labor. It inclosed one nearly elliptical area, and one other, which, though separated from the first by a lesser mound, appeared to be connected with it. The spaces thus inclosed abounded in fragmentary remains. Among them I saw a stocking without a foot, sewed up at its edge, and a mitten not so much the worse for use as to have been without value to its owner. Shavings of wood were strewed freely on the southern side of the mound, as if they had been collected there by the continued labor of artificers, and not far from these, a few hundred yards lower down, was the remnant of a garden. Weighing all the signs carefully, I had no doubt that this was some central shore establishment, connected with the squadron, and that the lesser area was used as an observatory, for it had large stones fixed as if to support instruments, and the scantling props still stuck in the frozen soil.

Travelling on about a quarter of a mile further, and in the same direction, we came upon a deposit of more than six hundred preserved-meat cans, arranged in regular order. They had been emptied, and were now filled with limestone pebbles, perhaps to serve as convenient ballast on boating expeditions.

These were among the more obvious vestiges of Sir John Franklin's party. The minor indications about the ground were innumerable: fragments of canvas, rope, cordage, sail-cloth, tarpaulins; of casks, iron-work, wood, rough and carved; of clothing, such as a blanket lined by long stitches with common cotton stuff, and made into a sort of rude coat; paper in scraps, white, waste, and journal; a small key; a few odds and ends of brass-work, such as might be part of the furniture of a locker; in a word, the numberless reliquiæ of a winter resting-place. One of the papers, which I have preserved, has on it the notation of an astronomical sight, worked out to Greenwich time.

With all this, not a written memorandum, or pointing cross, or even the vaguest intimation of the condition or intentions of the party. The traces found at Cape Riley and Beechy were still more baffling. The cairn was mounted on a high and conspicuous portion of the shore, and evidently intended to attract observation; but, though several parties examined it, digging round it in every direction, not a single particle of information could be gleaned. This is remarkable; and for so able and practiced an Arctic commander as Sir John Franklin, an incomprehensible omission.

In a narrow interval between the hills which come down toward Beechy Island, the searching parties of the Rescue and Mr. Murdaugh of our own vessel found the tracks of a sledge clearly defined, and unmistakable both as to character and direction. They pointed to the eastern shores of Wellington Sound, in the same general course with the traces discovered by Penny between Cape Spencer and Point Innes.

Similar traces were seen toward Caswell's Tower and Cape Riley, which gave additional proofs of systematic journeyings. They could be traced through the comminuted limestone shingle in the direction of Cape Spencer; and at intervals further on were scraps of paper, lucifer matches, and even the cinders of the temporary fire. The sledge parties must have been regularly organized, for their course had evidently been the subject of a previous reconnoissance. I observed their runner tracks not only in the limestone crust, but upon some snow slopes further to the north. It was startling to see the evidences of a travel nearly six years old, preserved in intaglio on a material so perishable.

The snows of the Arctic regions, by alternations of congelation and thaw, acquire sometimes an ice-like durability; but these traces had been covered by the after-snows of five winters. They pointed, like the Sastrugi, or snow-waves of the Siberians, to the marches of the lost company.

Mr. Griffin, who performed a journey of research along this coast toward the north, found at intervals, almost to Cape Bowden, traces of a passing party. A corked bottle, quite empty, was among these. Reaching a point beyond Cape Bowden, he discovered the indentation or bay which now bears his name, and on whose opposite shores the coast was again seen.

It is clear to my own mind that a systematic reconnoissance was undertaken by Franklin of the upper waters of the Wellington, and that it had for its object an exploration in that direction as soon as the ice would permit.

There were some features about this deserted homestead inexpressibly touching. The frozen trough of an old water channel had served as the wash-house stream for the crews of the lost squadron. The tubs, such as Jack makes by sawing in half the beef barrels, although no longer fed by the melted snows, remained as the washers had left them five years ago. The little garden, too: I did not see it; but Lieutenant Osborn describes it as still showing the mosses and anemones that were transplanted by its framers. A garden implies a purpose either to remain or to return: he who makes it is looking to the future. The same officer found a pair of Cashmere gloves, carefully "laid out to dry, with two small stones upon the palms to keep them from blowing away." It would be wrong to measure the value of these gloves by the price they could be bought for in Bond Street or Broadway. The Arctic traveler they belonged to intended to come back for them, and did not probably forget them in his hurry.

The facts I have mentioned, almost all of them, have been so ably analyzed already, that I might be excused from venturing any deductions of my own. But it was impossible to review the circumstances as we stood upon the ground without forming an opinion; and such as mine was, it is perhaps best that I should express it here.

In the first place, it is plain that Sir John Franklin's consort, the Terror, wintered in 1845–6 at or near the promontory of Beechy; that at least part of her crew remained on board of her; and that some of the crew of the flag-ship, the Erebus, if not the ship herself, were also there. It is also plain that a part of one or both these crews was occupied during a portion of the winter in the various pursuits of an organized squadron, at an encampment on the isthmus I have described, a position which commanded a full view of Lancaster Sound to the east of south, and of Wellington Channel extending north. It may be fairly inferred, also, that the general health of the crews had not suffered severely, three only having died out of a hundred and thirty odd; and that in addition to the ordinary details of duty, they were occupied in conducting and computing astronomical observations, making sledges, preparing their little anti-scorbutic garden patches, and exploring the eastern shore of the channel. Many facts that we ourselves observed made it seem probable that Franklin had not, in the first instance, been able to prosecute his instructions for the Western search; and the examinations made so fully since by Captain Austin's officers have proved that he never reached Cape Walker, Banks' Land, Melville Island, Prince Regent's Inlet, or any point of the sound considerably to the west or southwest. The whole story of our combined operations in and about the channel shows that it is along its eastern margin that the water-leads occur most frequently: natural causes of general application may be assigned for this, some of which will readily suggest themselves to the physicist; but I have only to do here with the recognized fact.

So far I think we proceed safely. The rest is conjectural. Let us suppose the season for renewed progress to be approaching; Franklin and his crews, with their vessels, one or both, looking out anxiously from their narrow isthmus for the first openings of the ice. They come: a gale of wind has severed the pack, and the drift begins. The first clear water that would meet his eye would be close to the shore on which he had his encampment. Would he wait till the continued drift had made the navigation practicable in Lancaster Sound, and then retrace his steps to try the upper regions of Baffin's Bay, which he could not reach without a long circuit; or would he press to the north through the open lead that lay before him? Those who know Franklin's character, his declared opinions, his determined purpose, so well portrayed in the lately published letters of one of his officers, will hardly think the question difficult to answer: his sledges had already pioneered the way. We, the searchers, were ourselves tempted, by the insidious openings to the north in Wellington Channel, to push on in the hope that some lucky chance might point us to an outlet beyond. Might not the same temptation have had its influence for Sir John Franklin? A careful and daring navigator, such as he was, would not wait for the lead to close. I can imagine the dispatch with which the observatory would be dismantled, the armorer's establishment broken up, and the camp vacated. I can understand how the preserved meat cans, not very valuable, yet not worthless, might be left piled upon the shore; how one man might leave his mittens, another his blanket coat, and a third hurry over the search for his lost key. And if I were required to conjecture some explanation of the empty signal cairn, I do not know what I could refer it to but the excitement attendant on just such a sudden and unexpected release from a weary imprisonment, and the instant prospect of energetic and perilous adventure.

CHAPTER XXII.

"*August* 28. Strange enough, during the night, Captain Austin, of her majesty's search squadron, with his flag-ship the Resolute, entered the same little indentation in which five of us were moored before. His steam-tender, the Pioneer, grounded off the point of Beechy Island, and is now in sight, canted over by the ice nearly to her beam ends. He has come to us not of design, but under the irresistible guidance of the ice. We are now seven vessels within hailing distance, not counting Captain Ommanney's, imbedded in the field to the westward.

"I called this morning on Sir John Ross, and had a long talk with him. He said that, as far back as 1847, anticipating the 'detention' of Sir John Franklin—I use his own word—he had volunteered his services for an expedition of retrieve, asking for the purpose four small vessels, something like our own; but no one listened to him. Volunteering again in 1848, he was told that his nephew's claim to the service had received a recognition; whereupon his own was withdrawn. 'I told Sir John,' said Ross, 'that my own experience in these seas proved that all these sounds and inlets may, by the caprice or even the routine of seasons, be closed so as to prevent any egress, and that a missing or shut-off party must have some means of falling back. It was thus I saved myself from the abandoned Victory by a previously constructed house for wintering, and a boat for temporary refuge.' All this, he says, he pressed on Sir John Franklin before he set out, and he thinks that Melville Island is now the seat of such a house-asylum. 'For, depend upon it,' he added, 'Franklin will be expecting some of us to be following on his traces. Now, may it be that the party, whose winter quarters we have discovered, sent out only exploring detachments along Wellington Sound in the spring, and then, when themselves released, continued on to the west, by Cape Hotham and Barrow's Straits?' I have given this extract from my journal, though the theory it suggests has since been disproved by Lieutenant M'Clintock, because the tone and language of Sir John Ross may be regarded as characteristic of this manly old seaman.

"I next visited the Resolute. I shall not here say how their perfect organization and provision for winter contrasted with those of our own little expedition. I had to shake off a feeling almost of despondency when I saw how much better fitted they were to grapple with the grim enemy, Cold. Winter, if we may judge of it by the clothing and warming appliances of the British squadron, must be something beyond our power to cope with; for, in comparison with them, we have nothing, absolutely nothing.

"The officers received me, for I was alone, with the cordiality of recognized brotherhood. They are a gentlemanly, well-educated set of men, thoroughly up to the history of what has been done by others, and full of personal resource. Among them I was rejoiced to meet an old acquaintance, Lieutenant Brown, whose admirably artistic sketches I had seen in Haghe's lithotints, at Mr. Grinnell's, before leaving New York. When we were together last, it was among the tropical jungles of Luzon, surrounded by the palm, the cycas, and bamboo, in the glowing extreme of vegetable exuberance: here we are met once more, in the stinted region of lichen and mosses. He was then a junior, under Sir Edward Belcher: I—what I am yet. The lights and shadows of a naval life are nowhere better, and, alas! nowhere worse displayed, than in these remote accidental greetings.

"Returning, I paid a visit to Penny's vessels, and formed a very agreeable acquaintance with the medical officer, Dr. R. Anstruther Goodsir, a brother of assistant surgeon Goodsir of Franklin's flag-ship.

"In commemoration of the gathering of the searching squadrons within the little cove of Beechy Point, Commodore Austin has named it, very appropriately, Union Bay. It is here the Mary is deposited as an asylum to fall back upon in case of disaster.

"The sun is traveling rapidly to the south, so that our recently glaring midnight is now a twilight gloom. The coloring over the hills at Point Innes this evening was sombre, but in deep reds; and the sky had an inhospitable coldness. It made me thoughtful to see the long shadows stretching out upon the snow toward the isthmus of the Graves.

"The wind is from the north and westward, and the ice is so driven in around us as to grate and groan against the sides of our little vessel. The masses, though small, are very thick, and by the surging of the sea have been rubbed as round as pebbles. They make an abominable noise."

The remaining days of August were not characterized by any incident of note. We had the same alternations of progress and retreat through the ice as before, and without sensibly advancing toward the western shore, which it was now our object to reach. The next extracts from my journal are of the date of September 3

"After floating down, warping, to avoid the loose ice, we finally cast off in comparatively open water, and began beating toward Cape Spencer to get round the field. Once there, we got along finely, sinking the eastern shore by degrees, and nearing the undelineated coasts of Cornwallis Island. White whales, narwhals, seals—among them the Phoca leonina with his puffed cheeks—and two bears, were seen.

"The ice is tremendous, far ahead of any thing we have met with. The thickness of the upraised tables is sometimes fourteen feet; and the hummocks are so ground and distorted by the rude attrition of the floes, that they rise up in cones like crushed sugar, some of them forty feet high. But that the queer life we are leading—a life of constant exposure and excitement, and one that seems more like the 'roughing it' of a land party than the life of shipboard—has inured us to the eccentric fancies of the ice, our position would be a sleepless one.

"*September* 4, 2 A.M. Was awakened by Captain De Haven to look at the ice: an impressive sight. We were fast with three anchors to the main floe; and now, though the wind was still from the northward, and therefore in opposition to the drift, the floating masses under the action of the tide came with a westward trend directly past us. Fortunately, they were not borne down upon the vessels; but, as they went by in slow procession to the west, our sensations were, to say the least, *sensations*. It was very grand to see up-piled blocks twenty feet and more above our heads, and to wonder whether this fellow would strike our main-yard or clear our stern. Some of the moving hummocks were thirty feet high. They grazed us; but a little projection of the main field to windward shied them off.

"I killed to-day my first polar bear. We made the animal on a large floe to the northward while we were sighting the western shores of Wellington, and of course could not stop to shoot bears. But he took to the water ahead of us, and came so near that we fired at him from the bows of the vessel. Mr. Lovell and myself fired so simultaneously, that we had to weigh the ball to determine which had hit. My bullet struck exactly in the ear, the mark I had aimed at, for he had only his head above water. The young ice was forming so rapidly around us that it was hard work getting him on board. I was one of the oarsmen, and sweated rarely, with the thermometer at 25°.

"On the way back I succeeded in hitting an enormous seal; but, much to my mortification, he sunk, after floating till we nearly reached him.

"Without any organization, and with very little time for the hunt, the Advance now counts upon her game list two polar bears, three seals, a single goose, and a fair table allowance of loons, divers, and snipes. The Rescue boasts of four bears, and, in addition to the small game, a couple of Arctic hares. Our solitary goose was the Anas bernicla, crowds of which now begin to fly over the land and ice in cunoid streams to the east of south. It was killed by Mr. Murdaugh with a rifle, on the wing.

"How very much I miss my good home assortment of hunting materials! We have not a decent gun on board; as for the rifle I am now shooting, it is a flint-lock concern, and half the time hangs fire."

The next morning found me at work skinning my bear, not a pleasant task with the thermometer below the freezing point. He was a noble specimen, larger than the largest recorded by Parry, measuring eight feet eight inches and three quarters from tip to tip. I presented the skin, on my return home, to the Academy of Natural Sciences at Philadelphia.

The carcass was larger than that of an ordinary ox fatted for market. We estimated his weight at nearly sixteen hundred pounds. In build he was very solid, and the muscles of the arms and haunch fearfully developed. I once before compared the posterior aspect of the Arctic bear to an elephant's. All my messmates used the same comparison. The extreme roundness of his back and haunches, with the columnar character of the legs, and the round expansion of the feet give you the impression of a small elephant. The plantigrade base of support overlapped by long hair heightens the resemblance. The head and neck, of course, are excluded from the comparison.

At five in the afternoon we succeeded in reaching within a quarter of a mile of the shore off Barlow's Inlet, and made fast there to the floe. This inlet is but a few miles from Cape Hotham, and is marked on the charts as a mere interruption of the coast line. Parry, who named it, must have had wonderfully favoring weather to sight so accurately an insignificant cove. He was a practiced hydrographer.

The limestone cliffs rise on each side, forming stupendous piers gnarled by frost degradation, between which is the entrance, about a quarter of a mile wide. The moment our little vessel entered the shadow of these cliffs, a quiet gloom took the place of bustling movement. We ground our way into the newly-formed ice, and, after making a couple of ships' lengths, found ourselves within a sort of cape of land floe, surrounded by high hummocks and anchored bergs. It was a melancholy spot; not one warm sun tint; every thing blank, repulsive sterility.

"*September* 6. The captain, Mr. Murdaugh, Mr. Carter, and myself started on a walk of exploration. The distance between the brig and the shore is not over three hundred yards, but the travel was arduous. The ice was eight and ten feet thick, studded with broken bergs and hummocks. These fragments were seldom larger than our Rensselaer dining-room, some twenty feet square, and, owing either to the rise and fall of the tides or the piling action of storms, deep crevices were formed around their edges, partially masked by the snow which had found its way into them, and by an icy crust over the surface. Alternately jumping these crevices and clambering up the hummocks between them made it a dangerous walk. We had some narrow escapes. Reaching the shore, we pushed forward about a mile and a quarter to the head of the inlet, and then crossed over on the ice to a cairn that stood near it. We found nothing but a communication from Captain Ommanney, whose vessels we saw as we entered the lead yesterday, informing the Secretary of the Admiralty that he had been off this place since the 24th, and that 'no traces are to be found on Cornwallis Island of the party under Sir John Franklin'—a somewhat too confident assertion perhaps, seeing that the island, if it be one, is more than fifty miles across, and that the observations can hardly have extended beyond the coast line.

"*September* 7. The spot at which we have been lying is in front of Barlow's Inlet. There is no barrier between it and our vessels but the young ice, which has now attained a thickness of three inches. On the east we have the drift plain of Wellington Channel, impacted with floes, hummocks, and broken bergs; and to the south we look out upon a wild aggregation of enormous hummocks. These hummocks are totally unlike any thing we saw in Baffin's Bay. They seem to have been so disintegrated by the conflicting forces that raised them as to have lost altogether the character of tables. If hogshead upon hogshead of crushed sugar had been emptied out at random, two or three in one pile, and two or three ship loads in another, and the summits of these irregular heaps were covered over with a succession of layers of snow, and the heaps themselves multiplied in number indefinitely, and crowded together in a disordered phalanx, they would look a good deal like the hummock field some twenty yards south of us. These fearful masses are all anchored, solid hills, rising thirty feet above the level from a bottom twenty-two feet below it.

"Our situation might be regarded as an ugly one in some states of the wind, but for the solid main floe to the north of us. This projected from the cliff, which served as an abutment for it; and, after forming a sort of cape outside of our position, extended with a horseshoe sweep to the northward and eastward, as far as the eye could reach, following the trend of the shore. It formed, of course, a reliable breakwater. Commodore Austin's vessels were made fast to it some distance to the north and east of us.

"The barometer had given us, in the early morning of the 4th, 29·90, since when it rose steadily till the 5th, at 6 A.M., when it stood at 30·38. For the next twenty-four hours it fluctuated between ·33 and ·37; but at 6 A.M. of the 6th, it again began to rise; by midnight, it had reached 30·44; and before ten o'clock P.M. of the 7th, it was at the unwonted height of 30·68. At 2 P.M. the wind had changed from S.S.E. to N.N.E., and went on increasing to a gale.

"We were seated cosily around our little table in the cabin, imagining our harbor of land ice perfectly secure, when we were startled by a crash. We rushed on deck just in time to see the solid floe to windward part in the middle, liberate itself from its attachment to the shore, and bear down upon us with the full energy of the storm. Our lee bristled ominously half a ship's length from us, and to the east was the main drift. The Rescue was first caught, nipped astern, and lifted bodily out of water; fortunately, she withstood the pressure, and rising till she snapped her cable, launched into open water, crushing the young ice before her. The Advance, by hard warping, drew a little closer to the cove; and, a moment after, the ice drove by, just clearing our stern. Commodore Austin's vessels were imprisoned in the moving fragments, and carried helplessly past us. In a very little while they were some four miles off."

The summer was now leaving us rapidly. The thermometer had been at 21° and 23° for several nights, and scarcely rose above 32° in the daytime. Our little harbor at Barlow's Inlet was completely blocked in by heavy masses; the new ice gave plenty of sport to the skaters; but on shipboard it was uncomfortably cold. As yet we had no fires below; and, after drawing around me the India-rubber curtains of my berth, with my lamp burning inside, I frequently wrote my journal in a freezing temperature. "This is not very cold, no doubt"—I quote from an entry of the 8th—"not very cold to your forty-five minus men of Arctic winters; but to us poor devils from the zone of the liriodendrons and peaches, it is rather cool for the September month of water-melons. My bear with his arsenic swabs is a solid lump, and some birds that are waiting to be skinned are absolutely rigid with frost."

In the afternoon of this day, the 8th, we went to work, all hands, officers included, to cut up the young ice and tow it out into the current: once there, the drift carried it rapidly to the south. We cleared away in this manner a space of some forty yards square, and at five the next morning were rewarded by being again under weigh. We were past Cape Hotham by breakfast-time on the 9th, and in the afternoon were beating to the west in Lancaster Sound.

"The sound presented a novel spectacle to us; the young ice glazing it over, so as to form a viscid sea of sludge and *tickly-benders*, from the northern shore to the pack, a distance of at least ten miles. This was mingled with the drift floes from Wellington Channel; and in them, steaming away manfully, were the Resolute and Pioneer. The wind was dead ahead; yet, but for the new ice, there was a clear sea to the west. What, then, was our mortification, first, to see our pack-bound neighbors force themselves from their prison and steam ahead dead in the wind's eye, and, next, to be overhauled by Penny, and passed by both his brigs. We are now the last of all the searchers, except perhaps old Sir John, who is probably yet in Union Bay, or at least east of the straits.

"The shores along which we are passing are of the same configuration with the coast to the east of Beechy Island; the cliffs, however, are not so high, and their bluff appearance is relieved occasionally by terraces and shingle beach. The lithological characters of the limestone appear to be the same.

"We are all together here, on a single track but little wider than the Delaware or Hudson. There is no getting out of it, for the shore is on one side and the fixed ice close on the other. All have the lead of us, and we are working only to save a distance. Ommanney must be near Melville by this time: pleasant, very!

"Closing memoranda for the day: 1. I have the rheumatism in my knees; 2. I left a bag containing my dress suit of uniforms, and, what is worse, my winter suit of furs, and with them my double-barrel gun, on board Austin's vessel. The gale of the 7th has carried him and them out of sight.

"*September* 10. Unaccountable, most unaccountable, the caprices of this ice-locked region! Here we are again all together, even Ommanney with the rest. The Resolute, Intrepid, Assistance, Pioneer, Lady Franklin, Sophia, Advance, and Rescue; Austin, Ommanney, Penny, and De Haven, all anchored to the 'fast' off Griffith's Island. The way to the west completely shut out."

CHAPTER XXIII.

THE succeeding pages are very little else than a transcript from my journal. It would have been easy to condense them into a more attractive form; but they relate to the furthest limits of our cruise, "*longarum meta viarum*;" and some of the topics which they embrace may perhaps invite that sort of evidence which is best furnished by a contemporary record.

"*September* 11, Wednesday. Snow, light and fleecy, covering the decks, and carried by our clothes into our little cabin. The moisture of the atmosphere condenses over the beams, and trickles down over the lockers and bedding. We are still along side of the fixed ice off Griffith's Island, and the British squadron under Commodore Austin are clustered together within three hundred yards of us. Penny, like an indefatigable old trump, as he is, is out, pushing, working, groping in the fog. The sludge ice, that had driven in around us and almost congealed under our stern, is now by the ebb of the tide, or at least its change, carried out again, although the wind still sets toward the floe.

"*September* 12, Thursday. We have had a rough night. About 4 P.M., the heavy snow which had covered our decks changed to a driving drift; the wind blew a gale from the northwest, and the thermometer fell as low as +16°. All the squadron of search, with the exception of Penny, were fastened by ice-anchors to the main ice; but the great obscurity made us invisible to each other.

"At three the Rescue parted her cable's hold, and was carried out to sea, leaving two men, her boat, and her anchors behind. We snapped our stern-cable, lost our anchor, swung out, but fortunately held by the forward line. All the English vessels were in similar peril, the Pioneer being at one time actually free; and Commodore Austin, who in the Resolute occupied the head of the line, was in momentary fear of coming down upon us. Altogether I have seldom seen a night of greater trial. The wind roared over the snow floes, and every thing about the vessel froze into heavy ice stalactites. Had the main floe parted, we had been carried down with the liberated ice. Fortunately, every thing held; and here we are, safe and sound. The Rescue was last seen beating to windward against the gale, probably seeking a lee under Griffith's Island. This morning the snow continues in the form of a fine cutting drift, the water freezes wherever it touches, and the thermometer has been at no time above 17°.

"*September* 12, 10 P.M. Just from deck. How very dismal every thing seems! The snow is driven like sand upon a level reach, lifted up in long curve lines, and then obscuring the atmosphere with a white darkness. The wind, too, is howling in a shrill minor, singing across the hummock ridges. The eight vessels are no longer here. The Rescue is driven out to sea, and poor Penny is probably to the southward. Five black masses, however, their cordage defined by rime and snow, are seen with their snouts shoved into the shore of ice: cables, chains, and anchors are covered feet below the drift, and the ships adhere mysteriously, their tackle completely invisible. Should any of us break away, the gale would carry us into streams of heavy floating ice; and our running rigging is so coated with icicles as to make it impossible to work it. The thermometer stands at 14°.

"At this temperature the young ice forms in spite of the increasing movement of the waves, stretching out from the floe in long, zigzag lines of smoothness resembling watered silk. The loose ice seems to have a southerly and easterly drift; and, from the increasing distance of Griffith's Island, seen during occasional intervals, we are evidently moving *en masse* to the south.

"Now when you remember that we are in open sea, attached to precarious ice, and surrounded by floating streams; that the coast is unknown, and the ice forming inshore, so as to make harbors, if we knew of them, inaccessible, you may suppose that our position is far from pleasant. One harbor was discovered by a lieutenant of the Assistance some days ago, and named Assistance Harbor, but that is out of the question; the wind is not only a gale, but ahead. Had we the quarters of Capua before us, we should be unable to reach them. It is a windward shore.

"11 P.M. Captain De Haven reports ice forming fast: extra anchors are out; thermometer +8°. The British squadron, under Austin, have fires in full blast: we are without them still.

"12 M. In bed, reading or trying to read. The gale has increased; the floes are in upon us from the eastward; and it is evident that we are all of us drifting bodily, God knows where, for we have no means of taking observations.

"*September* 13, 10 A.M. Found, on awaking, that at about three this morning the squadron commenced getting under weigh. The rime-coated rigging was cleared; the hawsers thashed; the ice-clogged boats hauled in; the steamers steamed, and off went the rest of us as we might. This step was not taken a whit too soon, if it be ordained that we are yet in time; for the stream-ice covers the entire horizon, and the large floe or main which we have deserted is barely separated from the drifting masses. The Rescue is now the object of our search. Could she be found, the captain has determined to turn his steps homeward.

"11 20 A.M. We are working, *i. e.*, beating our way in the narrow leads intervening irregularly between the main ice and the drift. We have gained at least two miles to windward of Austin's squadron, who are unable, in spite of steamers, to move along these dangerous passages like ourselves. Our object is to reach Griffith's Island, from which we have drifted some fifteen miles with the main ice, and then look out for our lost consort.

"The lowest temperature last night was +5°, but the wind makes it colder to sensation. We are grinding through newly-formed ice three inches thick; the perfect consolidation being prevented by its motion and the wind. Even in the little fireless cabin in which I now write, water and coffee are freezing, and the mercury stands at 29°.

"The navigation is certainly exciting. I have never seen a description in my Arctic readings of any thing like this. We are literally running for our lives, surrounded by the imminent hazards of sudden consolidation in an open sea. All minor perils, nips, bumps, and sunken bergs are discarded; we are staggering along under all sail, forcing our way while we can. One thump, received since I commenced writing, jerked the time-keeper from our binnacle down the cabin hatch, and, but for our strong bows, seven and a half solid feet, would have stove us in. Another time, we cleared a tongue of the main pack by riding it down at eight knots. Commodore Austin seems caught by the closing floes. This is really sharp work.

"4 P.M. We continued beating toward Griffith's Island, till, by doubling a tongue of ice, we were able to force our way. The English seemed to watch our movements, and almost to follow in our wake, till we came to a comparatively open space, about the area of Washington Square, where we stood off and on, the ice being too close upon the eastern end of Griffith's Island to permit us to pass. Our companions in this little vacancy were Captain Ommanney's Assistance, Osborne's steam tender the Pioneer, and Kater's steamer the Intrepid. Commodore Austin's vessel was to the southward, entangled in the moving ice, but momentarily nearing the open leads.

"While thus boxing about on one of our tacks, we neared the north edge of our little opening, and were hailed by the Assistance with the glad intelligence of the Rescue close under the island. Our captain, who was at his usual post, conning the ship from the foretop-sail yard, made her out at the same time, and immediately determined upon boring the intervening ice. This was done successfully, the brig bearing the hard knocks nobly. Strange to say, the English vessels, now joined by Austin, followed in our wake—a compliment, certainly, to De Haven's ice-mastership.

"We were no sooner through, than signal was made to the Rescue to 'cast off,' and our ensign was run up from the peak: the captain had determined upon attempting a return to the United States."

It could not be my office to discuss the policy of

this step, even if the question were one of policy alone. But it was one of instructions. The Navy Department, imitating in this the English Board of Admiralty, had, in its orders to our commander, marked out to him the course of the expedition, and had enjoined that, unless under special circumstances, he should "endeavor not to be caught in the ice during the winter, but that he should, after completing his examinations for the season, make his escape, and return to New York in the fall." In the judgment of Commodore De Haven, these special circumstances did not exist; and he felt himself, therefore, controlled by the general terms of the injunction. I believe that there was but one feeling among the officers of our little squadron, that of unmitigated regret that we were no longer to co-operate with our gallant associates under the sister flag. Our intercourse with them had been most cordial from the very first. We had interchanged many courtesies, and I should be sorry to think that there had not been formed on both sides some enduring friendships.

In a little while we had the Rescue in tow, and were heading to the east. She had had a fearful night of it after leaving us. She beat about, short-handed, clogged with ice, and with the thermometer at 8°. The snow fell heavily, and the rigging was a solid, almost unmanageable lump. Steering, or rather beating, she made, on the evening of the 12th, the southern edge of Griffith's Island, and by good luck and excellent management succeeded in holding to the land hummocks. She had split her rudder-post so as to make her *unworkable*, and now we have her in tow. An anchor with its fluke snapped—her best bower; and her little boat, stove in by the ice, was cut adrift.

We were now homeward bound, but a saddened homeward bound for all of us. The vessels of our gallant brethren soon lost themselves in the mist, and we steered our course with a fresh breeze for Cape Hotham.

"As we passed the sweep of coast between Capes Martyr and Hotham, and were making the chord of the curve, our captain called my attention to a point of the coast line about six miles off. On looking without a glass, I distinctly saw the naked spars of a couple of vessels. 'Brigs!' said I. 'Undoubtedly,' said De Haven; and then both of us simultaneously, 'Penny!' On looking with the glass, the masts, yards, gaffs, every thing but the bowsprits, were made out distinctly. Lovell was called and saw the same. Murdaugh, who was half undressed, was summoned; and he, examining with the glass, saw a third, which De Haven, after a look, confirmed as a top-sail schooner, 'The Felix' of old Sir John.

"We changed our course, ran in, and determined to convince ourselves of their character, and perhaps to speak them. The fog, however, closed around them. Still we stood on. Presently, a flaw of wind drove off the vapor; and upon eagerly gazing at the spot, now less than three miles off, no vessels were to be seen.

"I can hardly comment upon this strange circumstance. It was a complete puzzle to all of us. Refractive distortion plays strange freaks in these Arctic solitudes; but this could hardly be one of its illusions. Four persons saw the same image with the naked eye, and the glass confirmed the details. There was no disagreement. As plainly as I see these letters did I see those brigs; and although we supposed the Lady

Franklin and Sophia to be ice-caught at or toward Cape Walker, I did not hesitate to name them as the vessels before us. Ten minutes of obscurity, we sailing directly toward them, a sudden interval of brightness—and they had passed away.

"Some large hummocks of grounded ice were near them, and we try to convince ourselves that they may have been closed in by changes in our relative positions; but this is hard to believe, for we should have seen their upper spars above the ice. I gazed long and attentively with our Fraünhofer telescope, at three miles' distance, but saw absolutely no semblance of what a few minutes before was so apparent."

We were obliged several times the next day to bore through the young ice; for the low temperature continued, and our wind lulled under Cape Hotham. The night gave us now three hours of complete darkness. It was danger to run on, yet equally danger to pause. Grim winter was following close upon our heels; and even the captain, sanguine and fearless in emergency as he always proved himself, as he saw the tenacious fields of sludge and pancake thickening around us, began to feel anxious. Mine was a jumble of sensations. I had been desirous to the last degree that we might remain on the field of search, and could hardly be dissatisfied at what promised to realize my wish. Yet I had hoped that our wintering would be near our English friends, that in case of trouble or disease we might mutually sustain each other. But the interval of fifty miles between us, in these inhospitable deserts, was as complete a separation as an entire continent; and I confess that I looked at the dark shadows closing around Barlow's Inlet, the prison from which we cut ourselves on the seventh, just six days before, with feelings as sombre as the landscape itself.

The sound of our vessel crunching her way through the new ice is not easy to be described. It was not like the grinding of the old formed ice, nor was it the slushy scraping of sludge. We may all of us remember, in the skating frolics of early days, the peculiar reverberating outcry of a pebble, as we tossed it from us along the edges of an old mill-dam, and heard it dying away in echoes almost musical. Imagine such a tone as this, combined with the whir of rapid motion, and the rasping noise of close-grained sugar. I was listening to the sound in my little den, after a sorrowful day, close upon zero, trying to warm up my stiffened limbs. Presently it grew less, then increased, then stopped, then went on again, but jerking and irregular; and then it waned, and waned, and waned away to silence.

Down came the captain: "Doctor, the ice has caught us: we are frozen up." On went my furs at once. As I reached the deck, the wind was there, blowing stiff, and the sails were filled and puffing with it. It was not yet dark enough to hide the smooth surface of ice that filled up the horizon, holding the American expedition in search of Sir John Franklin imbedded in its centre. There we were, literally frozen tight in the mid-channel of Wellington's Straits.

"*September* 15. The change of tide, or, rather, those diurnal changes in the movement of the ice which seem to be indirectly connected with it, gave us a little while before noon a partial opening in the solid ice around us. We made by hard work about a mile, and were then more fast than ever. The ice along side will now bear a man: the wind, however, is hauling around to the westward. With a strong northwester, there might still be a hope for us.

"This afternoon, at 6h. 20m., a large spheroidal mass was seen floating in the air at an unknown distance to the north. It undulated for a while over the ice-lined horizon of Wellington Channel; and after a little while, another, smaller than the first, became visible a short distance below it. They receded with the wind from the southward and eastward, but did not disappear for some time. Captain De Haven at first thought it a kite; but, independently of the difficulty of imagining a kite flying without a master, and where no master could be, its outline and movement convinced me it was a balloon. The Resolute dispatched a courier balloon on the 2d; but that could never have survived the storms of the past week. I therefore suppose it must have been sent up by some English vessel to the west of us.

"I make a formal note of this circumstance, trivial as it may be; for at first Franklin rose to my mind, as possibly signalizing up Wellington Channel."

Cape Hotham was at this time nearly in range, from our position, with the first headland to the west of it; and our captain estimated that we were about thirty miles from the eastern side of the strait. The balloon was to leeward, nearly due north of us, more so than could be referred to the course of the wind as we observed it, supposing it to have set out from any vessel of whose place we were aware. It appeared to me, the principal one, about two feet long by eighteen inches broad; its appendage larger than an ordinary dinner-plate. The incident interested us much at the time, and I have not seen any thing in the published journals of the English searchers that explains it.

CHAPTER XXIV.

THE region, which ten days before was teeming with animal life, was now almost deserted. We saw but one narwhal and a few seal. The Ivory gull too, a solitary traveler, occasionally flitted by us; but the season had evidently wrought its change.

Several flocks of the snow bunting had passed over us while we were attached to the main ice off Griffith's Island, and a single raven was seen from the Rescue at her holding grounds. The Brent geese, however, the dovekies, the divers, indeed all the anatidæ, the white whales, the walrus, the bearded and the hirsute seal, the white bear, whatever gave us life and incident, had vanished.

The following Sunday, the 15th, was signalized by the introduction of a bright new "Cornelius" lard lamp into the cabin, a luxury which I had often urged before, but which the difficulties of opening the hold had compelled the captain to deny us. The condensation of moisture had been excessive; the beams had been sweating great drops, and my bedding and bunk-boards bore the look of having been exposed to a drizzling mist. The temperature had been below the freezing point for a week before. The lamp gave us the very comfortable warmth of 44°, twelve degrees above congelation. It was a luxury such as few but Arctic travelers can apprehend.

For some days after this, an obscurity of fog and snow made it impossible to see more than a few hundred yards from the ship. This little area remained fast bound, the ice bearing us readily, though a very slight motion against the sides of the vessel seemed to show that it was not perfectly attached to the shores. But as I stood on deck in the afternoon of the 16th, watching the coast to the east of us, as the clouds cleared away for the first time, it struck me that its configuration was unknown to me. By-and-by, Cape Beechy, the isthmus of the Graves, loomed up; and we then found that we were a little to the north of Cape Bowden.

The next two days this northward drift continued without remission. The wind blew strong from the southward and eastward, sometimes approaching to a gale; but the ice-pack around us retained its tenacity, and increased rapidly in thickness.

Yet every now and then we could see that at some short distance it was broken by small pools of water, which would be effaced again, soon after they were formed, by an external pressure. At these times our vessels underwent a nipping on a small scale. The smoother ice-field that held us would be driven in, piling itself in miniature hummocks about us, sometimes higher than our decks, and much too near them to leave us a sense of security against their further advance. The noises, too, of whining puppies and swarming bees made part of these demonstrations, much as when the heavier masses were at work, but shriller perhaps, and more clamorous.

I was aroused at midnight of the 16th by one of these onsets of the enemy, crunching and creaking against the ship's sides till the masses ground themselves to powder. Our vessel was trembling like an ague-fit under the pressure; and when so pinched that she could not vibrate any longer between the driving and the stationary fields, making a quick, liberating jump above them that rattled the movables fore and aft. As it wore on toward morning, the ice, now ten inches thick, kept crowding upon us with increased energy; and the whole of the 17th was passed in a succession of conflicts with it.

The 18th began with a nipping that promised more of danger. The banks of ice rose one above another till they reached the line of our bulwarks. This, too, continued through the day, sometimes lulling for a while into comparative repose, but recurring after a few minutes of partial intermission. While I was watching this angry contest of the ice-tables, as they clashed together in the darkness of early dawn, I saw for the first time the luminous appearance, which has been described by voyagers as attending the collision of bergs. It was very marked; as decided a phosphorescence as that of the fire-fly, or the fox-fire of the Virginia meadows.

Still, amid all the tumult, our drift was toward the north. From the bearings of the coast, badly obtained through the fogs, it was quite evident that we had passed beyond any thing recorded on the charts. Cape Bowden, Parry's furthest headland, was at least twenty-five miles south of us; and our old landmarks, Cape Hotham and Beechy, had entirely disappeared. Even the high bluffs of Barlow's Inlet had gone. I hardly know why it was so, but this inlet had some how or other been for me an object of special aversion: the naked desolation of its frost-bitten limestone, the cavernous recess of its cliffs, the cheerlessness of its dark shadows, had connected it, from the first day I saw it, with some dimly-remembered feeling of pain. But how glad we should all of us have been, as we floated along in hopeless isolation, to find a way open to its grim but protecting barriers.

I return to my journal.

"*September* 19, Thursday. About five o'clock this morning the wind set in from the northward and eastward; but the ice was tightly compacted, and for a while did not budge. Presently, however, we could see the water-pools extending their irregular margins. Ahead of us, that is, still further to the north, was ice apparently more solid than the ten-inch field around us. It shot up into larger hummocks and heavier masses, and was evidently thicker and more permanent. It had been for the past two days not more than fifty yards ahead, and we called it in the log the 'fixed ice.' By breakfast-time this opened into two long pools on our right, and one on the left, which seemed to extend pretty well toward the western shore. It was evident that we were now drifting to the southward again.

"The sun, so long obscured, gave us to-day a rough meridian altitude. Murdaugh, always active and efficient, had his artificial horizon ready upon the ice, and gave us an approximate latitude. We were in 75° 20′ 11″ north. A large cape and several smaller headlands were seen, together with apparently an inlet or harbor, all on the western side. They remain unchristened. From our mast-head, no *positive* land was visible to the north. Tides we have not had the means of observing. Our soundings on the 17th gave us bottom at 110 fathoms, nearly in mid-channel.

"*September* 19, 11 20 P.M. The wind continued all day from the northward and westward, freshening gradually to a gale. The barometer fell from 29° 73· to 32, and our maximum temperature was 26°. A heavy fall of snow covered the deck.

"*September* 20. I have been keeping the first watch, and anxiously observing the ice; for I am no sailor, and in emergency can only wake my comrades. The darkness is now complete. The wind has changed again. At three A.M. it set in from the southward and eastward, increasing gradually to a fresh gale. Perhaps it may be the breaking up of the season, or some unusual premonition of stern winter; but certain it is that our experience of Lancaster Sound has given us any thing but tranquillity of winds. We entered on the wings of a storm; and ever since, with the exception of about three days off Cape Riley, we have had nothing but gales, rising and falling in alternating series from the north to northward and westward, and from the south to southward and eastward. The day was as usual ushered in with snow, and the thermometer rose to the height of 29°; yet to sensation it was cold. There is something very queer about this discrepancy between the thermometrical register and the effects of heat. It thawed palpably to-day at 28°; and yet all complain of cold, even without the influence of the wind.

"We are now, poor devils! drifting northward again. Creatures of habit, those who were anxious have forgotten anxiety: glued fast here in a moving mass, we eat, and drink, and sleep, unmindful of the morrow. It is almost beyond a doubt that, if we find our way through the contingencies of this Arctic autumn, we must spend our winter in open sea. Many miles to the south, Captain Back passed a memorable term of vigil and exposure. Here, however, I do not anticipate such encounters with drifting floes as are spoken of in Hudson's Bay. The centre of greatest cold is too near us, and the communication with open sea too distant.——

"I was in the act of writing the above, when a startling sensation, resembling the spring of a well-drawn bow, announced a fresh movement. Running on deck, I found it blowing a furious gale, and the ice again in motion. I use the word motion inaccurately. The field, of which we are a part, is always in motion; that is, drifting with wind or current. It is only when other ice bears down upon our own, or our own ice is borne in against other floes, that pressure and resistance make us conscious of motion.

"The ice was again in motion. The great expanse of recently-formed solidity, already bristling with hummocks, had up to this moment resisted the enormous incidence of a heavy gale. Suddenly, however, the pressure increasing beyond its strength, it yielded. The twang of a bow-string is the only thing I can compare it to. In a single instant the broad field was rent asunder, cracked in every conceivable direction, tables ground against tables, and masses piled over masses. The sea seemed to be churning ice.

"By the time I had yoked my neck in its *serape*, and got up upon deck, the ice had piled up a couple of feet above our bulwarks. In less than another minute it had toppled over again, and we were floating helplessly in a confused mass of broken fragments. Fortunately the Rescue remained fixed; our hawser was fast to her stern, and by it we were brought side by side again. Night passed anxiously; *i. e.*, slept in my clothes, and dreamed of being presented to Queen Victoria.

"*September* 21, Saturday. We have drifted still more to the northward and eastward An observation gave us latitude 75° 20′ 38″ N. We are apparently not more than seven miles from the shore. It is still of the characteristic transition limestone, very uninviting, snow-covered, and destitute; but we look at it longingly. It would be so comforting to have landed a small depôt of provisions, in case of accident or impaction further north.

"No snow until afternoon. Thermometer, maximum 22°, minimum 19°, mean 20° 35′. Wind gentle, and now nearly calm, from southward and eastward to southward.

"About tea-time (21st), the sun sufficiently low to give the effects of sunset, we saw distinctly to the north by west a series of hill-tops, apparently of the same configuration with those around us. The trend of the western coast extending northward from the point opposite our vessel receded westward, and a vacant space, either of unseen very low land or of water, separated it from the Terra Nova, which we see north of us. Whether this Grinnell Land, as our captain has named it, be a continuation of Cornwallis Island, or a cape from a new northern land, or a new direction of the eastern coast of North Devon, or a new island, I am not prepared to say. We shall probably know more of each other before long.

"*September* 22, Sunday. A cloudless morning: no snow till afternoon. Our drift during the night has been to the northward; and, except an occasional crack or pool, our horizon was one mass of snow-covered ice.

"The beautifully clear sky with which the day opened gave us another opportunity of seeing the unvisited shores of Upper Wellington Sound. Our latitude by artificial horizon was 75° 24′ 21″ N., about sixty miles from Cape Hotham. Cape Bowden, on the eastern side, has disappeared; and on the west, Advance Bluff, a dark, projecting cape, from which we took sextant angles, was seen bearing to the west of south. To the northward and westward low land was seen, having the appearance of an island,* and mountain tops terminating the low strip ahead. The trend of the shore on our left, the western, is clearly to the westward since leaving Advance Bluff. It is rolling, with terraced shingle beach, and without bluffs. It terminates, or apparently terminates, abruptly, thus:

after which comes a strip without visible land, and then the mountain tops mentioned above. Beyond this western shore, distant only seven miles, we see mountain tops, distant and very high, rising above the clouds.

"*September* 25, Wednesday. The wind has changed, so that our helpless drift is now again to the north. The day was comparatively free from snow; but not clear enough to give us an observation, or to exhibit the more distant coast-lines. We can see the western shore very plainly covered with snow, and stretching in rolling hills to the north and west. A little indentation, nearly opposite the day before yesterday, is now in nearly the same phase—if any thing, a little to the southward. We have therefore changed our position by drift not so much as on the preceding days. The

* I have followed my journal literally. I find, however, in my copy of the log-book, below the entry of the watch-officer which mentions this island, a note made by me at the time: "I can see no island, but simply this prolongation or tongue."

winds, however, have been very light. Advance Bluff is now shut in by 'Cape Rescue,' the westernmost point yet discovered of Cornwallis Island. This shows that we are nearing the shore.

"Toward the north and a little to the west is a permanent dark cloud, a line of stratus with a cumulated thickening at the western end. This is the same during sunshine and snow-storm, night and day. It is thought by Captain De Haven to be indicative of open water. It may be that Cornwallis Island ends there, and that this is a continuation of the present channel trending to the westward. Or this dark appearance may be merely the highland clouds over the mountains seen on Sunday; but De Haven suggests that it is rather a vacant space, or water free from ice; the exemption being due to the island and adjacent western shore (not more than seven miles from it), acting as a barrier to the northern drift of the present channel."

CHAPTER XXV.

I HAVE copied literally from my journal the observations which I noted during our northward drift, because some of them bear on a question, unhappily made one of controversy, as to the extent and character of the discoveries which were due to the American squadron.

It has been seen that on the 19th of September, 1850, we were in latitude 75° 20′ 11″ N., and probably some seven miles from the western shore of Wellington Sound. At this time I observed, but not with certainty, a large cape, several minor headlands, and an inlet or harbor, in the direction of Cornwallis Island. These may, perhaps, have been the Cape De Haven, Point Decision, and Helen Haven or Harbor, discovered and named by Captain Penny in May of the following year.

On the 21st, our latitude was 75° 20′ 38″. The sky being clear, and the position of the sun favorable, I saw distinctly, bearing north by west, a series of hill-tops, not mountains, apparently of the same configuration with those around us, and separated from Cornwallis Island by a strip of low beach or by water. I have sometimes thought that this was the Baillie Hamilton Island, also discovered by Captain Penny in 1851.

On the 22d, our latitude was 75° 24′ 21″. I now saw land to the north and west; its horizon that of rolling ground, without bluffs, and terminating abruptly at its northern end. Still further on to the north came a strip without visible land, and then land again, with mountain tops distant and "rising above the clouds." This last was the land which received from Captain De Haven the name of Mr. Grinnell.

Captain De Haven's official report, made on the 4th of October, 1851, immediately after our return to the United States, speaks of a small, low island, discovered about seven miles to the north-northwest on the 22d of September, 1850. "A channel," he says, "of three or four miles in width separated it from Cornwallis Island. This latter island, trending northwest from our position, terminated abruptly in an elevated cape, to which I have given the name of Manning, after a warm personal friend and ardent supporter of the expedition. Between Cornwallis Island and some distant high land visible in the north, appeared a wide channel leading to the westward. A dark, misty-looking cloud which hung over it (technically termed frost-smoke) was indicative of much open water in that direction. * * * To the channel, which appeared to lead into the open sea, over which the cloud of 'frost-smoke' hung as a sign, I have given the name of Maury, after the distinguished gentleman at the head of our National Observatory, whose theory with regard to an open sea to the north is likely to be realized through this channel. To the large mass of land visible between northwest to north-northeast, I gave the name of Grinnell, in honor of the head and heart of the man in whose philanthropic mind originated the idea of this expedition, and to whose munificence it owes its existence.

"To a remarkable peak bearing N.N.E. from us, distant about forty miles, was given the name of Mount Franklin. An inlet or harbor immediately to the north of Cape Bowden was discovered by Mr. Griffin in his land excursion from Point Innes on the 27th of August, and has received the name of Griffin Inlet. The small island mentioned before was called Murdaugh's Island, after the acting master of the Advance.

"The eastern shore of Wellington Channel appeared to run parallel with the western; but it became quite low, and, being covered with snow, could not be distinguished with certainty, so that its continuity with the high land to the north was not ascertained."

These discoveries, with the exception of Murdaugh Island, present themselves on the English maps in new forms and with different names. I do not refer to those which were published in the newspapers and by the Hydrographic Office in September, 1851; though in both of them the name of Prince Albert has the place which our commander had inscribed a year before with that of Mr. Grinnell: the authors of these two charts could hardly have been informed of the American discoveries. I regret that there is not an equally obvious apology for those who have followed since.

Mr. Arrowsmith's map of the "Discoveries in the Arctic Seas" bears the date of the 21st of October, 1851; though it was not completed, in fact, for several weeks afterward. This is clear from some of the discoveries it records; particularly those of Dr. Rae, which were first announced to the Admiralty on the 10th of November.* The hydrographical map of the British Admiralty, with a similar title, is dated in April, 1852. Both of these documents reassert the name of Albert Land for the large tract of high lands seen by us to the north. In the former, Arrowsmith's,

* See Remarks made at the meeting of the National Institute at Washington, in May, 1852, by the President of the Institute, Peter Force, Esq.

the inscription runs thus: "ALBERT LAND: seen (on the birth-day of H. R. H. Prince Albert) from H. M. S. Assistance, 26th August, 1850.—CAPTAIN OMMANNEY'S JOURNAL: independently seen and explored by Captain Penny and his officers." The other, from the hydrographer of the Admiralty, goes further: it not only inscribes Albert Land on the region we had named after Mr. Grinnell, but explains the error of our claim, by announcing, in a note, that Baillie Hamilton Island is the "Grinnell Land of the American squadron."

The controversy is perhaps of little moment. The time has gone by when the mere sighting of a distant coast conferred on a navigator or his monarch either ownership of the soil or a right to govern its people: even the planting a flag-staff, with armorial emblazonments at the top and a record-bottle below it, does not insure nowadays a conceded title. Yet the comity of explorers has adopted the rule of the more scientific observers of nature, and holds it for law every where that he who first sees and first announces shall also give the name. I should be sorry to withdraw from the extreme charts of northern discovery any memorial, even an indirect one, of that Lady Sovereign, whose noble-spirited subjects we met in Lancaster Sound. It was only by accident that we preceded them, under the guidance of causes that can assert for us little honor, since they were beyond our control, and we should have been glad to escape them. But we *did* precede them; and the most northern land on the meridian of 94° west must retain, therefore, the honored name which it received from the American commander.

A very brief review of the facts will establish this

beyond the chance of doubt. To those who have read Captain De Haven's Report, even though it were not confirmed in its leading particulars by the extracts from my journal, it must be plain that on the 22d of September, 1850, the officers of the American expedition saw, or thought they saw, from a point in latitude 75° 24′ 21″, a large tract of land, extending in the distance from the northwest to the north-northeast, and that they gave to it the name of Grinnell Land. The accounts, which filled the American newspapers immediately after our return in September, 1851, announced this fact widely, and the rude charts that were inserted in several of them indicated both the locality and the name. When this announcement was made, it was not known or supposed that any other party had ever sighted this high northern tract. There was no one from whom the Americans could have borrowed the knowledge of its existence, position, or outline. The fact, more recently ascertained, that others also have seen a similar tract in the same direction, may confirm the truth of the American statement; but it is difficult to imagine how it can be regarded as impeaching it. It only proves that the land is there, as the American commander said it was; while to those who doubt his assertion that he discovered it, it leaves the somewhat puzzling question, how it came to pass that he knew of its existence.

But it is not alone the report of Captain De Haven, corroborated by memoranda made on the spot—it is not on these alone that the asserted discovery rests. All the officers of the American squadron were present at the time when it is said to have taken place; they were all of them in New York when the accounts of it were in the newspapers; they have all of them read the official report of their commander; and there is not a man among them who would have given for a single moment the countenance of his silence to a fabricated claim. I can not allow myself to discuss this branch of the question any further.

A glance at the map is the fitting reply to the intimation of the British hydrographer, that the Grinnell Land of the American squadron was in fact Baillie Hamilton Island. Baillie Hamilton Island, as it is marked on all the maps, bears considerably to the west of northwest from the position of our vessel on the 22d of September. What Captain De Haven saw, and described and plotted, was a tract extending from the northwest to the north-northeast of the same position. It is scarcely a warranted assumption that the American explorers mistook the bearings of the land some sixty or seventy degrees.*

If it be conceded, then, that the American squadron did in fact discover the land in question in September, 1850, we are ready for the next inquiry, Had any one discovered it before them?

No doubt it was visited by Mr. Stewart, one of Captain Penny's officers, on the 24th of May, 1851; and it is certain that, after Captain Penny's return, it was announced as his discovery, and took the name of Albert Land on the maps of Arrowsmith and of the Admi-

* Our expedition was well supplied with chronometers. Besides several of the best English manufacture, carefully selected and tested at the National Observatory, we had three from Bliss and Creighton, of New York. One of these, under the charge of Mr. Murdaugh, our master, varied from its given rate, between the 18th of May, 1850, and the 3d of October, 1851, 10 min. 45′; showing a daily error of $\frac{18}{1000}$ of a second of time. Such an error, computed up to the 22d of September, 1850, would be equal, in latitude 75° 24′ 11″, to an error of position of less than a mile and a half. The weather, however, was rarely favorable for astronomical observations. The most reliable one which I find noted in my copy of the Log gives for our longitude, in our extreme drift to the north, 93° 31′ 10″ W.

ralty of September, 1851. But this was eight months after it had been seen by us and received its American designation.

The Arrowsmith map of October 21, or rather, as we have seen, of November, 1851—it is immaterial which is regarded as the true date—was completed after the discovery of Grinnell Land by the Americans had been made known in England. Our squadron arrived at New York on the 30th of September, 1851, and the intelligence crossed the Atlantic by the next steamer. It was in the maps published immediately after this that it was first made known to the world that the English discovery was older by nine months than had been supposed before; and that the very name of Albert Land, which this region had received either from Penny or the hydrographer, after Penny's return in September, 1851, had, by a coincidence as striking as it was happy, been conferred upon it on the 26th of August, 1850, by another officer, in honor of the day on which he had himself seen it; a day doubly fortunate as the natal day of the prince consort and of Captain Ommanney's discovery.

Yet another notice, in the recent work of Dr. Sutherland, defines the authorship of this discovery still more precisely. Passing by the American claim without remarking even that it ever was asserted, this writer allots the honor alternatively to Captain Penny's party in May, 1851, or to Captain Ommanney, of the Assistance, and Mr. Manson, mate of the Sophia, on the 26th of August, 1850.

It was for me a matter of curious inquiry, upon what evidence this newest claim of discovery might rest. I have examined with all care Captain Ommanney's report to Commodore Austin of the 10th of September, 1850, and Commodore Austin's official reports of subsequent date, and have looked through the different letters of Captain Penny, who was the commander of Mr. Manson, without discovering one word in any of them that could suggest, or imply, or support such a claim. Indeed, I am not aware that either Captain Ommanney or Mr. Manson has authorized the assertion of it. Happily, the question may be decided without appealing to negative evidence. It is a fact, susceptible of demonstration, that neither of them did or could make the discovery which is now imputed to them.

On the 26th of August, 1850, Captain Ommanney was on board his own vessel, the Assistance. He had been detached by Commodore Austin to make a thorough examination of the coast about Cape Hotham, and on the evening of the 25th he was fairly imbedded and fast in the ice between that point and Barlow's Inlet. He was seen there by Mr. Penny, by Commodore Austin, and by every one on board the Advance. He may not have been seen there by some of his British associates on the 26th, for a reason which I shall advert to presently; but on the 27th he was there still, and his own report shows that he remained there till the 3d of September. Now he who feels interest enough in the question to extend a scale upon any of the charts, will prove for himself that on the 26th of August, Captain Ommanney, being then off Cape Hotham, was at the distance of a hundred miles from the land he is supposed to have that day discovered. We had drifted more than sixty miles to the north of his position before we saw that land, and it was then some forty miles still further to the north. We lost it again when we had drifted back ten miles to the south.

On the 26th we were off Cape Innis, and Captain Ommanney about ten miles further to the south. Our log-book speaks of two vessels beset in the ice off Cape Hotham, which were no doubt his; but the state of the atmosphere was such as to make it impossible to recognize any thing at that distance. My meteorological record for the day shows this: it was dull and heavy, till it was relieved by a fall of snow.

The journal recently published by Dr. Sutherland shows it also. Under the date of August 26th, it says: "At one o'clock A.M. the ships were made fast to the floe, to take some water from it, and to wait until the weather should clear up;" and "during the day the weather was almost perfectly calm, the sky was overcast with a dense misty haze, and toward evening there was a great deal of soft snow."—Vol. i., p. 296, 298. Captain Ommanney himself, writing on the 10th of September, says: "During the day (the 25th of August), we kept along the solid field of ice, extending from Cape Innis to Barlow's Inlet, which bounded the horizon to the northward, and where *no land was visible*. When six miles east of Barlow's Inlet, the pack-ice closed in and stopped my further progress. In this position we continued beset in Wellington Channel from the 25th ultimo to the 3d instant, strong south-easterly winds and thick weather prevailing." The question of discovery by Captain Ommanney on the 26th of August resolves itself, therefore, into this, Could he, when objects were not distinguishable at ten miles distance, make discoveries at the distance of a hundred?

As to Mr. Manson, he was on board the Sophia on the 25th, and does not appear, from Dr. Sutherland's journal, to have left her for some time afterward. On the 26th, Captain Penny was on board the Advance, in company with some of the officers of the Sophia, Mr. Manson perhaps among the rest; and it is enough for me to say that, among the many interesting pieces of information which we derived from that honest and communicative seaman, the crowning fact of such a discovery by his mate was not included. For the rest, the journals I have already quoted show that no one on board the Sophia could that day have made any distant discovery at all.

I pass gladly to other topics. The nobility of character and feeling that distinguished our British friends of Union Bay, and the weighty obligations I am under to the generous men who preside in the departments of the British Admiralty, especially the hydrographic, have made this discussion a most unwelcome one. My recollections as a subordinate, and my much more limited experience as a superior, have taught me that the principal should not always be held answerable for that which bears the sanction of his name; and I am, besides, old enough to know, that the charity I extend to the erroneous opinions of others, may often be invoked more properly for errors of my own.

THE ADVANCE IN THE ICE, 26TH SEPTEMBER, 1850.

CHAPTER XXVI.

I AM reluctant to burden my pages with the wild, but scarcely varied incidents of our continued drift through Wellington Channel. We were yet to be familiarized with the strife of the ice-tables, now broken up into tumbling masses, and piling themselves in angry confusion against our sides—now fixed in chaotic disarray by the fields of new ice that imbedded them in a single night—again, perhaps, opening in treacherous pools, only to close round us with a force that threatened to grind our brigs to powder. I shall have occasion enough to speak of these things hereafter. I give now a few extracts from my journal; some of which may perhaps have interest of a different character, though they can not escape the saddening monotony of the scenes that were about us.

I begin with a partial break-up that occurred on the 23d.

"*September* 23. How shall I describe to you this pressure, its fearfulness and sublimity! Nothing that

I have seen or read of approaches it. The voices of the ice and the heavy swash of the overturned hummock-tables are at this moment dinning in my ears. 'All hands' are on deck fighting our grim enemy.

"Fourteen inches of solid ice thickness, with some half dozen of snow, are, with the slow uniform advance of a mighty propelling power, driving in upon our vessel. As they strike her, the semi-plastic mass is impressed with a mould of her side, and then, urged on by the force behind, slides upward, and rises in great vertical tables. When these attain their utmost height, still pressed on by others, they topple over, and form a great embankment of fallen tables. At the same time, others take a downward direction, and when pushed on, as in the other case, form a similar pile underneath. The side on which one or the other of these actions takes place for the time, varies with the direction of the force, the strength of the opposite or resisting side, the inclination of the vessel, and the weight of the superincumbent mounds; and as these conditions follow each other in varying succession, the vessel becomes perfectly imbedded after a little while in crumbling and fractured ice.

"Perhaps no vessel has ever been in this position but our own. With matured ice, nothing of iron or wood could resist such pressure. As for the British vessels, their size would make it next to impossible for them to stand. Back's 'Winter' is the only thing I have read of that reminds me of our present predicament. No vessel has ever been caught by winter in these waters.

"We are lifted bodily eighteen inches out of water. The hummocks are reared up around the ship, so as to rise in some cases a couple of feet above our bulwarks—five feet above our deck. They are very often ten and twelve feet high. All hands are out, laboring with picks and crowbars to overturn the fragments that threaten to overwhelm us. Add to this darkness, snow, cold, and the absolute destitution of surrounding shores.

"This uprearing of the ice is not a slow work: it is progressive, but not slow. It was only at 4 P.M. that the nips began, and now the entire plain is triangulated with ice-barricades. Under the double influence of sails and warping-hawsers, we have not been able to budge a hair's-breadth. Yet, impelled by this irresistible, bearing-down floe-monster, we crush, grind, *eat* our way, surrounded by the ruins of our progress. In fourteen minutes we changed our position 80 feet, or 5.71 per minute.

"Sometimes the ice cracks with violence, almost explosive, throughout the entire length of the floe. Very grand this! Sometimes the hummock masses, piled up like crushed sugar around the ship, suddenly sink into the sea, and then fresh mounds take their place.

"Our little neighbor, the Rescue, is all this time within twenty yards of us, resting upon wedges of ice, and not subjected to movement or pressure—a fact of interest, as it shows how very small a difference of position may determine the differing fate of two vessels.

"*September* 24. The ice is kinder; no fresh movements; a little *whining* in the morning, but since then undisturbed. The ice, however, is influenced by the wind; for open water-pools have formed—three around the ship within eye distance. In one of these, the seals made their appearance toward noon; no less than five disporting together among the sludge of the open water. I started off on a perilous walk over the ruined barricades of last night's commotion; and, after cooling myself for forty minutes in an atmosphere ten degrees above zero, came back without a shot. The condensed moisture had so affected my powder that I could not get my gun off.

"This condensation is now very troublesome, dripping down from our carlines, and sweating over the roof and berth-boards. When we open the hatchway, the steam rises in clouds from the little cabin below.

"We have as yet no fires; worse! the state of uncertainty in which we are placed makes it impossible to resort to any winter arrangements. Yet these lard lamps give us a temperature of 46°, which to men like ourselves, used to constant out-door exercise, exposure, and absence of artificial heat, is quite genial. But for the moisture—that wretched, comfortless, rheumatic drawback—we would be quite snug.

"Our captain is the best of sailors; but, intent always on the primary objects and duties of his cruise, he is apt to forget or postpone a provident regard for those creature-comforts which have interest for others. To-day, with the thermometer at 10°, we for the first time commenced the manufacture of stove-pipes. I need not say that the cold metal played hob with the tinkers. If they go on at the present rate, the pipes will be nearly ready by next summer.

"*September* 26. The hummocks around us still remain without apparent motion, heaped up like snow-covered barriers of street rioters. We are wedged in a huge mass of tables, completely out of water, cradled by ice. I wish it would give us an even keel. We are eighteen inches higher on one quarter than the other.

"The two large pools we observed yesterday, one on

each side of us, are now coated by a thick film of ice. In this the poor seals sometimes show themselves in groups of half a dozen. They no longer sport about as they did three weeks ago, but rise up to their breasts through young ice, and gaze around with curiosity-smitten countenances.

"The shyness of the seal is proverbial. The Esquimaux, trained from earliest youth to the pursuit of them, regard a successful hunter as the great man of the settlement. If not killed instantaneously, the seal sinks and is lost. The day before yesterday, I adopted the native plan of silent watching beside a pool. Thus for a long time I was exposed to a temperature of +8°; but no shots within head-range offered; and I knew that, unless the spinal column or base of the brain was entered by the ball, it would be useless to waste our already scanty ammunition.

"To-day, however, I was more fortunate. A fine young seal rose about forty yards off, and I put the ball between the ear and eye. A boat was run over the ice, and the carcass secured. This is the second I have killed with this villainous carbine: it will be a valuable help to our sick. We are now very fond of seal-meat. It is far better than bear; and the fishiness, which at first disturbed us, is no longer disagreeable. I simply skin them, retaining the blubber with the pelt. The cold soon renders them solid. My bear, although in a barrel, is as stiff and hard as horn.

"Took a skate this morning over some lakelets recently frozen over. The ice was tenacious, but not strong enough for safety. As I was moving along over the *tickly-benders*, my ice-pole drove a hole, and came very near dropping through into the water.

"*September* 27. This evening the thermometer gave

3° above zero. A bit of ice, which I took into my mouth to suck, fastened on to my tongue and carried away the skin. When we open the cabin hatch now, a cloud of steam, visible only as the two currents meet, gives evidénce of the Arctic condensation.

"Afar off, skipping from hummock to hummock, I saw a black fox. Poor desolate devil! what did he, so far from his recorded home,. seven miles from even the naked snow-hills of this dreary wilderness? In the night-time I heard him bark. They set a trap for him; but I secretly placed a bigger bait outside, without a snare-loop or trigger. In the morning it was gone, and the dead-fall had fallen upon no fox. How the poor, hungry thing must have enjoyed his supper! half the guts, the spleen, and the pluck of my seal.

"Lovell raised a swing; cold work, but good exercise. He rigged it from the main studding-sail boom. Murdaugh and Carter are building a snow-house. The doctor is hard at work patching up materials for an overland communication with the English squadron —an enterprise fast becoming desperate. Yet, drifting as we are to unknown regions north, it is of vast importance that others should know of our position and prospects."

Our position, however, at the end of September, thanks to the rapidly-increasing cold, gave promise of a certain degree of security and rest. The Advance had been driven, by the superior momentum of the floes that pressed us on one side, some two hundred and fifty feet into the mass of less resisting floes on the other; the Rescue meanwhile remaining stationary; and the two vessels were fixed for a time on two adjacent sides of a rectangle, and close to each other. The unseen and varying energies of the ice movements had occasionally modified the position of each; but their relation to each other continued almost unchanged.

We felt that we were fixed for the winter. We arranged our rude embankments of ice and snow around us, began to deposit our stores within them, and got out our felt covering that was to serve as our winter roof. The temperature was severe, ranging from 1°.5, and 4° to +10°; but the men worked with the energy, and hope too, of pioneer settlers, when building up their first home in our Western forests.

The closing day of the month was signalized by a brilliant meteor, a modification of the parhelion, the more interesting to us because the first we had seen.

"*October* 1, Tuesday. To-day the work of breaking hold commenced. The coal immediately under the main hatch was passed up in buckets, and some five tons piled upon the ice. The quarter-boats were hauled about twenty paces from our port-bow, and the sails covered and stacked; in short, all hands were at work preparing for the winter. Little had we calculated the caprices of Arctic ice.

"About ten o'clock A.M. a large crack opened nearly east and west, running as far as the eye could see, sometimes crossing the ice-pools, and sometimes breaking along the hummock ridges. The sun and moon will be in conjunction on the 3d; we had notice, therefore, that the spring tides are in action.

"Captain Griffin had been dispatched with Mr. Lovell before this, to establish on the shore the site for a depôt of provisions: at one o'clock a signal was made to recall them. At two P.M., seeing a seal, I ran out upon the ice; but losing him, was tempted to continue on about a mile to the eastward. The wind, which had been from the westward all the morning, now shifted to the southward, and the ice-tables began to be again in motion. The *humming of bees* and upheaving hummocks, together with exploding cracks, warned me back to the vessel.

"At 3 20, while we were at dinner, commenting with some anxiety upon the condition of things without, that unmistakable monitor, the '*young puppies*,' began. Running on deck, we found a large fissure, nearly due north and south, in line with the Advance. A few minutes after, the entire floe on our starboard side was moving, and the ice breaking up in every direction.

"The emergency was startling enough. All hands turned to, officers included. The poor land party, returning at this moment, tired and dinnerless, went to work with the rest. Vreeland and myself worked like horses. Before dark, every thing was on board except the coal; and of this, such were the unwearied efforts of our crew, that we lost but a ton or two.

"This ice-opening was instructive practically, because it taught those of us who did not understand it before how capriciously insecure was our position. It revealed much, too, in relation to the action of the ice

"1. The first crack was nearly at right angles to the axis of the channel; the subsequent ones crossed the first; the wind being in the one case from the westward, and afterward changing to the southward.

"2. The next subject of note was the disintegration of the old floes. It took place almost invariably at their original lines of junction, well marked by the hummocky ridges. This shows that the cementation was imperfect after seventeen days of very low temperature; a circumstance attributable, perhaps, to the massive character of the up-piled tables, which protected the inner portion of them from the air, and to the constant infiltration (*endosmose*) of salt-water at the abraded margins.

"3. The extent to which the work of super and infra position had been carried during the actions may be realized, when I say that the floe-piece which separated from us to starboard retained the exact impression of the ship's side. There it was, with the gangway stairs of ice-block masonry, looking down upon the dark water, and the useless embankment embracing a sludgy ice-pool.

"We could see table after table, more properly layer after layer, each not more than seven inches thick, extending down for more than twenty feet. Thus, it is highly probable, may be formed many of those enormous ice-tables, attributed by authors to direct and uninterrupted congelation.

"The quantity of ice adhering to our port-side must be enormous; for although the starboard floe, in leaving us, parted a six-inch hawser, it failed to budge us one inch from the icy cradle in which we are set."

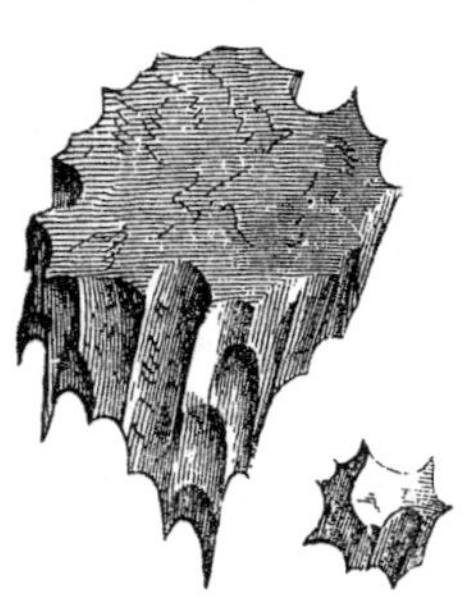

THE ADVANCE, OFF CROKER'S BAY.

CHAPTER XXVII.

THREE days after this entry the thermometer had fallen to 11° below zero. Our housings were not yet fixed, and we had no fires below; indeed, our position was so liable to momentary and violent change that it would have been impracticable to put up stoves. Still, our lard-lamp in the cabin gave us a temperature of +44°; and so completely were our systems accommodated to the circumstances in which we were, that we should have been quite satisfied but for the condensed moisture that dripped from every thing about us. Our commander had allowed me to place canvas gutters around the hatchways, and from these we emptied every day several tin cans full of water, that would otherwise have been added to the slop on our cabin floor. But the state of things was, on the whole, exceedingly comfortless, and, to those whom the scurvy had attacked, full of peril. I remember once, when the lard-lamp died out in the course of the night, the mercury sunk in the cabin to 16°. It was not till the 19th that we got up our stoves.

The adaptation of the human system to varying temperatures struck me at this time with great force. I had passed the three winters before within the tropics—the last on the plains of Mexico—yet I could now watch patiently for hours together to get a shot at seals, with the thermometer at +10°. I wrote my journal in imaginary comfort with a temperature of 40°, and was positively distressed with heat when exercising on the ice with the mercury at +19°.

I return to my diary.

"*October* 3. I write at midnight. Leaving the deck, where I have been tramping the cold out of my joints, I come below to our little cabin. As I open the hatch, every thing seems bathed in dirty milk. A cloud of vapor gushes out at every chink, and, as the cold air travels down, it is seen condensing deeper and deeper. The thermometer above is at 7° below zero.

"The brig and the ice around her are covered by a strange black obscurity—not a mist, nor a haze, but a peculiar, waving, palpable, unnatural darkness: it is the frost-smoke of Arctic winters. Its range is very low. Climbing to the yard-arm, some thirty feet above the deck, I looked over a great horizon of black smoke, and above me saw the heaven without a blemish.

"*October* 4. The open pools can no longer be called pools; they are great rivers, whose hummock-lined shores look dimly through the haze. Contrasted with the pure white snow, their waters are black even to inkyness; and the silent tides, undisturbed by ripple or wash, pass beneath a pasty film of constantly forming ice. The thermometer is at 10°. Away from the ship, a long way, I walked over the older ice to a spot where the open river was as wide as the Delaware. Here, after some crevice-jumping and *tickly-bender* crossing, I set myself behind a little rampart of hummocks, watching for seals.

"As I watched, the smoke, the frost-smoke, came down in wreaths, like the lambent tongues of burning turpentine seen without the blaze. I was soon enveloped in crapy mist.

"To shoot seal, one must practice the Esquimaux tactics of much patience and complete immobility. It is no fun, I assure you after full experience, to sit motionless and noiseless as a statue, with a cold iron musket in your hands, and the thermometer 10° below zero. But by-and-by I was rewarded by seeing some overgrown Greenland calves come within shot. I missed. After another hour of cold expectation, they came again. Very strange are these seal. A countenance between the dog and the mild African ape—an expression so like that of humanity, that it makes gun-murderers hesitate. At last, at long shot, I hit one. God forgive me!

"The ball did not kill outright. It was out of range, struck too low, and entered the lungs. The poor beast had risen breast-high out of water, like the treading-water swimmers among ourselves. He was thus supported, looking about with curious, expectant eyes, when the ball entered his lungs.

"For a moment he oozed a little bright blood from his mouth, and looked toward me with a sort of startled reproachfulness. Then he dipped; an instant after, he came up still nearer, looked again, bled again, and went down. A half instant afterward, he came up flurriedly, looked about with anguish in his eyes, for he was quite near me; but slowly he sunk, struggling feebly, rose again, sunk again, struggled a very little more. The thing was drowning in the element of his sportive revels. He did drown finally, and sunk; and so I lost him.

"Have naturalists ever noticed the expression of this animal's phiz? Curiosity, contentment, pain, reproach, despair, even resignation I thought, I saw on this seal's face.

"About half an hour afterward, I killed another. Scurvy and sea-life craving for fresh meat led me to it; but I shot him dead.

"On returning to the ship, I found one toe frost-bitten—a tallow-looking dead man's toe—which was restored to its original ugly vitality by snow-rubbing. Served me right!

"Spent the afternoon in unsuccessful seal stalking, and in rigging and contriving a spring-gun for the Arctic foxes: a blood-thirsty day. But we ate of fox to-day for dinner; and behold, and it was good.

"*October* 5, Saturday. The wind evidently freshens up. The day has been bitterly cold. Although our lowest temperature was zero and —1°, we felt it far more than the low temperature of yesterday. Our maximum was as high as 4°; yet, with this, it required active motion on deck to keep one's self warm.

"At 12h. 55m., we had an interval of clear sunshine. The utmost, however, to which it would raise one of the long register Smithsonian thermometers was 7°. The air was filled with bright particles of frozen moisture, which glittered in the sunshine—a shimmering of transparent dust.*

"At the same time, we had a second exhibition of parhelia, not so vivid in prismatic tints as that of the 30th of September, but more complete. The sun was expanded in a bright glare of intensely-white light, and was surrounded by two distinct concentric circles, delicately tinted on their inner margins with the red of the spectrum. The radius of the inner, as measured

* Under the microscope these again showed obscure modifications of the hex agon

by the sextant, was 22° 04′; that of the outer, 40° 15′. The lower portions of both were beneath the horizon, and of course not seen.

"From the central disk proceeded four radii, coincident with the vertical and the horizontal diameters of the circles.

"Their visible points of intersection were marked by bright parhelia; each parhelion having its circumference well defined, but compressed so as to have no resemblance to the solar disk.

Six of these were visible at the same moment; those of the outer circle being fainter than the inner. Touching the upper circumference of this outer circle was the arc of a third, which extended toward the zenith. Indeed, at one time I thought I saw a luminosity overhead, which may have corresponded to its centre. The tints of this supplemental circle were very bright. The glowing atmosphere about the sun was very striking.

"The strange openings in the water of a few hours ago are now great rivers, lined by banks of hummocks, and wreathed in frost smoke. The continually increasing wind from the northward explains this southern drift of the ice, and with it these unwelcome openings. We are stationary, and the detached ice is leaving us.

"The strong floe of ice-table under ice-table, and hummock upon hummock, makes our position one of nearly complete solidity. We are glued up in ice; and to liberate us, some fearful disruption must take place. Twenty-five feet of solid ice is no feeble matrix for a brig drawing but ten. Yet the water is wider, and still widening around us; so that now we hold on—that is, our floe holds on, to the great mass to the north of us, like a little peninsular cape.

"To the south every thing is in drifting motion—water, sludge, frost-smoke—but no seals.

"We caught a poor little fox to-day in a dead-fall. We ate him as an anti-scorbutic.

"*October* 6, Sunday. A dismal day; the wind howling, and the snow, fine as flour, drifting into every chink and cranny. The cold quite a nuisance, although the mercury is up again to +6°. It is blowing a gale. What if the floe, in which we are providentially glued, should take it into its head to break off, and carry us on a cruise before the wind!

"8 P.M. Took a pole, and started off to make a voyage of discovery around our floe. After some weary walking over hummocks, and some uncomfortable sousings in the snow-dust, found that our cape has dwindled to an isthmus. In the midst of snow and haze, of course, I did not venture across to the other ice.

"We look now anxiously at the gale—turning in, clothes on, so as to be ready for changes.

"12 Midnight. They report us adrift. Wind, a gale from the northward and westward. An odd cruise this! The American expedition fast in a lump of ice about as big as Washington Square, and driving, like the shanty on a raft, before a howling gale.

"*October* 7, Monday. Going on deck this morning, a new coast met my eyes. Our little matrix of ice had floated at least twenty miles to the south from yesterday's anchorage. The gale continues; but the day is beautifully clear, and we have neared the western coast enough to recognize the features of the limestone cliffs, although many a wrinkle of them is now pearl-powdered with snow-drift.

"Prominent among these was Advance Bluff; and to the south of it, a great indentation in the limestone escarpment, which ran back into a gray distance—a sort of gorge, with a summer water-course. Further off, Point Innes again, and the shingle beach of 'the Graves;' and a high bluff-like cape or headland to the southward and westward, which the captain supposes to be Barlow's Inlet.

"10 P.M. Our master got an observation this evening of *a* Aquila (circum-meridian altitude), giving us a latitude of 74° 54′ 07″. The seat of our late resting-place was in latitude 75° 24′ 52″ N. We have therefore voyaged 30 miles 45 seconds since this new start. At this rate, should the wind continue, another day will carry us again into Lancaster Sound.

"*October* 8. Still we drift. Barlow's Inlet is nearly abreast of us, and Cape Hotham seen distinctly. The broad, unterminated expanse of ice to the south is Lancaster Sound, sixty miles distant when we first began our prisoner's journey. Thermometer at +8°.

"To-day seemed like a wave of the handkerchief from our receding summer. Winter is in every thing. Yet the skies came back to us with warm ochres and pinks, and the sun, albeit from a lowly altitude, shone out in full brightness. It was a mockery of warmth, however, scarcely worthy the unpretending sincerity of the great planet; for the mercury, exposed to the full radiance of his deceitful glare, rose but two degrees: from +7° to 9°. In spite of this, the day was beautiful to remember, as a type of the sort of thing which we once shared with the world from which we are shut out; a parting picture, to think about during the long night. These dark days, or rather the dark day, will soon be on us. The noon shadows of our long masts almost lose themselves in the distance.

"A little white fox was caught alive in a trap this

morning. He was an astute-visaged little scamp; and although the chains of captivity, made of spun-yarn and leather, set hardly upon him, he could spare abundant leisure for bear bones and snow. He would drink no water. His cry resembled the inter-paroxysmal yell of a very small boy undergoing spanking. The note came with an impulsive vehemence, that expressed not only fear and pain, but a very tolerable spice of anger and ill-temper."

He was soon reconciled, however. The very next day he was tame enough to feed from the hand, and had lost all that startled wildness of look which is supposed to characterize his tribe. He was evidently unused to man, and without the educated instinct of flight. Twice, when suffered to escape from the vessel, he was caught in our traps the same night. Indeed, the white foxes of this region—we caught more than thirty of them—seemed to look at us with more curiosity than fear. They would come directly to the ship's side; and, though startled at first when we fired at them, soon came back. They even suffered us to approach them almost within reach of the hand, ran around us, as we gave the halloo, in a narrow circle, but stopped as soon as we were still, and stared us inquisitively in the face. One little fellow, when we let him loose on the ice after keeping him prisoner for a day or two, scampered back again incontinently to his cubby-hole on the deck. There may be matter of reflection for the naturalist in this. Has this animal no natural enemy but famine and cold? The foxes ceased to visit us soon after this, owing probably to the uncertain ice between us and the shore: they are shrewd ice-masters.

Drawn by J. Hamilton, after a Sketch by Dr. E. K. Kane, U.S.N.—Engraved by J. Sartain.

CHAPTER XXVIII.

We remained during the rest of this month ice-cradled, and drifting about near the outlet of Wellington Channel. Occasionally a strong southerly wind would set us back again to the north, as far, perhaps, as Barlow's Inlet; but it was soon apparent that the greater compactness of the barrier that had come down after us, and the force of some unknown current, were resisting our progress in that direction. A northerly wind, on the other hand, seemed to have no counteracting influences. A little while after it began to blow, open leads would present themselves under our lee, and the floe which imbedded us moved gradually and without conflict through them toward the south. Our thoughts turned irresistibly to the broad expanse of Lancaster Sound, which lay wild and rugged before us, and to the increasing probability that it was to be our field of trial during the long, dark winter—perhaps our final home.

With this feeling came an increasing desire to communicate with our late associates of Union Bay. I had volunteered some weeks before to make this traverse, and had busied myself with arrangements to carry it out. The Rescue's India-rubber boat was to carry the party through the leads, and, once at the shore, three men were to press on with a light tent and a few days' provisions. The project, impracticable perhaps from the first, was foiled for a time by a vexatious incident. I had made my tent of thin cotton cloth, so that it weighed, when completed, but fourteen pounds, soaking it thoroughly in a composition of caoutchouc, ether, and linseed oil, the last in quantity. After it was finished and nearly dried, I wrapped it up in a dry covering of coarse muslin, and placed it for the night in a locked closet, at some distance from the cook's galley, where the temperature was between 80° and 90°. In the morning it was destroyed. The wrapper was there, retaining its form, and not discolored; but the outer folds of the tent were smoking; and, as I unrolled it, fold after fold showed more and more marks of combustion, till at the centre it was absolutely charred. There was neither flame nor spark.

In a few days more the tumult of the ice-fields had made all chance of reaching the shore hopeless. But the mean time was not passed without efforts.

"*October* 23. I started with a couple of men on another attempt to reach the shore. After five miles of walking, with recurring alternations of climbing, leaping, rolling, and soaking, we found that the ice had driven out from the coast, and a black lane of open water stopped our progress. This is the seventh attempt to cross the ice, all meeting with failure from the same cause. The motion of ice, influenced by winds, tides, and currents, keeps constantly abrading the shore-line. Any outward drift, of course, makes an irregular lane of water, which a single night converts into ice; the returning floes heap this in tables one over another; and the next outward *set* carries off the floes again, crowned with their new increment.

"The haze gathered around us about an hour after starting, and the hummocks were so covered with snow that the chasms often received us middle deep. We walked five hours and a half, making in all but eleven miles; and even then were at least a mile from the beach.

"At one portion of our route, the ice had the crushed sugar character; the lumps varying in size from a small cantaloupe to a water-melon, but hard as frozen water at zero ought to be. Over this stuff we walked in tiptoe style—and a very miserable style it was.

"At another place, for a mile and a half, we trod on the fractured angles of upturned ice. Call these curb-stones; toss them in mad confusion, always taking care that their edges shall be uppermost; dust them over with flour cooled down to zero; and set a poor wretch, loose, in the centre of a misty circle, to try for a pathway over them to the shore!

"At another place, break-water stones, great quarried masses of ice, let you up and down, but down oftener than up. At another time, you travel over rounded dunes of old seasoned hummock, covered with slippery glaze. Again, it is over snow, recent and soft, or snow, recent and sufficiently crusty to bear you five paces and let you through the sixth—a trial alike to temper and legs.

"At last, to crown the *deliciæ* of our Arctic walk, we come to a long meadow of recent ice, just enough covered with snow to keep you from slipping, and just thin enough to make it elastic as a Polka floor. Over this, with a fine bracing air, every nerve tingling with the exercise, and the hoary rime whitening your beard, you walk with a delightful sense of ease and enjoyment.

"One of my attendants had both ears frost-bitten; the whole external cartilage (*Pinna*) was of tallow, jaundiced. Snow-rubbing set him right. I have ordered the men to take ear-rings from their ears. Wilson, a Livournese, rejoiced in a couple of barbaric pendules, doubtless of bad gold, but good conducting power."

The indications of winter were still becoming more and more marked. On the 11th, the sun rose but 9° at meridian; on the 15th but 6°; and on the 7th of November, at the same hour, it almost rested on the horizon. The daylight, however, was sometimes strangely beautiful. One day in particular, the 8th, a rosy tint diffused itself over every thing, shaded off a little at the zenith, but passing down from pink to violet, and from violet to an opalescent purple, that banded the entire horizon.

The moon made its appearance on the 13th of October. At first it was like a bonfire, warming up the ice with a red glare; but afterward, on the 15th, when it rose to the height of 4°, it silvered the hummocks and frozen leads, and gave a softened lustre to the snow, through which our two little brigs stood out in black and solitary contrast. The stars seemed to have lost their twinkle, and to shine with concentrated brightness as if through gimlet-holes in the cobalt canopy. The frost-smoke scarcely left the field of view. It generally hung in wreaths around the horizon; but it sometimes took eccentric forms; and one night, I remember, it piled itself into a column at the west, and Aquila flamed above it like a tall beacon-light. We were glad to note these fanciful resemblances to the aspects of a more kindly region; they withdrew us sometimes from the sullen realities of the world that encompassed us—ice, frost-smoke, and a threatening sky.

We had parhelia again more than once, but developed imperfectly; a mass of incandescence 22° from the sun, with prismatic coloring, but without the circular and radial appearances that had characterized it before. On the 27th, a partial paraselene was visible, the first we observed—merely the limbs of two broken arcs, destitute of prismatic tint, stretching like circumflexes at about 23° distance on each side the moon; the moon about 20° high, thermometer −10°, barometer 30°.55′, atmosphere hazy. The sky clearing shortly afterward, it shone out with increased beauty for a while, but died away as the haze disappeared.

The thermometer was now generally below the zero point, sometimes rising for a little while about noon a few degrees above it, once only as high as +13°. When there was no wind, even the lowest of its range was quite bearable; and while we were exercising actively, it was difficult to believe that our sensations could be so strikingly in contrast with the absolute temperature. But a breeze, or a pause of motion till we could raise the sextant to a star or make out some changing phasis of the ice-field, never failed to persuade us, and that feelingly, that the mercury was honest. Night after night the bed-clothes froze at our feet; and a poor copy of the New York Herald, that lay at the head of the captain's bunk, was glazed with ice.

"*November* 8. Tempted by the over-arching beauty of the sky, I started off this morning with Captain De Haven on a walk of inspection shoreward. The open water, frozen since October 2d, is now nearly two feet thick, and at this low temperature (−15°) it becomes hard and brittle as glass. Wherever the nipping has caught two of the floes, they have been driven with a force inconceivable one above the other, rising and falling until they now form a ridge fifteen or twenty feet high.

"The tension of the great field of ice over which we passed must have been enormous. It had a sensible curvature. On striking the surface with a walking-pole, loud reports issued like a pistol-shot, and lines of fissure radiated from the point of impact. It seemed as if the blow of an axe would sever the keystone, and break up by a shock the entire expanse. In one place the ice suddenly arched up like a bow while we were looking at it, burst into fragments, collapsed at the exterior margins of fracture, and by the work of a moment created a long barrier line of ruins ten feet high. Our position was one of peril. We had crossed two miles of ice. A change of tide relieved the strain, and we returned.

"The nearest break-up to our homestead floe is about one hundred and fifty yards off. It is now to the south; though our position, constantly changing, alters the bearing by the hour. Very many of the masses that compose it are as large as the grapery at home, two hundred feet long perhaps, and lifted up, barricade-fashion, as high as our second story windows."

The next day our winter arrangements were completed. They were simple enough, and hardly worth describing in detail. A housing of thick felt was drawn completely over the deck, resting on a sort of ridge-pole running fore and aft, and coming down close at the sides. The rime and snow-drift in an hour or two made it nearly impervious to the weather. The cook's galley stood on the kelson, under the main hatch; its stove-pipe rising through the housing above, and its funnel-shaped apparatus for melting snow attached below. The bulkheads between cabin and forecastle had been removed; and two stoves, one at each end of the berth-deck, distributed their heat among officers and seamen alike. We had of course a community of all manner of odors; and as our only direct ventilation was by the gangway, we had the certainty of a sufficient diversity of temperatures.

The exemption from gales, that has attracted the notice of other travelers in this region, had not yet been confirmed by our experience. On the contrary, our approach to Lancaster Sound, and the earlier part of our drift after we entered it, were marked by frequent storms. Some of these had all the sublimity that could belong to a mingled sense of danger and discomfort. They reminded me of the sand-storms of the Sahara. "The fine particles of snow flew by us in a continuous stream. When they met the unprotected face, the sensation was like the puncture of needles. Standing under the lee of our brig, and watching the drift as it scudded on the wings of the storm through the interval between the two vessels, the lines of sweeping snow were so unbroken that its filaments seemed woven into a mysterious tissue. Objects fifty yards off were invisible: no one could leave the vessels."

The month of November found us oscillating still with the winds and currents in the neighborhood of Beechy Island. Helpless as we were among the floating masses, we began to look upon the floe that carried us as a protecting barrier against the approaches of others less friendly; and as the month advanced, and the chances increased of our passing into the sound, our apprehensions of being frozen up in the heart of the ice-pack gave place to the opposite fear of a continuous drift. We had seen enough, and encountered enough of the angry strife among the ice-floes in the channel, to assure us of disaster if we should be forced to mingle in the sterner conflicts of the older ice-fields of the sound. Yet, as the new fields continued forming about us, thickening gradually from inches to feet, and locking together the floes in one great amorphous expanse, we retained a hope to the last that our island floe, thickening like the rest, and piling its wall of hummocks around us, would continue to ward us from attack, till the all-pervading frost had made it a stationary part of the great winter covering of the Arctic Sea. It encountered almost daily immense hummocks, some of them impinging against us while we were apparently at rest; some, apparently motionless, receiving the impact from us. At such times our floe would be deflected at an angle from its normal course, or would rotate slowly round its centre, and pass on—not, however, always in the same direction; sometimes nearing the western shore, sometimes closing in upon the beach of "the Graves," and sometimes fluctuating slowly to the northward. The chart opposite page 12 will show the capricious nature of this drift.

But our general course was toward the south and east. On the 17th we were fairly in the sound. It welcomed us coldly. The mercury stood for a while at −19°, and sunk during the night to −27°.

The next day, however, a shift of wind, gradually increasing in force, combined with a tidal influence to drive us back to our old position. The thermometer was at this time lower than we had ever seen it, and the sky seemed to sympathize with the temperature. The moon had a solid look, resting upon the snow-hills of Cape Riley, like a great viscid globe of illumination. In the morning the sky combined all the tints of the spectrum in regular zones, a broad band of orange girding the horizon with an almost uniform intensity of color. The stars shone during the entire day. At daybreak on the 18th, Leopold's Island rose by refraction above the ice, standing with its unmistakable outline clearly black against the orange sky; but it went down as the sun neared the horizon, and passed to the south of his low circuit. My journal for the next two days shows the degree of illumination at the different hours.

"*November* 20, Wednesday. The winds are unlike those encountered by Parry, our only predecessor in this region at this season of the year. It has been very providential, and very unexpected for us, this predominance of breezes from the southward and eastward. It has prevented our drifting into the dreaded sound, there to be carried, if it pleased Fortune, into Baffin's Bay by the easterly current.

"We had a heavy gale from 2 P.M. of yesterday

(19th) until this morning at 9 A.M., hauling round from southeast to east-southeast. After this last hour, it gradually died away; and now, at 3 P.M., we have a gentle breeze from the same quarter. The wind has left the north since the 18th.

"Our temperature, which on the 18th gave us $-27°$, the lowest we have yet recorded, was at the close of the next day but $-6°$; and to-day its extreme was $-4°$. Now, by gradual elevation, it has reached zero.

"Zero once more, and a positive sensation of warmth! There was no wind; and the haze vapors so softened this once greatest cold, that I walked about with bare hands and sweating body.

"The daylight is hardly now worthy of the name, according to the Philadelphia notions of the blessing; but to us it is the last leaf of the sibyl. Here is a little record of its incomings and outgoings.

"9 A.M. Breakfast over; furs on; deck covered in with black felt, the frozen condensation patching it with large white wafers of snow. A lantern makes it barely light enough to walk. No red streak to the east: one misty haze of visible darkness.

"10 A.M. A twilight gloom: can just see the Azimuth, with its tripod stand, thirty yards off on the ice. Snow whirling in drifts.

"11 A.M. Can read newspaper print by going to open daylight, *i. e.*, twilight—the twilight of a foggy sunrise at home.

"12 M. Noonday. A streak of brown red looms up above the mist to the south. Save a little more light from the 'foggy sunrise' of 11 A.M., no great perceptible difference; yet I can now read the finest print easily.

"1 P.M. Very decidedly more hazy than at 11, the

corresponding hour before meridian. Can read with difficulty the newspaper—London Illustrated News.

"2 P.M. A hazy darkness, but so compounded with the fast-rising light of the dear moon, that it is far lighter than the corresponding hour before meridian.

"Day is over. Moonlight begins!

"This is a fair specimen of our usual day. The occasional clear day, such as we had the 18th, is far lighter, and full of variety and interest.

"*November* 21, Thursday. The day is clear; but the moonlight, an absolute *clair de lune*, so confounds itself with the day as to make a merely solar register impossible.

"8 A.M. The whole atmosphere bathed in pellucid clearness. The moon, like a luminous sphere, not a circle, as with us, is away up the straits in the northern sky. Not a speck betokens sunrise.

"9 A.M. The southeastern horizon is zoned with a mellow uniform band of light. Nothing we have seen has its extension or its uniformity. The visual angle is an unbroken tint, rising from the ice with a raw sienna, mellowing into pink, and softened again into an orange yellow, which runs sometimes through a gradation of green into the clear blue sky. The moon absorbs all perception of other light.

"10 A.M. The light of dawn begins to mingle with the moonlight; I can not say where or how, but I am conscious of an interfering light. To the southward all is orange, and red, and solar. To the northward, from a cobalt sky of even tint, the moon 'shineth down alone'—alone, save the bright planet Saturn to the northward, and the broad zone of red sunrise at the south.

"11 A.M. Day upon us on one side, and moon bright

on the other: moonlight and sunlight blend overhead. To the north and south, each keeps its separate dominion. I read the finest print readily.

"12 M. Walked out to see the ice. I have no change of words left to describe noonday. The sunlight zone of color was more light and less bright, perhaps—and the moon was more bright and less light, perhaps; but both were there.

"1 P.M. The light hardly dimmed; but the moon shines out so emulously, that it is hard to measure the sunlight.

"2 P.M. It is evidently no longer day, although the southwestern horizon is flared with red streaks, and a softening of yellow into the blue of heaven says that the sun is somewhere below it. The moon has confused the day; and coming as she does at this commencement of our long night, I bless her for the grateful service. I make my four to six hours of daily walk, and hardly miss the guidance of day

"3 P.M. Moonlight!!"

CHAPTER XXIX.

"*November* 22. I walked yesterday, and to-day again, to the open water that separates us from Wellington Channel. It is a bold and rapid river, as broad as the Delaware at Trenton or the Schuylkill at Philadelphia, rolling wildly between dislocated hummock crags, and whirling along in its black current the abraded fragments of its shores. Ice of recent growth had cemented the gnarled masses about its margin into a ragged wall some twenty feet high, and perhaps thirty paces wide. I stood with perfect safety on a tall, spire-like pinnacle, and endeavored to trace its course. It could be seen reaching from a remote point in the southeastern part of the channel, and is probably connected with the open shore leads that stretch from Cape Riley past Cape Spencer toward the further coasts of North Devon. It passed about a mile and a half to the northwest of our vessels, and was lost in the distant ice-fields to the east.

"Returning with Captain De Haven, we saw the recent prints of a bear and two cubs, that had evidently been scenting our foot-marks of the day before. The old bear was not large, measuring by her trail only six feet four inches; the young ones so small as to surprise us, their track not much bigger than that of a Newfoundland dog. At what breeding season were these cubs produced?

"I have been for some evenings giving lectures on topics of popular science, the atmosphere, the barometer, &c., to the crew. They are not a very intellectual audience, but they listen with apparent interest, and express themselves gratefully.

"*November* 25. Great clouds of dark vapor were seen to the southward to-day, the crape-wreaths of our first imprisonment. This frost-smoke is an unfailing indication of open water, and to us, poor prison-bound vagrants, is suggestive of things not pleasant to think about. It streamed away on the wind in black drifts.

"Our daylight to-day was a mere name, three and a half hours of meagre twilight. I was struck for the first time with the bleached faces of my mess-mates. The sun left us finally only sixteen days ago; but for some time before he had been very chary of his effective rays; and our abiding-place below has a smoky atmosphere of lamplit uncomfortableness. No wonder we grow pale with such a cosmetic. Seventy-seven days more without a sunrise! twenty-six before we reach the solstitial point of greatest darkness!

"The temperature continues singularly mild. Parry, at Melville Island, had $-47°$ before this, twenty degrees lower than our minimum; and even in the more southern regions of Port Bowen and Prince Regent's Straits, the cold was much greater. For some days now, zero has not been an uncommon temperature; and to-day we are in $-14°$, here far from unpleasantly cold. May not much of this moderated intensity of the weather be referred to the influence of the open water around us?

"We are still in our old neighborhood, at the brink of the channel, a mile or so from Cape Riley, and both shores in view.

"*November* 28. The sunlight, a mere band of red cloud; the day, a poor apology. Walked eastward toward Beechy Island, dimly seen. The ice river is clogged with ground masses of granular ice: toward the south it is more open.

"The wind to-day is getting stronger from the west. with some northing, of all winds the most to be feared: the north drives us into Lancaster; the west comes in aid of the current to keep us there, and speed us back toward Baffin.

"Our thermometer does not fall below −11°. The frost-smoke is all around us in bistre-colored vapor. Can it be that we are again detached, our floe independent altogether of the field? We have heard noises of grinding ice, distant, but bodingly distinct.

"In my walks for some days past, I have been studying the topography of our ice-island residence. Here are my elements:

"1. To the north; over broken ice and edge-hummocks, that is to say, hummocks formed at the margin of floes and afterward cemented there, all of this season's growth. Several large masses, resembling berg-ice; one, the largest, twenty-seven feet high. The water-lead margined by rude hummocky crags trend ing to the westward and southward from the southward and eastward, forming a rude, broken horseshoe. Distance to water, one mile.

"2. To the south; over long floes of recent ice, young. snow-covered, and smooth, with few indications of heavy pressure at their junctions. Distance to open water, glazed over with young ice, two miles: trend of this lead east and west. The diameter of the floe, north and south, is three miles from water to water.

"3. To the east, *i. e.*, northeast by east; rough, mixed ice, with lines of recent heavy hummocks. Thickness of ice, averaging four feet to five feet eight inches; ice of the early part of last August. Distance to open river, one and three fourths to two miles Marks of recent action excessive here; hummock banks massive; and tables sometimes five feet thick, rising to a height of eighteen feet. From the east and northeast, the trend of the break is to the southward at first, and some two miles below to the westward.

"4. To the west; over the broken region of varied ice, traveled over in my attempts to reach Barlow's Inlet some days ago. Distance to lead, one mile. Chasm very irregular; but from the point I visited at the north and east, trending nearly due west, and pointing to the southward of Cape Hotham.

"From all this it is clear enough that we are a moving floe, comparatively isolated. The only point of our circumscribed horizon I have not visited, and where no frost-smoke asserts the near proximity of water, is the northwest. Whether on that side the ice of Lancaster is blocked against us by the easterly current, or whether the frost has made our floe one more speck in the massive field, is the only question remaining.

"*November* 29. The doubt is gone. Our floe, ice-cradle, safeguard, has been thrown round. Its eastern margin is grinding its way to the northward, and the west is already pointing to the south. Our bow is to Baffin's Bay, and we are traveling toward it. So far, ours has been a mysterious journeying. For two months and more, not a sail has fluttered from our frozen spars; yet we have passed from Lancaster Sound into the highest latitude of Wellington Channel, one never attained before, and have been borne back again past our point of starting, along a capriciously varied line of drift. Cape Riley is bearing, by compass, S. ½ E., N.N.E ½ E. (true); and Beechy Head, by compass, S.E. ½ E., N. ½ E. (true). Cape Hurd is visible to the northward and eastward, and to the east are the ice-clogged waters of Lancaster Sound.

"*November* 30. When I came on deck this morning, the lanterns were burning at ten o'clock, and the southern sky had not even a trace of red. Our head had slewed rather more to the southward; and off on our starboard beam sundry dark lines on the ice had a suspicious look. I walked toward them with some of our officers. After sundry groping tumbles, we came, sure enough, upon open water, one hundred yards to the south of the brig. Returning on our track, and taking a new departure toward the east—open water again. Off to the dim, hazy north—still open water. Off to the hummocky west, feeling our way with walking-poles—open water all round us. Once more, then, we are launched on a little ice-island, to float wherever God's mercy may guide us.

"The India-rubber boat inflated, and a few clothes stowed away, ready for a sudden break out; and all hands turn in for the night.

"*December* 1. There was a rude murmur in the night, that mingled its tones of admonition with the wind. But we are habituated pretty thoroughly to sounds of this sort, and they have ceased to disturb us. Walking after breakfast toward the northeast, to an ice-quarry, from which we have obtained our fresh water of late, we found that a water-crack we observed yesterday had undergone severe pressure during the night, and that the action was still going on. A low, hazy twilight just allowed us to distinguish near objects. A level, snow-covered surface was rising up in inclined planes or rudely undulating curves. These, breaking at their summits, fell off on each side in masses of twenty tons' weight. Tables of six feet in thickness by twenty of perpendicular height, and some of them fifteen yards in length, surging up into the misty air, heaving, rolling, tottering, and falling with a majestic deliberation worthy of the forces that impelled them. When a huge block would rise vertically, tremble for a moment, and topple over, you heard the heavy *sough* of the snow-padding that received it; but this was only the deep bass accompaniment to a wild, yet not unmusical chorus. I can not attempt to describe the sounds. There was the ringing clatter of ice, made friable by the intense cold and crumbling under lateral force; the low whine which the ice gives out when we cut it at right angles with a sharp knife, rising sometimes into a shriek, or sinking to the plaintive outcry of our night-hawk at home; the whirr of rapidly-urged machinery; the hum of multitudes: and all these mingled with tones that have no analogy among the familiar ones of unadventurous life.

"So slowly and regularly did these masses roll, rise, break, and fall, that, standing upon a broad table, ice-pole in air, we rolled when it rolled, rose when it rose, balanced when it broke, and jumped as it fell. What would our quiet people in brick houses say to such a ride? Temperature at 30° below zero.

"On deck; looming up in the very midst of the haze, land! so high and close on our port beam, that we felt like men under a precipice. We could see the vertical crevices in the limestone, the recesses contrasting in black shadow. What land is this? Is it the eastern line of Cape Riley, or have we reached Cape Ricketts?

"There is one thing tolerably certain: the Grinnell expedition is quite as likely to be searched for hereafter as to search. Poor Sir John Franklin! this night-drift is an ugly omen.

"Do you remember, in the Spanish coasting craft, down about Barcelona and the Balearics, the queer little pictures of Saint Nicholas we used to see pasted up over the locker—a sort of mythic effigy, which the owner looked upon pretty much as some of our old commodores do the barometer, a mysterious something, which he sneers at in fair weather, but is sure, in the strong faith of ignorance, to appeal to in foul! Well, very much such a Saint Anthony have we down in the cabin here, staring us always in the face. Not a vermilion-daubed puerility, with a glory in Dutch leaf stretching from ear to ear; but a good, genuine, hearty representative of English flesh and blood, a mouth that speaks of strong energies as well as a kindly heart, and an eye—the other one is spoiled in the lithography—that looks stern will. Many a time in the night have I discoursed with him, as he looked out on me from his gutta percha frame—'Sir John Franklin; presented by his wife;' and sometimes I have imagined how and where I was yet to shake the glorious old voyager by the hand. I see him now while I am writing; his face is darkened by the lamp-smoke that serves us for daylight and air, and he seems almost disheartened. So far as help and hope of it are afloat in this little vessel, Sir John, well you may be!

"It is Sunday: we have had religious service as usual, and after it that relic of effete absurdity, the reading of the 'Rules and Regulations.'

"We had the aurora about 7 P.M. The thermometer at -33° and falling; barometer, Aneroid, 30°. 74; attached thermometer, 86°. Wind steady, W.N.W. The meteor resembled an illuminated cloud; illuminated, because seen against the deep blue night sky;

otherwise it resembled the mackerel fleeces and mare's tails of our summer skies at home.

"It began toward the northwestern horizon as an irregular flaring cloud, sometimes sweeping out into wreaths of stratus; sometimes a condensed opaline nebulosity, rising in a zone of clearly-defined whiteness, from 3° to 5° in breadth up to the zenith, and then arching to the opposite horizon. This zone resembled more a long line of white cirro-stratus than the auroral light of the systematic descriptions. There was no approach to coruscations, or even rectangular deviations from the axis of the zone. When it varied from a right line, its curvatures were waving and irregular, such as might be produced by wind, but having no relation to the observed air-currents at the earth's surface. It passed from the due northwest, between the Pleiades and the Corona Borealis; the star of greatest magnitude in the latter of these constellations remaining in the centre, although its waving curves sometimes reached the Pleiades. At the zenith, its mean distance from the Polar Star was 7° south, and it passed down, increasing in intensity, near Vega, in Lyra, to the southeast.

"There was throughout the arc no marked seat of greatest intensity. Around the Corona of the north, its light was more diffused. The zone appeared narrowed at the zenith, and bright and clear, without marked intermission, to the southeast. The frost-smoke was in smoky banks to the northwest; but the aurora did not seem to be affected by it, and the compass remained constant.

"*December* 2. Drifting down the sound. Every thing getting ready for the chance of a hurried good-by to our vessels. Pork, and sugar, and bread put up in small bags to fling on the ice. Every man his knapsack and change of clothing. Arms, bear-knives, ammunition out on deck, and sledges loaded. Yet this thermometer, at −30°, tells us to stick to the ship while we can.

"This packing up of one's carpet-bag in a hurry requires a mighty discreet memory. I have often wondered that seamen in pushing off from a wreck left so many little wants unprovided for; but I think I understand it now. After bestowing away my boots, with the rest of a walking wardrobe, in a snugly-lashed bundle, I discovered by accident that I had left my stockings behind.

"4 P.M. Brooks comes down while we are dining to say we are driving east like a race-horse, and a crack ahead: 'All hands on deck!' We had heard the grindings last night, and our floe in the morning was cut down to a diameter of three hundred yards: we had little to spare of it. But the new chasm is there, already fifteen feet wide, and about twenty-five paces from our bows, stretching across at right angles with the old cleft of October the 2d.

"Our floe, released from its more bulky portion, seems to be making rapidly toward the shore. This, however, may be owing to the separated mass having an opposite motion, for the darkness is intense. Our largest snow-house is carried away; the disconsolate little cupola, with its flag of red bunting, should it survive the winter, may puzzle conjectures for our English brethren.

"Mr. Griffin and myself walked through the gloom to the seat of hummock action abeam of the Rescue. A dark, hard walk: no changes. The crack, noticed some time ago as parallel to and alongside of the Rescue, has not opened. Her officers have brought their private papers on board the Advance, and such indispensable articles as may be needed in case of her destruction.

"Our ship's head is toward a point of land to the northeastward, but her position changes so constantly that there is little use of recording it. Caught a fox this morning; have now two on board.

"Our bearings, taken by azimuth compass this morning at eleven, gave Cape Hurd, S. by W. ¼ W.; Western Bluff, of Rigsby's Inlet, S.E. ¼ S.; Table-hill of Parry, S.E. by S. ½ S.; Cape Ricketts, E. by N.

"Wind changed at 9 P.M. to N.N.W.; thermometer, minimum, −26°; maximum, −22°; mean, 23° 82′.

"*December* 4, Wednesday. This morning showed us an interval of over two hundred yards already covered with stiff ice: so much for our chasm of last night! All around us is a moving wreck of ice-fields.

"Our drift seems to have been to the westward. We have certainly left the coast, which yesterday seemed almost over us, though it is still too near for good fellowship.

"This is the first clear day—truly clear, that we have had since my record of the changing daylight. Compared with the gloomy haziness of its predecessors, it was cheering. The southern horizon was a zone of red light; and although the clear blue soon absorbed it, we could read small print with a little effort at noonday by turning the book to the south. The stars were visible all the time, except where the horizon was lighted up."

The next four days were full of excitement and anxiety. One crack after another passed across our floe, still reducing its dimensions, and at one time bringing down our vessel again to an even keel. An hour afterward, the chasms would close around us with a sound like escaping steam. Again they would open under some mysterious influence; a field of ice from two to four inches thick would cover them; and then, without an apparent change of causes, the separated sides would come together with an explosion like a mortar, craunching the newly-formed field, and driving it headlong in fragments for fifty feet upon the floe till it piled against our bulwarks. Every thing betokened a crisis. Sledges, boats, packages of all sorts, were disposed in order; contingencies were met as they approached by new delegations of duty; every man was at work, officer and seaman alike; for necessity, when it spares no one, is essentially democratic, even on shipboard. The Rescue, crippled and thrown away from us to the further side of a chasm, was deserted, and her company consolidated with ours. Our own brig groaned and quivered under the pressure against her sides. I give my diary for December 7.

"*December* 7, Saturday. The danger which surrounds us is so immediate, that in the bustle of preparation for emergency I could not spend a moment upon my journal. Now the little knapsack is made up again, and the blanket sewed and strapped. The little home Bible at hand, and the ice-clothes ready for a jump.

Dec. 1.

Dec. 4.

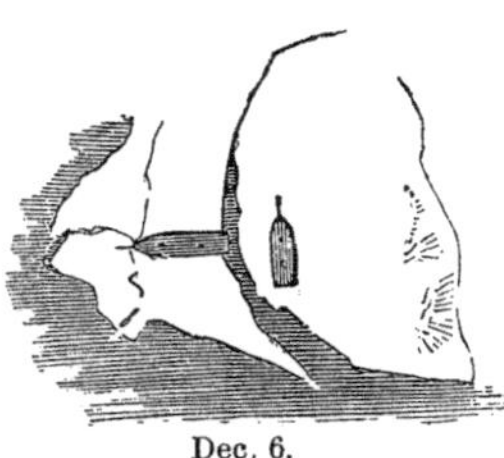
Dec. 6.

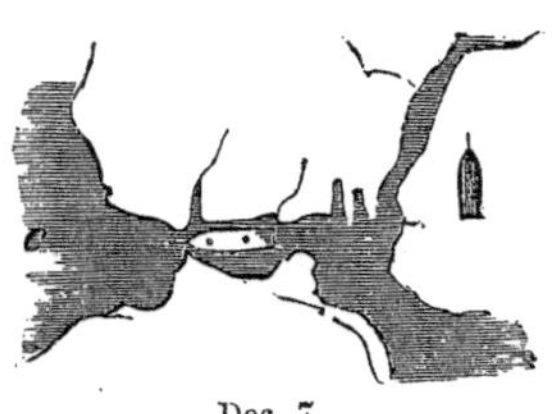
Dec. 7.

"The above is a rough idea of our last three days' positions and changes.

"From this it is evident that a gradual process of breaking up has taken place. We are afloat.

"The ice, as I have sketched it, December 7, began to close at 11 A.M., and, at the same time, the brig was driven toward the open crack of December 4 (*c*). At 1 P.M. this closed on us with fearful nipping.

"1 P.M. Ran on deck. The ice was comparatively quiescent when I attempted to write; but it recommenced with a steady pressure, which must soon prove irresistible. It catches against a protruding tongue forward, and is again temporarily arrested.

"4 P.M. Up from dinner—'all hands!' The ice came in, with the momentum before mentioned as 'irresistible,' progressive and grand. All expected to betake ourselves sledgeless to the ice, for the open space around the vessel barely admits of a foot-board. The timbers, and even cross-beams protected by shores, vibrated so as to communicate to you the peculiar tremor of a cotton-factory. Presently the stern of the brig, by a succession of jerking leaps, began to rise, while her bows dipped toward the last night's ice ahead. Every body looked to see her fall upon her beam-ends, and rushed out upon the ice. After a few anxious breath-compressed moments, our nobly-strengthened little craft rose up upon the encroaching floes bodily.

Her dolphin-striker struck the ice ahead; her bows began to feel the pressure; and thus lifted up upon the solid tables, we have a temporary respite again.

"Stores are now put out upon the ice, and we await —time. Cape Fellfoot, S. by W. ¼ W. Remarkable perpendicular bluff, S.S.E. Cape Hurd, E.N.E. ½ E., by compass; Cape Hurd, N.W. by W. ½ W. (true).

"We are at least fifty miles from Beechy Island and Union Bay—about forty-five miles from Leopold Harbor stores. Leopold Harbor, or our more distant English friends, about one hundred and twenty miles off, are our only places of refuge. We are daily, hourly, drifting further from both. It is this nakedness of resources, even more than perpetual darkness and unendurable cold, that makes our position one of bitterness. Drift a little westward; thermometer 17°."

My journal does not tell the story; but it is worth noting, as it illustrates the sedative effect of a protracted succession of hazards. Our brig had just mounted the floe, and as we stood on the ice watching her vibration, it seemed so certain that she must come over on her beam-ends, that our old boatswain, Brooks, called out to "stand from under." At this moment it occurred to one of the officers that the fires had not been put out, and that the stores remaining on board would be burned by the falling of the stoves. Swinging himself back to the deck, and rushing below, he found two persons in the cabin; the officer who had been relieved from watch-duty a few minutes before, quietly seated at the mess-table, and the steward as quietly waiting on him. "You are a meal ahead of me," he said; "you didn't think I was going out upon the ice without my dinner."

"*December* 8, Sunday, 8 P.M. This has thus far been a day of rest. Our vessel, lifted up upon the heavy ice, has borne without injury a few fresh pressures. The wind has been still from the eastward, and we have drifted about six miles to the westward again. This wind was almost a gale; yet its influence upon the eastern drift is barely able to produce this limited westing. I now regard it as past a doubt, that should we survive the collisions of the journey, we must float into Baffin's Bay.

"A small auroral light was seen to the northwest at 9 A.M., the second within two days. Its axis was 16° W. of the magnetic meridian. The mean temperature of the day has been −12° 70′. Wind more gentle from the eastward.

"Mr. Griffin, who is now the executive officer of our consolidated squadron, has undertaken a systematic drill of the crew. He has mustered them for an ice-march, with knapsacks fitted to their backs, and sledge equipments, just such as will be required when the worst comes. Every thing is rigorously inspected; the provisions and stores of all sorts are packed snug, and have their places marked; and the men are instructed as to their course in the moment of emergency.

"Here is a sketch of the present position of our vessel. It looks extravagant, but it is in truth the very opposite. Every thing like locomotion on board is up and down hill.

"*December* 9, Monday. Like its three predecessors, clear; that is to say, for three scanty hours of scanty twilight, you see the skeleton shore cliffs, and the bright stars, a little paled, but bright. The moon, a second-quarter crescent, was for a while on the northern and western horizon, distorted and flaming like a crimson lamp.

"Last night, mounted as we are, the nipping caused our timbers to complain sadly. We had to send out parties to crow-bar away the ice from our bowsprit. The bob-stays were forced up and broken. Our floe movement continued to the southeast, driving the heavy ice in upon the Rescue. She rose up under the pressure, and is now surrounded by hummock ruins like ourselves. She is not more than fifty yards distant from us, astern."

From this time to the 21st our drift was without intermission. As one headland after another defined itself against the horizon, it was apparent that we were skirting the northern coast of the sound. At first this gave us some anxiety, when our floe, pressing hard against the shore-ice as we doubled some projecting point, threatened to wreck us among its fragments. But as we drew nearer to the outlet, and began to compute the new hazards of entering Baffin's Bay, this very circumstance became for us an important ground of hope. Theory, as well as the accounts of the whalers, made the southeastern cape of Lancaster Sound the seat of intense hummock action. The greater the distance from that point, the broader must be the curvature of the meeting currents, and the less perilous the conflict of the ice-masses in their rotation. There was, of course, no escape for us from this encounter; and the only question was of the degrees of hazard it must involve.

On the 19th, the tall, mural precipices to the northward, and the cape in which they terminated toward the east, convinced us that we had almost reached the western headland of Croker's Bay. We had drifted one hundred and eleven miles since the beginning of the month. Our course had been without any cheering incident. There was the same wretched succession of openings and closings about our floe, somewhat dangerous, but too uniform to be exciting; and we had drilled with knapsack and sledge, till we were almost martinets in our evolutions on the ice. I group the few entries of my journal that have any interest.

"*December* 11. Wind last night fierce from the north; to-day as fierce from the west. It has carried us clear of the great cape that stretches out east of Maxwell's Bay, and that threatened us with the variety of a lee shore. The Rescue has had another trial: her sternpost is carried away, her pintle and gudgeon wrenched off. A party of officers and men are out, trying the experiment of a night upon the ice, tented and bag-bedded. I wish them luck; but the thermometer fifty-seven degrees below freezing is unfavorable to a *fête champêtre.*

"*December* 12. Every thing solid, and looking as if it had always been so; yet, a few days ago, I had this journal of mine stitched up in its tarred canvas-bag, and ready for a fling upon the ice four times in the twenty-four hours. The floes have stopped abrading each other, and are driving ahead right peaceably, with our brig mounted on top: how far we are from the edges, it is too dark to see.

"*December* 13. A little clearer than yesterday, but too dark to read small print at noon. Something like a long reach of land looming up to southward: it can not be Croker's Bay?

"All our mess took our tour of practice to-day, with a sledge and four hundred pounds of provender. Hard work, and sweating abundantly; but we feel already the good effects of this sort of exercise. Thermometer at −11°.

"*December* 14. A quiet day; the winds at rest, and the stars twinkling through the hazy sky as I never saw them before. The moon, too, is in high heaven, almost a three-quarter disk. She is a great comfort to us; her high northern declination makes her visible all the time. It looks strangely this undying fortnight moon. The frost-smoke is wreathing the red zone of our southern horizon. It would be a good night-scene for a painter.

"At 7 P.M. the thermometer rose from −3° to −1°. At 10 o'clock it was −4°. Its maximum was +10°, a temperature mild and comfortable. The wind changed from west by south to west by north, and the ice and the drift are as yesterday.

"A poor bear, fired at last night by Mr. Carter, was found this morning, about three hundred yards from the ship, dead. He was wedged between two slabs of ice, and in his agony had rubbed his muzzle deep into the frozen snow. Twice he had stopped to lie down during his death-walk, marking each place with a large puddle of blood, which branched out over the floe like crimson-streaked marble. He measured eight feet four inches from tip to tip. I killed a fox; but missing his head, opened the large arteries of the neck, and spoiled his pelt. The temperature at the orifice of the ball was +92°. The crew were at work till eleven, leveling our rugged floe, and heaping up snow against the sides of the brig. The position of our vessel, high perched in air, and dipping head foremost in a way most Arctic and uncomfortable, makes the protection of snow very desirable. We feel the cold against her walls. The crew had an hour of sledging, as well by way of exercise as of preparation for their expected trials.

"A point supposed to be Cape Crawfurd bore, by compass, west. Our distance from the north shore is about five miles."

ARCTIC HOOD.

CHAPTER XXX.

I EMPLOYED the dreary intervals of leisure that heralded our Christmas in tracing some Flemish portraitures of things about me. The scenes themselves had interest at the time for the parties who figured in them; and I believe that is reason enough, according to the practice of modern academics, for submitting them to the public eye. I copy them from my scrap-book, expurgating only a little.

"We have almost reached the solstice; and things are so quiet that I may as well, before I forget it, tell you something about the cold in its sensible effects, and the way in which as sensible people we met it.

"You will see, by turning to the early part of my journal, that the season we now look back upon as the perfection of summer contrast to this outrageous winter was in fact no summer at all. We had the young ice forming round us in Baffin's Bay, and were measuring snow-falls, while you were sweating under your grass-cloth. Yet I remember it as a time of sunny recreation, when we shot bears upon the floes, and were scrambling merrily over glaciers and murdering rotges in the bright glare of our day-midnight. Like a complaining brute, I thought it cold then—I, who am blistered if I touch a brass button or a ramrod without a woolen mit.

"The cold came upon us gradually. The first thing that really struck me was the freezing up of our water-casks, the drip-candle appearance of the bung-holes, and our inability to lay the tin cup down for a five-minutes' pause without having its contents made solid. Next came the complete inability to obtain drink without manufacturing it. For a long time we had collected our water from the beautiful fresh pools of the icebergs and floes; now we had to quarry out the blocks in flinty, glassy lumps, and then melt it in tins for our daily drink. This was in Wellington Channel.

"By-and-by the sludge which we passed through as we traveled became pancakes and snow-balls. We were glued up. Yet, even as late as the 11th of September, I collected a flowering Potentilla from Barlow's Inlet. But now any thing moist or wet began to strike me as something to be looked at—a curious, out-of-the-way production, like the bits of broken ice round a can of mint-julep. Our decks became dry, and studded with botryoidal lumps of dirty foot-trodden ice. The rigging had nightly accumulations of rime, and we learned to be careful about coiled ropes and iron work. On the 4th of October we had a mean temperature below zero.

"By this time our little entering hatchway had become so complete a mass of icicles, that we had to give it up, and resort to our winter door-way. The opening of a door was now the signal for a gush of smoke-like vapor: every stove-pipe sent out clouds of purple steam;

and a man's breath looked like the firing of a pistol on a small scale.

"All our eatables became laughably consolidated, and after different fashions, requiring no small experience before we learned to manage the peculiarities of their changed condition. Thus, dried apples became one solid breccial mass of impacted angularities, a conglomerate of sliced chalcedony. Dried peaches the same. To get these out of the barrel, or the barrel out of them, was a matter impossible. We found, after many trials, that the shortest and best plan was to cut up both fruit and barrel by repeated blows with a heavy axe, taking the lumps below to thaw. Saurkraut resembled mica, or rather talcose slate. A crow-bar with chiseled edge extracted the *laminæ* badly; but it was perhaps the best thing we could resort to.

"Sugar formed a very funny compound. Take *q. s.* of cork raspings, and incorporate therewith another *q. s.* of liquid gutta percha or caoutchouc, and allow to harden: this extemporaneous formula will give you the brown sugar of our winter cruise. Extract with the saw; nothing but the saw will suit. Butter and lard, less changed, require a heavy cold chisel and mallet. Their fracture is conchoidal, with hæmatitic (iron-ore pimpled) surface. Flour undergoes little change, and molasses can at −28° be half scooped, half cut by a stiff iron ladle.

"Pork and beef are rare specimens of Florentine mosaic, emulating the lost art of petrified visceral monstrosities seen at the medical schools of Bologna and Milan: crow-bar and handspike! for at −30° the axe can hardly chip it. A barrel sawed in half, and kept for two days in the caboose house at +76°, was still as refractory as flint a few inches below the surface

A similar bulk of lamp oil, denuded of the staves, stood like a yellow sandstone roller for a gravel walk.

"Ices for the dessert come of course unbidden, in all imaginable and unimaginable variety. I have tried my inventive powers on some of them. A Roman punch, a good deal stronger than the noblest Roman ever tasted, forms readily at −20°. Some sugared cranberries, with a little butter and scalding water, and you have an impromptu strawberry ice. Many a time at those funny little jams, that we call in Philadelphia 'parties,' where the lady-hostess glides with such nicely-regulated indifference through the complex machinery she has brought together, I have thought I noticed her stolen glance of anxiety at the cooing doves, whose icy bosoms were melting into one upon the supper-table before their time. We order these things better in the Arctic. Such is the 'composition and fierce quality' of our ices, that they are brought in served on the shaft of a hickory broom; a transfixing rod, which we use as a stirrer first and a fork afterward. So hard is this terminating cylinder of ice, that it might serve as a truncheon to knock down an ox. The only difficulty is in the processes that follow. It is the work of time and energy to impress it with the carving-knife, and you must handle your spoon deftly, or it fastens to your tongue. One of our mess was tempted the other day by the crystal transparency of an icicle to break it in his mouth; one piece froze to his tongue, and two others to his lips, and each carried off the skin: the thermometer was at −28°.

"Thus much for our Arctic grub. I need not say that our preserved meats would make very fair cannon-balls, canister-shot!!

"Now let us start out upon a walk, clothed in well-fashioned Arctic costume. The thermometer is, say −25°, not lower, and the wind blowing a royal breeze, but gently.

"Close the lips for the first minute or two, and admit the air suspiciously through nostril and mustache. Presently you breathe in a dry, pungent, but gracious and agreeable atmosphere. The beard, eyebrow, eyelashes, and the downy pubescence of the ears, acquire a delicate, white, and perfectly-enveloping cover of venerable hoar-frost. The mustache and under lip form pendulous beads of dangling ice. Put out your tongue, and it instantly freezes to this icy crusting, and a rapid effort and some hand aid will be required to liberate it. The less you talk, the better. Your chin has a trick of freezing to your upper jaw by the luting aid of your beard; even my eyes have often been so glued, as to show that even a wink may be unsafe. As you walk on, you find that the iron-work of your gun begins to penetrate through two coats of woolen mittens, with a sensation like hot water.

"But we have been supposing your back to the wind; and if you are a good Arcticized subject, a warm glow has already been followed by a profuse sweat. Now turn about and face the wind; what a devil of a change! how the atmospheres are wafted off! how penetratingly the cold trickles down your neck, and in at your pockets! Whew! a jack-knife, heretofore, like Bob Sawyer's apple, 'unpleasantly warm' in the breeches pocket, has changed to something as cold as ice and hot as fire: make your way back to the ship!! I was once caught three miles off with a freshening wind, and at one time feared that I would hardly see the brig again. Morton, who accompanied me, had his cheeks frozen, and I felt that lethargic numbness mentioned in the story books.

"I will tell you what this feels like, for I have been twice 'caught out.' Sleepiness is not the sensation. Have you ever received the shocks of a magneto-electric machine, and had the peculiar benumbing sensation of 'can't let go,' extending up to your elbow-joints? Deprive this of its paroxysmal character; subdue, but diffuse it over every part of the system, and you have the so-called pleasurable feelings of incipient freezing. It seems even to extend to your brain. Its inertia is augmented; every thing about you seems of a ponderous sort; and the whole amount of pleasure is in gratifying the disposition to remain at rest, and spare yourself an encounter with these latent resistances. This is, I suppose, the pleasurable sleepiness of the story books.

"I could fill page after page with the ludicrous miseries of our ship-board life. We have two climates, hygrometrically as well as thermometrically at opposite ends of the scale. A pocket-handkerchief, pocketed below in the region of stoves, comes up unchanged. Go below again, and it becomes moist, flaccid, and almost wet. Go on deck again, and it resembles a shingle covered with linen. I could pick my teeth with it.

"You are anxious to know how I manage to stand this remorseless temperature. It is a short story, and perhaps worth the telling. 'The Doctor' still retains three luxuries, remnants of better times—silk next his skin, a tooth-brush for his teeth, and white linen for his nose. Every thing else is Arctic and hairy—fur, fur, fur. The silk is light and washable, needing neither the clean dirt of starch nor the uncomfortable trouble of flat-irons. It secures to me a clean screen between my epidermoid and seal-skin integuments.

"I try to be a practical man as to clothing and the et ceteras of a traveler. All baggage beyond the essential I regard as *impedimenta*, and believe in the wisdom of Titian Peale, who, when preparing for an exploring tour around the world, purchased—a tin cup. For the sake of poor devils condemned to cold winters, I give in detail my dress, the result of much trial, and, I think, nearly perfect. Here it is, from tip to toe.

"1. Feet. A pair of cotton socks (Lisle thread) covered by a pair of ribbed woolen stockings, rising above the knee and half way up the thigh. Over these a pair of Esquimaux water-proof boots, lined by a sock of dog-skin, the hair inside; the leg of dressed seal-hide; a sole with the edges turned up, and crimped so as to form a water-tight cup; the furred edge of a dog-skin sock inserted as a lining; and some clean straw laid smoothly at the bottom, which forms the elastic cushion on which you tread.

"2. Legs. A pair of coarse woolen drawers, and a pair of seal-skin breeks over them, stitched with reindeer tendon.

"3. Chest. A jumper or short coat, double, of seal-skin and reindeer fur. This invaluable article I got at Disco on my fur journey, obtaining a good number besides for men and officers. It consists of an inner-hooded shirt of reindeer-skin with the hair inside, reaching as far as the upper ridge of the hips, so as to allow free swing to the legs, and fitting about the throat very closely. It is drawn on like the shirt, and, except at the neck, is perfectly loose and unbinding.

"4. Head. Our people generally wear fur caps. I wear an ear-ridge, a tiara, to speak heroically, of wolf-skin. Excellent is this Mormon fur! Leaving the entire poll bare to the elements, it guards the ears and forehead effectually: in any ordinary state of the wind above −15°, I am not troubled with the cold. Before I resorted to this, my cap was full of frozen water, stiff and uncomfortable, all the condensation turning to ice the moment I uncovered. When the weather is very cold, I up hood; when colder, say −40°, with a middling breeze—quite cold enough, I assure you —I wear an elastic silk night-cap in addition, one of a pair forced on me by a certain brother of mine as I was leaving New York, drawn over my head and face, and lined with a mask of wolf-skin. To prevent excessive condensation, I cut only two eye-holes, and leave a large aperture below the point of the nose for talking and breathing. A grim-looking object is this wolf-skin mask, its openings lined with water-proof oiled silk.

"The only changes in the above are a pair of cloth pants for fur, when the thermometer strays above −15°, and a pair of heavy woolen wad-mail leggins, drawn over my fur pants, and worn, stocking fashion, within my boots, in windy weather, when we get down to −30° or thereabouts. A long waist-scarf, worn like the kummerbund of the Hindoos, is a fine protection while walking, to keep the cold from intruding at the pockets and waist: it consummates, as it floats martially on the breeze, the grotesque harmonies of my attire."

ARCTIC MASK.

OFF CROKER'S BAY, DEC. 23.

CHAPTER XXXI.

"*December* 21, Saturday. To-day at noon we saw, dimly looming up from the redness of the southern horizon, a low range of hills; among them some cones of great height, mountains of a character differing from the naked table-lands of the northern coast. The land on the other side of Croker's Bay, with one high headland, supposed to be Cape Warrender, is in view. From all of which it is clear that we are drifting regularly on toward Baffin's Bay.

"An opening occurred last night in the ice to the northward. It is not more than a hundred yards from us, and it is already seventy wide. It was explored for about a mile in a northwest and southeast course. Another of the same character is about half a mile to the south of us.

"Our floe has now remained in peace for nearly three weeks; and, with the happy indifference of sailors' human nature, we are beginning to forget the driving ice and the groaning pressures which have perched us thus upon a lump of drift. I look, however, to the spring-tides for a renewal of the trouble. The ice about us is apparently as strong and solid as the slow growth of Wellington Channel; but we know it to be recent, and less able to withstand pressure. Every thing now depends upon preserving our vessel and stores. A breaking up must take place, and for us the later in the spring the better. At the present rate of progress, we shall be in Baffin's Bay by the latter end of January. There the daylight will be with us again; most providentially, for the icebergs are wretched enemies in darkness. Thirty more days, and we may take a noonday walk; forty-four, and the sun comes back.

"Our men are hard at work preparing for the Christmas theatre, the arrangements exclusively their own. But to-morrow is a day more welcome than Christmas—the solstitial day of greatest darkness, from which we may begin to date our returning light. It makes a man feel badly to see the faces around him bleaching into waxen paleness. Until to-day, as a looking-glass does not enter into an Arctic toilet, I thought I was the exception, and out of delicacy said nothing about it to my comrades. One of them, introducing the topic just now, told me, with an utter unconsciousness of his own ghostliness, that I was the palest of the party. So it is, 'All men think all men,' &c. Why, the good fellow is as white as a cut potato!"

In truth, we were all of us at this time undergoing changes unconsciously. The hazy obscurity of the nights we had gone through made them darker than the corresponding nights of Parry. The complexions of my comrades, and my own too, as I found soon afterward, were toned down to a peculiar waxy paleness. Our eyes were more recessed, and strangely clear. Complaints of shortness of breath became general. Our appetite was almost ludicrously changed: ham-fat frozen, and saur-kraut swimming in olive-oil were favorites; yet we were unconscious of any tendency toward the gross diet of the Polar region. Most of my companions would not touch bear; indeed, I was the only one, except Captain De Haven, that still ate it. Fox, on the other hand, was a favorite. Things seemed to have changed their taste, and our inclination for food was at best very slight.

Worse than this, our complete solitude, combined with permanent darkness, began to affect our *morale*. Men became moping, testy, and imaginative. In the morning, dreams of the night — we could not help using the term—were narrated. Some had visited the naked shores of Cape Warrender, and returned laden with water-melons. Others had found Sir John Franklin in a beautiful cove, lined by quintas and orange-trees. Even Brooks, our hard-fisted, unimaginative boatswain, told me, in confidence, of having heard three strange groans out upon the ice. He "thought it was a bear, but could see nothing!" In a word, the health of our little company was broken in upon. It required strenuous and constant effort at washing, diet, and exercise to keep the scurvy at bay. Eight cases of scorbutic gums were already upon my black-list. One severe pneumonia left me in anxious doubt as to its result. There was, however, little bronchitis.

"*December* 22, Sunday. The solstice!—the midnight of the year! It commences with a new movement in the ice, the open lead of yesterday piling up into hummocks on our port-beam. No harm done.

"The wind is from the west, increasing in freshness since early in the morning. The weather overcast; even the moon unseen, and no indications of our drift. We could not read print, not even large newspaper type, at noonday. We have been unable to leave the ship unarmed for some time on account of the bears. We remember the story of poor Barentz, one of our early predecessors. One of our crew, Blinn, a phlegmatic Dutchman, walked out to-day toward the lead, a few hundred yards off, in search of a seal-hole. Suddenly a seal rose close by him in the sludge-ice: he raised his gun to fire; and, at the same instant, a large bear jumped over the floe, and by a dive followed the seal. Blinn's musket snapped. He was glad to get on board again, and will remember his volunteer hunt. Thermometer, minimum, −18°; maximum, −6°. A beautiful paraselene yesterday!!

"*December* 23, Monday. Perfect darkness! Drift unknown. Winds nearly at rest, with the exception of a little gasp from the westward. Thermometer never below −12°, nor above −7°.

"*December* 24, Tuesday. 'Through utter darkness borne!'

"*December* 25. 'Y^e^ Christmas of ye Arctic cruisers!' Our Christmas passed without a lack of the good things of this life. 'Goodies' we had galore; but that best of earthly blessings, the communion of loved sympathies, these Arctic cruisers had not. It was curious to observe the depressing influences of each man's home thoughts, and absolutely saddening the effort of each man to impose upon his neighbor and be very boon and jolly. We joked incessantly, but badly, and laughed incessantly, but badly too; ate of good things, and drank up a moiety of our Heidsiek; and then we sang negro songs, wanting only tune, measure, and harmony, but abounding in noise; and after a closing bumper to Mr. Grinnell, adjourned with creditable jollity from table to the theatre.

"It was on deck, of course, but veiled from the sky by our felt covering. A large ship's ensign, stretched from the caboose to the bulwarks, was understood to hide the stage, and certain meat-casks and candle-boxes represented the parquet. The thermometer gave us $-6°$ at first; but the favoring elements soon changed this to the more comfortable temperature of $-4°$.

"Never had I enjoyed the tawdry quackery of the stage half so much. The theatre has always been to me a wretched simulation of realities; and I have too little sympathy with the unreal to find pleasure in it long. Not so our Arctic theatre: it was one continual frolic from beginning to end.

"The 'BLUE DEVILS:' God bless us! but it was very, very funny. None knew their parts, and the prompter could not read glibly enough to do his office. Every thing, whether jocose, or indignant, or commonplace, or pathetic, was delivered in a high-tragedy monotone of despair; five words at a time, or more or less, according to the facilities of the prompting. Megrim, with a pair of seal-skin boots, bestowed his gold upon the gentle Annette; and Annette, nearly six feet high, received it with mastodonic grace. Annette was an Irishman named Daly; and I might defy human being to hear her, while balanced on the heel of her boot, exclaim, in rich masculine brogue, 'Och, feather!' without roaring. Bruce took the Landlord, Benson was James, and the gentle Annette and the wealthy Megrim were taken by Messrs. Daly and Johnson.

"After this followed the Star Spangled Banner; then a complicated Marseillaise by our French cook, Henri; then a sailor's hornpipe by the diversely-talented Bruce; the orchestra—Stewart, playing out the inter vals on the Jews-harp from the top of a lard-cask. In fact, we were very happy fellows. We had had a foot-race in the morning over the midnight ice for three purses of a flannel shirt each, and a splicing of the main-brace. The day was night, the stars shining feebly through the mist.

"But even here that kindly custom of Christmas-gifting was not forgotten. I found in my morning stocking a jack-knife, symbolical of my altered looks, a piece of Castile soap—this last article in great request—a Jews-harp, and a string of beads! On the other hand, I prescribed from the medical stores two bottles of Cognac, to protect the mess from indigestion.* So passed Christmas. Thermometer, minimum, $-16°$; maximum, $-7°$. Wind west.

"*December* 26, Thursday. To-day, looming up high in the air, we catch a sight of new unknown land. Of our drift, save by analogy, we know nothing.

"*December* 27, Friday. The shores of this coast seem to have changed their scale. At Cape Riley, as my sketches show, the limestone rises in a mural face, based by a deposit of detritus, which extends out in tongues, indentations, and salient capes; and between these, a cemented shingle, full of corallines and encrinites, forms a beach of varying extent.

"Sometimes this beach is backed by rolling dune-like hills of the scaly mountain limestones; but after a mile or two of intermission, the high cliffs rise up again in abutments, and continue unbroken until another interval occurs. As we proceeded east, these escarped masses became more buttress-like and monumental, rising up into plateau-topped masses, separated

* An offense which I thus publicly acknowledge in advance of the court-martial, to which this illegal dispensation of the public stores may subject me

by chasms, which seem mere ruptures in the continuous hill-line. Now, however, a trace is seen in the clouds indicative of distant land, higher, more mountainous, rolling, and broken. It may be the Cunninghame Mountains toward Cape Warrender.

"The wind is quietly blowing from the west, and the misty haze gives us barely a vestige of daylight.

"*December* 28, Saturday. From my very soul do I rejoice at the coming sun. Evidences not to be mistaken convince me that the health of our crew, never resting upon a very sound basis, must sink under the continued influences of darkness and cold. The temperature and foulness of air in the between-deck Tartarus can not be amended, otherwise it would be my duty to urge a change. Between the smoke of lamps, the dry heat of stoves, and the fumes of the galley, all of them unintermitting, what wonder that we grow feeble. The short race of Christmas-day knocked up all our officers except Griffin. It pained me to see my friend Lovell, our strongest man, fainting with the exertion. The symptoms of scurvy among the crew are still increasing, and becoming more general. Faces are growing pale; strong men pant for breath upon ascending a ladder; and an indolence akin to apathy seems to be creeping over us. I long for the light. Dear, dear sun, no wonder you are worshiped!

"Our drift is still eastward, with a slow but unerring progress. The high land mentioned yesterday took, in spite of the obscuring haze, a distinguishable outline. It is not more than eight miles off, and so high that, with its retiring flanks on either side, it can be none other than the projecting Cape Warrender. Its structure is unmistakably gneissoid. We have now left the limestones.

"This cape is the great entering landmark of the northern shores of Lancaster Sound. Just one hundred days ago we passed it, urged by the wings of the storm; our errand of mercy filling us with hope, and the gale calling for our best energies. We were then but a few hours from Baffin's Bay, and not over twenty-four from the coast of Greenland. How differently are we journeying now!

"The Bay of Baffin, with its moving ice and opposing icebergs, bathed in foggy darkness and destitute of human fellowship or habitable asylum, is before us; and we, so utterly helpless, hampered, and non-resistant, must await the inevitable action of the ice. This nearness to Cape Warrender makes us feel that our silent marches have brought us near to another conflict.

"*December* 29, Sunday. The drift shows an indent of the cape now abaft our beam. We are slowly making easting. The day is one of the same obscure and dimmed fog which for the past week has wrapped us in darkness. The ice gives no change as yet: the same great field of moving whiteness.

"*December* 30, Monday. By a comparison of our several days' positions, I find that from the 18th to the 28th we have drifted fifty-two miles and a half, something over five miles a day. The winds during this period have been from the westward, constant though gentle; and our progress has been of the same steady but gentle sort. At this rate, we will in a few days more be within the Baffin's Bay incognita.

"Looking round upon my mess-mates with that sort of scrutiny that belongs to my craft and my position, I am startled at the traces, moral and physical, of our Arctic winter life. Those who con it over theoretically can hardly realize the operation of the host of retarding influences that belong to a Polar night. If I were asked to place in foremost rank the item that has been most trying, it would be neither the perpetual cold, nor the universal sameness, nor our complete exclusion from the active world of our brother men, but this constant and oppressing gloom, this unvaried darkness.

"To-day was clear toward the south, so that the blessing of light came to us more largely than of late. I walked about a mile on the recent lead, now frozen to a level meandering lane. We see to the north the Cunninghame Mountains of Cape Warrender, but can not make out our change of position definitely. To the south, an outlined ridge of doubtful mountain land shows itself high in the clouds; probably a part of the high ridges east of Admiralty Inlet.

"The thermometer fell at eight this morning to −21°. By noonday it gave us −26° and −27°. It is now −22°. The wind is gentle and cold, but not severe.

"*December* 31, Tuesday. The ending day of 1850! So clear and beautiful is this parting day, that I must take it as a happy omen. Pellucid clearness, and a sky of deep ultra-marine, brought back the remembrance of daylight. I give the record of the day.

"9 A.M. The stars visible even to the lesser groups; but a deep zone of Italian pink rises from the south, and passes by prismatic gradations into the clear blue. The outline of the shore to the northward is well defined.

"10. The day is growing into clearness. The thermometer is at twenty-seven degrees below zero. Your lungs tingle pleasantly as you draw it in.

"11. Can read ordinary over-sized print. Started on a walk, the first time for twenty-odd days. Saw the great lead, and traveled it for a couple of miles, expanding into a plain of recent ice.

"M. Passed noon on the ice. Can read diamond type. Stars of the first magnitude only visible. Saturn magnificent!

"1 P.M. With difficulty read large type. The clouds gathering in black stratus over the red light to the south.

"2. The heavens studded with stars in their groupings. Night is again over every thing, although the minor stars are not yet seen.

"Since the first of this month, we have drifted in solitude one hundred and seventy miles, skirting the northern shores of Lancaster Sound. Baffin's Bay is ahead of us, its current setting strong toward the south. What will be the result when the mighty masses of these two Arctic seas come together!"

WINTER IN THE PACK: CABIN OF THE ADVANCE.

CHAPTER XXXII.

1851, *January* 1, Wednesday. The first day of 1851 set in cold, the thermometer at −28°, and closing at −31°. We celebrated it by an extra dinner, a plum-cake unfrosted for the occasion, and a couple of our residuary bottles of wine. But there was no joy in our merriment: we were weary of the night, as those who watch for the morning.

It was not till the 3d that the red southern zone continued long enough to give us assurance of advancing day. Then, for at least three hours, the twilight enabled us to walk without stumbling. I had a feeling of racy enjoyment as I found myself once more away from the ship, ranging among the floes, and watching the rivalry of day with night in the zenith. There was the sunward horizon, with its evenly-distributed bands of primitive colors, blending softly into the clear blue overhead; and then, by an almost magic transition, night occupying the western sky. Stars of the first magnitude, and a wandering planet here and there, shone dimly near the debatable line; but a little further on were all the stars in their glory. The northern firmament had the familiar beauty of a pure winter night at home. The Pleiades glittered "like a swarm of fire-flies tangled in a silver-braid," and the great stars that hang about the heads of Orion and Taurus were as intensely bright as if day was not looking out upon them from the other quarter of the sky. I had never seen night and day dividing the hemisphere so beautifully between them.

On the 8th we had, of course, our national festivities, and remembered freshly the hero who consecrated the day in our annals. The evening brought the theatricals again, with extempore interludes, and a hearty splicing of the main-brace. It was something new, and not thoroughly gladsome, this commemoration of the victory at New Orleans under a Polar sky. There were men not two hundred miles from us, now our partners in a nobler contest, who had bled in this very battle. But we made the best of the occasion; and if others some degrees further to the south celebrated it more warmly, we had the thermometer on our side, with its $-20°$, a normal temperature for the "laudatur et alget."

But the sun was now gradually coming up toward the horizon: every day at meridian, and for an hour before and after, we were able to trace our progress eastward by some known headland. We had passed Cape Castlereagh and Cape Warrender in succession, and were close on the meridian of Cape Osborn. The disruptions of the ice which we had encountered so far, had always been at the periods of spring-tide. The sun and moon were in conjunction on the 21st of December; and, adopting Captain Parry's observation, that the greatest efflux was always within five days after the new moon, we had looked with some anxiety to the closing weeks of that month. But they had gone by without any unusual movement; and there needed only an equally kind visitation of the January moon to give us our final struggle with the Baffin's Bay ice by daylight.

Yet I had remarked that the southern shore of Lancaster Sound extended much further out to the eastward than the northern did; and I had argued that we might begin to feel the current of Baffin's Bay in a very few days, though we were still considerably to the west of a line drawn from one cape to the other. The question received its solution without waiting for the moon.

I give from my journal our position in the ice on the 11th of January:

"*January* 11, Saturday. The floe in which we are now imbedded has been steadily increasing in solidity for more than a month. Since the 8th of December, not a fracture or collision has occurred to mar its growth. The eye can not embrace its extent. Even from the mast-head you look over an unbounded expanse of naked ice, bristling with contorted spires, and ridged by elevated axes of hummocks. The land on either side rises above our icy horizon; but to the east and west, there is no such interception to our winteryness.

"The brig remains as she was tossed at our providential escape of last month, her nose burrowing in the snow, and her stern perched high above the rubbish. Walking deck is an up and down hill work. She retains, too, her list to starboard. Her bare sides have been banked over again with snow to increase the warmth, and a formidable flight of nine ice-block steps admits us to the door-way of her winter cover. The stores, hastily thrown out from the vessel when we expected her to go to pieces, are still upon the little remnant of old floe on our port or northern side. The Rescue is some hundred yards off to the south of east."

The next day things underwent a change. The morning was a misty one, giving us just light enough to make out objects that were near the ship; the wind westerly, as it had been for some time, freshening perhaps to a breeze. The day went on quietly till noon, when a sudden shock brought us all up to the deck. Running out upon the ice, we found that a crack had opened between us and the Rescue, and was extending in a zigzag course from the northward and eastward to the southward and westward. At one o'clock it had become a chasm eight feet in width; and as it continued to widen, we observed a distinct undulation of the water about its edges. At three, it had expanded into a broad sheet of water, filmed over by young ice, through which the portions of the floe that bore our two vessels began to move obliquely toward each other. Night closed round us, with the chasm reduced to forty yards and still narrowing; the Rescue on her port-bow, two hundred yards from her late position; the wind increasing, and the thermometer at $-19°$.

My journal for the next day was written at broken intervals; but I give it without change of form:

"*January* 13, 4 A.M. All hands have been on deck since one o'clock, strapped and harnessed for a farewell march. The water-lane of yesterday is covered by four-inch ice; the floes at its margin more than three feet thick. These have been closing for some time by a sliding, grinding movement, one upon the other; but every now and then coming together more directly, the thinner ice clattering between them, and marking their new outline with hummock ridges. They have been fairly in contact for the last hour: we feel their pressure extending to us through the elastic floe in which we are cradled. There is a quivering, vibratory hum about the timbers of the brig, and every now and then a harsh rubbing creak along her sides, like waxed cork on a mahogany table. The hummocks are driven to within four feet of our counter, and stand there looming fourteen feet high through the darkness. It has been a horrible commotion so far, with one wild, booming, agonized note, made up of a thousand discords; and now comes the deep stillness after it, the mysterious ice-pulse, as if the energies were gathering for another strife.

"6½ A.M. Another pulse! the vibration greater than we have ever yet had it. If our little brig had an animated centre of sensation, and some rude force had torn a nerve-trunk, she could not feel it more — she fairly shudders. Looking out to the north, this ice seems to heave up slowly against the sky in black hills; and as we watch them rolling toward us, the hills sink again, and a distorted plain of rubbish melts before us into the night. Ours is the contrast of utter helplessness with illimitable power.

"9 50 A.M. Brooks and myself took advantage of the twilight at nine o'clock to cross the hummocky fields to the Rescue. I can not convey an impression of the altered aspects of the floe. Our frozen lane has disappeared, and along the line of its recent course the ice is heaped up in blocks, tables, lumps, powder, and rubbish, often fifteen feet high. Snow covered the decks of the little vessel, and the disorder about it spoke sadly of desertion. Foot-prints of foxes were seen in every imaginable corner; and near the little hatchway, where we had often sat in comfortable good-fellowship, the tracks of a large bear had broken the snow crust in his efforts to get below.

"The Rescue has met the pressure upon her port-bow and fore-foot. Her bowsprit, already maimed by her adventure off Griffith's Island, is now completely forced up, broken short off at the gammoning. The ice, after nipping her severely, has piled up round her three feet above the bulwarks. We had looked to her as our first asylum of retreat; but that is out of the question now; she can not rise as we have done, and any action that would peril us again must bear her down or crush her laterally.

"The ice immediately about the Advance is broken into small angular pieces, as if it had been dashed against a crag of granite. Our camp out on the floe, with its reserve of provisions and a hundred things besides, memorials of scenes we have gone through, or appliances and means for hazards ahead of us, has been carried away bodily. My noble specimen of the Arctic bear is floating, with an escort of bread barrels, nearly half a mile off.

"The thermometer records only $-17°$; but it blows at times so very fiercely that I have never felt it so cold: five men were frost-bitten in the attempt to save our stores.

"9 P.M. We have had no renewal of the pressure since half past six this morning. We are turning in;

the wind blowing a fresh breeze, weather misty, thermometer at −23°."

The night brought no further change; but toward morning the cracks, that formed before this a sort of net-work all about the vessel, began to open. The cause was not apparent: the wind had lulled, and we saw no movement of the floes. We had again the same voices of complaint from the ship, but they were much feebler than yesterday; and in about an hour the ice broke up all round her, leaving an open space of about a foot to port, indented with the mould of her form. The brig was loose once more at the sides; but she remained suspended by the bows and stern from hummocks built up like trestles, and canted forward still five feet and a quarter out of level. Every thing else was fairly afloat: even the India-rubber boat, which during our troubles had found a resting-place on a sound projection of the floe close by us, had to be taken in.

This, I may say, was a fearful position; but the thermometer, at a mean of − 23° and − 24°, soon brought back the solid character of our floating raft. In less than two days every thing about us was as firmly fixed as ever. But the whole topography of the ice was changed, and its new configuration attested the violence of the elements it had been exposed to. Nothing can be conceived more completely embodying inhospitable desolation. From mast-head the eye traveled wearily over a broad champaigne of undulating ice, crowned at its ridges with broken masses, like breakers frozen as they rolled toward the beach. Beyond these, you lost by degrees the distinctions of surface. It was a great plain, blotched by dark, jagged shadows, and relieved only here and there by a hill of upheaved rubbish. Still further in the distance came an unvarying uniformity of shade, cutting with saw-toothed edge against a desolate sky.

Yet there needed no after-survey of the ice-field to prove to us what majestic forces had been at work upon it. At one time on the 13th, the hummock-ridge astern advanced with a steady march upon the vessel. Twice it rested, and advanced again—a dense wall of ice, thirty feet broad at the base and twelve feet high, tumbling huge fragments from its crest, yet increasing in mass at each new effort. We had ceased to hope; when a merciful interposition arrested it, so close against our counter that there was scarcely room for a man to pass between. Half a minute of progress more, and it would have buried us all. As we drifted along five months afterward, this stupendous memento of controlling power was still hanging over our stern. The sketch at the head of the next chapter represents its appearance at the close of the month.

ERODED ICE-FLOE.

THE ADVANCE, FEBRUARY, 1851.

CHAPTER XXXIII.

We had lost all indications of a shore, and had obviously passed within the influences of Baffin's Bay. We were on the meridian of 75°; yet, though the recent commotions could be referred to nothing else but the conflict of the two currents, we had made very little southing, if any, and had seen no bergs. But on the 14th the wind edged round a little more to the northward, and at six o'clock in the morning of the 15th we could hear a squeezing noise among the ice-fields in that direction. By this time we had become learned interpreters of the ice-voices. Of course, we renewed our preparations for whatever might be coming. Every man arranged his knapsack and blanket-bag over again with the practiced discretion of an expert. Our extra clothing sledge, carefully repacked, was made free on deck. The India-rubber boat, only useful in this solid waste for crossing occasional chasms, was launched out upon the ice for the third time. Our former depôts on the floe had fared so badly that we were reluctant to risk another; but our stores were ready to be got out at the moment.*

Now began, with every one after his own fashion, the discussion what was best to be done in case of a wreck. Should we try our fortunes for the while on board the Rescue? She would probably be the first to go, and could hardly hope for a more protracted fate than her consort. Or should we try for the shore, and what shore? Admiralty Inlet, or Pond's Bay, or the River Clyde? We have no reason to suppose the Esquimaux are accessible on the coast in winter; and if they are, they can not have provisions for such a hungry re-enforcement as ours; besides, the chance of reaching land from the drift-field through the broken ice between them is slender at the best for men worn down and sick; much more if they should attempt to carry two months' stores along with them. There was only one other resort, to camp out on the floe, if it should kindly offer us a foothold, and then move as best we might from one failing homestead to another, like a band of Arabs in the desert. Happily, Captain De Haven was spared the necessity of choosing between the alternatives: the ice-storm did not reach us.

"*January* 15. The moon is now nearly full. Her light mingles so with the twilight of the sun that the stars are quite sobered down. Walking out at 4 P.M.,

* I have avoided speaking of my brother officers. From myself, a subordinate, only accidentally recording their exertions, it would be out of place; yet I should speak the sentiment of all on board were I to recognize how much we owed to our executive officer, Mr. Griffin. All our systematized preparation for the contingencies which threatened us, the sledges, the knapsacks, the daily training, and the provision depôts, were due to him. Our commander, then so ill with scurvy that we feared for his recovery, was compelled to delegate to his second in command many executive duties which he would otherwise have taken on himself.

with the thermometer at −24°, to find, if I could, the cause of a sound a good deal like that of the surf, I was startled by a noise like a quarry blast, explosive and momentary, followed by a clatter like broken glass. Some ten minutes afterward, it was repeated, and a dark smoke-like vapor rose up in the moonlight from the same quarter. These things keep us on the *qui vive.*

"*January* 16. In the course of a tramp to-day about noon, the thermometer standing at −18°, I came across a wonderful instance of the yielding elasticity of ice under intense pressure. About two hundred yards from the brig, on her starboard quarter, was an unbroken plain of level ice, which before our recent break-up used to form one of my daily walks. It measured one hundred and thirty paces in its longer diameter and eighty-five in its shorter, and its thickness I ascertained this morning was over five feet. I found in crossing it to-day that the surface presented a uniform curve, a segment whose versed sine could not have been less than eight feet, abutted on each side by a barricade of rubbish. It strikes me that the dehiscence, lady's slipper or Rupert's drop fashion, of such tensely-compressed floes, must be the cause of the loud explosions we have heard lately. At −30° or −40° the ice is as friable and brittle as glass itself; besides, one of those yesterday was followed by a ringing clatter.

"*January* 18. The extreme stillness, and the facility with which sound travels over these Polar ice-plains, make us err a good deal in our estimates of distance at night. I went out to-day with Dr. Vreeland in search of a violent disruption of the ice, which our look-outs declared they had heard at the very side of the brig. We had some difficulty in finding it: it was the closing of a fissure considerably more than half a mile off.

"As we were returning we noticed some additional results of the ice action of the 13th. Among them was a table of ice, four feet thick, eighteen long, and fifteen broad, so curved without destroying its integrity as to form a well-arched bridge across a water chasm. It had evidently reared up high in air, and then, toppling over, bent into its present form—a mark-

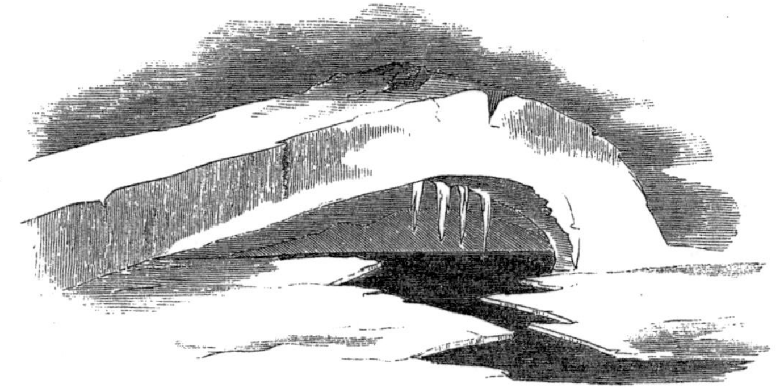

ed instance of the semi-solid or viscous character which forms the basis of Professor Forbes's glacial theory. It is not, however, the first extreme change of form that I have noticed in apparently matured ice at a low temperature: its plasticity at $+32°$ must be much greater.

"Observations by meridian altitudes of Saturn and Aldebaran give us to-day a latitude of 73° 47′ north. Yesterday we were at 73° 5′. This progress to the south is shown also by the bearing of the Walter Bathurst coast in the neighborhood of Possession Bay. We are fully inside of Baffin's Bay, and with the wind at northwest. There are some signs of ice trouble ahead; a crack has been gradually opening toward our quarter, and has got within eight hundred yards of us."

The day after this the crack approached us till it was only about three hundred yards off, and then began closing again, with the usual accompanying phenomena. The ice between it and us was apparently quiescent; but our ship quivered and jumped under the transmitted pressure. Soon after, in the midst of a heavy snow-drift, and with a temperature of −30°, another crack showed itself close upon our cut-water. The shocks which reached us during these commotions are noted in the log-book as "apparently lifting the vessel aft:" the feeling was, indeed, not unlike that which has been observed during an earthquake, immediately before and sometimes during a vibration.

"*January* 20. The ice sounded last night like some one hammering a nail against the ship's side, clicking at regular intervals. Another crack on the other side of the Rescue, now showing open water, was perhaps the cause.

"We already begin to experience the change in our axis of drift. The changes of the wind and the currents of Baffin's Bay have impressed the great system which surrounds us with a marked progress to the south.

"Throughout last night, and until nine o'clock this morning, a column of illumination depended from the moon. Viewing it obliquely, its penciled rays could be seen reaching nearly to the horizon; while in its direct aspect a manifest but intermitting interval was apparent. It struck me as an illustration, perhaps, of Sir John Herschell's remark when observing the Pleiades, that the centre of the retina is not the seat of greatest sensibility.

"Our snow-water has been infected for the past month by a very perceptible flavor and odor of musk, to such a degree sometimes that we could hardly drink it. After many attempts to find out its cause, and at least as many philosophical disquisitions to account for it without one, I accidentally saw to-day a group of foxes on the floes about our brig, who resolved our doubts by an illustration altogether simple and natural.

"*January* 22. On reaching the deck at half past eight this morning, after my usual sleepless night in the murky den below, I found the horizon free from cloud stratus, and the feeble foreshadowings of day bathing the snow with a neutral tint. By nine we could see to walk; and as late as five in the afternoon, the refracted twilights hung about the western sky. How delicious is this sensation of coming day! In less than a fortnight the great planet will be lifted by the bountiful refraction of the Arctic circle into clear eye presence.

"I long for day. The anomalous host of evils which hang about this vegetation in darkness are showing themselves in all their forms. My scurvy patients, those I mean on the sick-list, with all the care that it is possible to give them, are perhaps no worse; but pains in the joints, rheumatisms, coughs, loss of appetite, and general debility, extend over the whole company. Fifteen pounds of food per diem are consumed reluctantly now, where thirty-two were taken with appetite on the 20th of October. We are a ghastly set of pale faces, and none paler than myself. I find it a labor to carry my carbine. My fingers cling together in an ill-adjusted *plexus*, like the toes in a tight boot, and my long beard is becoming as rough and rugged as Humphrey of Gloster's in the play.

"12 M. The thermometer keeps steadily at −20°, but to-day is the coldest I have ever felt. It blows a young gale. Brooks and myself have been flying kites. The wind was like prickling needles, and the snow smoked over the moving drifts.

"I am struck more and more with the evidences of gigantic force in the phases of our frozen *pedragal.* Returning from a chase after an imaginary bear, we came across, yesterday, a suspended hummock, so imposing in its form, that, half frozen as we were, we stopped to measure it. It was a single table of massive ice, supported upon a pile of rubbish, and inclined about 15° to the horizon. Its length was ninety-one feet six inches, its breadth fifty-one feet, and its average solid thickness eight feet. At its lower end it was seven feet above the level of the adjacent floe; at its upper, twenty-seven. The weight of such a mass, allowing 113 lbs. to the cubic foot, would be 1883 tons. I almost begin to realize Baron Wrangell's account of the hummocks on the coast of Siberia. We have here, perhaps, some five hundred fathoms of water: the six, or twelve, or twenty fathoms of slimy mud, that he speaks of as forming the inclined plane of the shore, must facilitate very much the upheaval of ice-tables.

"10 P.M. The wind has freshened to a gale of the first order, and it howls outside like the dog-chorus of outer Constantinople. But cheerless as these heavy winds are in all out-of-the-way, undefended places, it is only when they announce or accompany a change of direction that we fear them. So stable and so elastic withal is the cementing effect of the cold here, that the strongest gales do not break up the ice after it has been once set in the line of the wind. On the other hand, a trifling breeze, if it deviates a very few points from the axis of the last set, puts every thing into commotion.

"*January* 23. The gale of last night subsided into the usual quiet but fresh westerly breeze, sometimes inclining to the W.N.W. To-day is very clear; the stars, except one or two of the northern magnates, invisible at noonday; and two or three well-marked crimson lines streaking the dawning zone above the sun. The hills around Walter Bathurst and Possession Bay, the entering southern headlands of Lancaster Sound, have sunk in the distance. Two summits, bearing southwest by west, probably belonging to Possession Mount, are all that remains of the coast. We are more than fifty miles from land, and still drifting rapidly to the east. To the southwest, by compass (true S.E. ½ E.), little volumes of smoke have been rising; but after a tolerably long walk, I could not find any further signs of the open water. We are now in latitude 73° 10′.

"The daylight is very sensibly longer: the noon was quite joyous with its little crimson flocculi; and five, or even five and a half hours afterward, when we looked toward the day quarter, instead of a grim blackness, or, as we had it more recently, a stain of Indian-red, we saw the pale bluish light, so gratefully familiar at home."

The appearances which heralded the sun's return had a degree of interest for us which it is not easy to express in words. I have referred more than once already to the effects of the long-continued night on the health of our crowded ship's company. It was even more painful to notice its influence on their temper and spirits. Among the officers this was less observable. Our mess seemed determined, come what might, to maintain toward each other that honest courtesy of manner, which those who have sailed on long voyages together know to be the rarest and most difficult proof of mutual respect. There were of course seasons when each had his home thoughts, and revolved perhaps the growing probabilities that some other Arctic search party might seek in vain hereafter for a memorial of our own; yet these were never topics of conversation. I do not remember to have been saddened by a boding word during all the trials of our cruise.

With the men, however, it was different. More deficient in the resources of education, and less restrained by conventional usages or the principle of honor from communicating to each other what they felt, all sympathized in the imaginary terrors which each one conjured up. The wild voices of the ice and wind, the strange sounds that issued from the ship, the hummocks bursting up without an apparent cause through the darkness, the cracks and the dark rushing water that filled them, the distorted wonder-workings of refraction; in a word, all that could stimulate, or sicken, or oppress the fancy, was a day and nightmare dream for the forecastle.

We were called up one evening by the deck-watch to see for ourselves a "ball of fire floating up and down above the ice-field." It was there sure enough, a disk of reddish flame, varying a little in its outline, and flickering in the horizon like a revolving light at a distance. I was at first as much puzzled as the men; but glancing at Orion, I soon saw that it was nothing else than our old dog-star friend, bright Sirius, come back to us. Refraction had raised him above the hills, so as to bring him to view a little sooner than we expected. His color was rather more lurid than when he left us, and the refraction, besides distorting his outline, seemed to have given him the same oblateness or horizontal expansion which we observe in the disks of the larger planets when nearing the horizon.

For some days the sun-clouds at the south had been changing their character. Their edges became better defined, their extremities dentated, their color deeper as well as warmer; and from the spaces between the lines of stratus burst out a blaze of glory, typical of the longed-for sun. He came at last: it was on the 29th. My journal must tell the story of his welcoming, at the hazard of its seeming extravagance: I am content that they shall criticise it who have drifted for more than twelve weeks under the night of a Polar sky.

"*January* 29. Going on deck after breakfast at eight this morning, I found the dawning far advanced. The whole vault was bedewed with the coming day; and, except Capella, the stars were gone. The southern horizon was clear. We were certain to see the sun, after an absence of eighty-six days. It had been arranged on board that all hands should give him three cheers for a greeting; but I was in no mood to join the sallow-visaged party. I took my gun, and walked over the ice about a mile away from the ship to a solitary spot, where a great big hummock almost hemmed me in, opening only to the south. There, Parsee fashion, I drank in the rosy light, and watched the horns of the crescent extending themselves round toward the north. There was hardly a breath of wind, with the thermometer at only $-19°$, and it was easy, therefore, to keep warm by walking gently up and down. I thought over and named aloud every one of our little circle, F. and M., T. and P., B. and J., and our dear, bright little W.; wondered a while whether there were not some more to be remembered, and called up one friend or relative after another, but always came back to the circle I began with. My thoughts were torpid, not worth the writing down; but I was not strong, and they affected me. It was not good 'Polar practice.'

"Very soon the deep crimson blush, lightening into a focus of incandescent white, showed me that the hour was close at hand. Mounting upon a crag, I saw the crews of our one ship formed in line upon the ice. My mind was still tracing the familiar chain of home affections, and the chances that this one or the other of its links might be broken already. I bethought me of the Sortes Virgilianæ of my school-boy days: I took a piece of candle paper pasteboard, cut it with my bowie-knife into a little carbine target, and on one side of this marked all our names in pencil, and on the other a little star. Presently the sun came: never, till the grave-sod or the ice covers me, may I forego this blessing of blessings again! I looked at him thankfully with a great globus in my throat. Then came the shout from the ship—three shouts—cheering the sun. I fixed my little star-target to the floe, walked backward till it became nearly invisible; and then, just as the completed orb fluttered upon the horizon, fired my '*salut.*' I cut M in half, and knocked the T out of Tom. They shall draw lots for it if ever I get home; for many, many years may come and go again before the shot of an American rifle signalizes in the winter of Baffin's Bay the conjunction of sunrise, noonday, and sunset.

"The first indications of dawn to-day were at forty-five minutes past five. By seven the twilight was nearly sufficient to guide a walking party over the floes. I have described the phenomena at eight. At nine the deck-lantern was doused. By 11h. 14m. or 15m. those on board had the first glimpses of the sun. At 5 P.M. we had the dim twilight of evening.

"Our thermometric records on board ship can not be relied on. I mention the fact for the benefit of those who may hereafter consult them. My wooden-cased Pike thermometer, hung to a stanchion on the northern beam of the brig, gave at noonday $-19°$; exposed to the sun's rays on the southern, $-14°$. The observation repeated at 12h. 30m., gave $-20°$ for the northern, and $-15°$ for the southern side; the difference in each case being five degrees. The same thermometer, carefully exposed about a hundred yards from the ship, gave at noon, on the north and windward side, $-21°$; on the south, exposed to the sun, $-18°$; and at thirty minutes afterward (nearly), on the north, $-20° 5'$; toward the sun, $-16°$. The difference in these last observations of $3°$ in the first and $4° 5'$ in the second was owing unmistakably to the effect of the solar rays. The ship's record for the same hours was simply $-19°$ and $-18°$. The fact is, that there is always a varying difference of two to five degrees of temperature between the lee and weather sides of the brig; the quarter of the wind and its intensity, the state of our fires, the open or shut hatches, and other minor circumstances, determining what the difference shall be at a particular time.

"*January* 30. The crew determined to celebrate 'El regresado del sol,' which, according to old Costa, our Mahonese seaman, was a more holy day than Christmas or All-Saints. Mr. Bruce, the diversely talented, favored us with a new line of theatrical exhibition, a *divertissement* of domestic composition, 'The Countryman's first Visit to Town;' followed by a pantomime. I copy the play-bill from the original as it was tacked against the main-mast:

ARCTIC THEATRE.

To be performed, on the night of Thursday, the 30th day of January, the Comic Play of the COUNTRYMAN. After which, a PANTOMIME.

To begin with

A Song .... By R. Bruce.

THE COUNTRYMAN.

Countryman .... R. Baggs.
Landlady .... C. Berry.
Servant .... T. Dunning.

PANTOMIME.

Harlequin .... James Johnson.
Old Man .... R. Bruce.
Rejected Lover .... A. Canot.
Columbine .... James Smith.

Doors to be opened at 8 o'clock. Curtain to rise a quarter past 8 punctually
No admittance to Children; and no Ladies admitted without an escort.

STAGE MANAGER,
S. BENJAMIN.

The strictest order will be observed both inside and outside.

We sat down as usual on the preserved-meat boxes, which were placed on deck, ready strapped and becketed (*nauticè* for trunk-handled) for flinging out upon the ice. The affair was altogether creditable, however, and every body enjoyed it. Here is an outline of the pantomime, after the manner of the newspapers. An old man (Mr. Bruce) possessed mysterious, semi-magical, and wholly comical influence over a rejected lover (M. Auguste Canot, ship's cook), and Columbine (Mr. Smith) exercised the same over the old man. Harlequin (Mr. Johnson), however, by the aid of a split-shingle wand and the charms of his "motley wear," secures the affections of Columbine, cajoles the old man, persecutes the forlorn lover, and carries off the prize of love; the fair Columbine, who had been industriously chewing tobacco, and twirling on the heel of her boot to keep herself warm, giving him a sentimental kiss as she left the stage. A still more sentimental song, sung in seal-skin breeks and a "*nor-wester*," and a potation all round of hot-spiced rum toddy, concluded the entertainments.

The thermometer stood at -7°.

THE RESCUE, IN LANCASTER SOUND.

CHAPTER XXXIV.

On the 2d of February the sun rose up in full disk at a quarter before eleven. The atmosphere was clear, but filled with minute spiculæ. The cold was becoming more intense: our ship thermometers stood at −32°, my spirit standard at −34°, and my mercurial at −38°. The ice that had formed between the floes since our break-up of January 12th was already twenty-seven inches thick, and was increasing at the rate of five inches in the twenty-four hours. The floes crackled under the intense frost, and we heard loud explosions around us, which one of our seamen, who had seen land service in Mexico, compared very aptly to the sound of a musket fired in an empty town.

The 6th was still colder. At seven in the evening my spirit standard was at −40°. The day, however, had been graced with some hours of sunshine, and we worked and played foot-ball out on the ice till we were many of us in a profuse perspiration. The next morning my mercurial thermometer had frozen, leaving its parting record at −42°; and at half past eight one of the spirit standards indicated the same point. Up to this period, it was our lowest temperature. The frozen mercury resembled in appearance lead, recently chilled after melting. You could cut the thinner edges easily enough with a penknife; but where it was heaped up, nearer the centre of the solid mass, it was tenacious and resisting. I wished to examine it under the microscope, but was unable to procure a fractured surface.

Between six and eight o'clock in the evening of the 2d, we had a magnificent though nearly colorless exhibition of the aurora; and on the 7th, at 10h. 20m. A.M., the southern sky presented the appearance of a day aurora attending on the sun. The observations which I made of these two phenomena may be the subject of a distinct chapter; I will only say here, that it was difficult to doubt their identity of character or cause. We had several displays of the paraselene, too, in the earlier days of the month, and an almost constant deposition of crystalline specks, which covered our decks with a sort of hoar-frost. The rate of this deposition on the vessel was about a quarter of an inch in six hours; but in an ice-basin on the floes, surrounded by hummocks, and thus protected from the wind, I found it nine inches deep.

When accumulated in this manner, it might, on a hurried inspection, be confounded with snow; but it differs as the dew does from rain. It is directly connected with radiation, and is most copious under a clear sky. Snow itself, the flaky snow of a clouded atmosphere, has not been noticed by us when the temperature was lower than −8° or at most −10°. Our last snow-fall was on the 1st of February and the day preceding. It began with the thermometer at −1°, and continued after it had sunk to −9°; but it had ceased some time before it reached −13°.

"*February* 9. To-day we had a sky of serene purity, and all hands went out for a sanitary game of romps in the cold light. Presently three suns came to greet us—strange Arctic parhelia—and a great golden cross of yellow brightness uniting them in one system. Under the glare of these we played foot-ball.

"At meridian we made a rough horizon of the ice,

and found ourselves in latitude about 72° 16′. At this time another marvel rose before us—Land. The monster was to the W.S.W., in the shape of two round-topped hills, lifted up for the time into our field of view. An hour or two later, while the day was waning, these hills became mountains, and then a line of truncated cones, the spectre of some distant coast. Looking a few minutes later out of the little door in our felt house, the port gangway of the log-book, to where for this last fortnight a bleak sameness of snow has been stretching to the far north, we saw a couple of icebergs standing alone in the sky, and at their shadowy tops their phantom repetitions inverted. By this time the mountains also had become twain, and the long line of resurrected coast was duplicated in the clouds. A stratum of false horizon separated the two sets of images.

"We have been now for many months without seeing the icebergs. They were beautiful objects, monuments of power, when we met them on the coast of Greenland, floating along on a liquid sea. Now they admonish us only of our helplessness and of perils before us. We should be glad to keep them in the clouds.

"The sun begins to make himself felt, though as yet feebly enough. My large spirit thermometer, in the shade of a hummock some hundred yards from the brig, gave us at noon −21° 5′, and on the sunny side of the same hummock −12°. The same thermometer, before a blackboard exposed to the sun, was at −7°. Twenty minutes later, the thermometer at the blackboard rose to +2°, and twenty minutes later still it was at −2°. The ice formed within the twenty-four hours in the fire-hole measured four and a quarter inches; three quarters of an inch less than our measurements of it a week ago. A thermometer plunged two feet deep in a bank of light snow-drift indicated −12°.

"*February* 10. A hazy day; with moonlight, and a drizzling fall of broken spiculæ following it. Mr. Murdaugh obtained observations for meridian altitude and time-sights of Aldebaran: our latitude is 72° 19′, our longitude 68° 55′. The winds have been unfavorable to the rapidity of our drift, which has been reduced in its rate since our observation on the 29th of January from five and a quarter to four miles a day. It may be that our approach to the narrower parts of the bay and the increased cold together have been disturbing causes in the movement of the great pack; but the wind has been the most important in its influence.

"To look at the completely unbroken area which shows itself from our mast-head, motion would be the last idea suggested. In Lancaster Sound the changing phases of the coast gave us a feeling of progress, movement, drift—that sensation of change so pleasing to one's incomprehensible moral machinery. But here, with this circle of impenetrable passive solidity every where around us, it is hard to realize that we move. But for the stars, my convictions of rest would be absolute. Yet we have thus traveled upward of three hundred miles. I shall not soon forget this inevitable march, with its alternations of gloomy silence and fierce disruptions.

"*February* 11, Wednesday. Day very hazy, and nothing to interrupt its monotony. It requires an effort to bear up against this solemn transit of unvarying time.

"I will show you how I spend one of these days—

that is, all of them. It is the only palliation I can offer for my meagreness of incident. As for the study we used to talk about—even you, terrible worker as you are, could not study in the Arctic regions.

"Within a little area, whose cubic contents are less than father's library, you have the entire abiding-place of thirty-three heavily-clad men. Of these I am one. Three stoves and a cooking galley, four Argand and three bear-fat lamps burn with the constancy of a vestal shrine. Damp furs, soiled woolens, cast-off boots, sick men, cookery, tobacco-smoke, and digestion are compounding their effluvia around and within me. Hour by hour, and day after day, without even a bunk to retire to or a blanket-curtain to hide me, this and these make up the reality of my home.

"Outside, grim death, in the shape of $-40°$, is trying—most foolishly, I think—to chill the energy of these his allies. My bedding lies upon the bare deck, right under the hatch. A thermometer, placed at the head of my cot, gives a mean temperature of 64°; at my feet, under the hatchway, $+16°$ to $-4°$—ice at my feet, vapor at my head. The sleeping-bunks aft range from 70° to 93°; those forward, regulated by the medical officer, from 60° to 65°.

"We rise, the crew at six bells, seven o'clock, and the officers at seven bells, half an hour later. Thus comports himself your brother. He sits up in the midst of his blankets, and drinks a glass of cold water; eyes, nose, and mouth chippy with lampblack and undue evaporation. Oh! how comforting this water is! That over, a tin-basin, in its turn, is brought round by Morton, mush-like with snow; and in this mixt ure, by the aid of a hard towel, with a daily regularity that knows no intermission, he goes over his entire skeleton, frictionizing.

"This done, comes the dressing—the two pairs of stockings, the three under-shirts, the fur outer robing, and the seal-skin boots; and then, with a hurried cough of disgust and semi-suffocation, he is on deck. There the air, pure and sharply cold, now about 26° or 30°, last week 40° below zero, braces you up like peach and honey in a Virginia fog, or a tass of mountain dew in the Highlands. Then to breakfast. Here are the mess, with the fresh smell of overnight undisturbed, and on our table griddle cakes of Indian meal, hominy, and mackerel: with hot coffee and good appetites, we fall to manfully.

"Breakfast over, on go the furs again; and we escape from the accumulating fumes of 'servants' hall,' walking the floes, or climbing to the tops, till we are frozen enough to go below again. One hour spent now in an attempt at study—vainly enough, poor devil! But he does try, and what little he does is done then. By half past ten our entire little band of officers are out upon the floes for a bout at anti-scorbutic exercise, a game of romps: first foot-ball, at which we kick till our legs ache; next sliding, at which we slide until we can slide no more: then off, with carbine on shoulder, and Henri as satellite, on an ice-tramp.

"Coming back, dinner lags at two. Then for the afternoon—God spare the man who can with unscathed nose stand the effluvium. But night follows soon, and with it the saddening question, What has the day achieved? And then we stretch ourselves out under the hatches, and sleep to the music of our thirty odd room-mates.

"*February* 14, Friday. A glorious day, with the sun from nine to half past two. Three bergs seen by refraction. The mercury rose to +2 over a black surface turned toward the sun. To-day the usual foot-ball.

"Our Arctic theatre gave us to-night 'The Mysteries and Miseries of New York,' followed by a pantomime. The sitting temperature was −20°; that outside, −36°; behind the scenes, −25°. A flat-iron used by the delicate Miss Jem Smith gave the novel theatrical effect of burning by cold. Poor Jem suffered so much in her bare sleeves and hands, that whenever the iron touched she winced. Cold merriment; but it concluded with hotchpot and songs.

"*February* 15, Saturday. Another glorious day; the sun visible from 9 A.M. to 3 P.M., and embanked during the remaining time. Much to our surprise, at the moment of setting, a startling ridge of mountain peaks rose into sight to the westward. Their distance, as estimated by the latest charts, was no less than 76 miles.

"*February* 22, Saturday. 'Some things can be done as well as others:' so at least Sam Patch said, when he scrambled up after his jump at Niagara. I walked myself into a comfortable perspiration this morning, with the thermometer at −42°, seventy-four degrees below the freezing point. My walk was a long one. When about three miles from the brig, a breeze sprang up: it was very gentle; but instantly the sensation came upon me of intense cold. My beard, coated before with massive icicles, seemed to bristle with increased stiffness. Henri, who walked ahead, began to suffer: his nose was tallow white. Before we had rubbed it into circulation, my own was in the same condition; and an unfortunate hole in the back of my mitten stung like a burning coal. We are so accustomed to cold that I did not suffer during our walk back, though it was more than an hour of hummock crossing.

"The sensation most unendurable of these extremely low temperatures is a pain between the eyes and over the forehead. This is quite severe. It reminded me of a feeling which I have had from over-large quantities of ice-cream or ice-water, held against the roof of the mouth. I reached the brig in a fine glow of warmth, having skated, slid, and made the most of my time in the open air.

"An increased disposition to scurvy shows itself. Last week twelve cases of scorbutic gums were noted at my daily inspections. In addition to these, I have two cases of swelled limbs and extravasated blotches, with others less severely marked, from the same obstinate disease. The officers too, the captain, Mr. Lovell, and Mr. Murdaugh, complain of stiff and painful joints and limbs, with diarrhœa and impaired appetite: the doctor like the rest. At my recommendation, the captain has ordered an increased allowance of fresh food, to the amount of two complete extra daily rations per man, with potatoes, saurkraut, and stewed apples; and we have enjoined more active and continued daily exercise, more complete airing of bedding, &c. I have commenced the use of nitro-muriatic acid, as in syphilitic and mercurial cases, by external friction.

"The state of health among us gives me great anxiety, and not a little hard work. Quinine, the salts of iron, &c., &c., are in full requisition For the first time I am without a hospital steward.

"It is Washington's birth-day, when 'hearts should be glad;' but we have no wine for the dinner-table, and are too sick for artificial merriment without it. Our crew, however, good patriotic wretches, got up a theatrical performance, 'The Irish Attorney;' Pierce O'Hara taken by the admirable Bruce, our Crichton.

The ship's thermometer outside was at $-46°$. Inside, among audience and actors, by aid of lungs, lamps, and housings, we got as high as 30° below zero, only sixty-two below the freezing point!! probably the lowest atmospheric record of a theatrical representation.

"It was a strange thing altogether. The condensation was so excessive that we could barely see the performers: they walked in a cloud of vapor. Any extra vehemence of delivery was accompanied by volumes of smoke. The hands steamed. When an excited Thespian took off his hat, it smoked like a dish of potatoes. When he stood expectant, musing a reply, the vapor wreathed in little curls from his neck. This was thirty degrees lower than the lowest of Parry's North Georgian performances.

"*February* 23, Sunday. Mist comes back to us. After our past week of glorious sunshine, this return to murkiness is far from pleasing. But it might be worse: one month ago, and a day like this would have made our winter-stricken hearts bound with gladness.

"Caught a cold last night in attending the theatre. A cold here means a sudden *malaise*, with insufferable aches in back and joints, hot eyes, and fevered skin. We all have them, coming and going, short-lived and long-lived: they leave their mark too. This Arctic work brings extra years upon a man. A fresh wind makes the cold very unbearable. In walking to-day. my beard and mustache became one solid mass of ice. I inadvertently put out my tongue, and it instantly froze fast to my lip. This being nothing new, costing only a smart pull and a bleeding abrasion afterward, I put up my mittened hands to 'blow hot' and thaw the unruly member from its imprisonment. Instead of succeeding, my mitten was itself a mass of ice in a moment: it fastened on the upper side of my tongue, and flattened it out like a batter-cake between the two disks of a hot griddle. It required all my care, with the bare hands, to release it, and that not without laceration.

"*February* 25. A murky day. Two hundred and forty-four fathoms of line gave no bottom at the air-hole. Scurvy getting ahead. Began using the remnant of our fetid bear's meat: nasty physic, but we will try it. It is colder to-day, with the wind and fog at −15°, than a few days ago at −46°. Wind south by east: sun not seen.

"*February* 26, Wednesday. The sun came back again with such vigor, that my spirit standard rose over black to +14°; my glass—cased, to +35°. The difference between shade and sunshine is 30°: a thermometer freely suspended in shade and in sun gave −32° and −2°. Black surfaces begin to scale off their snowy covering, not by thawing attended by moisture, but with a manifest diminution in the tenacity and adhesiveness of the snow. We observe these indications of returning heat closely.

"The scurvy has at last fairly extended to our own little body, the officers. Pains in the limbs, and deep-seated soreness of the bones, seem to be its most common demonstration. The complaint is of 'a sort of tired feeling,' or as if 'they had had a beating.' Our usual supper, the saur-krout, has become excessively popular. Even the abused bear is not quite as bad as it was.

"The crew have been snow-rubbing their blankets. The snow is so fine and sand-like, that under these low Arctic temperatures it acts mechanically, and is an effectual cleanser. Withal, if you beat it well out of the tissue, it is not a damp application. The only trouble is that, on taking the bedding below, the condensation covers it with dew-drops. With drying-lines on the lower decks, the resort would be excellent.

"The setting sun, now fast approaching the home quarter of setting suns, the west, gave us again the spectral land about Cape Adair, eighty miles off.

"Sirius is beautifully resplendent on the meridian. What a fine exhibition it is! As it rises from the banked horizon, it gives us nightly freaks of terrestrial refraction. Its colors are blue, crimson, and white; its shapes oval, hour-glass, rhomboid, and square. Sometimes it is extinguished; sometimes flashing into sudden life: it looks very like a revolving light.

"To-day, in putting my hand inside my reindeer hood, I felt a something move. The something had a crepitating, insectine wriggle. Now, at home and every where else, without being a nervous man as to insects—for I have eaten locusts in Sennaar and bats in Dahomey—I rather dislike the crawl of centipede or slime of snail. Here, with an emotion hard to describe, surprise, pleasure, and a don't-know-why wonderment, I caught my bug gently between thumb and finger.

"An air insect would be, in this dreary waste of cold, an impossibility greater than the diamond in the snow-drift. Save a seal and a fox, nothing sharing our principle of vitality has greeted us for months. The teeming myriads of life which characterized the Arctic summer have gone. The anatidæ are clamoring in the great bays and water-courses of the middle south. The gulls have sought the regions of open water. The colymbi and Auks are lining the northern coasts of my own dear home. The croaking raven, dark bird of winter, clings to the in-shore deserts. The tern are far away, and so, thank Heaven, are the musquitoes. There are no bugs in the blankets, no nits in the hair, no maggots in the cheese. No specks of life glitter in the sunshine, no sounds of it float upon the air. We are without a single sign, a single instinct of living thing.

"If now, with the thermometer eighty degrees below the freezing point, and the new sun casting a cold gray sheen upon the snow, you leave the thirty-one, to whom you are the thirty-second, and walk out upon the ice away off—so far that no click of hammer nor drone of voice places you in relation with that little outside world—then you will know how I felt when I caught that 'creeping wonder' on my reindeer hood. It was a frozen feather.

"*February* 27, Thursday. An aurora passing through the zenith, east and west, at 3h. 30m. this morning. What little wind we have is coming feebly from the west and southwest. The thermometer has traveled from $-40°$ to $-31°$, and the sun is out again in benign lustre. A difference of 27°, due to his influence, was evident as early as 10h. 20m., viz.: Green's spirit standard gave, in shade, $-33°$; over black surface, in sunshine, $-7°$ and $-6°$. At noonday, the same thermometer gave +2. My glass—cased, hot-house like, gave the pleasant deception of $+40°$.

"Still the scurvy increases. I am down myself to-day with all the premonitories. It is strangely depressing: a concentrated 'fresh cold' pain extends searchingly from top to toe. I am so stiff that it is only by an effort that I can walk the deck, and that limpingly. Once out on the floes, my energies excited and my blood warmed by exercise, I can tramp away freely; back again, I stiffen.

"Walked with our other cook, Auguste Canot. Queer changes these Frenchmen see! Canot's father, a captain in the French army, was shot while serving with Oudinot, beneath the infernal 'barricades' of Rome—Canot the younger looking on. A few months after, the son had figured upon the list of condemned for the affair at Lyons, and was a fugitive *emigré* to the United States. The same sergeant-major, Canot, is now cooking salt junk in Baffin's Bay. His *confrère*, the modest but gifted Henri, although a worse soldier, is a better cook. He first saw ice among the glaciers of La Tour. He has scullionized at the '*Trois Frères*,' and played *chêf* to a London club-house. He passed through this latter ordeal, strange to say, unscathed; and, but for an amorous temperament, might be now at Delmonico's, upon good wages and bad Bordeaux. Henri is a boy of talent, pensive by temperament, and withal ambitious. Were it not for the somewhat unequal distribution of two molars and an incisor, his entire stock of teeth, he would be an insufferable coxcomb. As it is, he treats his infirmity with amiable, if not philosophic contempt. He made me this morning an idea of white bear's liver, *à la brochette*. The idea was good, the liver hippuric and detestable. Henri prides himself upon that most difficult simplicity, the *filet*. He prepares thus a sea-gull *à merveille*.

"*February* 28, Friday. The most wintery-looking day I have ever seen. The winds have been let loose, and the cheering novelty of a northwester breaks in on our calm. The drifting snow either rises like smoke from the levels, or whirls away in wreaths from the hummocks. The atmosphere has an opaline ashy look; in the midst of which, like a huge girasole, flashes the round sun. The clouds are of a sort seldom seen, except in the conceptions of adventurous artists, quite undefinable, and out of the line of nature, defying Howard's nomenclature. They are blocked out in square, stormy masses, against a pearly, misty blue —harsh, abrupt, repulsive, quite out of keeping with the kindly lightness of things belonging to the sky."

The lowest temperature we recorded during the cruise was on the 22d of this month, when the ship's thermometer gave us −46°; my offship spirit, −52°; and my own self-registering instruments, purchased from Green, placed on a hummock removed from the vessels, −53°, as the mean of two instruments. This may be taken as the true record of our lowest absolute temperature.

Cold as it was, our mid-day exercise was never interrupted, unless by wind and drift storms. We felt the necessity of active exercise; and although the effort was accompanied with pains in the joints, sometimes hardly bearable, we managed, both officers and crew, to obtain at least three hours a day. The exercise consisted of foot-ball and sliding, followed by regular games of romps, leap-frog, and tumbling in the snow. By shoveling away near the vessel, we obtained a fine bare surface of fresh ice, extremely glib and durable. On this we constructed a skating-ground and admirable slides. I walked regularly over the floes, although the snows were nearly impassable.

With all this, aided by hosts of hygienic resources, feeble certainly, but still the best at my command, scurvy advanced steadily. This fearful disease, so often warded off when in a direct attack, now exhibited itself in a cachexy, a depraved condition of system sad to encounter. Pains, diffuse, and non-locatable, were combined with an apathy and lassitude which resisted all attempts at healthy excitement.

These, of course, were not confined to the crew alone: out of twenty-four men, but five were without ulcerated gums and blotched limbs; and of these five, strange to say, four were cooks and stewards. All the officers were assailed. Old pains were renewed, old wounds opened; even old bruises and sprains, received at barely-remembered periods back, came to us like dreams. Our commander, certainly the finest constitution among us, was assailed like the rest. In a few days purpuric extravasations appeared on his legs, and a dysentery enfeebled him to an extent far from safe. An old wound of my own became discolored, and, curious to say, painful only at such points of old suppuration, three in number, as had been relieved by the knife. The seats of a couple of abscess-like openings were entirely unaffected and free from pain.

The close of the month found this state of things on the increase, and the strength of the party still waning.

AURORA SEEN SOUTH OF CAPE FAREWELL.

CHAPTER XXXV.

It might be supposed, at first view, that the accession of solar light would be accompanied by increase of temperature. This, however, was far from being the case. Though February had brought back the sun, it was the first month throughout which the ice-fields remained frozen in their wintery rest. It was our coldest month. This effect was due to the greatly increased evaporation; a subject of frequent notice in my journal, confirming in this the experience of Ermann and other Siberian travelers.

The renewed alternation of day and night, with their increased range of diurnal temperatures, gave us in full perfection those different forms of meteoric exhibition which affect peculiarly the Arctic zone. The aurora, with a host of phenomena dependent upon the modifications of light, halos, coronæ, tangent circles, parhelia, anthelia, and paraselenæ, came to us in rapidly-varying succession; and refraction, with its preternatural augmentation of the visual hemisphere, revisited us under new and startling forms.

The scintillation of the stars, that phenomenon so connected with alternating changes in the refractive media, was wonderfully apparent. The fixed stars, whose distance made the least displacement sensible to the eye, were especially influenced; yet even the planets shared in the change, and twinkled like the stars at home. I have alluded to the gorgeous changes of Sirius and Aldebaran; but these descriptions give a feeble index of their Protean varieties of shape and color, which, with every grade of intensity, greeted us nightly.

The red coloring of the clouds reminded me of the rose-tints of the Alps. Cirro-cumuli of every imaginable form began again to deck the horizon. The twilight too, that long Arctic crepusculum, seemed, contrary to theory, to be disproportionally increased in its duration. Eighteen degrees is certainly a very arbitrary limit to its extent. How noble a field for research would, with intellectual capacity, adequate instruments, and sympathizing co-operation, have been the ice-plain of Baffin's Bay!

The auroras to the north and northeast of the American magnetic pole are not the brilliant displays described by Biot and Lottin in Northern Europe, or the English explorers in Canadian America. Those of Lancaster, Wellington, Prince Regent's, and the North Baffin waters, partake of the same general character; and though somewhat modified perhaps, did not, as I observed them, differ materially from those described by Fisher and Parry. This last great navigator constantly expresses his disappointment at the feebleness of the auroral displays, as compared with those of the Northern Atlantic, on the European side. I had the same feeling.

Their changes seemed to be dependent upon modifications rather of intensity than form. They were characterized by neither active movement nor varied coloring. My tabular observations will be published elsewhere, but I subjoin a rude attempt at analysis of their distinctive features.

1st. A mere illumination, apparently emerging from a dark cloud some five degrees above the horizon, more resembling a nebulous patch or a moonlight cirrus than the auroral light.

2d. Detached bands of illumination, impressed against the sky, like a condensed nebulosity, unconnected with any visible central arc, and distributed near about the line of the magnetic axis between the horizon and the zenith. These were sometimes stratiform, converging by perspective, and reminding one of the auroral plates, *plaques aurorales* of Lottin.

3d. A well-marked zone or band, or sometimes several concentric ones, either broken or continuous, unaccompanied by the ordinary segments of light or cloud, passing through or near the zenith in a direction which, according to the mean of some fourteen observations, was sixteen degrees east of the magnetic meridian. These bands were constantly varying, not by active scintillation, but by changes of intensity—rapid flashing augmentation, sudden subsidence, or complete extinction—a wavy oscillation, resembling wind action.

4th. Bistre-colored clouds, assuming a segmentary or arch-like form, and throwing out rays of white light; these streaming toward the zenith, and sometimes across to the opposite horizon, with more of coruscating movement than any other form. It was somewhat remarkable, that of six such displays observed in October and February, every one was in the direction of the sun, then not more than eight degrees below the horizon, and in one instance above it—a true daylight aurora. These jets, although not colored, might be looked upon as rudimentary forms of those dependent rays, now recognized by observers as corresponding in direction with the local magnetic inclination.

If we regard these forms as characterizing generally the auroras of this region, we can not help being struck with their departure from the indications observed by Lieut. Hood, in the Franklin Expedition of 1820. His observations may be referred to two general classes. The first commencing with arches, either to the east or west of the magnetic meridian, or coincident with it, sometimes four or five in number, rising in concentric series, and never less than 5° in altitude: these, upon reaching the zenith, become broad, irregular streams, never crossing each other, but coruscating with a rapid interior motion, rich with chromatic displays.

Those of the second class propagate themselves from points of the compass between the north and west, toward the opposite quarters, or sometimes from the southeast, and extending themselves to the northwest: they are arch-like in form; with beaming wreaths, flashing "merry dancers," and jets of pea-green, purple, and violet light, like the spark in an exhausted receiver. But in both classes the arches are in a plane seldom deviating more than two points from the magnetic meridian. Mr. Hood has not described a vibratory motion without colors.

In the auroras seen by the American Expedition, a distinct scintillation was rare; and I observed a prismatic tinting in only a single instance. The movements of the auroral bands were so wave-like that they were at once suggestive of wind-action, although no correspondence was noted between them and the direction of the lower atmospheric currents. This effect, which I had repeated occasion to observe, heightened the resemblance of our Arctic aurora to illuminated cirro-stratus, and, I confess, always impressed me with its want of altitude.

Let me condense from my Journal and Meteorological Record a description of the aurora, as we sometimes saw it.

The 2d of February came to us with sunshine, the atmosphere in yellow light, and full of minute spiculæ; our thermometers at 32°, my spirit standard at 34°, and Green's mercurial at 38°. Drawing the finger through the mercury of our artificial horizon gave the sensation of scalding water. The evaporation and increased dryness were very perceptible: a brass clinometer, which was coated with hoar-frost, became perfectly clean on exposure to the solar ray. The haze disappeared from the southern horizon, and the sky became strikingly clear. As late as half past eight A.M., I saw the North Star in the zenith, the tail of the Bear, and stars of the third and fourth magnitude. By nine every one had gone, leaving Arcturus and Capella in possession of the field.

Between the hours of six and eight P.M., we had an interesting display of the aurora. It was of a luminous white, not much more marked than any of the isolated nebulæ seen through a telescope, which it indeed resembled. This white light stretched in cumulated masses from the northwest to the southeastern horizon, forming to the northward an arch of some regularity. From the inner circumference of this great arch proceeded a series of scintillating processes, at apparent right angles to the plane of the horizon, and constantly shifting their positions, so as to produce an effect nearly like that of the "merry dancers." To the south, however, the arch became irregular and changing; its diameter varied from five to thirty degrees, the augmentation being by a broken series of parallel bands, no one exceeding six or eight degrees.

At the period of its greatest intensity, 7h. 10m., it enveloped Procyon and the Pleiades, obscuring the larger portion of Taurus, and actually hiding Aldebaran. A process extended obliquely from about twelve degrees above the horizon to Castor and Pollux, whose brightness it sensibly dimmed. The zone then narrowed, passing about eleven degrees to the west of Polaris, and ascending in a regular arch to the northwest. It faded gradually, and by 9h. 20m. had disappeared. Neither a silk-suspended magnetic needle nor our rude electrometers detected any disturbance.

The foggy segment which forms the characteristic feature of the incipient aurora, as observed by Biot, Mairan, Lottin, and others, was in a rudimentary form visible with us. The deep bistre-colored arc, which I have arbitrarily spoken of as No. 4, is in many of its features analogous to that of the Shetland and Bossekop Observations.

The well-known aurora of Mairan begins with a dark mist or foggy cloud to the northward, not unlike the "bistre-colored segment," taking gradually an arc-like form. The visible portion of this arc soon becomes surrounded with a pale light, followed by the formation of other concentric arcs: next come jets and colored rays from the dark part of the segment, breaking up its continuity, and indicating a general movement throughout its mass—"internal shocks," as Lardner calls them—which issue from it as flames from a conflagration.

Lottin's observations at Bossekop, in Finland, latitude 70°, which embrace no less than a hundred and forty-five exhibitions, begin with a "tinting of the constantly prevailing sea-fog," the upper border of which was fringed with auroral light.

If these, and the more familiar accounts of the aurora in the middle United States, be taken as good types of this phenomenon, I would say that the matured Arctic aurora resembled their incipient stages; but that the same law of correspondence, which marks the centre of the segment in or about the magnetic axis, gave to us, situated as we were in the immediate proximity of the magnetic pole of our earth, the strange spectacle of a complete arch passing through or near the zenith, and embracing an amplitude of nearly one hundred and eighty degrees. The zone or band-like character of this auroral arch was its pervading characteristic. It seldom exceeded thirty, and was generally within ten degrees in width, a floating, waving band of nebulous illumination.

The likeness between some of the auroral appearances and a lower range of meteorological phenomena has been repeatedly noticed. The *bandes polaires* of Humboldt, the *plaques aurorales* of Lottin, the cirro-cumulated resemblances of Hood and Richardson, are among these: and I have alluded more than once myself to the apparent wind-movements of our exhibitions in Lancaster Sound.

I have quoted the "fog or cloud-like segment" as forming a prominent feature in the Continental descriptions, for the purpose of introducing from my journal two anomalous exhibitions of aurora in the same connection. One was in direct conjunction with the diffracted solar ray; the other a true daylight aurora. I give them verbatim from my notes.

"*February* 7. Cold and clear: thermometer, at 8h. 40m. A.M., at 38°, while on the vessel's stern; and at 42° when freely suspended by the bows outside: my Green's spirit standard, some fifty paces from the vessel, at −48°: one more illustration of the local influences of ship-board, and of the irregularity of our system of registration.

"The sun was completely visible at about ten A.M.; but his rays were subdued by a slight haziness, caused by myriads of crystallized specks that filled the atmosphere. These, when examined by my traveling Frauenhofer at two hundred diameters, gave in some few cases regular hexagonal prisms, with well-defined terminations; but this symmetry of form was generally obscured by groupings, and long oblique truncations. I have now made eight careful examinations of these crystalline spiculæ at varying temperatures, when they came to us accompanied by parhelia, halos, or anomalous columns proceeding from the sun. In every case there was a decided approach to the six-sided form.

"The sun to-day exhibited an unusual phenomenon. At 10h. 20m., while very low, a column of light was observed stretching from the upper summit of its disk to an approximate height of 15°. This expanded, fan-fashion, as it rose, and was lost by its penciled radiations blending with the illuminated sky. Thus far it did not differ materially from the vertical or crepuscular rays accompanying rudimentary forms of parhelia. But by eleven o'clock this fan-like column had enlarged to a cloudy shaft of bright yellow light, twenty to twenty-four degrees in height, and proceeding from a complete segment of illumination, which was thickly studded with cirrous clouds. The upper terminus of this column, unlike the parhelia which we had seen before, assumed a curvilinear wedge shape not unlike the section of a pear, from whose sides rose tangentially a series of penciled illuminations terminating in streaks of cloud strata.

"The feature about this phenomenon of greatest interest was a distinct play of light, a series of coruscating changes resembling the scintillations of the aurora. The rays which shot out from the three-curved summit sometimes extended twelve or fifteen degrees, with a sudden movement of increased energy almost resembling ignition: then again they retired, until represented by but a few feeble points. The cloud-like segment showed in a lesser degree the same movements; and at the periods of most active display, the vertical or fan-like shaft flashed up into more intense illumination. The diameter of this shaft at its entering base could not have been less than eighty degrees."

This singular exhibition recalled irresistibly the analogous phenomena of the aurora, with those anomalous displays of coronæ which have been referred to the diffraction of light by atmospheric vesicles or icy spiculæ. I give it from my notes, as a simple detail of facts, without comment or opinion.

A daylight aurora has been described by other observers. I witnessed several, one of them interesting enough to be worth transcribing.

"About ten o'clock, going out to exercise at football, I noticed that the usual cloud-bank of the horizon had nearly cleared away at the south. One or two feathery cirri hung about the zenith, and the northern horizon retained its usual deep obscurity. This was in the course of my usual cursory examination for my weather record. Half an hour after, I observed one spot where the banking remained, attracting attention by its nearness to the sun and its well-defined segmentary character. Its margin was distinctly and regularly arched; its tinting a peculiar purple, slightly warmed or bronzed at its margins, but deepening into a heavy brown at the line of the horizon. The centre of the segment bore south twenty degrees west (magnetic), its altitude eight degrees, nearly. Smoke and vapor from ship's fires, purple-tinted; distant objects not very clearly visible; atmosphere filled with ice spiculæ.

"Soon from the circumference of this arch proceeded a fimbriated or fringy series of purple cirri, delicately tinted at their edges, increasing with wonderful regularity, and extending in long, ray-like processes of cloud to an altitude of some twenty degrees above the horizon. Before eleven o'clock these processes had become long, stratiform illuminated clouds, beautifully marked, of a breadth, measured roughly by the eye, of four or five degrees, interrupted where they crossed the illuminated region of the sun, but every where else extending over the heavens to the south and west (true); and although still diminishing in intensity, extending nearly to the eastern quarter of the sky. By coalescing at their bases, these radiating processes augmented the size of the central segment. The intervals between them appeared, by contrast, to be artificially illuminated.

"Till now there had been no movement; but at 11h. 20m. these cloud-like processes or radiations strikingly resembled the rays or beams of a coruscating auroral arch. Dr. Vreeland and myself witnessed repeatedly interruptions of their continuity; then sudden shootings out, or increasings of their length; and then a rapid and momentary formation, followed by a sudden and complete disappearance.

"At this time, too, a strange wavy movement was seen about the shorter prolongations in the neighborhood of the vertex of the mass. These resembled the rising wreaths of 'frost-smoke' seen in Wellington Channel, and had an appearance almost of combustion.

"During all these phases, the cloud-like character was singularly preserved: the rays appeared to modify the processes, as light would behind our ordinary clouds. The whole exhibition was a daylight one, perfectly cloud-like, differing only in the elements of shape, movement, and radiated illumination. It was a day aurora.

The appearance continued until twenty minutes of meridian. At 11h. 10m., when it was at its maximum, the rayed prolongations stretched nearly across the sky; and the centre of the mass from which they emanated was fifteen degrees west from the south pole of the needle. At about the same deviation, viz., N. by E. ½ E., and at a rude altitude of about fifteen or twenty degrees, was an irregular cirro-cumulated cloud of the same purple tint, but not so much illuminated. From its eastern margin, rays or processes were seen stretching as high as fifty degrees, and as far as due east.

"Before the sun had reached his meridian altitude, the prolongations had become faint, and passed into detached feathery clouds, which collected at the zenith and lost the radiated arrangement altogether. The mass of cloud stratus to the south (magnetic), also, had blended with the usual bank about the horizon."

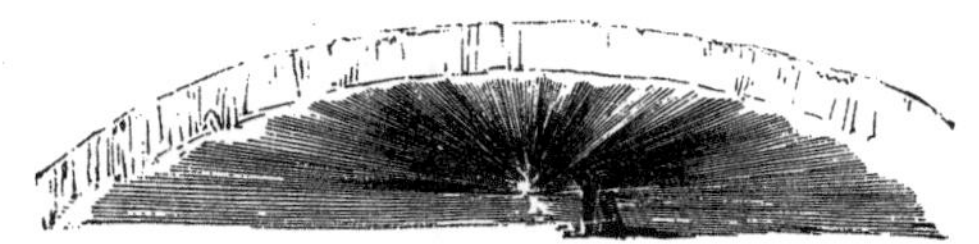

THE RESCUE IN HER ICE-DOCK.

CHAPTER XXXVI.

Our brig was still resting on her cradle, and her consort on the floe a short distance off, when the first month of spring came to greet us. We had passed the latitude of 72°.

To prepare for our closing struggle with the ice-fields, or at least divide its hazards, it was determined to refit the Rescue. To get at her hull, a pit was sunk in the ice around her, large enough for four men to work in at a time, and eight feet deep, so as to expose her stern, and leave only eighteen inches of the keel imbedded. This novel dry-dock answered perfectly. The hull was inspected, and the work of repair was pressed so assiduously, that in three days the stern-post was in its place, and the new bowsprit ready for shipping. We had now the chances of two ships again in case of disaster.

Since the middle of February the felt housing of our vessel had shown a disposition to throw off its snowy crust. There was an apparent recession, or, rather, want of adhesion about it, that spoke of change. But it was not till the 7th of March that we witnessed an actual thaw. On the black planking of the brig's quarter, in full sun glare, the snow began to move, and fell, leaving a moist stain. This was either evaporated or frozen instantly; but still it had been there, unequivocal moisture. A sledge, too, alongside the vessel, kept laden to meet emergencies, with a black felt cover, gave on its southern side a warm impression to the unmittened hand; and several drops of water rolled from its mounting of snow, and formed in minute icicles.

With these cheering signs of returning warmth came a sensible improvement in my cases of scurvy. I ascribed it in a great degree to the free use of saurkraut and lime-juice, and to the constant exercise which was enforced as part of our sanitary discipline. But I attributed it also to the employment of hydrochloric acid, applied externally with friction, and taken internally as a tonic. The idea of this remedy, hitherto, so far as I know, unused in scurvy, occurred to me from its effects in cachectic cases of mercurial syphilis. I am, I fear, heterodox almost to infidelity as to the direct action of remedies, and rarely allow myself to claim a sequence as a result; but, according to the accepted dialectics of the profession, the *Acid. chlorohyd. dilut.* may be recommended as singularly adapted to certain stages of scorbutus.

The great difficulty that every one has encountered in treating this disease is in the reluctance of the patient to rouse himself so as to excite the system by cheerful, glowing exercise, and in the case of seamen, to control their diet. My ingenuity was often taxed for expedients to counteract these predispositions. Some that I resorted to were ludicrous enough.

James Stewart, with purpuric blotches and a stiff

knee, had to wag his leg half an hour by the dial, opposite a formidable magnet, each wag accompanied by a shampooing knead. Stewart had faith; the muscular action, which I had enjoined so often ineffectually, was brought about by a bit of steel and a smear ing of red sealing-wax. They cured him.

Another, remarkable for a dirty person, of well used-up capillary surface, a hard case—one of a class scarcely ever seen by any but navy doctors—sponged freely and regularly from head to foot in water colored brown by coffee, and made acid with vinegar. His gums improved at once. He would never have washed with *aqua fontana*.

Another set of fellows adhered pertinaciously to their salt junk and hard tack, ship bread and beef. These conservative gentlemen gave me much trouble by repelling vegetable food. The scurvy was playing the very deuce with them, when the bright idea occurred to me of converting the rejected delicacies into an abominable doctor-stuff. It was an appeal to their spirit of martyrdom: they became heroes. Three times a day did these high-spirited fellows drink a wine glass of olive-oil and lime-juice, followed by raw potato and saur-kraut, pounded with molasses into a damnable electuary. They ate nobly, and got well.

But the causes of scurvy were relaxing their energies only for the time. Before the month was out, the disease had come back with renewed and even exacerbated virulence. Some of its phases were curious. The joint of Captain De Haven's second finger became the seat of severe pain, accompanied by a distinct tubercle cartilaginous to the touch. It exactly recalled, he said, the appearance and feeling of the part for some months after it had been hurt by a schoolmaster's ruler twenty-five years before. One of the crew had his tongue completely excoriated. Another, who had lost a molar tooth seven years ago, spit from the cavity a conoidal wedge: I had no chance of examining it by the microscope; but an impression of the cavity in wax showed the sides perfectly smooth, and the vertex intersected by lines of ossification. I have spoken already of my lance mark in the groin: it had been healed some three years; but it now threatened suppuration again wherever it bore the marks of the surgeon's knife.

We had unfortunately almost exhausted our supply of antiscorbutic drinks, and were driven to the manufacture of substitutes not always the most palatable. One of them, which served at least as a vehicle for lime-juice and muriate of iron, was, however, a recognized exception. It was a beer, of which a remnant of dried peaches and some raisins, with barley and brown sugar, formed the fermenting basis. The men drank it in most liberal quantities.

On the 10th we had an exhibition of the day aurora again, less brilliant than the one I have described a few pages back, but quite well marked. It was followed at night by the paraselene. Another atmospheric display, which occurred a few days afterward, attracted more notice.

"*March* 13. Again a day of bright sunshine, but to my feelings colder than our lowest temperatures. The thermometer stood at $-24°$ in the shade at noon, and the wind was very light. Yet there was a cutting asperity about it that made your face tingle—a sensation as if evaporation was going on under the skin—quite a painful one. At four in the afternoon the atmosphere was studded with glistening particles. I have never seen them so manifest and so numerous. Our slide, a polished surface of clear ice, became clouded in a few minutes, and before five o'clock it was perfectly white. The microscope gave me the same broken hexagonal prisms, mixed with tables closely resembling the snow-crystal. A haze surrounded the horizon, rising for some six degrees in a bronzed, purple bank; after which it gradually blended with the sky, a clear blue, undisturbed by cirri.

"Accompanying this redundancy of atmospheric spiculæ was a parhelion of remarkable intensity. There was no halo round the sun, and no vertical or horizontal column; but at the distance of 22° 04′ from the sun's centre were three solar images, one on each side, and the other immediately above the sun. This latter image was intensely luminous, but not prismatic; the others had the rudiments of an arc, highly colored, the red upon the inner margin. The haze rose as high as these horizontal images; and the arc, which in so short a segment presented no visible curvature, expanded as it descended, so as to form an elongated pyramid or column, the prismatic tints increasing in intensity as they approached the horizon. The effect of this was that of two illuminated beacons or rainbow towers, the sun blazing between them. As we stood a little way off on the ice, it was very beautiful to see the brig, with its spars and rigging cutting like tracery against the central light, with these prismatic structures on each side, capped by a spectral sun."

Two evenings later, the parhelia gave us another spectacle of interest. Two mock suns, which had accompanied the sun below the horizon, sent up an illuminated and colored arc some eight or ten degrees in height. Midway rose a brush-like column of crimson (*baryta*) light. A series of flame-colored strata, alternating with an incomprehensible black cloud, was so completely eclipsed by the vertical column, that it seemed to cut its way without a diminution of its brightness. The whole atmosphere was as warmly tinted as in the evenings of Melville Bay.

Indeed, from the beginning of the month, the skies had undergone a sensible change of aspect. Instead of the heavy-banked or linear stratus about the horizon, and the light, cold cirri above, we were getting back to something like the fall skies of our own climate, the misty bands of morning becoming fleecy as the day wore on, and taking the marbled or mackerel character before they blended with the western skies.

I am tempted to apologize, once for all, for the imperfect character of these observations. Our stock of instruments on board was scanty at the best, and the routine observances of a ship of war do not favor the prosecution of merely scientific researches. We had no actinometer to mark the daily increments of solar radiation: our thermometers were generally of rude construction, and were not so placed as to give the highest value to their results; and an entry which I find in my journal explains why my barometrical records were so few.

"*March* 12. To-day, for the first time during the cruise, I had the pleasure of seeing our mountain barometer released from its stowage, and an attempt made to compare it with our aneroids. Before we began our drift to the north, when we had no fires below to give us a constantly vibrating temperature, and the aneroid of the Rescue had not come into the overcrowded cabin of our vessel to divide the formalities of registration with our own, it might have been well to make a careful comparison of the two with those of the British vessels, and with our mountain barometer also. The index error of this instrument on its zero point could have been adjusted then by reference to others that were just from Greenwich, and it would have been practicable, perhaps, to give something of increased value to our log-book records of the atmospheric pressure. Under all the circumstances, I have not thought it necessary to transfer them to my journal."

As the middle of March approached, our drift became gradually slower, until we almost reached a state of rest. For several days we advanced at an average rate of scarcely half a mile a day. We were at this time some seventy miles east of Cape Adair, our nearest Greenland shore being somewhere between Upper Navik and Disco; and the idea of encountering the final break-up among the closely-impacted masses that surrounded us, or of being carried back to the north by some inopportune counter-current, was far from pleasant. But our log-line, in an attempt at soundings, showed still a marked under-draught toward the south; and in a few days more we were moving southward again with increased velocity.

The 19th gave us a change of scene. I was aroused from my morning sleep by the familiar voice of Mr. Murdaugh, as he hurried along the half-deck: "Ice opening"—"Open leads off our starboard quarter"—"Frost-smoke all around us!" Five minutes afterward, Henri had been summoned from the galley; and, carbine in hand, I was tumbling over the hummocks.

After a heavy walk of half a mile, sure enough there it was—the open lead—stretching with its film of forming ice far in a narrowing perspective to the east and west. Balboa himself never looked out upon an ocean with more grateful feelings than I did upon this open chasm, the first inbreak upon complete solidity which we had known since the 15th of January. It was a breach in our prison-walls. The undulatory movement of the mercury and the varied appearance of the clouds were now explained. Although only discovered this morning, the rupture must have been going on for days, perhaps a week. Our winds had favored the separation of cracks into wide channels; but how such changes could have taken place puzzled me.

The ice, as shown by my measurements, was from four to eight feet; and even now, when I recall the fearful sounds which accompanied the Lancaster Sound commotions, I can hardly realize that such extensive chasms should have been formed almost in silence. We could only guess what had been the extent of our ice-field at this time. Baffin's Bay was nearly three hundred miles across, and the field may have been twice as long in the other direction. Perhaps the wave action of a heavy sea, great sub-glacial billows, unfelt at our fast-cemented little vessel, may have broken the tables without the crash and tumult of a collision.

The lead where I first reached it, to the southeast of our brig, was nearly three hundred yards across; not, however, three hundred yards of open water, but a separation between the two sides of the original floe of about that distance. The sides still showed their clean-edged fracture, diversified by drift and hummock, and rising above the intervening level, like the banks of a tideless river, margined by new ice and crusted with efflorescing snow. But at its further or southern side, a long strip, narrow and very black, gave evidence of open water. In this, surrounded by exhaling mist and frost-smoke, were our old friends, the seal; grave, hirsute-looking fellows, who rose out of the water breast-high, and gazed upon us with the curious faces of old times. Near them was a solitary dovekie, dressed in its gray winter plumage, the first bird I had seen for days; here, too, had crossed the tracks of a bear.

All this was very cheering. To see something, no matter what, checkering the waste of white snow, was like a shady grove to men sun-tired in a prairie; but to see life again—life, tenanting the desolate air and inhospitable sea—was a spring of water in the desert. My old hostility to gun-murder was forgotten. I wasted, of course, some small remnant of poetic sympathy with fellow-life thus springing up out of the wilderness; but then, in the midst of my sympathies, came the destructive instinct which longed to make it subservient to my wants. The scurvy, the scurvy patients, myself among the rest!—but the seal and the dovekies kept themselves out of shot.

At this lead we saw the recent frost-smoke within a few yards of us in pointed tongues of vapor: further off, the long, wreathy brown clouds were rising. I never before, not even in Wellington Channel, saw this phenomenon in greater perfection: in Wellington it was an interesting, sometimes a gloomy feature; here it was imposing. As far back as the twelfth, we had caught glimpses of brown vapor in this very direction: we now learned to look upon it in certain phases as an unerring indication of open water, and wondered that we did not so regard it earlier.

The chasms were not limited to the long lead before us. They extended to the east and west indefinitely; and were intersected by transverse fissures, which so met each other as completely to surround our vessels. From this circuit the frost-smoke was rising. The thermometer stood at $-20°$, fifty-two degrees below the freezing point in the shade; but the sun was shining brilliantly, raising the mercury to $+10°$. Under these circumstances, theoretically so favorable, this Arctic phenomenon became the most prominent feature in the scene.

As I stood upon a tall knob of hummock, the entire horizon seemed to be sending up, exhaling a bronzine smoke—not the lambent, smoky wreaths which I have compared to burning turpentine, but a peculiar russet brown smoke, tongued and wreathy when near, but at a distance rolling in cumulated masses. These seemed to cling at their bases to the surface from which they rose, like the discharges of artillery over water, or a locomotive steaming over a cold, wet meadow. They were wafted by the wind, so as to drive them out in lines two or three hundred yards long; but they clung tenaciously to the water and young ice, giving us a varying but always narrow horizon of smoke. The Rescue was enveloped with the heavy, sooty clouds of repeated broadsides. If I had seen the flashing of guns or the glimmer of burning prairie-grass, I should have been less impressed; so strange, very strange, was this ordinary attendant on conflagration rolling in the midst of our winteriness.

THE ICE-PACK OPENING, MARCH 21.

CHAPTER XXXVII.

"*March* 20. Thursday, the 20th of March, opens with a gale, a regular gale. On reaching deck after breakfast, I found the wind from the southeast, the thermometer at zero, and rising. These southeast storms are looked upon as having an important influence on the ice. They are always warm, and by the sea which they excite at the southern margin of the pack, have a great effect in breaking the floes. Mr. Olrik told me that they were anxiously looked for on the Greenland coast as precursors of open water. The date of the southeast gale last year, at Uppernavik, was April 25th. Our thermometer gave +5° at noonday, +7° at one, and +8° at three o'clock!!

"This is the heaviest storm we have had since entering Lancaster Sound, exactly seven months and a day ago. The snow is whirled in such quantities, that our thick felt housing seems as if of gauze: it not only covers our decks, but drives into our clothes like fine dust or flour. A plated thermometer was invisible fourteen feet from the eye: from the distance of ten paces off on our quarter, a white opacity covers every thing, the compass-stand, fox-traps, and all beyond: the Rescue, of course, is completely hidden. This heavy snow-drift exceeds any thing that I had conceived, although many of my Arctic English friends had discoursed to me eloquently about their perils and discomforts. As to facing it in a stationary position, nothing human could; for a man would be buried in ten minutes. Even in reaching our little Tusculum, we tumble up to our middle, in places where a few minutes before the very ice was laid bare. The entire topography of our ice is changing constantly.

"7 P.M. 'The wind is howling.' Our mess begin to talk again of sleeping in boots, and the other luxuries of Lancaster Sound. For my own part, better, far better this, with the spicy tingling of a crisis, than the corroding, scurvy-engendering sameness of the past two months. Every moment now is full of expectation.

"*March* 21. The wind changed this morning to the westward, and by daylight was blowing freshly. After breakfast, Murdaugh and myself started on a tramp to the 'open water,' to see the effects of the gale. The drift was beyond conception; sufficient, in many places, to have covered up our whole ship's company. The wind made it as cold at -5° as I have seen it at -30°, and the fine snow pelted our faces; but the surface was frozen so hard that we walked over the crust, and in a little over half an hour we reached the lead.

"Planting a signal pole, with a red silk handkerchief as a mark, and taking compass-bearings to guide us back again, we began to look around us. Oui expectations of hummock action were agreeably disappointed. We thought that the storm would have driven the ice from the southward, and that the change of wind would have marshaled opposing floes to meet it. But it was not so. Even the young, marginal ice, though warped, was unbroken. The pressure had evidently taken place, but with little effect. After the gigantic upheavings of Lancaster Sound, excited by winds much weaker, no wonder I was surprised. Upon thinking it over, I came to the conclusion that the absence of a *point d'appui*, either of land or land-ice, was the cause of these diminished actions. We were now in a great sea, surrounded by consolidated floes, and away from salient capes or shore-bound ice. The pressure was diffused throughout a greater mass, without points of special or even unequal resistance. If this reasoning hold, we will not experience the expected tumult until we drift into a region where forces are more in opposition; perhaps not until we reach the contraction of Davis' Straits.

"The young ice margin of this open lead had the appearance of a beautiful wave-flattened sand beach. The lead itself had opened so far that its opposite shores were barely visible. The wind checked the immediate formation of new ice; and, to our inexpressible joy, there, glittering in the cold sunlight, were little rippling waves. So long have we been pent up by this wretched circle of unchanging snow, that I make myself ridiculous by talking of trifles, with which you, milk-drinking, sun-basking, melted-water-seeing people at home can have no sympathy.

In spite of the winds and the snow-drift, I could hear the babbling of these waves as they laughed in their temporary freedom.

"*March* 22, Saturday. I started again for the ice-openings. There had evidently been a good deal of commotion in the night; but nothing so violent as to negative my yesterday's conclusions. Still there were hummocks of young tables, and some ugly twists of the beach line; and matters had not yet settled themselves into rest. As the great floe on which I stood traveled, under the influence of the west wind, obliquely eastward, I heard once more the familiar sounds of our *noctes Lancastrianæ*. The grating of nutmegs, the cork rubbing of old-fashioned tables, the young puppies, and the bee-hives; all these were back again; but we missed pleasantly the wailing, the howling, the clattering, the exploding din, which used to come to us through the darkness. The pulse-like interval was there too, like a breathing-time; but the daylight modified every thing, my feelings most of all. They became almost pleasant, as I listened, after a lullaby fashion, to the bees and puppies; and something very like gratitude came over me, as I thought of the uncertain gloom or palpable midnight which accompanied a few weeks ago the 'voices of the ice.' The thermometer was 21° below zero, and the wind blowing: naturally enough, my nose became a tallow nose in the midst of my reverie. So I rubbed the nose, blew the nose, buffeted my armpits until my fingers tingled, and then started off on a tramp.

"Seal were seen, curious as usual, but indulging in the weakness afar off. Presently two poor winter-mated little divers met my meat-seeking senses. One of these I killed with my rifle, covetously regretting that my one ball could not align his mate. This was the first game we had obtained since the fall: he was divided, poor fellow, between two of my scurvy patients. In getting this bird out, I came very near getting myself in; and that, when a ducking means a freezing, is no fun.

"10 P.M. To-night finds me knocked up. Be it known, that after crawling on my belly, not like the wisest of animals, for two hours, I came nearly within shot of a week's fresh meat. The fresh meat dived, first shaking his whisker tentacles at my disconsolate beard, leaving me half frozen and wholly discontented. Fool-like, after the long walk back, the warming, the drying, and the feeding, I returned by the other long walk to the ice-openings, tramped for two hours, saw nothing but frost-smoke, and came back again, dinnerless, with legs quaking, and spirits wholly out of tune.

"Our drift to-day, at meridian, was in the neighborhood of 9 miles; our latitude was 71° 9′ 18″.

"*March* 23, Sunday. After divine service, started for the ice-openings. We are now in the centre of an area, which we estimated roughly as four miles from north to south, and a little more east and west. On reaching what was yesterday's sea-beach, I was forced to recant in a measure my convictions as to the force of the opposing floes. Yesterday's beach existed no longer; it was swallowed up, crushed, crumbled, submerged, or uplifted in long ridges of broken ice.

"The actions were still in progress, and fast intruding upon the solid old ice which is our homestead. The ice-tables now crumbling into hummocks were from eight to fourteen inches thick, generally ten. Not even in Lancaster Sound did the destruction of surface go on more rapidly. The wind was a moderate breeze from the northwest, and the floes were advancing on each other at a rate of a knot and a half an hour, building up hummock tables along their line of collision. Several rose in a few minutes to a height of ten or twelve feet. I have become so accustomed to these glacial eruptions, that I mounted the upheaving ice, and rode upon the fragments—an amusement I could hardly have practiced safely before I had studied their changes.

"The snow-covered level upon which Brooks and myself were walking was about thirty paces wide, between the older ice on one side and the encroaching hummock-line on the other. Upon our return, after a walk of a short half mile, we found our footsteps obliterated, and the hummock-line within a few yards of this older ice. Things are changing rapidly.

"A new crack was reported at one o'clock, about the third of a mile from our ship; and the bearings of the sun showed that our brig had, for the first time since entering Baffin's Bay, rotated considerably to the northward. Here were two subjects for examination. So, as soon as dinner was over, I started with Davis and Willie, two of my scurvy henchmen, on a walk to the openings. Reaching the recent crack, we found the ice five feet four inches thick, and the black water, in a clear streak a foot wide, running to the east and west.* I had often read of Esquimaux being carried off by the separation of these great floes; but, knowing that our guns could call assistance from the brig, we jumped over and hurried on. We were well paid.

* This direction, transverse to the long axis of Baffin's Bay, seems to be that of most of our fissures.

"The hummockings of this morning had ceased; the wind so gentle as hardly to be perceptible: the lead before me was an open river of water, and in it were narwhals (*M. monoceros*), in groups of five or six, rolling over and over, after the manner of the dolphin tribe. They were near me; so near that I could see their checkered backs, and enjoy the rich coloring that decorates them. The horn, that monodontal process which gives them their name of sea-unicorn, was perfectly examinable. Rising in a spirally indented cone, this beautiful appendage appeared sometimes eight and ten feet out of water; one especially, whose tall curvetings astonished my body-guard. I never saw a more graceful, striking, and beautiful exhibition than the unrestrained play of these narwhals.* In the same open water, almost in company with the narwhals, were white whales (*Delphinopterus albicans*, or *Beluga:* these cetacea have so many names, they puzzle me), and seal besides.

"I was tempted to stay too long. The wind sprang up suddenly. The floe began to move. I thought of the crack between me and the ship, and started off. The walking, however, was very heavy, and my scurvy patients stiff in the extensors. By the time I reached the crack, it had opened into a chasm, and a river as broad as the Wissahiccon ran between me and our ship. After some little anxiety—not much—I saw our captain ordering a party to our relief. The sledges soon appeared, dragged by a willing par-

* I have seen many of these fish since, but never under such circumstances. I stood on a ledge of hummock within short gunshot. The animals were entirely unapprehensive. The non-symmetrical character of the "horn" (an unduly developed tooth, say the naturalists) was not seen; and as this long lance-like process played about at a constantly varying angle, it reminded me of the mast of some sunken boat swayed by the waves.

ty; the India rubber boat was lowered into the lead, and the party ferried over. So ends this last trip to these ice-openings.

"It is evident that these gradual crack-formings and chasm-openings, with the hummocking and other attendant actions, are but preludes to a complete breaking up. Our previous observations show that the disruption of these large areas can not be effected suddenly. It is a gradual process; so gradual, even in Lancaster Sound, as to allow time for personal escape, although the vessel be a victim.

"From the 12th of January, the date of our last break-up, down to the present movement, is two months. The intense cold, with feeble winds and the absence of impact or collisions, have kept up the integrity of this great pack. I think it may reasonably be doubted whether it will now close again before our liberation or destruction. The excessive thickness of the tables, the wave and tidal actions, the mildening temperature, and the probable continuance of winds, all point to this. We have already a system of fissures within a third of a mile of us; and a continued augmentation of their number must soon place us in a centre of commotion. It is pleasant by one's ice-experience to anticipate the state of things: and now that the battle is coming on again, I make a record of these reasoned expectations, to show you hereafter how well I am reasoning.

"One thing more: the days have stolen upon us—longer, and longer, and longer, until now the long twilight lets me read on deck as late as eight P.M. In fact, the sun's greatest depression below the horizon is now 18°, the limit of theoretical twilight.

"*March* 26, Wednesday. The same peculiar crisping or crackling sound, which I noted on the 2d of February, was heard this morning in every direction. This sound, as the 'noise accompanying the aurora,' has been attributed by Wrangell and others, ourselves among the rest, to changes of atmospheric temperature acting upon the crust of the snow. We heard it most distinctly between seven and eight A.M., when the solar ray should begin to affect the snow. The mercury stood at −27° at five, rising to −19° by nine A.M., and attaining a maximum of −2° by noonday. But this is not to be regarded as indicating the temperature of the snow surface. The snow, when horizontal, according to all my observations, differs but little in temperature from the atmosphere, owing probably to its oblique reception of the solar ray; while the snow-coverings of the hummocks and angular floe-tables, which receive the rays at right angles, show by repeated trials a marked augmentation. I venture, therefore, to refer this peculiar crisping sound to the unequal contraction and dilatation of these unequally presenting surfaces, not to a sudden change of atmospheric temperature acting upon the snow.

"To-day we saw a couple of icebergs looking up in the far south.

"*March* 27, Thursday. The sun shone out, but not as yesterday. The little cirrous clouds interfere with its brightness, and affect very perceptibly its warmth. To the eye, however, the day is undimmed.

"The wind, which we watch closely as the index of our ice-changes, our leading variety, came out at seven in the evening from the northward; and with it came a rise of black frost-smoke to the south, showing that the old ice-opening had gaped again. I had started before this at half past five, with old Blinn, my faithful satellite, for a bright plain, glittering in the low sunshine some three miles to the west, a new direction. We did not get back till eight.

"Let me make a picture for you without a jot of fancy about it, and you may get H. to put it into colors if he can. The sun was low, very low; and his long, slanting beams, of curious indescribable purple, fell upon old Blinn and myself as we sat on a crag of ice which overhung the sea. The chasm was perhaps a mile wide, and the opposite ice-shores were so painted by the glories of the sunshine, that they appeared like streaks of flame, licking continuous water. The place to which we had worked ourselves had been subjected to forces which no one could realize, so chaotic, and enormous, and incomprehensible were they. A line of old floe, eight feet thick and four miles long, had been powdered into a pedragal of crushed sugar, rising up in great efflorescing knobs fifteen and twenty feet high; and from amid these, like crystal rocks from the foam of a cataract, came transparent tables of blue ice, floating, as it were, on unsubstantial whiteness. Some of these blocks measured eight feet in thickness by twenty-two long, and of indeterminate depth, one side being obliquely buried in the mass. On one of these tables, that stretched out like a glass spear-point, directly over the water, were straddled your brother and his companion. Underneath us the narwhals were passing almost within pole-reach. As they rolled over, much after the fashion of our own porpoises, I could see the markings of their backs, and the great suction of their jaws throwing the water into eddies. Seal, breast-high, were treading water with their horizontal tails, and the white whale was blowing purple sprays into the palpable sunshine.

"*March* 23, Friday. I visited the western opening of yesterday. The sea has dwindled to a narrow lane. flanked by the heavy hummocks, whose rupture formed the sides. Although the aperture was so distant yesterday that I could barely see the further banks, here and there dotting the horizon, it has now closed with such nice adaptation of its line of fracture, that, but for a few yards of lateral deviation, this 'yesternight sea' would be nothing but a crack in the ice-field. The area of filmy ice that was between the edges of the lead had been thrust under the floe, thus aiding the process of re-cementation. These ice-actions are very complicated and various.

"Retracing my steps by a long circuit to the southward, I came to a spot where, without any apparent axis of fracture (chasm), the ice presented all the phenomena of table-hummocks. It was very old and thick, at least nine feet in solid depth. About a little circle of a hundred yards diameter, it had been thrown up into variously-presenting surfaces, with a marked bearing toward a focus of greatest energy and accumulation, presenting an appearance almost eruptive. The crushed fragments exuding and falling over, and rolling down toward the level ice, so as to cover it for feet in depth with powdery, granulated rubbish:

REMAINS OF A BERG.

THE FLOE IN APRIL.

CHAPTER XXXVIII.

My journal for the closing days of March and the early ones of April is full of varying drifts and alternating temperatures. Still, it seemed as if, by some gradual though scarcely explicable process, the work of our extrication was going on. Sometimes the wind would come to us from the southeast—the breaking-up wind, as we called it, because as it subsided the reaction of the floes developed itself in fissures; but more frequently from the north, expediting our course to a more genial latitude. The floes themselves were, however, much more massive and gnarled than any we had seen before: every party that left the vessel for an ice-tramp came back with exaggerated impressions of the mighty energies that had hurled them together. We felt that it would have been impossible for any organized structure of wood and metal to resist such Maelstroms of solid ice as had left these memorials around us, and looked forward with scarcely pleasurable anticipations to the equivalent forces that might be required to obliterate them. Some extracts from my journal may show how far other causes were in the mean time operating our release.

"*April* 7, Monday. For the last fortnight the ice has been perceptibly moist at the surface. The open crack near our brig to the south has now been closed for nearly a fortnight; yet the snow which covers it is quite slushy. The trodden paths around our ship are in muddy pulp, adhering to the boots. All this can hardly be the direct influence of the sun upon the surface; for the thermometer seldom exceeds +16°, and is more generally below +10° at noonday. Yet this temperature has an evident influence upon the status of the ice, increasing its permeability, and permitting some changes analogous to thawing, but which I can not explain. May it be that the crystalline structure of the ice is undergoing some modification, that increases its capilarity, or develops an action like the endosmose and exosmose!

"It is a mere puzzle, of course, for we have not data enough to make it a question. Yet there is another like it that I can not help setting down. Can it be that our thermometers, so notorious in this Polar region for their imperfect coincidence with 'sensations of cold,' are equally fallacious as measures of absolute increments or decrements of sensible caloric? It will not do, I suppose, to admit such a supposition; yet the marvels which come constantly before me may almost justify it. You know that I am no heat-maker. Well! my winter trials, as you may imagine, have not increased my vital energies. Suppose me, then, as you knew me when I left New York. For the past week I have almost lived in the open air—genial, soft, bland, and to sensation just cool enough to be pleasantly tonic. I walk moderately, and am in comfortable, glowing warmth. I walk over the hummocks or ice floes, and am oppressed with perspiration and lassitude. This at a temperature of zero in the shade, and +11° in the sun!!! I can not realize it. To-day the thermometer gave +10° in the shade of the ship, obviously affected not a little by radiation, +34° in the sun over the ship's painted side, +13° by my own observation of an instrument suspended at a distance from the ship, and under the same circumstances in the shade, *zero!* Yet the day seemed spring-like and delicious. The early breezes (8 A.M.) from the southeast came with a sensation of reviving coolness, although to their warmth we perhaps owed our sensations of pleasant heat. While I am writing, the skaters come in to say that 'it is too warm to skate:' yet the sun is low, and my shade thermometer gives some ten degrees below the point of freezing.

"I have often alluded to this discrepancy between our feelings and the recorded temperature. I have read of the same thing in the Arctic voyages, with a reference to contrast for the explanation. But I never until to-day realized so fully that we were warmed from within by a mysterious, and, I must believe, unknown system of functional compensation. I wish Liebig could make a Polar voyage!! As you feel open-windowed at the first breaking-in day of Spring, with your thermometers at vernal 60°, so feel I with the thermometer at zero!!

"*April* 10, Thursday, 2 P.M. The southeaster blows on with steady endurance. It is now east by south; a snow-storm reminding me of home, so soft and flaky, drifting every where; and the thermometer rising steadily to +32 at noonday. Once more at the freezing point!! it seems hard to realize. The decks are wet, the housing dripping, the snow adhesive and slushy.

"9 P.M. The gale continues. Our thermometer outside at a maximum of +33°. Every thing wet, warm, and summer-like.

"I have a story to tell—a foolish adventure; but I was ennuied past all bearing. Walking the deck, beast-like, in our damp cage, it occurred to me that I would climb the rigging. Climb the rigging I did; and, by a glimpse between the long wreaths of drift, saw Water! The temptation was a sore one: I yielded to it, came down from my perch, donned my sealskin, shouldered my carbine, and walked off with my face toward the wonder. None of the crew would accompany me: my messmates did not volunteer: so I was alone.

"It was a walk to be remembered. Snow up to the neck; drift moist and blinding; and a gale, luckily not a cold one, in my face. But after a mile of such promenading as no other region can boast of, I reached the water at last. Water it was; dark, surging water; no pellicles of glazing ice; no sludgy streams of pancake; but the liquid element itself, such as we saw last summer, and you see every day, stretching out as broad as the Delaware, and in contrast with the snow at its margin as black as Styx.

"I took a good look at it, and turned to come back. The wind had wiped out my footsteps: all within the horizon was a waste of sleet. I had neither compass nor signal pole to show me the way; but I kept the gale behind me, and waded onward. I do not know how far I might have traveled before reaching the vessel; but I had buffeted the elements quite long enough to content me, when I heard Captain Griffin hailing me through the drift. He had been uneasy at my stay, and was out in search of me. We took a new departure together, were blown over a few times, and tumbled over, no matter how often; but we hit the ships to a notch.

"This crack is the old transverse one from northeast to southwest, off the Rescue's port beam. The gale, with such a temperature, must be achieving much upon the ice to the southward. It can hardly reach men so imbedded as we are; but it may so break up the southern edge of the pack as to give us a ready drift, should we have a favoring wind. As it is, we are undoubtedly flicking it to the north again.

"*April* 15. The sun perceptibly warmer, and the indications of thaw unequivocal. To guard as far as we can against the chance of the two vessels being separated among the floes when the general break-up comes, we began a trench to-day from one to the other. It goes down through the snow to the solid ice; and we are going to strew rock-salt in it, remembering that even a slight scratch on the surface will determine the line of fracture. We will try it at any rate, even across the entire floe to the present seat of hummocking at the open water, though it is a distance of nearly or quite two miles. We are looking to our approaching disruption with absorbing interest; and, whether our theories are good or bad, they give us something to think and talk about. Our ice-cutting machine belongs to the same family. We finished it to-day, and it will be tested to-morrow.

"The ice in the neighborhood of the fire-hole is wet and overflowed. It seems to be depressed below the water-level. The snow has piled up some seven or eight feet high on the vessels' side, and this, with the radiating heat, may possibly explain this depression. But I am strongly inclined to believe in endosmotic actions in the ice.

"*April* 16. To-day the salting continues. The men call it our spring-seed sowing. On board the Rescue, a party are at work preparing for the return to her. The ice-cutting machine proves a failure.

"This afternoon a solitary snow-bunting was seen flitting around our vessel. The last time we saw this little animal was at Griffith's Island, in the midst of the terrible storm which we were sharing with our English brethren. Goodsir saw the same bird on the 13th, in latitude 54°; but he was not at Winter Island till the 27th. Since then, the little family have made their migratory journey, and are now on their way again to these Polar seas. They breed seldom or never south of 62°, and linger late among the Northern snows. This poor little wanderer was an estray from his fellows. He paused at the treasures which surrounded our ship, refreshed himself from our dirt pile, and then flew away again on his weary journey.

"*April* 17. A memorable day. We put out our cabin lamps, and are henceforward content with daylight, like the rest of the world. Our latitude is 69° 52′; our longitude, 63° 03′.

"This afternoon, while walking deck, this endless deck, with Murdaugh, we discovered a bear walking tranquilly alongside, nearly within gunshot. We have lost so many opportunities by the bustle and ignorance of a universal chase, that I crawled out to attack him alone. To my sorrow, the brute, who had been gazing at the ship dog-fashion and curious, turned tail. He was out of range for my carbine, but I gave him the ball as he ran in his right hind-quarter. He fell at once, and I thought him secure; but rising instantly, he turned upon his wounded haunch, and, very much as a dog does at a bee-sting, bit spasmodically at the wound. For a little while he spun round, biting the bloody spot with a short, probing nip; and then, before I could reload my piece, started off at a limping but rapid gait. I mention this movement on account of the very curious fact which follows. The animal had found the ball, seized it between the incisors, and *extracted it.* The bullet is now in my possession, distinctly marked by his teeth.

"After a very tedious and harassing pursuit, I came up to him at the young ice. He stood upon the brink of the lead. I was within long shot, and about to make preparations for a more deliberate and certain aim, when he took to the water, and then to the opposite young ice, bleeding and dropping every few yards.

"Joined by Daly, a bold bull-headed Irishman, I crossed by a circuitous channel, and then took to the young ice myself, and tried to run him down. It was very exciting; and I fear I was not as prudent as I ought to have been; for a dense fog had gathered around us, and the young floe, level as the sea which it covered, was but two nights old. The bear fell several times; and at last, poor fellow, dragged himself by his fore feet, trailing his hind quarters over the incrusted snow, so as to leave a long black imprint stained by blood.

"The fog was getting more and more dense, and the frail ice—we were now walking, as it were, over the sea itself—bent under us so much, that I, like a prudent man, ordered a return. This chase cost us at least ten miles of journey, part of it at an Indian trot. We dripped like men in a steam bath.

"*April* 20, Sunday. Daly started with a company of sailors after the wounded bear. They walked, by their own account, six miles before they found him.

He was unable to retreat—stood at bay; and the fools were so scared at his 'growlings' and his 'bloody tongue,' that they returned without daring to attack him.

"*April* 21, Monday. I have more than common cause for thankfulness. A mere accident kept me from starting last night to secure our bear. Had I done so, I would probably have spared you reading more of my journal. The ice over which we traveled so carelessly on Saturday has become, by a sudden movement, a mass of floating rubbish. An open river, broader than the Delaware, is now between the old ice and the nearest part of the new, over which I walked on the 19th more than three miles.

"In the walk of this morning, which startled me with the change, I saw for the first time a seal upon the ice. This looks very summer-like. He was not accessible to our guns. To-day, for the first time too, the gulls were flying over the renovated water. Coming back we saw fresh bear tracks. How wonderful is the adaptation which enables a quadruped, to us associated inseparably with a land existence, thus to inhabit an ice-covered ocean. We are at least eighty miles from the nearest land, Cape Kater; and channels innumerable must intervene between us and terra firma. Yet this majestic animal, dependent upon his own predatory resources alone, and, defying cold as well as hunger, guided by a superb instinct, confides himself to these solitary, unstable ice-fields.

"Parry, in his adventurous Polar effort, found these animals at the most northern limit of recorded observation. Wrangell had them as companions on his first Asiatic journey over the Polar ocean. Navigators have found them also floating upon berg and floe far out in open sea; and here we have them in a region some seventy miles from the nearest stable ice. They have seldom, or, as far as my readings go, never—if we except Parry's Spitzbergen experience—been seen so far from land. In the great majority of cases, they seem to have been accidentally caught and carried adrift on disengaged ice-floes. In this way they travel to Iceland; and it may have been so perhaps with the Spitzbergen instances. Others have been reported thirty miles from shore in this bay. I myself noticed them fifty miles from the Greenland coast last July.

"There is something very grand about this tawny savage; never leaving this utter destitution, this frigid inhospitableness—coupling in May, and bringing forth in Christmas time—a gestation carried on all of it below zero, more than half of it in Arctic darkness—living in perpetual snow, and dependent for life upon a never-ending activity—using the frozen water as a raft to traverse the open seas, that the water *unfrozen* may yield him the means of life. No time for hibernation has this Polar tiger: his life is one great winter."

CHAPTER XXXIX.

"*April* 22. The past week has been one of dismantling, rubbish-creating, ship-cleaning torment. First, bull's-eyes were inserted in the deck; and the black felt housing, so comfortable in the winter darkness, but that now shut out the sunlight like a great pall, was triced up fore and aft, remaining only amidships. Next, the Rescue, with her new bowsprit in, received her crew and officers. They slept on board last night for the first time, but still walk over the ice to their meals.

"When I saw the little brig through the darkness, on the afternoon of the 13th of January, moving slowly past us and losing herself in the gloom, while sounds like artillery mingled with the shrieking, howling, and crashing of the ice, as the great ridges rose and fell—and when the India-rubber boat was launched, and the men took their knapsacks, and old Brooks called out to us to get out of the way of the rigging, believing the brig about to topple over—I did not think there would be a spring-time for the Rescue.

"We are now in the midst of those intestine changes which characterize the house-cleanings at home. The disgusting lamps have done smoking, the hatches are allowed to look out at the sun, and the galley, with its perpetual odors, is banished to the hurricane-house on deck. That peculiar interspace between the coal and the 'purser's slops,' so dark and full of head-bumping beams, exults in the full glare of day. What a wonderful hole we have been existing in! It, the half-deck, as it is called on board ship, is three feet six inches high, by fourteen feet long and seventeen broad. On it, forgetful of precedence and rank, our bedding separated from the loose planking by a canvas cot frame, slept Murdaugh, Vreeland, Brooks, De Haven, two cooks, and Dr. Kane. The last-named came on board last, and found, though he is not a very large man, a sufficiently narrow kennel between the companion-ladder and the dinner-table. Our clothing, as it now welcomed the sun, was black with lamp-soot; the beams above fringed, and festooned, and wreathed with the same. My bed-coverings, frozen over the feet in the winter, are bathed with inky water. But all this is to be removed to-day; and we go back to the luxuries of bunks, and daylight, and a long breath.

"The day was bright and sunny. I walked out to the open water. Marks of commotion, hummock ridges, and chasms. A new feature was the thaw. Heretofore I could stand upon the brink of the cleanly-separated fissures, and look down upon the bleak water as securely as from a quartz rock. To-day every thing around (pshaw! the snow and ice, I mean; we have no *things* here) was wet and crumbling. The snow covered deceitfully some very dangerous cracks: in one of these I sunk neck deep. My carbine caught across it, and Holmes pulled me out.

"We are very anxious to obtain fresh meat for the

invalids. Indeed, our longing for something fresh is itself a disease. To-day a tantalizing seal kept me prostrate upon the slushy ice for an hour and a half. In spite of all my seal craft, the prime secret of which is patience, I could not draw him into gunshot. With the characteristic curiosity of his tribe, the poor animal would rise breast high to inspect my fur cap. Presently a whale spouted, and off he went.

"The decks are clear! the barrels stowed away below, the fore-peak restored, the old bunks reoccupied, and my messmates snoozing away as in old times, a fire burning in the stove, and lard lamps flaming away vigorously upon my paper. Daylight still finds its way down the hatch, although it is eleven o'clock.

"*April* 24, Thursday. The snow falls in loose, flaky, home feathers. The decks are wet, and the misty air has the peculiar ground-glass translucency which I noticed last summer. When I came up before breakfast to look around, the thermometer gave +32°, the familiar temperature of old times: to me it was warm and sultry.

"The season of summer, if not now upon us, is close at hand. It seems but yesterday that we hailed the dawning day, and burned our fingers in the frozen mercury; now we have a summer snow-storm at 32°.

"This little table will show you how stealthily and how rapidly summer has trampled down winter:

Mean temperature for week ending March	14th, —23° 94′.	
" " " " " "	21st, —9° 07′;	gain, 14° 87′.
" " " " " "	28th, —16° 90′;	loss 7° 83′.
" " " " " April	4th, —4° 31′;	gain, 12° 39′.
" " " " " "	11th, +8° 59′;	gain, 12° 90′.
" " " " " "	18th, +9° 55′;	gain, 0° 55′.
" " " five days "	23d, +14° 56′;	gain, 5° 01′.

"Changes show themselves in the configuration of

the snow surfaces. The hummocks seem already to have diminished by evaporation. They are less angular, and blend in rounder lines with the snow drifts. Night has gone. I see still at midnight the circumpolar stars, and Jupiter, in his splendor, on the eastern sky; but I can read at midnight.

"*April* 25, Friday. Walked to open water to the northeast. The snow is melted through the crust. I sink up to my knees. Saw the tracks of a fox, very recent. The little fellow had come from the direction of the poor wounded bear, now cut off from us by the broken ice, swimming the lead at its narrowest crossing, some fifteen paces. So long as his patron could have supplied him with food, the little parasite would not have left him. It may be that the bear has perished from inability to hunt for both.

"Saw a right whale! Saw also a large flock of geese at 9 A.M., winging their way to the northward, and flying very low. They were so irregular in their order of flight, that I would have taken them for ducks —the *Somateria;* but my messmates say geese.

"*April* 26, Saturday. One of the changes which we must expect has brought back to us comparative winter. Yesterday gave us a noonday and morning temperature of +28°. It is now (10 P.M.) −9°. It was −7° at noonday, with a bright, clear sunshine. The change is due to a northerly wind. It has blown steadily throughout the day from northwest by north. We hope much from it in the way of drift. Our latitude was 69° 40′ 42″ N; our longitude, 63° 08′ 46″ W.

"The wind change has given us no new ruptures. Indeed, it seems to have shut up the environing 'leads' around us. This may be a good preface to a squeeze; for I can see no water from the mast-head.

"The stars at midnight remind me of our Lancaster Sound noondays. The peculiar zone of fairly blended light, stretching over an amplitude of some seventy degrees—the colors red, Indian red, Italian pink, with the yellows; and then a light cobalt, gradually deepening into intense indigo as it reaches the northern horizon.

"*April* 27, Sunday. The cold increases, and our northwest wind continues. The day's observation gives us 69° 35′ 50″, so that we still go south encouragingly, though slowly. This big floe is so solid, that some of us are beginning to fear it may resist the pressure, and not break up in the bay; leaving us to the thaws of summer and the stormy winds of September before our imprisonment ceases. The apprehension has no mirth in it.

"Walked to the open water to the northward, nearly ahead of us. The leads were so frozen over as to bear me. Looking across the level, letting my eyes wander from tussock to tussock of entangled floe-ice, as they had grouped themselves in freezing, I heard the blowing of a narwhal, followed by the peculiar swash of squeezing ice. A short walk showed me some six or eight conical elevations, forced upward upon the recently-formed ice, evidently by a force protruding from beneath. While looking at these, the sounds, though seemingly further off, increased to such a degree that I was convinced the ice was in action, and started off to double a cape of hummocks and see the commotion. Our steward, Morton, a shrewd, ob servant fellow, who was with me, suddenly called out, 'Look here, sir—here!'

"Each of these little cones was steaming like the salices or mud-volcanoes of Mexico, the broken ice on top vibrating, and every now and then tumbling, as if by some pulsatory movement below. Presently, in one concerted diapason, a group of narwhals, imprisoned by the congelation of the opening,* spouted their release, scattering spray and snow in every direction. I was not more than three yards from the nearest cone; yet I could see nothing of the animal except this jet.

"The noise was so great that I could hardly make the steward hear me. It had, moreover, more of voice mingled with its sibilant 'blow' than I had ever heard —a distinct and somewhat metallic tone, thrown out impulsively, and yet with the crescendo and diminuendo of an expiration. According to the views of some systematic naturalists, the cetacea have, strictly speaking, no voice. This opinion admits of much modification. The white whale in Wellington Sound whistled while submerged and swimming under our brig; and, in the present singular case, the ejaculatory character of the tone sounded like a gigantic bark.†

"*May* 1, Thursday. A little before ten this morning, the sun showed almost half his disk above the snow horizon, with his usual appanage of pearly opals and mellowed fire displayed about the southern heavens. At noon I walked out in the full glare, twenty-five degrees above the freezing-point on my face, and about as many below it on my back—a May-day frolic in the snow!

* I found afterward from the Danes that they assemble in this way when extensive areas are frozen. Mr. Moldrup, of Godhaven, mentions fifty being killed at one of these congregations.

† On this occasion, I heard the white whale singing under water—a peculiar note between the whistle and the Tyrolean yodel. Our men compared it to the Jews-harp. Once, off Cape James, it was so loud that we heard it in the cabin, as if proceeding from the cable-tier. I have often, in my walks over the ice-openings, been startled by the resemblance between the sudden spout of a near narwhal and the bark of an animal.

The crisp covering, over which I used to skim along a few weeks ago, broke through with me at every step. It was just strong enough to tantalize and deceive. Never, in the warmest days of summer harvest-time, have I felt the heat so much as on this Arctic May-day; and yet no life, no organization carried me back to the spring-time of reviving nature. Even the tinnitus of the idle ear, that inner droning that sings to you in the silent sunshine at home, was wanting. In fact, the silentness was so complete, and the reflection from the snow so excessive, though I had a green rag over my face, that when I got far away, and out of sight of every thing but the interminable ice, it made me feel as if the world I left you in and the world about me were not exactly parts of the same planet.

"And so I traveled back to my sick men. God bless us! here are old Blinn, and Carter, and Wilson, all on my list for fainting spells: the same scurvy syncope our officers complain of. Captain Griffin fainted dead away, and Lovell complains of strange feelings. We need fresh food sorely. I hardly think any organized expedition to these regions was ever so completely deprived of anti-scorbutic diet as we are at this time.

"Midnight. My old scurvy symptoms, it may be, that keep me from sleeping. But I write by the light of the sun; and it really seems to me that there is a something about this persistent day antagonistic to sleep. The idea thrust itself upon me last summer. Thinking the fact over afterward, I referred it to habit, acting unphilosophically, as it is apt to do; and concluded that my sleeplessness was not connected directly with the augmented or continued light. But this is not so. I neither get to sleep so easily nor sleep as long, nor, indeed, do I seem to need the same quantity of sleep as when we had the alternation of light and darkness. On the other hand, I think our long Arctic night solicited a more than common ration of the same restorative blessing, though my journal has shown you that our waking energies during that period were not so heavily taxed as to require more than their usual intermission."

The day after this entry superadded the visitation of snow blindness to our trials. Four of the party were attacked severely, myself among the rest; so severely, indeed, as to make it impossible for me to write, and, what was much more important in the estimation of our scurvy patients, impossible for me to hunt. The brief notes which were made in my journal by the kindness of a brother officer speak of our sensible approach toward a final disengagement from the ice-field. Though the winds were generally from the southwest, our drift tended very plainly to the south: in one day, we reduced our latitude eighteen miles, passing at the same time nearly a degree of longitude, twenty-two miles to the east. The ice, too, was becoming more infiltrated, and the heavy snow-banks that surrounded our vessel were saturated with water Spring was doing its office.

CUTTING OUT, MAY, 1851.

CHAPTER XL.

ON the 11th, I was well enough, or imprudent enough, to attempt a seal hunt. Our mean temperature had sunk to 19° 5′, and the snow-crust was strong enough to bear. A gale had swept away the loose, fleecy drifts of the fortnight before, exposing the familiar surface of the older snow. I walked over it as I did in April.

"Reaching the seat of the open water to the northward, I found it closed by young ice, an extensive surface frail and unsafe. About a quarter of a mile from the edge of the old floe, almost in the centre of this recent lead, was a seal. The temptations of the flesh were too much for me: I ventured the ice, crawled on my belly, and reached long-shot distance.

The animal thus laboriously stalked was large; a hirsute, bearded fellow, with the true plantigrade countenance. All his senses were devoted to enjoyment: he wallowed in the sludge, stretched out in the sunshine, played with his flippers, lying on his back, much as a heavy horse does in a skin-loosening roll. I rose to fire—and down he went. An unseen hole had received him: a lesson for future occasions. This hole was critically circular, beveled from the under surface, and symmetrically embanked round with the pulpacious material which he had excavated from the ice.

"Crawling back less actively than I had approached, my carbine arm broke through, carrying my gun and it up to the shoulder. It was very well, all things considered, that my body did not follow; for I was on a very rotten shell, and nearly two miles from the brigs, alone.

"Wednesday 12. For the last fortnight, our ice-saw, under Murdaugh's supervision, has been hard at work. To-day we have a trench opened to our gangway.

"The ice shows the advancing season. It is no longer splintery and quartz-like, spawling off under the axe in dangerous little chips; but sodden, infiltrated ice, such as we see in our ice-houses. The water has got into its centre, and the crow-bars, after the sawing out, break it readily up for hauling upon the field. The process is this: First, we cut two parallel tracks, four feet asunder, through six and five feet ice, with a ten-foot saw; then lozenged diagonals; then straps (ropes) are passed around the fragments, and a block and line, *nautice* jigger, or watch tackle, made fast to the bowsprit, hauls the lumps upon the floe, where they are broken up by the ice bars. A formidable barricade of dirty ice, about the size and shape of gneiss building stones, is already inclosing our vessel. Many a poor fellow has had an involuntary slide-bath into the freezing mixture alongside; but in most cases without unpleasant consequences."

I remember only one serious exception. It was that of our heroine of the Thespian corps, Jim Smith. The immediate result for him was an attack of scurvy, so marked, yet so blended with the active symptoms belonging to arthritic disease, as to incline me to an opinion for the time that there may be such a thing as acute scurvy, or a sudden inflammatory sthenic action, whose characteristics are scorbutic. He had immediately stitch, dyspnœa, pains in the back and joints, and in the alveolar and extensor muscles, just as in his previous attacks of scurvy, but without fever. The day after, he was so distressed by his stitch, that I feared pleuritis. On looking at his shins, I found large purpuric blotches, which were not there a week before. I commenced the anti-scorbutic tyranny at once; and the next morning his gums bled freely, his pains left him, and he took his place again at the ice-saw.

"Several laridæ flew about us: I heard them to-day for the second time—pleasant tones, with all their discord. Do you remember the skylark's song, 'a dropping from the sky,' in the 'Ancient Mariner?' I thought of it this morning when the gulls screeched over our motionless brig.

"*May* 18, Sunday. First, of late, in my daily records is this glorious wind, still from the northwest, fresh and steady. It is, as is every thing else for that matter, a Godsend. To-day's observation places us but thirty-two miles from Cape Searle, and seventy from Cape Walsingham, the abutting gate of Davis's Straits, where the channel is at its narrowest, and where our imprisonment ought to end.

"This welcome wind-visitor is still freshening: it is not perpetrating, I hope, an extra brilliancy before its *congé*.

"I found to-day a rough caricature drawing by one of the men: some of the mess call it a portrait of myself. By-the-way, suppose I tell you of my latest rig? Here it is. A long musket on shoulder; a bear knife in the leg of the left boot; a rim of wolf-skin around my head, leaving the bare scalp with its '*hairs*' open to the breeze; rough Guernsey frock, overlined by a red flannel shirt, in honor of the day on which thou shalt do no labor; legs in sailor pants of pilot cloth, slop-shop cut; feet in seal-hide socks or buskins, of Esquimaux fabric and Esquimaux smell; a pair of crimson woolen mittens, which commenced their career as a neck comforter; and a little green rag, the snow veil, fluttering over a weather-beaten face: place all this, for want of a better lay figure, on your brother of the Arctic squadron.

"With a delicacy which may possibly do me discredit, I have never before alluded to the garniture of my outer man. I may as well tell the truth at once. We are an uncouth, snobby, and withal, shabby-looking set of varlets. L'illustre Bertrand would be a very Beau Brummel alongside of us. We are shabby, because we have worn out all our flimsy wardrobes, and have of late resorted to domestic tailorization. We are snobby, because our advance in the new art does not yet extend to the picturesque or well-fitting.

I wish some of my soda-water-in-the-morning club friends could see me perspiring over a pair of pants, dorcassing a defunct sock. We do our own sewing, clothing ourselves cap-à-pie; and it astonishes me, looking back upon my dark period of previous ignorance, to feel how much I have learned. I wonder whether your friend the Philadelphia D'Orsay knows how to adjust with a ruler and a lump of soap the seat of a pair of breeches?

"Why, I have even made discoveries in—I forget the Greek word for it—the art which made George the Fourth so famous. Thus a method, adopted by our mess, of cutting five pair of stockings out of one hammock blanket—a thing hitherto deemed impossible—is altogether my own. In the abstract or speculative part of the profession, I claim to be the first who has reduced all vestiture to a primitive form—an integral particle, as it were. I can't dwell on this matter here: it might, perhaps, be out of place; perhaps, too, attributed in some degree to that personal vanity almost inseparable from invention. I will tell you, however, that this discovered type, this radical nucleus, is the 'bag.' Thus a bag, or a couple of parallelogramic planes sewed together, makes the covering of the trunk. Similar bags of scarcely varied proportion cover the arms; ditto the legs; ditto the hands; ditto the head: thus going on, bags, bags, bags, even to the fingers; a cytoblastic operation, having interesting analogies with the mycelium of the fungus or the saccine vegetation of the confervas.

"All this is a digression, perhaps; yet I am not the first traveler whose breeches have figured in his diary of wonders: you remember the geometrical artist of Laputa who re-enforced the wardrobe of Mr. Gulliver

But to return to less ambitious topics. The birds, in spite of the increasing wind, fly over in numbers, all seeking the mysterious north. What is there at this unreached pole to attract and sustain such hordes of migratory life? Since the day before yesterday, the 16th, we can not be on deck at any hour, night or day —they are one now—without seeing small bodies, rather groups than flocks, on their way to the unknown feeding or breeding grounds. Toward the west the field of a telescope is constantly crossed by these detachments. The ducks are now scarce: in fact, they have been few from the beginning. Geese are seen only in the forenoon and early morning. The guillemots, also, are not so numerous as they were two days ago; but from to-day we date the reappearance of the little Auk. This delicious little pilgrim is now on his way to his far north breeding grounds. Toward the open lead the groups fly low, sometimes doubtless pausing to refresh. At the water's edge I shot five, the first game of the season; and most valuable they were to our scurvy men. If this snow blindness permits me, I hope to-morrow to prove myself a more lucky sportsman.

"*May* 19, Monday. Jim Smith, little Jim Smith, reported 'Land.' We have become so accustomed to this great sameness of snow, that it was hard to realize at first the magnitude of our drift. Our last land was the spectral elevation upreared in the sunset sky of the 9th of February. The land itself must have been eighty miles off. Our drift, although now not absolutely fixed by observation, has probably carried us to within forty miles, perhaps thirty, of Cape Searle. Land it certainly is, shadowy, high, snow-covered, and strange. It is ninety-nine days since we looked at the refracted tops of the Lancaster Bay headlands, our last land.

"*May* 20, Tuesday. So snow-blind that I can barely see to write. A gauzy film floats between me and every thing else. I have been walking twelve miles upon the ice. No sun, but a peculiar misty, opalescent glare. I bagged thirty-three Auks; but my snow-blindness avenges them."

For some days after this entry my snow-blindness unfitted me for active duty. Several of the officers and men shared the visitation, Captain De Haven more severely than any of us. My next quotation from my journal dates of the 24th.

"*May* 24, Saturday. The ship shows signs of change, grating a little in her icy cradle, and rising at least nine inches forward. The work of removing the ice goes on painfully, but constantly. The blocks are now hoisted with winch and capstan by a purchase from the fore-yard; the saw, of course, pioneering. The blocks when taken out resemble great break-water stones, measuring sometimes eight by six feet.

"Thus far, by persevering labor, we have cut a four-feet wide trench to our starboard gangway, a little vacant pool of six yards by three in our bows, and a second trench now reaching amidships of our fore-chains.

"The difference of level between the deck at our bows and stern is still five feet three inches. It is proposed to launch the brig, as it were, from her ice-ways. To this purpose a screw jack is to be applied aft, and strong purchases on the ice ahead. The experiment will take place this afternoon. We have now been five months and a half, since the seventh of December, living on an inclined plane of about one foot in sixteen.

"10 P.M. The effort failed, as no doubt it ought to have done: we must wait for the great break-up to give us an even keel. From the mast-head we can see encroachments all around. The plains, over which I chased bear and shot at Auks, are now water. The floe is reduced to its old winter dimensions, three miles in one diameter, five in the other. We have not yet reached the narrow passage; and the wind, now from the southward, seems to be holding us back. Strange as it sounds, we are in hopes of a break-up at Cape Walsingham.

"*May* 25, Sunday. Howling a perfect gale; drift impenetrable. By some providential interference the wind returned last night to its old quarter, the northwest, a direction corresponding with the trend of the shore. It is undoubtedly driving us fast to the southward, and is, of all quarters, that most favorable to a passage without disruption. Once past Cape Walsingham, the expansion of the bay is sudden and extensive. If, then, our floe maintains its integrity through the strait, the relief from pressure may allow us to continue our drifting journey. So at least we argue.

"And just so, it may be, others have argued before us about chances of escape that never came: there is a cycle even in the history of adventure. It makes me sad sometimes when I think of the fruitless labors of the men who in the very olden times harassed themselves with these perplexing seas. There have been Sir John Franklins before, and searchers too, who in searching shared the fate of those they sought after. It is good food for thought here, while I am of and among them, to recall the heart-burnings and the failures, the famishings and the freezings, the silent, unrecorded transits of 'ye Arctic voyageres.'

"Mount Raleigh, named by sturdy old John Davis 'a brave mount, the cliffes whereof were as orient as golde,' shows itself still, not so glittering as he saw it two hundred and sixty-five years ago, but a 'brave mount' notwithstanding. No Christian eyes have ever gazed in May time on its ice-defended slope, except our own. Yet there it stands, as imperishable as the name it bears.

"I could fill my journal with the little histories of this very shore. The Cape of God's Mercy is ahead of us to the west, as it was ahead of the man who named it. The Meta Incognita, further on, is still as unknown as in the days of Frobisher. We have passed, by the inevitable coercion of ice, from the highest regions of Arctic exploration, the lands of Parry, and Ross, and Franklin, to the lowest, the seats of the early search for Cathay, the lands of Cabot, and Davis, and Baffin, the graves of Cortereal, and Gilbert, and Hudson—all seekers after shadows. Men still seek Cathay."

SEALS AT PLAY.

CHAPTER XLI.

"The storm broke in the early morning hours. We have drifted more than sixteen miles since Saturday. The true bearing of the prominent cape we supposed to be Cape Walsingham was found by solar distance to be S. 63° W.; while our observed position, by meridian altitude and chronometers, placed us but four miles north of Exeter Bay. Either, then, the protruding cape is not Walsingham, or our chronometers are at fault. This latter is probably the case; for if the coast line be correctly laid down on the charts, the true bearing cited above, projected from one present parallel of latitude, would place us thirty-six miles from the cape. More likely this than so near Exeter.

"Our latitude is about 66° 51′, a very few miles north of the projecting headland, the western Gades of our strait. The character of the land is rugged and inhospitable. Ridges, offsetting from the higher range, project in spurs laterally, creviced and water-worn, but to seaward escarped and bluff. Some of these are mural and precipitous, of commanding height. The main range does not retire very far from the sea; it seems to follow the trend of the peninsula, and most probably on the Greenland shore is but the abutment of a plateau. Its culminating points are not numerous: the highest, Mount Raleigh, is, by my vague estimate, about fifteen hundred feet high.

"*May* 27. The land is very near to the eye; but in these regions we have learned to distrust ocular measurements of distance. Though we see every wrinkle even to the crows' feet, on the cheeks of Mount Raleigh, I remember last year, on the west coast of Greenland, we saw almost under our nose land that was thirty-five miles off. A party from the Rescue measured a base upon the ice to-day, and attempted trigonometrical measurements with sextant angles. They make Cape Walsingham seven miles distant, and the height of the peak at the cape fifteen hundred feet. Our observation places us in latitude 66° 42′ 40″; our longitude by time sights, at 5h. 43m. P.M., was 60° 54′. According to the Admiralty chart, this plants us high and dry among the mountains of Cape Walsingham.

"It is evident that our rate of drift has increased. The northwest winds carried us forward eight miles a day while near the strait—a speed only equaled in a few of the early days of our escape from Lancaster Sound. What has become of all the ice that used to be intervening between us and the shore? At one time we had a distance of ninety miles: we are now close upon the coast. What has become of it? If it moves at the same rate as we do, why have we no squeezing and commotion at this narrow strait? Can it be that the ice to the westward of us has been more or less fixed to the land floe, and that we have been drifting down in a race-course, as it were, an ice-river whose banks were this same shore ice? Or is it, as Murdaugh suggests, that the in-shore currents, more rapid, have carried down the in-shore ice before us, thus widening the pathway for us? It is certainly very puzzling to find ourselves, at the narrowest passage, close into the land; and no commotion, no disturbance. On the contrary, from the mast-head abundant open water meets the eye; and could we escape from our imprisoning, but—thankfully I say it—protecting floe, we might soon be moving in open seas.

"*May* 28, Wednesday. The fact of the day is the rotation of our floe. In spite of its irregular shape, it has rotated a complete circle within the past twenty-four hours. It is still turning at the same rate, wheeling us down along the in-shore fields. The Rescue, early this morning, was between us and the land: the evening before, the same land was astern of us. Strange that no rupture takes place!

"*May* 29, Thursday. I have just been witnessing one of the oddest of Arctic freaks. We were all of us engaged in tracing out the rugged indentations on Mount Raleigh, as the floe was rolling our vessels slowly along past Cape Walsingham, when, at five o'clock in the afternoon—the thermometer at 27°, the barometer at 30.31, and the atmosphere of the usual pearly opalescence—the captain, sweeping shoreward with his glass, saw a large pyramidal hummock, with a well-defined figure projecting in front of it, evidently animated and moving. Murdaugh, looking afterward, declared it 'a man.' I saw it next, a large human figure, covered with a cloak, and motionless. Murdaugh took the glass again, and holding it to his eye, suddenly exclaimed, 'It moves:' 'it spreads out its arms:' 'it is a gigantic bird!'

"The hummock was within a mile of us. The words were hardly uttered before the object had disappeared, and the white snow was without a speck. A discussion followed. The size made us at once reject the bird idea: the shape, too, was that of a cloak-covered man; the motion, as if he had opened his mantle-covered arms. Convinced that it was a human being, an Esquimaux astray upon the ice, Murdaugh and myself started off, nearing the hummock with hearts full of expectation. The traces on the soft snow would soon solve the mystery, and remove our only doubt, whether the Rescues might not be playing us a trick.

"Whatever it was, it either did not perceive us approaching, or was willing to avoid us; for it kept itself hidden behind a crag. Reaching, however, the spot where it had stood, we found traces, coprolitic and recent, of a bird; footprints, as a learned professor would have said, of certain familiar animal processes, exaggerated and dignified by those of refraction.

"On returning to the brig, the watchers told us that we had been ourselves curiously distorted; and that, when perched on the little icy crag we had gone to scrutinize, we lengthened vertically into gigantic forms. The position of the bird, probably a glaucous gull, had been breast toward the brig: a vertical enlargement, with the white body and moving wings, explained the phenomenon.

"The 'Rescues' had a very large bear hovering around them all this morning. At one P.M. he came within reach of a carefully-prepared ambush, receiving four out of a half dozen balls, a number soon increased to nine. You may have some idea of the superb tenacity of life of this beast, when I tell you that he ran, thus perforated, with his skull broken and his shoulder shivered. He even attempted a charge, uttering a hissing sound, ejaculated by sudden impulse, like the 'blowing of a whale,' to use Captain Griffin's comparison. He measured eight feet five inches, only three inches less than my own big trophy, which, with one exception, is the largest recorded in the stories of the Polar American hunt. What a glorious feed for the scurvy-stricken ships!

"To-day, for the first time, we had a Tide, made evident by the changing phases of the shore. We made southing in the forenoon: now, at half past eight P.M., the alignment of the hills shows a northward drift. The ice is unchanged: our floe is rotating from west to south, against the sun, but not equably. We crossed the Arctic circle at some unknown hour this forenoon. To the eye every thing is as before; yet it cheats one into pleasant thoughts. I do not wish to see a midnight sun again.

"*May* 30. The seal are out upon the ice, one of the most certain of the signs of summer. They are few in number, and very cautious. We notice that they invariably select an open floe for their hole, and that they never leave it more than a few lengths. Their alertness is probably due to their vigilant enemy, the bear. Sometimes you will see them frolicking together like a parcel of swimming school-boys; sometimes they are solitary, but keenly alive always to the enjoyment of the sunshine. I have often crawled within fair eye-shot, and, seated behind a concealing lump of ice, watched their movements.

"The first act of a seal, after emerging, is a careful survey of his limited horizon. For this purpose he rises on his fore flippers, and stretches his neck in a manner almost dog-like. This maneuver, even during apparently complete silence, is repeated every few minutes. He next commences with his hind or horizontal flippers and tail a most singular movement.

allied to sweeping; brushing nervously, as if either to rub something from himself or from beneath him. Then comes a complete series of attitudes, stretching, collapsing, curling, wagging; then a luxurious, basking rest, with his face toward the sun and his tail to his hole. Presently he waddles off about two of his own awkward lengths from his retreat, and begins to roll over and over, pawing in the most ludicrous manner into the empty air, stretching and rubbing his glossy hide like a horse. He then recommences his vigil, basking in the sun with uneasy alertness for hours. At the slightest advance, up goes the prying head. One searching glance; and, wheeling on his tail as on a pivot, he is at his hole, and descends head foremost.

"I have watched so many without success, that to-night I determined to try the Esquimaux plan—patience and a snow-screen. This latter, the easier portion of the formula, I have just returned from completing; it was a mile's walk and an hour's snow-shoveling. The other, the patience, I attempt to-morrow, 'squat like a toad' on the ice for an unknown series of hours, with the sun blistering my nose, and blinking my eyes the while; a sort of sport so much like fishing, that it ought to be reserved for the Piscators of our Schuylkill Club.

"The walk over the snow to-night was very delightful. The opalescence, so painful to the eyes, had given place to a clear atmosphere; and the low sun was full of rich coloring. Land, too, that pleasing representative of the world we are cut off from, was refracted into grotesque knolls and long spires.

"The surface of the floes shows more and more the thawing influence of our sun, now half as high at meridian as in the torrid zone! The immediate surface to-day was often entire, though we plunged almost knee-deep in water below it. This you will easily understand when I tell you that the thermometer in the sun gave, for four successive hours to-day, a mean of nearly 80°. The surface thaw percolates through the loosely-compacted snow, and, forming a pasty substratum, is protected from re-freezing by the very snow through which it has descended. Our mean temperature of late has varied but little between 25° and 27° for any twenty-four hours.

"The infiltration of saline water through the ice assists the process of disintegration. The water formed by surface or sun thaw is, by the peculiar endosmitic action which I believe I have mentioned elsewhere, at once rendered salt, as was evident from Baumé's hydrometers and the test of the nitrate of silver. The surface crust bore me readily this evening at a temperature of 21° and 19°, giving no evidences of thaw. Beneath, for two inches, it was crisp and fresh. As I tried it lower, cutting carefully with my bear-knife, it became spongy and brackish; at eight inches markedly so; and at and below twelve, salt-water paste. On the other hand, all my observations, and I have made a great many, prove to me that cold, if intense enough, will, by its unaided action, independent of percolation, solar heat, depending position, or even depth of ice, produce from salt water a fresh, pure, and drinkable element.

"*May* 31, Saturday. Walked to-night to the southward in search of seal: found the ice in motion, and had some difficulty in getting back. Wind from southward, and freshening, after a day of nearly perfect calm. The drift is somewhat to the eastward. The tables were heaping up actively, and the chewing process of demolition was in full energy among them. I have some hope that the action may extend itself to the core of our veteran floe-circle; but for the present it is confined to those peripheral adjuncts that have grown up around it in more recent freezings. A bird's-eye view from the mast-head, corrected by my walks, enables me to map out its present shape with considerable accuracy."

The "month of roses" closed on us without adventure; but its last ten days were full of monitory changes. The increased temperature had been visibly acting upon the ice, softening down its rough angles, and reducing bowlders to mere knobs on the surface; its weary monotony becoming every day only more disgusting. From the 1st to the 19th we had drifted almost a hundred miles, and had been expecting daily to make the eastern shore, when land was reported ahead. It proved to be the Highlands around Cape Searle, about thirty-five miles off.

It was the first inbreak upon our desolate circle of ice and water that we had experienced in ninety-nine days. The hundredth gave us a complete range of dreary, snow-covered hills; but to men whose last recollections of terra firma were connected with the refracted spectres that followed us eighty miles from shore, just one hundred days since, the solid certainty of mountain ridges was inexpressibly grateful. We studied their phases, as we drew nearer to them, with an intentness which would have been ludicrous under different circumstances: every cranny, every wrinkle spoke to us of movement, of a relation with the shut-out world. Our drift which brought us this blessed variety was favored by an unusual prevalence of northwesterly winds. We made in the thirty-one days of May one hundred and ninety odd miles to the southward and eastward.

For the last four days of the month we were at the margin of the Arctic circle, alternating within and without it. We passed to the south of it on the 30th, to recross it on the 31st with an accidental drift to the northward. We were experiencing at this time the rapid transition of seasons which characterizes this climate. The mean of the preceding month, April, had been +7° 96′; that of May was 20° 22′—a difference of nearly twelve degrees. At the same time, there was a chilliness about the weather, an uncomfortable rawness, both in April and May, which we had not known under the deep, perpetual frosts of winter. Cold there seemed a tangible, palpable something, which we could guard against or control by clothing and exercise; while warmth, as an opposite condition, was realizable and apparent. But here, in temperatures which at some hours were really oppressing, 60° to 80° in the sun, and with a Polar altitude of 45°, one half the equatorial maximum, we had the anomaly of absolute discomfort from cold. I know that hygrometric conditions and extreme daily fluctuations of the thermometer explain much of this; but it was impossible for me to avoid thinking at the time that there must also be a physiological cause more powerful than either.

I have alluded in my journal to the return of the birds. They were most welcome visitors. Crowds of little snow-birds (*Emberiza* and *Plectrophanes*), with white breasts and jetty coverts, were attracted by the garbage which the thaw had reproduced around us, and twittered from pile to pile, chirping sweet music over their unexpected store-house. Some of the larger birds, too, were with us, returning to the mysterious North; the anatinæ, represented by the eiders (*Somateria*), followed by two of the uria genus, the grylle and the alke. We recognized the latter as our little fat friend of last summer, and gave him treatment accordingly. I shot thirty-three in one day, which my mess-mates made up to sixty.

The characteristic disease of May was the snow-blindness, severe and acute, leaving with some of us a disturbed, uncertain state of vision far from pleasing. The remedy most effective was darkness. A disk of hard wood, with a simple slit, admitting a narrow pencil of light, we found a better protection than the goggle or colored lens; the increased sensibility of the retina seeming to require a diminution of the quantity rather than a modification of the character of the ray. The slightest automatic movement varied, of course, the sentient surface affected by the impression.

HUMMOCK FORMED MARCH 23, 1851.

CHAPTER XLII.

As we neared the narrow Straits of Davis, our expectations of disruption and liberation underwent many changes. All our reasonings seemed to be negatived by the results. We were the illustration of powerless ignorance; what we hoped for one day, we congratulated ourselves that we had escaped the next. We were rotating on the disk of a great wheel, with a ragged and constantly changing periphery. Our position on this was eccentric, and our rate of motion variable, as the obstructions which our ice-field encountered made it revolve on one or another axis. We felt that our prison could not retain its integrity much longer against the diversified agencies that were assailing it: beyond this we scarcely framed a conjecture.

It was evident that other changes more constant, and probably more effective than those of disruption, were taking place in the great plain around us. The snowy crust began to yield under our feet, and the hummock ridges, which had so long bristled in every direction, were losing their sharpness or bending before the sunshine. We had seen this great field grow up from the bosom of the ocean; and, traveling back in memory, it seemed but a few days since our sails swelled useless against the mast, as this ominous and unyielding barrier closed us in.

What better type can we have of the universal principle of change than this solid immensity of varied ice, only three months ago a quiet liquid sea, and now resolving itself, under the resistless action of natural causes, into its normal element! The destructive and conservative energies, those great powers of displacement and renewal which sustain the equilibrium of the globe, may be seen, in an humble yet impressive scale, in the formation, growth, increase, degradation, and departure of this icy terra firma. The geological analogies exhibited by the changes in the configuration of this pack—changes involving the noblest dynamic forces, as well as those slower actions now operating upon the crust of our earth—would form a volume for the comprehensive record of Von Buch or Murchison.

Instead of sea and land, the two great reciprocating agents and subjects of geological change, if for a moment you read sea and ice, hosts of analogies come crowding upon you, which, even to an uneducated observer like myself, assimilate the theoretical genesis of the one to the practical eye-seen growth of the other. The conversion of sea into ice, and of ice to sea, the excavation of valleys, the degradation of hills, the transfer of material to other unkindred surfaces, the transition from dry ice-fields to marshes impregnated with salt, the anomalous influences of currents and winds, and the final depravation of crystalline structure, are marshaled with forces of upheaval and depression, the synclinal and anticlinal axes which characterize the splendid dynamics of ice in motion.

I intended, when I began to arrange this narrative, to offer my ice-notes as a contribution to the Smithsonian publications. But a new duty is before me in the same field; and it may perhaps be as well that I should hold them back, till the experience of a northern winter or two shall have enabled me to test the conclusions which they point to. For the present I content myself with a mere *resumé*. My immediate subject is the growth of the pack.

On the twelfth of September, while attempting with a free top-gallant breeze to make our way to the east, the thermometer indicating a mean daily temperature of +14° or 18° below the freezing point, the sea was observed to gradually thicken around us. A pasty sludge, formed of crystals broken up by the action of the waves, began to resolve itself into those polyhedral plates described by Scoresby under the name of pancake ice.

SLUDGE. PANCAKE.

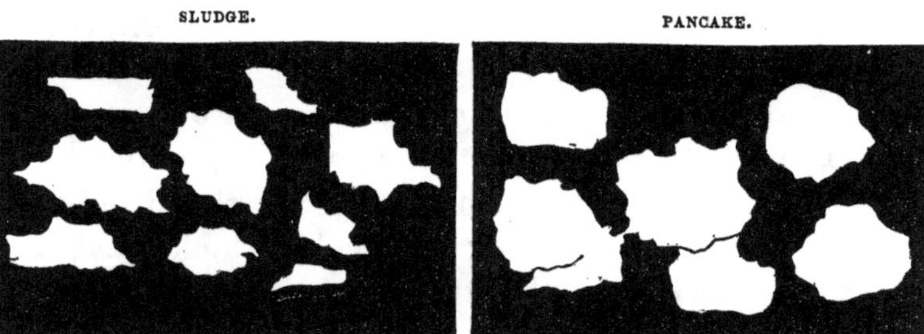

As the wind increased, these were rolled into actual spheroids; their forces being regulated by the laws which control equally compressed spheres, giving rise to a rudely pentagonal arrangement not unlike a tesselated pavement. To such an extent had

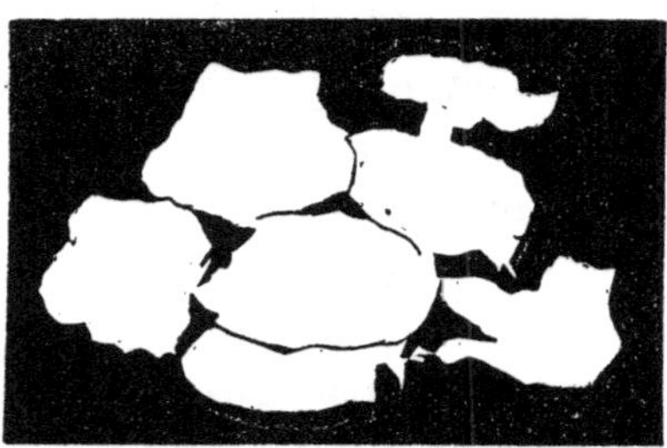

this increased by the night of the 13th, that we lost all power of progress.

When morning opened around us, we found ourselves in the midst of a great area of five-sided tiles, marked at their lines of junction by a slightly uplift-

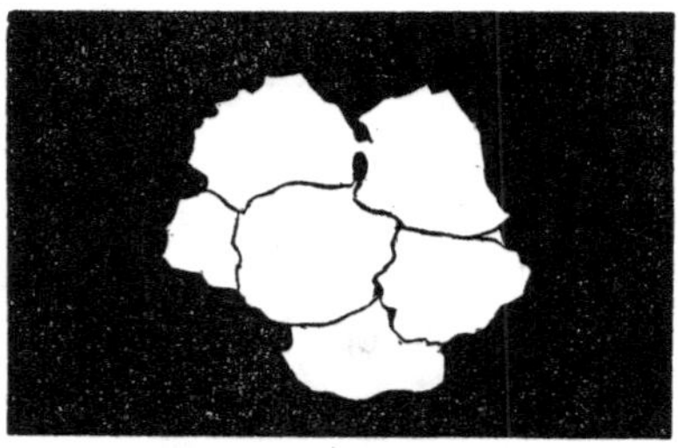

ed ridge: this would already bear a man. From this moment until the date of our escape, nine months after, our sails were without use; and our movements, as well as our destinies, were regulated by our ice-jailer. By the 20th of October, the floe immediately about us was twenty inches thick; and it had so interlocked itself with other ice-fields of different diameters, that to the eye it became a part of a great plain, terminated only by the headlands of the shores, and a narrow water-channel which separated us from them.

As long as we continued in Wellington Channel, our ice had not acquired its full firmness and tenacity: its structure was granular and almost spongy, its mass infiltrated with salt water, and its plasticity such that it crumbled and moulded itself to our form under pressures which would otherwise have destroyed us.

By the time we had reached the middle of Barrow's Straits, and the winter's midnight of December had darkened around us, our thermometers indicating a mean of 15° and 20° below zero, the ice attained a thickness of three feet, with an almost flinty hardness, and a splintery fracture at right angles to its horizontal plane. Such ice was at its surface completely fresh, and, when tested with nitrate of silver, gave not the slightest discoloration.

It was here, while drifting at a mean rate of twelve miles a day, through a channel compressed by the salient projection of the shore, that the most fearful of our ice-disruptions occurred. They seemed to combine the horrors of tempest, explosion, and earthquake. Our floe was severed to its centre. Dark rivers, exhaling that curious meteor, the frost-smoke, reticulated the entire surface; and our vessel, thrown alternately upon her beams, or plunged bows down into the ice, impressed us with a sense of immediate destruction.

This convulsion gave me an opportunity of witnessing, upon a scale which perhaps exceeded that of any previous experience, the operation called hummocking.

Imagine the flat, snow-covered floe surface, caught between two forces of great intensity, or two moving bodies several feet in thickness and miles in diameter, meeting at their marginal lines. The pure white surface of the snow remains unchanged. Presently, within some particular zone, determined by causes not to be entered into here, you see a slight crimping, followed by a dotted or Petersham-cloth appearance on the ice. This is followed again very rapidly by a multitude of transverse ridges or waves; and now for the first time you become conscious of a sharp, humming, grinding murmur.

Cast your eyes now over the level floe—level of a minute ago—and you will see that on each side of you there is a descent, and that the descending surface is curved. The snow is in motion, and small fissures fly over it in every direction, but principally parallel to the lines of pressure. The noises now become mingled with reports, not loud, but prolonged, like breaking the crust of a giant loaf of bread. Suddenly the lines of snow-fissures open into wedge-like chasms. Now run for it, without stopping to question; you have been standing all this time in the very centre of a forming hummock.

As you run, loud explosions, accompanied by a whirring as of spinning-jennies, and a whining as of young puppies, bring you up; and turning, you see the floe slowly part in the middle. The lines of previously marked fissures rise up into gigantic tables. Tables of one side oppose those of the other, and the margins of the floes from which they have arisen are pressing on with renewed energies to fill up the partial vacancy. Tables become more and more perpendicular; the edges beneath meet again, grind, fight,

rear themselves into fresh tables, thrusting over those first formed. New cracks rend the level ice. New curves fall into tabular masses; and thus in a few minutes the tranquil surface of frozen snow is covered by fragmentary barriers, grander and more massive than the Pharaonic rubbish of the Ramesium.

Differences of resistance along the margin of the floes, owing to irregularities in their lines of junction, give, of course, every irregularity conceivable to this action;* and it is only after it has continued sufficiently long to break all protruding edges, that the axis of the hummock approximates to a right line. My sections exhibit great diversity in this; but we learned, by the direction of the forces and the charac-

* The thickness of the ice, which the wood-cut on the following page is intended to represent, was between eight and nine feet. The height of one obliquely-fractured table was sixteen feet. The whole mass was thrown up from a previously solid floe in less than fifteen minutes. It was one of those on which Brooks and I practiced balancing during the commotion of the 23d of March.

ter of our floes, to determine pretty accurately beforehand the type of the approaching hummock.

Sometimes a hummock is as complete a jumble of confused tables as if Titans had been emptying rubbish carts of marble upon the floes. Sometimes they are so crumbled by the excessive action, that they look like crushed sugar; and, again, I have seen neatly-squared blocks piled regularly one above the other in a Cyclopean wall.

These pressures sometimes develop grotesque and singular forms. One of the most simple, an arch of ice four feet in thickness, bridging a fissure, is pictured literally in a former chapter. My friend, Mr. Murdaugh, pointed out to me two narrow tables forming the gable-end and the roof of a house. I am sorry I have lost the sketch I made of them.

Once, well on in November, while walking toward Barlow's Inlet with old Blinn, we came to a cross perched on a rounded dune, and sonorous when struck; and I remember, long after day had returned to us, during some of my walks upon the floes, coming to a little grave-yard of ice-tablets. They needed no inscription to record that winter had been. The two sketches that follow are of one of these monuments; the second drawing shows the action of gravity on the block after some weeks of exposure. It was more than fifty feet long.

It will readily be seen that these actions, renewed at intervals throughout many months, would essentially change the topography of our ice-country. In fact, although I have compared the primary and elemental forms of each floe to parts of a tesselated pavement, our great ice-field was one vast, broken, and confused mosaic-work, composed of ice-fields of different ages and thicknesses, and marked at their lines of junction by uplifted ridges of equally-varying dimensions.

Except that atmospheric deposit or hoar-frost, which seems in these Arctic regions to take the place of a more direct precipitation, we had no snow until late in November. Then we had those fine, dust-like snows, which, at low temperatures and in times of high wind, were hardly distinguishable from the driftings of former snow-fields. It was not until our closing month, with one exception, that the snow fell in the familiar flakes of home. All these tended to modify the aspect of our surface, rounding off edges, and filling up interstitial cavities; while those frozen vesicles, with modifications of the hexagon form, which I have alluded to as accompanying our parheliac and coronal phenomena, also contributed their share.

Thus, then, we continued drifting toward the south, sharing the movements of the icy system of which we were the centre, and only conscious of motion by the observation of that greater system which shone out above us. With March came a renewal of the ice-openings, and animal life, so long suspended, came back to us. The first bird seen was a diver (*C. Septentrionalis*), still in his winter plumage. On the same day we saw several seal. As the openings increased to rivers, and began to permeate the great pack more thoroughly, the narwhal and beluga, and, in two instances, the mysticetus, or right whale of the whalers, began to resort to them. The Laridæ, represented by the ivory, kittiwake, and the Burgomaster gulls, screamed over the floes. Our old friends, the mollemokes, fed once more upon the garbage around the vessels. The predatory jager (*Lestris parasitica*) soon joined them. Bears stalked about in numbers, accompanied by their satellites, the white foxes.

I have spoken of the first renewal of migratory life, as seen in that familiar little fringillide, the snow-bird. In company with the Plectrophanes, they crowded around our ships at a very early day; but it was only in the second week of May that the great Arctic migration really began. The air was checkered now with moving columns of birds: the families Uria and Somateria, the auks and the eiders, flew over us in continuous crowds.

It was at this time that the floe, which had so long been our homestead, began to show symptoms of decay. The mean thickness of our pack—the mean of many measurements—might be regarded as eight feet; although the ice-tables were in some cases so thrust one under the other, as to increase it to twenty and even thirty feet. Our great pack probably extended in a contiguous line from Lancaster Sound to Cape Walsingham, with a breadth of not less than two hundred miles.

It was interesting to observe the compensations by which Nature got rid of this vast accumulation. The simple effects of solar heat, whether from the atmosphere above or the heated currents below, do not satisfactorily explain the dissolution of this ice. Changes in its mechanical structure evidently took place, preparing the way for the subsequent actions of thaw. My attention was first called to this fact by hearing, through my friend, Lieutenant Brown, that the observatory of Sir James Ross at Leopold Island was moist and saggy, while the outside ice remained dry and firm. In the month of May, while our mean temperature was still below the freezing point, I noticed, during my walks over the ice, that certain surface-floes, which had been during the winter hard and fresh, began to yield under me as I walked, and gave a decidedly brackish taste to the palate. The ice, too, in many cases lost its tenacity and resistance. Our coal, which had been thrown out loosely on it, so depressed the little area around it, as to be surrounded by water; and some of the larger hummocks, whose colossal blocks had attracted my attention during the winter, were now wet and marshy to approach. Upon excavating blocks of ice with the saw and pickaxe, it was found, in many cases, to have lost its well-condensed character. It was divided by vertical lines into prisms, which stood prominently out, and ran continuously from the watery to the atmospheric surface, with an arrangement almost basaltic.*

Struck by this circumstance, I was led to test the ice of different localities by both the Marcet's bottle and the nitrate of silver, and discovered that the floes, which had formed in midwinter at temperatures below −30, were still fresh and pure, while the floes of slower growth, or of the early and late portions of the season, were distinctly saline. Indeed, ice which only two months before I had eaten with pleasure, was now so salt that the very snow which covered it was no longer drinkable.

This is a subject well worthy of future examination. The dissolution of the great ice-fields of the Polar regions bears upon physical questions of the highest importance; and it really seems to me that changes, independent of expansion and contraction, must take place in the molecular condition of the ice at temperatures greatly below the freezing point.

Another element in the disintegration of the floes, of which this was but a preliminary process, struck me forcibly a little later in the season. The invasion of the capillary structure of the ice by salt water from below would act, both chemically and mechanically in destroying its structure; but I am led to believe

* I am happy to find since my return, that this basaltic arrangement of the ice has been noticed also by Sir John Richardson.

that, in addition to the actions of simple infiltration, forces allied to endosmosis are called into play. I observed, during the month of May and in the last of April, that the surface snows, heated by the sun, formed pools in the most dependent portions of our ice. Where this occurred in ices formed either early or late in the season, and which presented, therefore, the prismatic arrangement I have described, the work of destruction went on with wonderful rapidity. Although our mean temperature was greatly below the freezing point, and these little pools were themselves coated nightly with a pellicle of ice, a very few days would render them unsafe. A boat-hook could be thrust nearly through them, and they were even dangerous for pedestrians. We had thus all the indications, except that of a membraneous interspace, which might invite endosmotic action; fluids of different densities above and below, and an intermediate structure abounding in capillary ducts.

The presenting face of the hummocks, approaching more or less nearly to the vertical, opposes them to the direct instead of the oblique rays of the sun; and their sides begin to thaw in consequence, while the more horizontal floes remain unchanged: and as these hummock ridges represent the lines of previous cementation, they are soon prepared to become those of first separation. Floes break up most readily along such lines of old cementation.

Before passing from these causes of disintegration and destruction in the pack, I would refer again to the fact which I have mentioned already of its being a great mosaic work, composed of tables of various thicknesses, and, of course, of varying resistance. Such ice, therefore, when subjected to mechanical pressure, whether by the action of currents and winds, or of protruding headlands, must present throughout its entire area a varying momentum and resistance. This, in connection with the fact of the hummock ridges or lines of junction being the soonest to give way, will explain the facility with which this great pack yields to assailing forces from without.

I believe I have adverted already to another most interesting and beautiful provision of nature to prevent the reconsolidation of the ice after it has been once broken up during the seasons of thaw. Fragmentary masses, which were fast cemented during the winter to the under surface of the floe, now rise through the water, interposing themselves between the opening tables, and acting as checks or wedges to prevent their reapposition and cementation.

By such impressive compensations does nature effect the equilibrium of the year. In a short and irregularly-graduated season, this great ice-raft, the growth of nine months of congelation, is returned to water by means almost independent of thaw, and resumes its office of tempering the climates of the distant south. As the views I have detailed in this chapter of the causes which effect the final disintegration of the pack may perhaps be novel, I venture to recite them in the form of a summary.

First. Changes in the molecular condition of the ice at temperatures below the freezing point, giving rise to infiltration of salt water and rapid decomposition of the ice in consequence.

Second. A greater intensity of this action, owing to the infraposition and superposition of two fluids of differing densities, inducing a rapid circulation allied to endosmosis.

Third. The facile disruption induced by transmitted forces throughout a plain of varying diameter and resistance.

Fourth. The softening down of hummock ridges, the lines of previous junction.

Fifth. The interposition of floating fragments or calves, preventing their reconsolidation.

ERODED BERG.

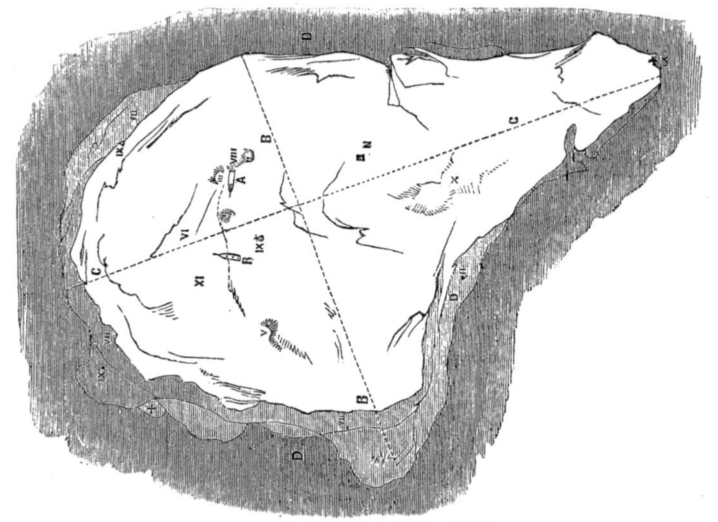

TOPOGRAPHY OF THE FLOE, MAY 31.

A. Advance. B B. Shorter diameter, 3½ miles.
R. Rescue. C C. Longer diameter, 5½ miles.
Distance between the vessels, 500 yards.

CHAPTER XLIII.

"*June* 1. June opens on us warm. Our mean temperature to-day has been above the freezing point, 34°; our lowest only 29°; and at 11 this morning it rose to 40°. The snow-birds increase in numbers and in confidence. It is delightful to hear their sweet jargon. They alight on the decks, and come unhesitatingly to our very feet. These dear little Fringillides have evidently never visited Christian lands.

"*June* 3. The day misty and obscure: no land in sight from aloft; and no change apparent in the floe. But we notice a distinct undulation in the ice trenches alongside, caused probably by some propagated swell.

"I walked out at night between 9 and 11 o'clock in

search of open water. We had the full light of day, but without its oppressive glare. The thawed condition of the marginal ice made the walk difficult, and forced us at last to give it up. But, climbing to the top of a hummock, we could see the bay rolling its almost summer waves close under our view. It was a grand sight, but more saddening than grand. It seems like our cup of Tantalus; we are never to reach it. And while we are floating close upon it, the season is advancing; and if we are ever to aid our brothers in the search, we should even now be hurrying back.

"*June* 4. Yesterday over again. But the water is coming nearer us. As we stand on deck, we can see the black and open channel-way on every side of us, except off our port quarter: it is useless to talk of points of the compass; our floe rotates so constantly from right to left, as to make them useless in description. To port, the extent of ice baffles the eye, even from aloft; it must, however, be a mere isthmus.

"*June* 5, Thursday. We notice again this morning the movement in the trench alongside. The floating scum of rubbish advances and recedes with a regularity that can only be due to some equable undulation from without to the north. We continue perched up, just as we were after our great lift of last December. A more careful measurement than we had made before, gave us yesterday, between our height aft and depression forward, a difference of level of 6 feet 4 inches. This inclination tells in a length of 83 feet—about one in thirteen.

"P.M. The BREAK-UP AT LAST! A little after five this afternoon, Mr. Griffin left us for the Rescue, after making a short visit. He had hardly gone before I heard a hail and its answer, both of them in a tone of more excitement than we had been used to for some time past; and the next moment, the cry, 'Ice cracking ahead!'

"Murdaugh and myself reached the deck just in time to see De Haven crossing our gangway. We followed. Imagine our feelings when, midway between the two vessels, we saw Griffin with the ice separating before him, and at the same instant found a crack tracing its way between us, and the water spinning up to the surface. 'Stick by the floe. Good-by! What news for home?' said he. One jump across the chasm, a hearty God-bless-you shake of the hand, a long jump back, and a little river divided our party.

"Griffin made his way along one fissure and over another. We followed a lead that was open to our starboard beam, each man for himself. In half a minute or less came the outcry, 'She's breaking out: all hands aboard!' and within ten minutes from Griffin's first hail, while we were yet scrambling into our little Ark of Refuge, the whole area about us was divided by irregular chasms in every direction.

"All this was at half past five. At six I took a bird's-eye sketch from aloft. Many of the fissures were already some twenty paces across. Conflicting forces were at work every where; one round-house moving here, another in an opposite direction, the two vessels parting company. Since the night of our Lancaster Sound commotion, months ago, the Rescue had not changed her bearing: she was already on our port-beam. Every thing was change.

"Our brig, however, had not yet found an even keel.

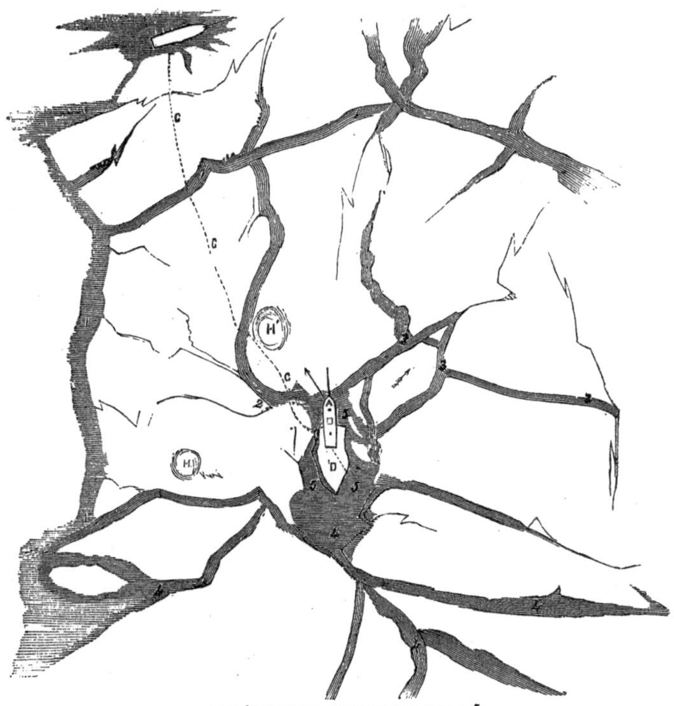

BIRD'S-EYE VIEW OF FLOE, JUNE 5.

A. Advance. D. Floe adhering to the Advance.
R. Rescue. C. Path between brigs before break-up.
H H. Hummocks.

The enormous masses of ice, thrust under her stern by the action of repeated pressures, had glued themselves together so completely, that we remained cradled in a mass of ice exceeding twenty-five feet in solid depth. Many of these tables were liberated by the swell, and rose majestically from their recesses, striking the ship, and then escaping above the surface for a moment, with a sudden vault.

"To add to the novelty of our situation, two cracks coming together obliquely, met a few yards astern of us, cleaving through the heavy ice, and leaving us attached to a triangular fragment of 14 by 22 paces. This berg-like fragment, reduced as it was, continued its close adhesion. Its buoyancy was so great, that it acted like a camel, retaining the brig's stern high in the air, her bows thrown down toward the water. We are so at this moment, 10 P.M."

All hands were in the mean time actively at work. The floe had been to us terra firma so long that we had applied it to all the purposes of land. Clothes and clothes' lines, sledges, preserved meats, kindling wood and planking, were now all bundled on board. The artificial horizon, which had stood for eight months upon a little ice-pedestal, was barely saved; and I had to work hard to get one of my few remaining thermometers from a neighboring hummock.

The cause of this sudden disruption—I mean the immediate cause, for the summer influences had prepared the floe for disintegration—was evidently the sea-swell setting from the southeast. This swell had given us minor manifestations of its existence as far back as the 1st of June. Whether it was increased without, or our floe made more accessible to it by the drifting away of other and protecting floes, I can not say. This, however, was clear, that the great undulations propagated by wave action caused our disruption. The proof of this I shall not forget.

Standing on our little deck, and looking out on the floe, we had the strange spectacle of an undulating solidity, a propagated wave borne in swell-like ridges, as if our ice was a carpet shaken by Titans. I can not convey the effect of this sublime spectacle. The ice, broken into polyhedric masses, gave at a few hundred yards no indications to the eye of the lines of separation; besides which, the infiltration of salt water had no doubt increased the plasticity of the material. Imagine, then, this apparently solid surface, by long association as unyielding to us as the shore, taking suddenly upon itself the functions of fluidity, another condition of matter. It absolutely produced something like the nausea of sea-sickness to see the swell of the ice, rising, and falling, and bending, transmitting with pliant facility the advancing wave.

A hummock hill, about midway between us and the Rescue, gave me an opportunity of measuring rudely the height of the swell. It rose till it covered her quarter boat; sinking again till I could see the side of the brig down to her water-line, an interval of five feet at least.

"As we walk along the edge of the open fissures, we see a wonderful variety in the thickness of the ice. Our apparently level surface is, in fact, a mosaic work of ices, frozen at separate periods, and tesselated by the several changes or disruptions which we have undergone. Thus I can see the tables under our stern extending down at least twenty-five feet: adjoining this is ice of four feet: next comes a field of six feet; and then hummock ridges, with tables choked below, so as to give an apparent depth of twenty.

"The 'calves' also, of which a great many have now risen to the surface, are worthy of note. These singular masses are evidently fragments of tables, of every degree of thickness, which have been forced down by pressure, and afterward, by some change in the temperature of the water, or by wave and tidal actions, have been liberated again from the floe, and find their way upward wherever an opening permits. We saw them honey-combed and cellular, water-sodden and in rounded bowlders, rising from the depths of the sea. Their density, so near that of the liquid in which they were submerged, made this rise slow and impressive. We could see them many fathoms below, voyaging again to the upper world. Once between the gaping edges of the lead, they effectually prevent the closing. They are about us in every direction, interposed between the fields.

"The appendage which sustains our brig has a good deal of this character. I will try to make an exact drawing of it as a curiosity, if it hangs on to us much longer. Its buoyancy indicates great submerged mass. A strong cable and ice anchor have been carried to a floe on our starboard bow, and the swell drives it upon us like a great battering-ram. This ingenious method of pounding us out of our tenacious cradle subjects us to a regular succession of heavy shocks, which would startle a man not used to ice navigation. At the time I write, 11 P.M., we have been nearly three hours subjected to this banging without any apparent impression. To-morrow we will, if not liberated, apply the saw; and then again to the warps!

"11 20 P.M. In the midst of fragments, few more than a hundred yards in length, nearly all much smaller. Between them are zigzag leads of open water. Astern of us is an expansion of some fifty yards across; ahead, a winding creek, wider than our brig. Thus closes the day.

"One thing more: a thought of gratitude before I turn in. This journal shows that I have been in the daily habit of taking long, solitary walks upon the ice, miles from the ship. Suppose this rupture to have come entirely without forewarning! I had greased my boots for a walk a few hours before the change, and only postponed it because I happened to get absorbed in a book.

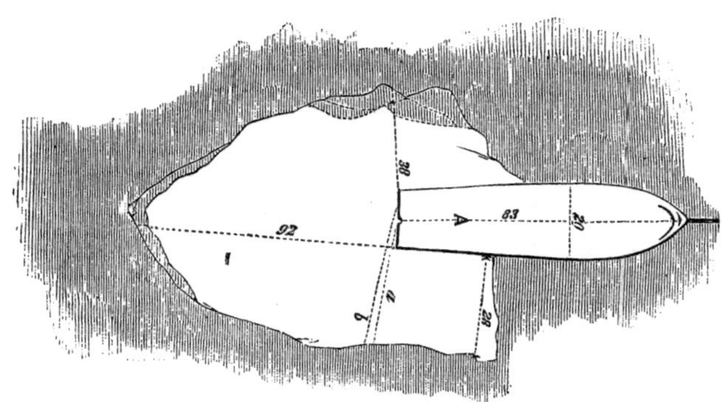

TOPOGRAPHY OF FLOE, JUNE 5.

PROFILE OF FLOE ; PORT SIDE.

PROFILE OF FLOE ; STARBOARD.

CHAPTER XLIV.

"*June* 6. Our bumping continued all night, without any apparent effect upon our sticking-plaster. Acting, as this impact does, at the long end of a lever, our stern being immovably fixed, it must be hard upon the rudder post, a beam that is now protruding from the least strengthened part of our brig into a transparent glue of tenacious ice. The twelve-feet saw, suspended from a tripod of spars, is at work, trying to cut a line across the mass to our keel. But for this appendage, we would be now warping through the fissures.

"7 P.M. The position of things continues unchanged. Our ice-saw with great labor buried its length in the floe, reaching nearly to our stern; but the submerged material is so thick that it has little or no effect. Wedging, by billets of wood between her sides and the mounding ice, was equally ineffectual. Gunpowder would perhaps release us; but that we can not spare.

"I tried to measure the depth of this inveterate companion of ours. Standing at our port gangway, I lowered the pump-rod twenty-four feet to a shelf projecting from the mass: beneath this, a prolongation or tongue stretched to a depth which I could not determine. On the other side, to starboard, the ice descends in solid mass some twenty feet. Adopting twenty-four feet as a mean depth, and ninety by fifty feet as the mean of dimensions at the surface, the solid contents of this troublesome winter relic would be 108,000 cubic feet. No wonder it lifts up our little craft bodily. I have made my drawings of it with all topographical accuracy.

"The wind has been hauling round from the south to the west, and by afternoon blew quite freshly. We made all sail, even to studding-sails, in hopes of forcing the cracks ahead, and tearing ourselves, as it were, from our impediment. Thus far all has failed.

"10 P.M. The ship is covered with canvas: she stands motionless amid the ice, although her wings are spread and tense. The wind is fresh and steady from the northwest. Our swell ceases with this wind, and the floes seem disposed to come together again; but the days of winter have passed by, and the interposing calves prevent the apposition of the edges.

"The effects of a constant force, slight as it seems,

have been beautifully shown by our brig. Pressing as we do, under full canvas, against heavy yet quiescent masses, we gradually force ahead, breasting aside the floes, and leaving behind us a pool of open water. Our rate is ten feet per hour! Remember that the old man of Sinbad still clings to us, and that we carry the burden in this slow progress. I hope that the Sinbad comparison will end here; for I can readily, without much imagination, carry it further.

"12 Midnight. Still advancing, dragging behind us this pertinacious mass. We have butted several times rudely against projecting floes, but it is as unmoved as solid rock. Very foggy: Rescue not visible. Thermometer at 29°.

"We recognize, among the floe fragments around us, old play-fellows. Here we played foot-ball; there we skated; by this hummock crag stood my thermometers; and here I shot a bear. We are passing slowly from them, or they from us. Now and then a rubbish pile will show itself, cresting the pure ice. Even an old Champagne basket, full of nothing but sadly-pleasant associations, is recognized upon a distant floe. This breaking up of a curtilage is not without its regrets. I wish that our 'old man' would loosen his griping knees: three hours would put us into comparatively open water.

"*June* 7, Saturday. The captain says that the shocks of the night of the fifth were the hardest our brig has experienced yet.

"This morning we made our incubus fast to one end of a passing floe, and ourselves fast to the other: double hawsers were used, blocks and tackle rigged, and all hands placed at our patent winch, the slack being controlled by a windlass. We parted our stern hawser, and that was all. Our resort now is to the fourteen-feet saw. With this, before the day closes, we shall cut a skerf as far as our fore-foot, and then try the efficacy of wedges.

"Toward evening the Rescue made sail, and forced her way slowly through the fragments. By eight P.M. she was snugly secured to the other side of our own floe. A beautiful sight it was to see once more, even in this labyrinth of rubbish, a moving sail-spread vessel. Once a momentary opening showed us the dark water, and beneath it the shadow of the brig.

"10 40. A crash! a low, grinding sound, followed by loud exclamations of 'Back,' 'back!' 'Hold on,' 'hold on!' I ran upon deck in time to add one cheer more to three which came from the ice. A large fragment, extending from her saw-crack along the bottom on the port side, had broken off, cutting the triangle in half, and leaving the crew behind floating and separated from the ship. All that now confined us was the mass (*a*) which remained on her starboard quarter. This descended some twenty or more feet, embracing our keel, and by its size sustaining us in our perched condition. We had settled but nine inches in consequence of our partial disengagement.

"Looking from the taffrail down the stern-post, we can now see the position of this portion of our brig distinctly. A strip of her false keel has been forced from its attachments, drawing the heavy bolts, and tearing away some of our sheathing. How far the injury extends, whether the entire length of the brig, or through some few yards, we can not tell. It must have occurred during the great ice commotion of December 7th and 8th. The disruption of January no doubt added to the thickness of the underlying tables;

but our keel probably received its shock at the same time that we received our elevation. We have escaped wonderfully.

"*June* 8, Sunday. Even keel again!! Once more floating ship-fashion, in a ship's element. It was between twelve and one o'clock this morning. Murdaugh went down upon the fragment, which was still adhering to our starboard side. He had hardly rested his weight upon it, when, with certain hurried, scarcely premonitory grindings, it cleared itself. He had barely time to scramble up the brig's side, tearing his nails in the effort, before, with crash and turmoil, it tumbled up to the surface, letting us down once more into clear water. When I reached the deck, I could hardly realize the level, horizontal condition of things, we have been accustomed to this up and down hill work so long.

"9 P.M. At 1 o'clock P.M. the wind freshened from the northward, enough to make sail. We cast off, and renewed the old times process of boring, standing irregularly among the fragments to the southward and eastward. We received some heavy bumps, but kept under weigh until 6 P.M., when an impenetrable ice-fog caused us to haul up to a heavy floe, to which we are now fast by three anchors. We estimate our progress at six miles. The Rescue is not visible.

"From the heavy floe to which we are secured we obtained fresh *thawed* water. This is the first time since the 15th of September that I have drunk water liquefied without fire. Eight months and twenty-four days: think of that, dear strawberry and cream eating family!

"We saw an ice-floe to-day, which had evidently come from the upper northern regions of Wellington, or the North Baffin's Straits. This ice, though pure and beautiful, could never have been created in any single winter. It has made me understand for the first time the startling stories of Wrangell. This floe is now more than two hundred and fifty yards long by four hundred wide; a size too large for infraposition of tables, while its purity precludes the idea of ground ice. Its depth, ascertained from its mean line of flotation, exceeds forty feet. Its surface is level, and the appearance, looking down into its pure depths, beautiful beyond description. It forms part of a great field, miles in circumference, as similar coaptating fragments are seen in every direction; the great swell of the 5th having no doubt destroyed its integrity. From what great winter basin comes this colossal ice?"

APPROACHING DISCO.

CHAPTER XLV.

We continued our progress through a labyrinth of ice, sometimes running into a berg, or grazing against its edge so close as to carry away a spar or stave a quarter-boat, but still making our way across to the Greenland shore. The sea was studded with low bergs and water-washed floes, wearing the fantastic forms which had surprised us the year before. Some were both complicated and graceful, supported generally by peduncular bases, which gave them a curious aspect of fragility. This was evidently due to the action of the waves at the water-line, aided by the warmth of the atmosphere. Some of these forms I have already given at the foot of chapters; others I group in the margin.

If we suppose a nearly symmetrical lump of ice, floating with that stable equilibrium which belongs to its excessive submergence, the atmosphere, which has now a temperature as high as 64° in the sunshine, will gradually round off and crease the edges, and at the same time will melt the portions of the mass which are above water. Its buoyancy increasing as its weight is reduced, the berg will now rise slowly, presenting a succession of new surfaces to the abrasion of the waves; and thus we shall have the familiar mushroom or fungoid appearance which is shown in many of the plates.

The process continuing under all the modifications of wave action, while the opposing face of the berg varies with every change of its gravitating centre, we may have eccentric resemblances to animated things sculptured in the ice, and at other times forms of classic symmetry, or the frets and garniture of mediæval art.

Our sail through this fanciful archipelago was a most uncomfortable one. Our stoves had been taken down; and the scurvy, exaggerated by the increased exposure to damp, began again to bear hard upon us. We devoured eagerly the seal, of which, by good fortune, we had several re-enforcements; but as the excitements of peril declined, the energies of the men seemed to relax more and more; and I had reason to fear that we should not be able to resume our search effectively, until the health of our party had undergone a tedious renovation.

It had been determined by our commander that we should refresh at Whale Fish Islands, and then hasten back to Melville Bay, the North Water, Lancaster Sound, and Wellington Channel; and certainly there was no one on board who did not enter heart and soul into the scheme. It was in pursuance of it that we were now bending our course to the east.

The circumstances that surrounded us, the daily incidents, our destination and purpose, were the same as when approaching the Sukkertoppen a year before. There were the same majestic fleets of bergs, the same legions of birds of the same varieties, the same anxious look-out, and rapid conning, and fearless encounter of ice-fields. Every thing was unchanged, except the glowing confidence of young health at the outset of adventure. We had taken our seasoning: the experience of a winter's drift had quieted some of our enthusiasm. But we felt, as veterans at the close of a campaign, that with recruited strength we should be better fitted for the service than ever. All, therefore, looked at the well-remembered cliffs, that hung over Kronprinsen, with the sentiment of men approaching home for the time, and its needed welcomes.

We reached them on the 16th. Mr. Murdaugh, and myself, and four men, and three bottles of rum, were dispatched to communicate with the shore. As we rowed in to the landing-place, the great dikes of injected syenite stood out red and warm against the cold gray gneiss, and the moss gullies met us like familiar grass-plots. Esquimaux crowded the rocks, and dogs barked, and children yelled. A few lusty pulls, and after nine months of drift, and toil, and scurvy, we were once more on terra firma.

God forgive me the revulsion of unthankfulness! I ought to have dilated with gratitude for my lot.

Winter had been severe. The season lagged. The birds had not yet begun to breed. Faces were worn, and forms bent. Every body was coughing. In one hut, a summer lodge of reindeer and seal skins, was a dead child. It was many months since I had looked at a corpse. The poor little thing had been for once washed clean, and looked cheerfully. The father leaned over it weeping, for it was a boy; and two little sisters were making lamentation in a most natural and savage way.

I gave the corpse a string of blue beads, and bought a pair of seal-skin boots for twenty-five cents; and we rowed back to the brig. In a very little while we were under sail for Godhaven.

We were but five days recruiting at Godhaven. It was a shorter stay than we had expected; but we were all of us too anxious to regain the searching ground to complain. We made the most of it, of course. We ate inordinately of eider, and codfish, and seal, to say nothing of a hideous-looking toad fish, a *Lepodogaster*, that insisted on patronizing our pork-baited lines; chewed bitter herbs, too, of every sort we could get; drank largely of the smallest of small-beer; and danced with the natives, teaching them the polka, and learning the pee-oo-too-ka in return. But on the 22d, by six o'clock in the morning, we were working our way again to the north.

We passed the hills of Disco in review, with their terraced summits, simulating the Ghauts of Hindostan; the green-stone cliffs round Omenak's Fiord, the great dockyard of bergs; and Cape Cranstoun, around which they were clustered like a fleet waiting for convoy. They were of majestic proportions; and as we wound our way tortuously among them, one after another would come into the field of view, like a temple set to be the terminus of a vista. At one time we had the whole Acropolis looking down upon us in silver; at another, our Philadelpia copy of the Parthenon, the monumental Bank of the United States, stood out alone. Then, again, some venerable Cathe-

dral, with its deep vaults and hoary belfries, would spread itself across the sky; or perhaps some wild combination of architectural impossibilities.

We moved so slowly that I had time to sketch several of these dreamy fabrics. The one which is engraved on the opposite page was an irregular quadrangle, projected at the extremity of a series of ice-structures, like the promontory that ends an isthmus: it was crowned with ramparts turreted by fractures; and at the water-line a great barreled arch went back into a cavern, that might have fabled as the haunt of sea-kings or smugglers. Another, much smaller, but still of magnificent size, had been excavated by the waves into a deep grotto; and the light reflected from the bay against its transparent sides and roofs colored them with a blue too superb for imitation by the brush or pencil.

In the morning of the 24th we made the pack; more to the south, therefore, than last year. It appeared at first like a firm neck, extending out among heavy bergs well into Haroë Island; and remembering our last year's experience, we moved cautiously. But after a while, our captain, now perhaps the best ice-master afloat, determined on boring. The dolphin-striker was triced up, the boats were taken on board, and the old sounds of conning the helm began again. This time we were lucky. In four hours we were through the tongue of the pack, and out in nearly an open sea.

We did not move long, however, before the navigation became embarrassed. The ice between Cape Lawson and Storoë was too compact to be wedged aside; and after some rude encounters with the floes, and a narrow escape from a reef of rocks which Captain Graah's charts do not mention, we found ourselves, on the 25th, nearly embayed by the noble headlands off Ovinde Oerme. The ice, in a horseshoe curve, completely shut us in to the north, and the tongue of the pack we had come through lay between us and the sea. The wind had left us. We were drifting listlessly in a glassy sea that reflected the green-stone terraces and strange pyramidal masses of its romantic shores.

We amused ourselves killing seals. There must have been hundreds of them of all varieties playing about us. Generally they were to be seen paddling about alone, but sometimes in groups, like a party of school-boys frolicking in the Schuylkill. One of their favorite sports was "treading water," rising breast-high, keeping up a boisterous, indefatigable splashing, and stretching out their necks, as if to pry into the condition of things aboard ship. We compared their behavior to that of the timorous but curious natives, when the Europeans first met them in the waters of America; and in our intercourse with them, conformed accurately to the Spanish precedent.

Occasionally only we obeyed our "manifest destiny" with reluctance. Some of the younger of these poor sea-dogs had overmuch of the honest expression of their land brethren: the truncation of the muzzle in others, with no external ear showing behind it, set their faces in almost perfect and human-like oval. When one of these would come up out of the water near us, and, raising his head and shoulders, that stooped like those of a hooded Esquimaux, gaze steadily at us with his liquid eye, then diving, come up a little nearer and stare again; so drawing nearer and nearer, diving and rising alternately, till he came within musket range; it sometimes went hard to salute him with a bullet.

We shot, among others, a very large beast (*P. bar-*

bata), lying upon a floating piece of ice. The captain's ball went through his heart; and my own, equally deadly, within a few inches of it; but the unwieldy creature continued struggling to reach the water, until a shot from Mr. Lovell, close upon him, drove a musket-ball through his head. He measured eight feet from tip to tip, five feet eleven inches in his greatest circumference, and five feet six inches in girth behind the fore-flippers. His carcass was a shapeless cylinder, terminating in an awkward knob to represent the head.

We lost two seals by sinking. Hitherto, when killed on the instant by perforation of the brain or spinal marrow, they had invariably floated. But the rule does not hold always. I wounded one so as to carry away the crown of his skull, and Captain De Haven gave him a second shot from within a few yards directly through the head, and yet we lost him. As the balls struck, he discharged, almost explosively, a quantity of air, and went down like a loon. The whalers say, wound your seals; but my own experience is, that, if they are fat, it is best to kill them at once. A Danish boy, who had joined us by stealth at Disco, told us that the animal's sinking was a proof that he had no blubber. He was probably right: we certainly did not secure any that were in good condition.

The next day gave us excitement of a different sort. We had been lying in the young ice-field, close under the southeast shore of Storoë, with the current setting strong toward it, and a grim array of bergs to the west of us. It was an ugly position; but we were fairly entangled, and there was no escape. Early in the morning, the wind freshened, and blew in toward the island; the ice piling against the rocky precipice under our lee, and opening in broken masses to windward The Rescue managed to make fast to a crag between us and the shore, but our ice-anchors missed. At four in the afternoon we were within rifle-shot of the land, and still drifting; the wind a gale, and the sea-swell coming in heavily.

We stopped, of course, or there would have been an end of my journal. But for some hours things looked squally enough. Our soundings had become small by degrees and beautifully less, till they were down to thirteen feet; and the black wall looked so near that you could have hit it with a filbert. It could not have been fifty yards off, when we brought up on some grounded floe-pieces. By eleven, our warps had headed us to windward, and our bow was off shore. For once, at least, we owed our safety to the ice.

The Rescue followed a few hours after; and we took the direction of the pack together to the N.N.W. By the next day at noon we were within twenty-three miles of Uppernavik, but a belt of ice lay between. We anchored to a berg, and for two days waited patiently for an opening.

My messmates in the mean time went off on a hunt to a flat, rocky ledge, that showed itself inshore, and I amused myself with a tramp on the ice-island to which we were fast. I had for company a noble Esquimaux slut, that Governor Moldrup had enabled me to get at Disco, and a dog of the same breed belonging to Mr. Lovell. I do not know what has become of Hosky, as Mr. Lovell named his favorite; but my poor Disco fell a martyr to our Philadelphia climate and his Arctic costume together, some three days after we got home.

I had a quiet day's walk. My companions rambled

with evident glee over the peaks and ravines of their familiar element. It was a magnificent pile of frost-work. But these crystal palaces of the ice, like every thing else under this northern sky, deceive one strangely in their apparent size. We thought, when we anchored, that the berg was a small one; yet we coursed more than the third of a mile in almost a direct line before we reached its further edge.

The pure surfaces which we traveled over were studded with irregular blocks of ice, evidently once detached and cemented on again. They varied in size and shape from a boy's playing-marble to a haystack;

and by their interesting distribution suggested most obtrusively the question of almost every Arctic traveler, how such fragments find their place on the plateau surfaces of the icebergs. I had answered the question for myself before; but I was glad to be confirmed by the observations I made in the course of this excursion. When first the mass separates from the land-berg or glacier, it is accompanied by a large quantity of disengaged fragments, with all varieties of detritus; and during the alternate risings and sinkings that follow the fall into the sea, a great deal of this is caught by the emerging surface of the berg, and adheres to it. I noticed valleys, where the subsequent roll had rounded the masses, and grouped them into something resembling bowlder-drift. I had seen similar valleys in some of the large bergs of Duneira Bay, supplying a bed for temporary water-streams, in which the bowlders were beautifully rounded, and arranged in true moraine fashion. I have given a sketch of one of these: it faces this chapter.

Off Storoë, a white fox (*C. lagopus*) came to us on the loose ice: his legs and the tip of his tail were black. He was the first we had seen on the Greenland coast.

He was followed the next day by a party of Esquimaux, who visited us from Pröven, dragging their kayacks and themselves over seven miles of the pack, and then paddling merrily on board. For two glasses of rum and a sorry ration of salt-pork, they kept turning somersets by the dozen, making their egg-shell skiffs revolve sideways by a touch of the paddle, and hardly disappearing under the water before they were heads up again, and at the gangway to swallow their reward.

The inshore ice opened on the thirtieth, and toward evening we left the hospitable moorage of our iceberg, and made for the low, rounded rocks, which the Hosky pointed out to us as the seat of the settlement. The boats were out to tow us clear of the floating rubbish, as the light and variable winds made their help necessary, and we were slowly approaching our anchorage, when a rough yawl boarded us. She brought a pleasant company, Unas the schoolmaster and parish priest, Louisa his sister, the gentle Amalia, Louisa's cousin, and some others of humbler note.

The baptismal waters had but superficially regenerated these savages: their deportment, at least, did not conform to our nicest canons. For the first five minutes, to be sure, the ladies kept their faces close covered with their hands, only withdrawing them to blow their noses, which they did in the most primitive and picturesque manner. But their modesty thus assured, they felt that it needed no further illustration. They volunteered a dance, avowed to us confidentially that they had educated tastes—Amalia that she smoked, Louisa that she tolerated the more enlivening liquids, and both that their exercise in the open air had made a slight refection altogether acceptable. Hospitality is the virtue of these wild regions: our hard tack, and cranberries, and rum were in requisition at once.

It is not for the host to tell tales of his after-dinner company. But the truth of history may be satisfied without an intimation that our guests paid niggard honors to the jolly god of a milder clime. The veriest prince, of bottle memories, would not have quarreled with their heel-taps. * * *

We were inside the rocky islands of Pröven harbor as our watches told us that another day had begun. The time was come for parting. The ladies shed a few kindly tears as we handed them to the stern-seats: their learned kinsman took a recumbent position below the thwarts, which favored a continuance of his nap; and the rest of the party were bestowed with seaman-like address—all but one unfortunate gentleman, who, having protracted his festive devotions longer than usual, had resolved not to "go home till morning."

The case was a difficult one; but there was no help for it. As the sailors passed him to the bottom of the boat, and again out upon the beach, he made the air vocal with his indignant outcries. The dogs—I have told you of the dogs of these settlements, how they welcomed our first arrival—joined their music with his. The Prövenese came chattering out into the cold, like chickens startled from their roost. The governor was roused by the uproar. And in the midst of it all, our little weather-beaten flotilla ran up the first American flag that had been seen in the port of Pröven.

OOMIAK.

PRÖVEN HILLS.

CHAPTER XLVI.

THE port of Pröven is securely sheltered by its monster hills. But they can not be said to smile a welcome upon the navigator. A smiling country, like a smiling face, needs some provision of fleshly integuments; and no earthly covering masks the grinning rocks of Pröven. They look as if the process of crumbling, and wrinkling, and splitting, and splintering had been at work on them since the first Arctic frost succeeded the last metamorphic fire; and even now great ledges are wedged off from the hillsides by the ice, and roll clattering down the slopes into the very midst of the settlement.

Summer comes slowly upon Pröven. When we arrived, the slopes of the hills were heavily patched with snow, and the surface, where it showed itself, was frozen dry. The water-line was toothed with fangs of broken ice, which scraped against the beach as the tides rose and fell; and an iceberg somehow or other had found its way into the little port. It was a harmless lump, too deep sunk to float into dangerous nearness; and its spire rose pleasantly, like a village church.

"*July* 3. I am writing in the 'Hosky' House of Cristiansen. Cristiansen is the Danish governor of Pröven, and this house of Cristiansen is *the House* of Pröven. Its owner is a simple and shrewd old Dane, hale and vigorous, thirty-one of whose sixty-four winters have been spent within the Arctic circle, north of 70° N. Lord in his lonely region—his four sons and five subordinates, oilmen, the only white faces about him, except when he visits Uppernavik—the good old man has the satisfaction of knowing no superior. His habits are three fourths Esquimaux, one eighth Danish, and the remainder Prövenish, or peculiarly his own. His wife is a half-breed, and his family, in language and aspect, completely Esquimaux.

"When the long, dark winter comes, he exchanges books with his friend the priest of Uppernavik. 'The Dantz Penning Magazin,' and 'The History of the Unitas Fratrum,' take the place of certain well-thumbed, ancient, sentimental novels; and sometimes the priest comes in person to tenant the 'spare room,' which makes it very pleasant, 'for we talk Danish.'

"Except this spare room, which elsewhere would be called the loft of the house, its only apartment is the one in which I am. And here eat, and drink, and cook, and sleep, and live, not only Cristiansen and all his descendants, but his wife's mother, and her children, grandchildren, and great-grandchildren who are growing up about her. It is fifteen feet broad by sixteen long, with just height enough for a grenadier, without his cap, to stand erect, and not touch the beams. The frame of the house is of Norway pine, coated with tar, with its interspaces caulked with moss, and small window-panes inserted in a deep casing of wood.

"The most striking decorative feature is a ledge or shelf of pine plank, of varying width, which runs round three of its sides. Its capacity is wonderful. It is the sofa and bed, on which the entire united family find room to loll and sleep; and upon it now are huddled, besides a navy doctor and his writing board, one ink-bottle, sundry articles of food and refreshment, one sleeping child, one lot of babies not in the least asleep, one canary-bird cage with its exotic and most sorrowful little prisoner, and an infinite variety of other articles too tedious to mention, comprising seal-skins, boots, bottles, jumpers, glasses, crockery both of kitchen and nursery, coffee-pots, dog-skin socks, canvas pillows, an eider-down comforter, and a sick bitch with a youthful family of whining puppies.

"Una, the second daughter, has been sick and under treatment; and she is now hard at work with her sisters, Anna, Sara, and Cristina, on a tribute of gratitude to her doctor. They have been busy all the morning whipping and stitching the seal-skins with reindeer tendon thread. My present is to be a complete suit of ladies' apparel, made of the richest seal-skin, according to the standard mode of Pröven, which may always be presumed to be the 'latest winter fashion.' It is a really elegant dress. To some the unmentionables might savor of mascularity; but having seen something of a more polite society, my feminine associations are not restricted to petticoats. Extremes meet in the Esquimaux of Greenland and Amazons of Paris.

"The large family is a happy one: so small a home could not tolerate a quarrelsome mess. The sons, the men Cristiansens, brave

and stalwart fellows, practiced in the kayack, and the sledge, and the whale-net, adroit with the harpoon and expert with the rifle, are constant at the chase, and bring home their spoil, with the honest pride becoming good providers of their household. And the women, in their nursing, cooking, tailoring, and housekeeping, are, I suppose, faithful enough. But what favorable impression that the mind gets through other channels can contend against the information of the nose! Organ of the aristocracy, critic and *magister morum* of all civilization, censor that heeds neither argument nor remonstrance—the nose, alas! it bids me record, that to all their possible godliness cleanliness is not superadded.

"During the short summer of daylight—it is one of the many apparent vestiges, among this people, of ancient nomadic habits—the whole family gather joyously in the summer's lodge, a tent of seal or reindeer skin, pitched out of doors. Then the room has its annual ventilation, and its cooking and chamber furniture are less liable to be confounded. For the winter the arrangement is this: on three sides of the room, close by the ledge I have spoken of, stand as many large pans of porous steatite or serpentine, elevated on slight wooden tripods. These, filled with seal-blubber, and garnished with moss round the edge to serve as a wick, unite the functions of chandelier and stove. They who quarrel with an ill-trimmed lamp at home should be disciplined by one of them. Each boils its half-gallon kettle of coffee in twenty minutes, and smokes—like a small chimney on fire; and the three burn together. There is no flue, or fire-place, or opening of escape.

"On the remaining side of the room stand a valued table and three chairs; and with these, like a buhl cabinet or fancy étagère, conspicuous in its modest corner, a tub. It is the steeping-tub for curing skins. Its contents require active fermentation to fit them for their office; and, to judge from the odor, the process had been going on successfully."

We warped out to sea again on the afternoon of the third, with our friend the cooper for pilot; the entire settlement turning out upon the rocks to wish us good-by, and remaining there till they looked in the distance like a herd of seal. But we found no opening in the pack, and came back again to Pröven on the fourth, not sorry, as the weather was thickening, to pass our festival inside the little port.

Our celebration was of the primitive order. We saluted the town with one of the largest balanced stones, which we rolled down from the cliff above;

and made an egg-nogg of eider eggs; and the men had a Hosky ball; and, in a word, we all did our best to make the day differ from other days—which attempt failed. Still, God ever bless the fourth!

The sixth was Sunday, and we attended church in the morning at the schoolmaster's. The service consisted of a long-winded hymn, and a longer winded sermon, in the Esquimaux—surely the longest of long-winded languages. The congregation were some two dozen men and women, not counting our party.

We put to sea in the afternoon. The weather was soft and warm on shore; but outside it was perfectly delightful: no wind—the streams of ice beyond enforcing a most perfect calm upon the water; the thermometer in the sunshine frequently as high as 76°, and never sinking below 30° in the shade. I basked on deck all night, sleeping in the sun.

And such a night! I saw the moon at midnight, while the sun was slanting along the tinted horizon, and duplicated by reflection from the water below it: the dark bergs to seaward had outlines of silver; and two wild cataracts on the shore-side were falling from ice-backed cliffs twelve hundred feet into the sea.

July 7. I was awakened from my dreamy sleep to receive the visits of a couple of boats that were working slowly to us through the floes. An English face—two English faces—twelve English faces: what a happy sight! We had had no one but ourselves to speak our own tongue to for three hundred days, and were as glad to listen to it as if we had been serving out the time in the penitentiary of silence at Auburn or Sing-Sing. Their broad North Briton was music. It was not the offensive dialect of the provincial Englishman, with the affectation of speaking his language correctly; but a strong and manly home-brew of the best language in the world for words of sincere and hearty good-will. They had to turn up their noses at our seal's-liver breakfast; but, when they heard of our winter trials, they stuffed down the seal without tasting it. I felt sorry after they were off, that I had not taken their names down every one.

The whaling vessels to which they returned were in the freer water outside the shore stream, the Jane O'Boness, Captain John Walker; and the Pacific, Captain Patterson. These gentlemen boarded us as soon as we got through the ice to them. They thought our escape miraculous; and it was some time before they found words to congratulate us. "Augh!" and "Wonderful!" with a peculiar interchange of looks, was all they said.

These burned children dread the fire; and their conversation opened our eyes to dangers we had gone through half unconsciously. Few masters in the whaling trade but have at some time suffered wreck. Two seasons ago, this veteran Patterson saw his ship thrust bodily through another, and then the transfixed and transfixing vessels were both eaten up together by the greedy floes. He stepped from the last remnant of his buried sail on to the hummocks: "And that's a' that e'e ha' seen o' her!"

They left us newspapers, potatoes, turnips, eggs, and fresh beef enough to eat out every taint of scurvy! They took letters from us for home, and cheered ship when we parted. I must not soon forget the Pacific and Jane O'Boness.

WHALERS NEAR THE PACK

INTERIOR OF A NATIVE HUT, UPPERNAVIK.

CHAPTER XLVII.

The next day, beating hard to windward, we made Uppernavik again. The scenery around it was very striking, exhibiting some magnificent mural sections of gneiss and slates. The entering headland was some fifteen hundred feet high. We found all the hills patched with snow to the water's edge, where their bases are abraded by the moving floes from one year's end to another.

Mr. Murdaugh and myself visited the town; that is to say, the priest's house, the governor's house, the oil house, the school-church house, and sundry native huts. The wood-cut at the head of the chapter gives the interior of one of them, in which we superintended the manufacture of a dish of coffee.

We were received by the governor, accompanied by an old friend of ours from Pröven, a sort of secretary there, "plenty-scribe-'em" as he styled himself. The old gentleman had arrived at two that morning, in a whale-boat, with his stalwart sons, after thirty-two miles of pulling through the ice against the wind. "Keesey ver bod," he said; "the ice was very bad."

The governor, superior in tone to Cristiansen, who is a self-made man, welcomed us with fine Danish good-breeding, and there is no good-breeding better. We found him out to be a desperate conservative, fearful of nothing but change. His house was after the fashion of Mr. Moldrop's, of Godhaven, and scrupulously clean. Coffee was served; and we had the honor of being introduced to three young ladies of the half-breed, absolutely with frocks on. I thought I could see that one of them had pantalettes of seal-skin peeping out from under her skirt, and a wiser critic than myself might have said that all their dresses were somewhat antique of fashion. But they met us, on the other hand, with a lady-like disregard of our own outlandish costume; and though our language was somewhat composite in its idiom, for I understand neither the Danish nor the Hosky, and they understood very little English, we managed to keep up quite an animated conversation. It was very pleasant to relapse in their company for a while, into the manners of society at home.

We saw also the family of Petersen, Penny's dog and Esquimaux manager, all neat and pleasing persons; the sons, frank, manly fellows, and the eldest daughter really quite refined and pretty. But we did not remain long. Our Aberdeen friends had transferred to us a full supply of newspapers which they had brought for Penny: so, after prescribing for the governor's child, and receiving a dog-skin jumper for my fee, we returned on board to review the annals of the outer world for the past year.

We now pursued our way very smoothly. We had delightful weather; not the best, indeed, for men whose errand lay ahead, but still very welcome to those who had roughed it of late so severely. Summer was concentrating all its strength and beauty in the long, sun-encircled day, and the sky looked as if its blue and gold sunshine could never cloud over or end.

It was surprising how beautifully the sea revived the colors of the atmosphere. Wherever we looked down into it, it showed deep, like an inverted sky. It was of the most pellucid clearness too. We could see the perfect jungle of sea-weed that was growing under us. Actinia, painted with gaudy colors, went streaming by on the tides; Entomostraca and Limacinæ grouped themselves among the branches; and Clios, the ideals of zoophytic *otium cum dignitate*, were flashing colored light in shady places from their ciliary vibrions, or lazily turning their crimsoned disks to the sunshine. Every now and then some exploring crab would rise from the tree-tops, and waddle down again into the protecting umbrage.

As we went on the bergs became numerous. We sailed through a town of them, grouped together as if on purpose for stage effect. There were two hundred and five, all in view at a time.

The whalers call Baffin's Islands the Duck Islands, on account of the number of these birds that breed there, and many of their precipitous headlands Loon-

SCENE AT BAFFIN'S ISLANDS.

heads, for a similar reason. It was fine sport for all hands to gather eggs from the rocky crevices in which they build. The birds, when disturbed by our predatory visits, literally darkened the air; and their quick, sharp cries, the hum of their wings flapping around us, and the surging noise of the sea as it broke against the base of their fortress below, all together might have startled a novice in the trade of plunder. It was something like "gathering samphire."

We found the eider also very numerous. In the selection of their nests, I remarked that these birds avoid the soft and apparently wind-protected slopes; a wise instinct, as the drip from the melted snows would expose them to wet there. They choose generally the knobbed face of some summit, where coarse sedges and mosses grow against the stone. Sometimes the nest is a mere depression in the moss, sparsely lined with down; but more generally it is constructed with considerable skill in the tussocks of a coarse grass, whose straw lasts from season to season. The duck and drake build it in company. They free the roots from mould, net the fibres together, cement them firmly by a glutinous excretion, and pad the whole of the interior with their own fine down, felting it well against the sides.

The eider is an awkward bird on the wing, and hardly graceful in the water. Its square and block-like head, set clumsily upon the neck, reminds one disagreeably of the Ptero-dactyls of fossil history. On the edges of the floes, while congregated together, quacking and feeding on the helpless Actinia, they seem another animal. The position of their legs, set very far back, throws the body, penguin-like, nearly upright; and they move about erect, but easily and animated. When in numbers and at rest, they are wary and hard to approach; but, like most of the Anatinæ, are not easily diverted from their line of flight. Their apparent stupidity in sweeping over certain headlands, after our repeated slaughter of their fellows, was like that of our own canvas-backs at home. We killed numbers by station shooting.

But the greatest enemies of the eider here are the whalers, who, whether from New York, New England, or Old England, are, like my friends the Van Nests in the veracious history of Mr. Knickerbocker, desperate robbers of birds' nests. We gathered two hundred eider eggs in one morning before breakfast; but this was gleaning a reaped field. The whaler, Jane O'Boñess, had four hundred and fifty dozen on board: she sent us a market-basketful. Parker's vessel, the Pacific, had nearly as many. And in the good old days of the fleet, when from sixty to ninety sail dared this

Melville Bay in a season, they would take from a couple of hundred thousand to half a million.

On the ninth we overtook a vessel, which proved to be the M'Lellan of New London, the bearer to us of letters and papers from home. My seals, thank God, were all in red wax; and I missed my count of twenty-four hours, by sitting up through the whole daylight night, reading them till it was breakfast-time.

The tenth, we came up with the whaling fleet lying at the Barrier; and before midnight had seven north country whaling captains from them, "holding clack" in our little cabin. The sturdy good fellows were overrunning with sympathy for dangers which they appreciated better than ourselves, but did not limit its expression to words of advice and warning. I must be excused for saying that our countryman, Quail, the master of the M'Lellan, made us pay freely for a few stores we obtained from him, lest the liberality of these good Britons should be esteemed a matter of course. Money could hardly have paid them for the luxuries which they insisted on giving up to us. Their malt, and brandy, and vegetables, and quarters of fresh beef, and haunches of venison shot on the islands, covered our decks.

On the twelfth, from the highest point of one of the Duck Islands, we descried with our object-glass a topsail schooner to the southward, which proved to be the Prince Albert, bound on the same errand as ourselves. Her commander, Mr. William Kennedy, boarded us at midnight between the sixteenth and seventeenth. He had more home letters for us, but he brought his own welcome with him besides. His demeanor announced his character at once. He had with him Dr. Cowrie, Hepburn — the Hepburn of poor Franklin's Coppermine River sufferings—and an excellent ice-master, named Leask. We saw also, in the course of the day, his second in command, M. Bellot, a volunteer from the French navy, an accomplished and gallant officer. I regret that the relations of confirmed friendship I have established with these gentlemen make it indelicate on my part to speak of them here as I could wish. I have no means of knowing if Mr. Kennedy is appreciated at home—his self-denying, philanthropic devotion, and unostentatious energy; but it has given me great pleasure to hear that M. Bellot has recently received from his government a deserved promotion.

We communicated our plans to each other, and agreed, as far as practicable, to pursue our course together. This companionship became a source of great satisfaction to us. We could not feel solitary while our three little vessels sailed in one fleet. We followed each other's leads, warped, tracked, and bored, and had all our conflicts with the ice together. When we were beset and at a stand-still, we enjoyed each other's company, ate pemmican and loon, went out hunting, and took long walks with each other.

One evening I remember enjoying a delightful tramp, with both M. Bellot and Mr. Kennedy. We began it by chasing a small specimen of the Polar bear. They made signals to guide us from the Albert, where they could see his course; and after puzzling through the floes, we reached a large berg, behind which he lay ensconced. Mr. Kennedy, and his follower, Gideon, took one side; M. Bellot and myself the other—it being our task to turn him toward them. We got within about one hundred and twenty yards of him before he galloped off. M. Bellot, in his excitement, tumbled down twice, and fired once.

Mr. Kennedy hallooed also repeatedly, and discharged his piece. I am perhaps warranted in believing that the bear heard both reports before leaving us to ourselves, which he did shortly after without further notice.

This failure put us in the mood for a long straightforward march. We proceeded due north to a region completely encumbered with bergs, thrown off from a great glacier hard by. About four miles from our brig they assumed a picturesque variety of shape, rarely seen in those found floating out at sea. It was not so much their size that impressed us—though they were very large, several measuring a third of a mile along the base—as the sharpness and boldness of the lines where they were caverned and cloven down.

We attributed some of this effect to their freshness and recent origin. They were in some cases so stained by earthy matter as to show plainly the different colors of the cliff-side they had rested on, some dyed with a burned umber, others with the black of an augite formation. One was a conglomerate of great ice-bowlders, stained of a dark tint, but cemented together by ice that was perfectly clear.

Another had the shape and the melancholy coloring of a half-torn-down old mansion-house. Some dusky earths, and ash-looking silt from the ground-up gneisses, streaked the gable-end, like the sooty chimney-flues; other ash-colored patches stood for old plaster and darkened whitewash; and the base was choked up with piles of building stone. There are few things to me more suggestive of sentimental moralizing, even ashore, than these zigzag smoke-passages and chambers torn open to the day. But I had not seen a real house for full fifteen months; and this dreamy profile of a deserted home called me back to firesides with blazing back-logs, and family circlings, and hallow-eves, and childish laughter, and all the rest: a whole year's mean temperature of six degrees (5° 92′) above zero makes the flesh tingle for a hearth-stone.

Some of the bergs were worn in deep, vault-like chasms, through which a way was practicable to broader caverns within. In these crystal solitudes the echoes were startling. A whistle, your own whistle—you could hardly recognize it for the length and clearness of the ring; the clang of a ramrod was heard running down the ranks of a whole army in review; and when you spoke, your words were repeated through the motionless and elastic atmosphere in syllables almost as long as your breath would hold out to make them. I tried a hexameter we used to quote at home, and it came back to me, in slow and distinct utterance, word for word. There is a certain cousin of mine, whom I remember envying in our school-boy days, for the dispatch with which he could say his prayers of a frosty night before jumping into bed. He may think, when he reads these pages, how odd it would have been to hear his devotional effort repeated at length by such a chorus of echoes in succession.

I have spoken of the rich lazulite blue that was reflected from the bergs. It combined curiously sometimes with the atmospheric tints. About two o'clock in the afternoon the sun shone out above a bank of mist with that metallic, yellow light which we sometimes see when it clears up of an evening after falling weather. Striking on a berg that we had just been remarking for the purity and depth of its color, it was reflected over us in a flood of unearthly green, that opaque, abominable green that the scene-painters are so fond of for their scenes of *diablerie*, without one ray in sympathy with the cheering verdure of vegetation. I have never witnessed the same effect in nature.

They were pleasant things these rambles on the ice with our new colleagues, and I should be sorry to forget them; but they were sometimes less poetical than the one I have been speaking of. There was a part of the ice-field that extended between the two vessels, which we had nicknamed the Albert Floe. A part of this had been broken up by the swell, and a space of some hundreds of yards close by us was filled up for the time with *skreed*, forming a floating platform of tesselated structure, but without a cement. Mr. Kennedy and M. Bellot were on their way to visit us, and had just reached this uncertain pathway. Knowing the difficulties they might encounter in the transit, and somewhat vain, I fear, of my own ice-craft, I took a boat-hook and started off to meet them. The ice happened not to be conveniently arranged for my progress in a direct line; and at the best of times it requires the composure of a well-balanced mind to make long leaps from one slippery fragment to another, especially when the dark water between is somewhat cold and deep. I was in a hurry, I suppose; for in one of my jumps I damaged the garniture of my nether limbs, and was constrained to halt long enough to administer some temporary repairs. It lost me a little time; but I jumped along for some hundred yards more, and was soon near enough to see M. Bellot up to his neck, and Mr. Kennedy trying to fish him out with a boat-hook. When I got up to them, which I did by a process of ferriage, using little blocks of floe for a raft, M. Bellot's Arctic attire presented an appearance strikingly aquatic and uncomfortable. With the unpretending pride that becomes a conscious superiority, I engaged to pilot him back safely to our little world of dry clothes. Of my success I am not constrained to speak; but should this book ever recall to him the adventures of the day, he shall be welcome to his laugh at my expense. I confess, when he was a second time swimming about in the sludge, I really feared his dip would be a deep one. I admit also, on the evidence of my shipmates, that, treated as a group, the effect is unique of a couple of human beings slipping heels up on an ice-margin while they are holding up a third by the strap of his shot-pouch.

Both our vessels were carrying home Esquimaux dogs. By continued kindness and over-feeding, I succeeded in quite changing the nature of ours: both Disco and Hosky were on the high road to civilization. But those on board the Rescue and the Albert were still as wild as jackals: let loose upon the ice, it was almost impossible to catch them again. One afternoon, a little below the Devil's Thumb, when the dogs of the Albert were out on the floe for exercise, a sudden breeze allowed her to work to windward through an open lead. One poor dog was left behind. Boats were sent out to recover him, and we all tried by voice and gesture to coax him toward us. But the half savage, though he stood gazing at us wildly when we were at a distance, ran skulking and wolf-like as soon as we were near. We were forced at last to abandon him to his fate. We could see him for hours, a dark speck upon the white floe; and afterward, as far off as the spy-glass served, still with his head raised and his body thrown back on his haunches. Worse than this; such was the quiet expanse of ice and water, that we heard the poor creature's howling, waxing fainter and fainter, for eight hours after we left the ice.

The training of these animals by the natives is of the most ungracious sort. I never heard a kind accent from an Esquimaux to his dog. The driver's whip of walrus hide, some twenty feet long, a stone or a lump of ice skillfully directed, an imprecation loud and sharp, made emphatic by the fist or foot, and a grudged ration of seal's meat, make up the winter's entertainment of an Esquimaux team. In the summer the dogs run at large and cater for themselves.

I remarked that there were comparatively few of them at Holsteinberg, and was told a melancholy story to account for it. It seems that the governor, and priest, and fisherman keep goats, veritable goats, housed in a fire-warmed apartment in winter, and allowed the rest of the year to crop the grasses of the snow valleys. Now the half-tutored, unfed Esquimaux dog would eat a goat, bones, skin, and, for aught I know, horns. The diet was too expensive. It became a grave question, therefore, how to reconcile the incompatibilities of dog and goat. The matter was settled very summarily. When the green season of sunshine and plenty came, the dogs were sent to a rocky islet, a sort of St. Helena establishment, about a mile from the main, with permission to live by their wits; and the goats remained to browse and grow fat at large. The results were tragical. The dogs were afflicted with sore famine. Great life battles began; the strong keeping themselves alive by eating the weak. By this terrible process of gradual reduction, the colony was resolved into some four or five scarred veterans, whose nightly combats disturbed even the milk drinkers at the settlement, until the remnant at last took to the water in desperation, and succeeded in reaching the shore. From these came the "parvum pecus" that we saw.

At Holsteinberg, however, the sledge is less necessary than further to the north. It is only when the winters are both long and close, for the state of the ice depends on the winds as well as temperature, that the Holsteinberger can make a run as far as Disco. In other seasons his dogs are used only for inner travel, along the peculiarly formed valleys, which stretch back like the fiords to interior lakes.

But there is a constant intercourse kept up by means of them between Omenak, Rittenbank, Cristianshaab, Egedesminde, and Disco; and for some three months, including January and February, they are able to follow the land-floe as far as Pröven and Uppernavik. At these last settlements the dogs are exceedingly numerous. Our friend, the cooper at Pröven, had twenty-seven, and each of the stalwart sons of Cristiansen had a team of twelve. Large numbers besides thronged the outskirts, like their pariah brethren of Constantinople and the Nile. They do not bark: I distinguish between the bark and the howl; and they have not the intelligent movement of the tail, which, like the fan of a Spanish señorita, I hold to be the most expressive and graceful of all the substitutes for voice. I succeeded, after a while, in making my poor Disco greet me with her tail erect; but she died before she had learned to wag it.

For the purposes of draught, the dogs are fastened by a simple breast-strap, eight, twelve, or even fourteen abreast—a single trace passing from each to a foot-board on the sledge. The long whip is the substitute for reins: a sharp hiss, accompanied by the lash, if need be, is the signal for greater speed; and a loud "*Aie!*" calls the halt. Harnessed in this manner, they will travel from Uppernavik to Disco in two days and a half, resting at night; and for shorter stages, as, for instance, between Pröven and Uppernavik, thirty-two miles of actual route, they have made fourteen miles an hour. The recent explorations of Mr. Kennedy have shown how valuable their services can be made to an exploring party.

The weather underwent a striking change on the thirteenth. The ice-studded sea, so indefinitely extended by refraction that a poet might have likened it to a turkois set with pearls, took a new character. A strange, palpable obscurity, wreathing up in long strata to the northward, gradually wrapped itself over every thing. The water grew intensely black beneath us, and vague and smoky as it receded. The ice-floes that used to cut so sharply against it were now lumps of whiteness without margin, and the bergs, always massive and monumental, flared up in distorted magnitude like white shadows. Every thing, in short, grew blurred and uncertain. The wild fowl seemed to leave a streak behind them as they cleaved the misty atmosphere; and from the little circle of water, still visible around us, the wake of our brig was prolonged like a tongue. These appearances announced the southeaster, the wind, of all others, the most fruitful, at this time of the year, of meteorological changes. It was, besides, a leading wind for our return to the North Water.

CHAPTER XLVIII.

I OUGHT perhaps, as a book-maker, to go on with a diary of our second progress toward the north. But my work is almost done. New excitements, more kindred to my habits than those of authorship, are urging me while I arrange these pages for the press; and I feel that my readers, like myself, must be tired of efforts that had no result.

From the 13th of July to the 13th of August we loitered along, impatient at the delays which every day forced on us. In the whole month we made but thirty-seven miles. Yet we had no lack of incidents, some of them novel, and some not without more stirring interest. But the scenery of the bergs, majestic and varied as it was, began to weary us. Even the hazards of our narrow, and tortuous, and almost critical navigation became things of use; and when we found ourselves at rest, as we did sometimes, safe and motionless in the surface of an ice-field, we were wasted with ennui.

After a while, the leads opened close into the shore, and we followed them almost to the base of the cliffs. From this position the indentations and occasional depressions of the coast enabled us to see into the country to a considerable distance.

That singular ejected rock, the Devil's Thumb, of which I have given several sketches, stands in the recess of a curve, of which Wilcox Point forms a headland. The shore in its immediate neighborhood is not lofty, but dotted here and there with hills jutting out through massive glaciers. At the northern sweep of the indentation this ice-wall becomes more imposing; and in front of it we found a progeny of bergs, crowded together so close that we could not count them.

These glaciers, though differing widely in form from their pinnacled brethren of the Alps, have an imposing character of their own. So far as dimensions go, the entire *mer de glace* might repose on the slope of this single ice-hill, and Aletsch in one of its ravines. Indeed, the whole country between the two abutting headlands, and extending back as far as the eye could reach, was filled up with one grand frozen mass, so that the sea and its open fiords seemed scarcely gateways enough for the mighty reservoir to pour forth its bergs. The length of this curve was estimated by Mr. Murdaugh at eighteen miles; but the ice extended many miles further along the coast without change.

We could not wonder, after this, at the enormous quantities of bergs which lay before us. At the escarped base of the glacier they were jammed and jumbled together in every variety of confusion; some of the mountain character with which we were familiar, others a congeries of rubbish, and illustrating every possible condition of libration. All three vessels were in a cul de sac of floe-cemented bergs, and were obliged to tie up and wait upon their movements.

The Alpine glaciers have engrossed, it seems to me, the field of scientific dissertation somewhat unduly. Those which crowd the western coast of Greenland have perhaps a higher interest; growing up, as they do, in a climate which is independent of altitude, besides being altogether superior in magnitude of scale.

The southernmost cape of this so-called peninsula is nearly in the latitude of 59°, some 500 miles south of the Arctic circle. This termination, which, like Good Hope and Comorin, illustrates Foster's law of South-trending peninsulas, is abrupt and precipitous. The influences of the surrounding sea give to its climate an insular character, and seem to prevent any great glacier accumulation.

As we travel, however, to the north, those great indentations known as the Fiords, which penetrate the metamorphic ridges at right angles to their long axes, serve as conduits to the interior ice. The settlements at Baal's River and Godhaab, the earliest inhabited upon the coast, and near the region of the ancient Icelandic colonists, are the seats of large glaciers. These do not abut directly upon the sea; but, as far as my inquiries extended, issue in troughs that enter the fiords from the north and south, and are connected with those great reservoirs, or *mers de glace*, which, like vast table-lands, occupy the unknown interior. The North and South Stromfiords, about Holsteinberg, receive similar glaciers; and the annual hunts for the reindeer, which seem to have carried the Esquimaux back from the coast, have disclosed great masses of ice, at whose bases the animals escaping from the musquitoes fall an easy prey to the hunter.

When we reach the latitude of 69°, where the greenstone dikes begin to modify the gneissoid character of the ranges, the glaciers approach more nearly to the actual coast. The crystalline schists, however, continue with lofty headlands as far as Wilcox Point; and it was only here, where the mean level of the coast seemed to be reduced, that the great glacier, properly speaking, began.

Taking a headland near Wilcox Point, which was known to be fifteen hundred feet above the level of the sea, and sweeping round to another headland of similar elevation, we made a rude approximation to the height of the glacier between: it was about seven hundred feet at the coast-line. Following it back from the sea with an excellent Fraunhofer telescope, we could see it rising slowly by a gradual talus till it was lost in the distance. Its undulations over the buried country, which it overlaid like a great tombstone, were marked by considerable diversity of surface. They were occasionally furrowed by ravines, indicating water action; and in these, wherever the cliffs protruded, a long earthen stain, garnished probably with detrited rubbish, extended down like the lines of a moraine. Sometimes the surface was smooth and unmarred; but more commonly, and especially on the faces of more abrupt descent, I recognized the crevasse character which I have noted in the bergs. I also observed escarpments of ice in some instances, great mural faces, beyond which the glacier was continued again; but these were rare.

The general color of the glacier, like that of the berg, was a dead white, varied only a little by alternations of light and shadow; and through this the higher land peaks rose like dark knobs. In two places I noticed a land spur, extending at right angles to the axis of the chain until it reached the sea, and thrusting itself boldly through the ice to the water-line, flanked on each side by the glacier face.

I thought too, though my observations with the glass were too rude to assure me of their correctness, that I could trace, in the general configuration of this great ice-surface, delta-like divisions, such as might be induced by surface streams expanding and divaricating as they approached the sea. In fact, hosts of geological analogies suggested themselves, which I do not venture to enlarge upon. It was evident that the accumulations had less variety of general configuration as they neared the coast, that their slopes became less sudden, their horizontalism more diffused, and that the water gorges were more ramiform.

Reaching the sea, the solid ice-mass terminated abruptly, presenting an escarped face with nearly vertical fracture, and varying in perpendicular height according to the profile of the protruding mass. The margin which defined this line of escarpment was clear and decided; the only departure from its regular continuity being at the gorges I have just referred to, or at cleanly-cut chasms, referable apparently to disruption.

I do not think the substance of the Greenland glacier differs materially from that of the Alpine. A fragment, examined by the microscope, exhibits the same vesicular structure; and it breaks into numerous pieces, whose separation is determined by their capillary structure. This fragmentary composition of the glacier ice enables you to walk on it without slipping. Its color is barely translucent, and at a distance as opaque as *matte* silver. It is only where cracks or chasms have been filled by waters and frozen up afterward, that we have a truly transparent ice.

I have examined the névé, which forms so interesting a feature in the study of glaciers, only once *in situ*. This was at the small glacier north of 76°, where this substance occupied the upper portion of its trough. But for the partial cementation of its particles, and a grain-like character which could be detected on close examination, I should have regarded it as a mere accumulation of snow-drift.

The change of the Arctic snows into névé or firn might be the subject of interesting examination. Even the surface drifts of our winter ice-floes underwent this granular transformation rapidly. After tossing about as a dry and almost impalpable powder during the long Polar winter, the returning sun, with its alternations of thaw and congelation, developed a grain-like or almost beaded structure. I have seen these crystalline pellets as large as a cherry-stone, diminishing down to the size of shot or mustard-seed.

The Polar glacier, as may be seen clearly when it has taken the berg form, is commonly coated over with this modified snow, and its valleys and minor depressions are often filled with it by drift-action. I have noted by sections strata of fifteen and twenty feet, whose composition was entirely analogous to the firn of the Alps. It may have been by observing portions of the berg like this, that Professor Forbes was led to the assertion that the iceberg is composed not of true ice, but of névé.

That the Polar glaciers obey the same law of movement as their Alpine brethren, I have seen no reason to doubt. The advance of the glacial faces at Jacobs' Harbor, of which Mr. Olrik informed me, is the only direct fact which I can add to those already noted on this subject. But the very circumstance of their offcasts, the bergs, being so numerous, seems to indicate a continuously protruding influence. It may be that in the more southern settlements of Greenland this advance is limited by atmospheric causes; but I am strongly inclined to believe that in those further north, the debacle or berg disgorgement is the most powerful countervailing agent.

It would be presumptuous, with my very meagre

data, to theorize as to the causes of this progression, or to become the advocate of any one view to the exclusion of others. But I confess that my observations of the bergs, and of the ice-fields of our winter-pack, point to the viscous or gelid flow of Professor Forbes.

The definition of a solid is at best comparative; and I have had abundant proofs that ice, even at very low temperatures, undergoes molecular changes which modify its external configuration very largely. On the 20th of March, while we were imbedded in the floe, with a temperature many degrees below zero, one of those great convulsions called hummocking had thrown up a table eight feet in thickness by twenty odd in width, and in such a position that it was only sustained by masses of ice at its two extremities. In the month of May, the thermometer never having risen in the interval to within many degrees of the freezing-point, I saw the same ice-table completely bent down, its centre depressed five feet, until arrested in its descent by a new support.*

This beautiful illustration of the semi-solid character of the ice during the depths of a Polar winter, when

* See the drawings of this ice-table on page 389.

its tenacity more resembled glass or granite than the familiar ice at home, was not a solitary one. The preceding sketch will exhibit an equally marked curvature in a larger mass, where the gravitating pressure was applied at the two extremities.

Contorted ices, natural bridges, and, as the season advanced, nodding, pendulous, stalactitic hummocks, were not unfrequent. These had a double interest, as bearing not only on the plasticity of ice, but on the influence which temperature exerts upon its condition at points below that of congelation, 32°.

I have already described the only glacier which I had an opportunity of surveying. It reminded me of La Brenva; and although I overlooked the *ribboned structure*, not having seen then the detailed work of Professor Forbes, I recollect that it had the peculiar scalloped shell summit, which he has regarded as illustrative of *mechanical advance.*

It was from the icebergs, however, that formed so characteristic a feature of the scene before us, that we derived our best idea of the glaciers from which they had come. To the eye they presented almost infinite diversity; but it required very little generalization to reduce them all to a few simple primary forms.

Thus the vertical fracture of the glacier, which would indicate the formation of a berg by debacle, would divide the mass into parallelopipedons or other rudely symmetrical solids; and where the surface of the original plateau was parallel to its base, the detached mass would float evenly upon the waters, a great table-land with perpendicular sides. This was the most frequent form of the bergs, and the most impressive. I have measured some that were thirteen hundred yards on a single face.

But the adjustment of the glacier to the country on which it is built generally prevents such a symmetrical equilibrium. One or another of its great sides will be inclined toward the water, destroying the vertical character of the rest, and giving the effect of a sloping hill rising from the sea. Over bergs of this form, and they also were very numerous, you walked as over a terrestrial surface, met by every diversity of configuration, valleys, gorges, hills, plains, and precipices.

A third form, so abnormal as to characterize a class, but at the same time comparatively rare, was that of a mass, which, probably by continued avalanche motion, had acquired such an irregular form, such a disproportion, perhaps, between its width and depth, that its centre of gravity, as it fell, was not within the submerged mass. Its equilibrium was therefore uncertain, and its side sometimes what had been at first its surface.

With some exceptions, the different forms of the berg could be derived from these; their subsequent changes being dependent on atmospheric or aqueous erosion, or both, or on accidental fractures, and on changes of equilibrium consequent on the others. These last were productive of the most eccentric diversities. Great tongues, which had become cavernous under the action of the waves, would rise bristling into the upper air; and gnarled peaks, stained with the silt through which they had plowed, cut in darkened pinnacles against the sky.

There was one great monster, that we called the Tower of Babel, nearly three hundred feet high, with a spiral stair-case as unsatisfactory as some of Martin's imaginings of infraterrene architecture. Another was an enormous honey-combed mass, studded all over with bowlders, and stained with syenitic detritus.

But curious among all the rest was the berg, of which a sketch is given on the opposite page. It was but partially overturned, and the exposed surface was marked all over by circular depressions, ten inches deep and a foot in diameter, so close together as nearly to touch at their upper edges. A smaller berg was so covered with these spot-like exca-

vations, and had withal so striking a form, that it could have no other nickname but the Giraffe. In my efforts to arrive at the cause of this strange leprosy, I once only found the bottom of the cavities filled with slimy diotomaceous life. It is possible that a vital action had determined this local thawing; but its symmetrical character still remains a puzzle.

It was very interesting to follow these secondary forms in their changes. Nothing can be more imposing than the rotation of a berg. I have often watched one, rocking its earth-stained sides in steadily-deepening curves, as if to gather energy for some desperate gymnastic feat; and then turning itself slowly over in a monster somerset, and vibrating as its head rose into the new element, like a leviathan shaking the water from its crest. It was impossible not to have suggestions thrust upon me of their agency in modifying the geological disposition of the earth's surface.

We were in an archipelago of stranded and of moving bergs. In some that had undergone this change

of equilibrium, the valleys were studded with irregularly angular and rounded rocks, and a detrital paste resembling till. In such cases, the deeply imbedded position of the larger fragments spoke of their having been there from the original structure of the berg, while the paste seemed to have been upturned afterward from the bottom through which the berg had furrowed its way; the occasional excess of both being due, in a greater or less degree, to atmospheric action. The preceding sketch shows the disposition of these fragments sufficiently well. They consisted of syenites, gneisses, rounded quartzes, green-stones, and clay slates; in fact, of all the characteristic rocks of our Plutonic coast-line. In a single instance, I found a piece of well-marked actinolite, eight inches in diameter, surrounded by crumbled chlorites and serpentines.

In the primary forms of berg, the disposition of the transported material did not seem to be determined by any law. Sometimes, but rarely, I could follow moraine traces, or rather lines indicating deposits from contiguous cliffs; but generally the fragment seemed to be cemented

into the glacier from the talus of some descending slope. I can not recall a case in which such fragments had the strictly angular character that belongs to a recent fracture. They were either complete bowlders, or partially rounded, as in the two preceding sketches.

The influences of the berg as a raft in the translation of masses of rock, with their accompanying paste, may be inferred to some extent from the facts I have thus hastily thrown together. Of nearly five thousand bergs which I have seen, there was, perhaps, not one that did not contain fragmentary rock. A walk over the berg would disclose them, either clinging partially imbedded in their slopes, or in the form of pebbles and still smaller fragments, penetrating in cylindrical cavities deep into the substance of the berg.

This form of deposit was even more marked than it seems to have been in the glaciers of the Alps. The constant daylight, without interruption of solar influence, and the absence of radiation during the night, will explain this. I have seen the surface of a berg completely covered, for perhaps a couple of acres, with the orifices of these perforating *crystallodromes.*

We did not often meet with the pinnacled character, which is so frequent in the Alps; a fact which may be due, perhaps, to the absence of the alternate freezing and thawing which attend the alternation of day and night.

When the berg was nearly melted down to the water's edge, the accumulation was more apparent, and the arrangement of drift upon its surface resembled that which the sketches I subjoin were intended to indicate.

The berg is beyond all doubt a most important agent in modifying the soundings upon the coast. The grounded bergs off Disco are known to leave troughs, plowed by their projecting tongues, as they float and ground with the rise and fall of the tides. Where the bottom is of mud and till, as is the case on the west coast generally, this action must be very marked; for on a berg I surveyed trigonometrically in July, which had grounded in soundings of five hundred and twenty feet, the great tap-root that anchored it to the bottom admitted of an easy rotation, and the berg swung upon its axis with each change of the tide. That such great tongues, though irregular in their shape, do in fact rock and rotate with the movements of the berg, might be inferred, indeed, from the facettes that are worn on the imbedded material; many of which are disposed about a convexity of uniform curvature.

We are to remember besides, in considering the geological eccentricities which are to be referred to the action of icebergs, the immense quantities of foreign material which I have spoken of as discoloring or staining so many of the bergs of Omenak, Ovinde, and Melville Bay. These ice-masses are of many millions of tons, all of them bearing the elements of gneissoid rocks, to be deposited in distant localities. A reference to my current chart will show that they pass, in the first instance, toward the north, and, descending along the western coast, perform the entire circuit of the bay. The extensive reaches of shoals, which are so marked a feature of this coast from Pond Bay to Cape Kater, may be due to this character of berg-drift. The islands and shallows about the mouth of Jones's Sound must, I suppose, be referred to it also.

BOWLDERS IN ICEBERG.

AMONG THE BERGS, MELVILLE BAY.

CHAPTER XLIX.

I RETURN from this long digression to my narrative.

In the night of the 15th of July a mist cleared away that had inclosed us for some days, and the atmosphere had the pellucid clearness of the Tropics after a rain. We then saw how completely surrounded we were by bergs. We had made fast, on the shore side, to one of magisterial proportions, that had anchored itself in the floe. As we looked coastward, others still closer in were so piled up against the land that it was impossible to separate them: a jagged wall of ice contrasting with the hills beyond was all that could be seen. To seaward, I counted seventy-three within the visual angle.

As the tide ebbed, the same phenomena of drift which had startled us last year in Melville Bay were renewed. The floes were choked in around us, so as to prevent the possibility of warping from our position; and the kingly bergs began their impressive march. Our anchorage seemed to be a fixed centre, influencing the general tidal streams. The set of the surface ice was rapid to the south; but where it struck against our island safeguard, the counter-stream worked its way toward the shore.

In the midst of this combination of floe-movements, the tide changed, and the inshore bergs began to bear down upon us, moving steadily against the surface current, and nearly against the wind. One of these, of quadrangular form, with a back like a table-land, and in bulk more than equal to two such as our own, advanced from the recesses of the land at the rate of a knot an hour, crumbling all opposing floes before it. Mr. Murdaugh and myself had accomplished a somewhat arduous journey over the ice to the Prince Albert. We returned just as the two bergs were about to meet, crushing our little vessels to atoms in their embrace. It was a sight to make "the bravest hold his breath;" more fearful by much than any whose peril we had shared. But we doubled a projecting crag; and it was past. Just as the drifting berg was about impinging on the other, it yielded a very little to some inexplicable counter-drift; moved slowly round on its axis to the northward; and, passing within fifty yards of the brigs, continued its majestic progress directly in the wind's eye. It was a narrow escape: the Rescue was heeled over considerably by the floes which were forced in upon her, driving in her port bulwarks and demolishing her monkey-rail.

The same fearful scene was renewed the next day. A second quadrangle stood out from the shore at the same rate as the other, and had approached within short biscuit-cast, when a deep, protruding tongue, altogether invisible to us, opposed itself against our advancing enemy, and with a shock that vibrated to our very centre brought him up. Why does not the attraction of these masses bring and retain them in apposition? Collisions between bergs are certainly rare; and my own experience, corroborated by the results of much inquiry among the Greenlanders and the fishermen, seems to say that a union between two bergs, except when one is aground—an exception on which I lay some stress—is almost unknown.

A few days after the scene I have described, we neared our hated landmark of last season, the Devil's Thumb. But here the leads closed; and our labyrinth of bergs attended us still, clogging our way, and wearying us with their monotony. Our commander had but one thought, and we all sympathized in it—how could our little squadron regain its position at the searching grounds? We had otherwise no lack of incidents. There were parhelia, intricate ones, with six solar images and eccentric circles of light, one of which had its circumference passing through the sun. And we had bear hunts now and then of mothers and cubs together; and sometimes we shot at a flock of birds.

But the spirit of the hunt had left us. We were close upon the middle of August. Less than four weeks remained for us to get rid of this vexatious entanglement, press on through Lancaster Sound, complete our explorations in Wellington Channel, and return to the open water of the bay. It was before the middle of September that we had been frozen in last year. And here we were in a perfect ice-trap, unable to win an inch of progress.

We were without the Albert too. As long ago as

the fifth, her good folks had determined to make south, despairing of success in a northward effort; and on the eleventh, while we were yet attached to the old land-floe, she found her way to an open lead, and disappeared on the thirteenth. We could hardly talk of the regrets we all felt at losing them. It seemed to me that for days after I could hear their broken-hearted little hand-organ grinding "The Garb of Old Gael;" and their gifts to me, Mr. Kennedy's pocket Bible, Bellot's French treatises, Cowrie's Shetland woolens, and Hepburn's gloves—it quite dispirited me to look at them.

GOOD-BY TO THE PRINCE ALBERT, MELVILLE BAY.

We perhaps thought of their departure the more, because it implied something of uncertainty as to our own fate. They had avowedly left us, fearless and enterprising as they were, to escape from hazards that we were continuing to brave. Mr. Leask, their veteran ice-master, thought, when he left us, that if we followed the northern leads there was almost a certainty of our being caught, like the Swan, and the York, and a host of others before us. A pleasant neighborhood, truly! Here perished the ships of '47. Here the North Star was beset in '48; hereabout, the year before last, the Lady Jane, and the Superior, and the Prince of Wales; and, coming to our own experience of last year, here it was, in this very devil's hole, that we wore out our three weeks' imprisonment.

Moreover, the season was more advanced than last year's had been. The thermometer, which stood at noon in the shade at 54°, sunk in the evening hours to 30°. At such a temperature the ice forms rapidly on the deeply chilled water, and the day sun barely melts it. We began to observe too flocks of the little Auk streaming south, as if to harbinger a change of season. It was evident that a very few days must decide where we should pass the approaching winter.

The crisis came soon enough. My journal is prolix throughout this period; but I venture to give it as it stands. I begin with the eleventh of the month.

"*August* 11, Monday. The wind has been nearly all day more or less from the northward. Now, though almost calm, it is from the eastern or shore side, accompanied by weather sunny and beautiful.

"We are still attached to the old land-floe. This so-called land-ice is rather a huge field, hemmed in by bergs, so as to be immovable. It is, however, young and frail, not exceeding eighteen inches in thickness, and perforated with water-pools, cracks, and seal-holes. It is so rotten that marginal pieces are continually breaking off, and carried into the chaos of floating drift outside. Were we to share the same chance, we must be involved helplessly in floating skreed, adrift, and at the mercy of the winds and currents. As our protecting floe gives way, therefore, men walk over the liberated tables, and plant our ice-hooks further off in the part that remains solid. This process is going on without intermission; so that now (12 o'clock M.) we have a hundred yards of cable out ahead and astern. We are surrounded by floes, and the channel outside is a compacted surface of floating rubbish.

"As far as the eye can reach, the sea, and, by refraction, the air, is studded with bergs, apparently concentering about our anchorage. Astern of us, stretching to the westward, are five, so nearly abreast as to resemble one ragged mountain precipice. There is not one of these smaller than our Washington Capitol; and one of them would fill the Capitol square. Directly ahead, only a hundred and fifteen yards off, is a huge one, black, gnarled, water-worn, and serrated with deep chasms; and streams of melted snow are pouring down in noisy cascades along its gullies. This berg is fast in the anchoring ice; but every now and then it breaks off in great masses with a report like artillery. Between it and the nearest astern of us the distance is about three hundred yards. On one side we have the equivalent of a rock-bound mountain coast: every where else a phalanx of serried bergs.

"2 P.M. The bergs are in motion again, and bearing for us.

"*August* 12, Tuesday. The berg ahead still holds its anchorage. It is an amorphous mass, so worn that it must have been sorely wrought before its release from the glacier. Its summit is a rolling country, stained with earth and rocks: you can walk up and down hill over it for nearly a mile in a single line.

"About one o'clock to-day, a fragment about as large as Independence Hall fell from it into the ice-sea below. The noise had not the usual sharp, reverberating character of these disruptions; but the effects of the avalanche upon the field into which it fell were very striking. At first, from the centre of turmoil came a circling series of large undulations clothed in foam. Next the floating rubbish began to roll in propagated waves; and these, passing our brig, extended themselves under the margin of the fast floe, breaking it up, and still expanding in one ridge beyond another till they disappeared in the distance. We counted at least five wave circles in the ice-field at one time. It reminded me of our scene in the pack on the fifth of June.

"*August* 15, Friday. The floe we have been fastened to so long still holds together, though traversed by innumerable cracks. The margin is constantly breaking away; but our whale lines are laid far out, and as one comes away we warp closer in by the others.

"This has kept us from drifting, but it has surrounded us with the off-shed fragments of the floes. These are already recemented about us, though constantly cracking and breaking away by the varying pressures; and outside of them the loose floes are drifting by, morning, noon, and night, like the foam-covered surface of a millrace when the ice gives way in a spring freshet. We may be said to be moored to an uncertain shore, a drifting beach of ice; while on every side, striving to tear us from this faithless anchorage, are the unquiet, grinding floes. But the bergs! it seems almost profanity to speak of them: where are they?

"I have compared the outside drift to the foam of

a millrace. The comparison was a wretched one. Imagine the horizon a great sea, visible here and there at the end of long marble vistas, one unbroken but moving whiteness. Let that sea be choked with jagged mountains, pale and chalky, but moving too. It is the panorama that surrounds us. They are not the same bergs that girded us a week ago. It is a constant series: as fast as one column passes another takes its place. At this moment, looking to the north, I recognize the terraces of a Babylonic tower, just losing itself behind the fast bergs to seaward. Yesterday that same berg emerged from the solid ice-mountain to the southward. Then it was the last of a long cavalcade; but they have all gone, and another train is now following it, so continuous and compact that I sometimes can not see the horizon. The procession, like a phantasmagorial dream of some giant theatre, glides slowly in from the left, passes across the front, and is lost far back to the right.

"Night before last, standing on the fast floe, I counted, between the two anchored bergs that serve as framings of the picture, thirty-two icebergs in a well-marshaled group. Standing afterward on the summit of our northern buttress, I counted two hundred and eighty, the glacier terminating the eastern view. Most of these bergs were above the standard height of two hundred and fifty feet; some exceeded three hundred; few were less than one hundred.

"We see no open water; but it is designated clearly by a dark sky, something between the bistre of the frost smoke and the indigo of our thunder clouds at home. The tint is deepest at the horizon, and fading as it ascends. We have seen these signs of water for the last four days. We confidently hope the southeasterly winds are driving the pack to the northward, for both the skreed drift and the bergs seem to have a northwesterly trend. It is probable that the leads may not be more than the third of a mile from us. We have been trying to warp toward them; but, after much hard labor, have moved not quite a hundred yards.

"*August* 16, Saturday. Our position is the same as yesterday, except that we are a day older in it. The bergs keep the same curved screen of bristling wall to seaward; and to the east, the glacier, with its black knobs of protruding mountain, shows dimly through the mist. The wind is from the northward and eastward; but we are so girded in that our floes can not relax. Outside, to the south, whenever a momentary opening permits a glimpse beyond, we have leads and a water-sky.

"It is evident now that our berth here is a horseshoe indentation, the loose ice of which is hemmed in by a rapidly changing army of bergs. Last night, or, to speak more accurately, this morning, though the wind was off-shore from the east, we experienced some tolerable nipping: the 'young puppies' were whining half the night. Under the circumstances, especially as the fast floe seems to yield very little, our captain has determined to try the warps again. The brig's head is pointed into the drift, and we are trying to spring her past the loose ice.

"9 P.M. While three men were out on a low berg this morning warping, one of them, Dunning, struck his ice-chisel against the mass. It parted instantly, with a short, sharp crack; one fragment sinking for a time nearly below the skreed, with two of the men on it. They had some difficulty in keeping their foothold, as it rose, and fell, and rocked about with them; but they managed to do it. Dunning was left on the other side: it see-sawed with him a good deal, but he jumped for it safely.

"The ice seems to relax morning and evening, probably under tidal influence. We have made three ship's lengths to-day, and are now clear of the floe that has been shielding us. The bergs are still keeping up their interminable procession, some of them making sublime evolutions as they pass. One to-day broke right before us in a vertical disruption, and rolled away in two nearly equal masses. Another seemed to stop to show us how he could oscillate, and then gracefully turned himself upside down and floated away.

"10 P.M. The thermometer has got up to 36°, and the air is transparent again. The sun is shining out, and the glacier glitters at its fractured face like satin spar and diamonds.

"*August* 17, Sunday. The same revolving wall of bergs meets us to the west, but the glacier on the other side is partially hidden by a new procession inshore. While profaning the day by an attempt to sketch these sublime monuments of creative power in my drawing-book, I was interrupted by a heavy undulation, rolling under the brig, and passing on to the solid inshore floe. It was followed by a number of others, coming in quick succession, and breaking up the floe drift in every direction. The action continued for some minutes. It must have been caused by some very large and probably irregular berg overturning at a distance; but it was without noise, and indeed without premonition of any sort. The direction of the wave where it struck us was from the northwest. Up to this moment, all the heavy heaving and warping of to-day had been without any effect. Now the floes separated as if by magic: there was relaxation every where; and we made at least two hundred yards before the ice closed again.

"This afternoon, the captain, with Murdaugh and myself, walked and climbed over this same ice, to make a reconnoissance of the region beyond the bergs. By the aid of boat-hooks and some slippery jumping we achieved it, and were at last able to climb one of the imprisoning bergs, and look from its crest to the other side.

"It was a sermon such as uninspired man has never preached. There, there, far down below us, there was the open water, stretching wide away to the south; placid and bright, bearing on its glazed surface fleets of bergs and rafts of floes, but open water still; and yet further on, the unbroken water-sky. Our little brig was under us, the tiny fretwork of her spars traced clean and sharp against the arena of ice; but, thank God! she is nearing the gates of her prison-house. De Haven was right. One quarter of a mile! Now, lads, for the warps again!

"*Midnight.* We are out: at ten minutes past eleven we shipped our rudder, the first time in three weeks; and made sail, the first time since the 26th of July.

"We owe it all to a relaxation of the floes. The wind was from the northward: the bergs that hemmed in the loose drift around us yielded a little toward the west, and the skreed began to separate. The main-brace was spliced; springs took the place of warps; and the men went gallantly to their work. They were as anxious to get out as any of us.

"At last we reached an opening: two immense

bergs, overhanging and ragged; and down toward the water-line, an opening between them like a gateway. Shall we pass? We have seen so many disruptions, and capsizings, and accidents of all sorts in this work of anchor-planting: sometimes a mere breath brings down masses that would bury half a dozen such vessels as ours; and these bergs are so water-washed and pendulous. Murdaugh waited for the order. De Haven gave it; and, in deep silence, we passed the Gades of the Devil's Trap.

"*August* 19, Tuesday. The Rescue is close astern of us: she got through about noon yesterday. Our commodore has resolved on an immediate return to the United States."

The game had been played out fairly. Lancaster Sound was out of the question; and for our scurvy-riddled crew, a nine months' winter in the ice of North Baffin would have been disastrous.

CHAPTER L.

After our escape from the congregated bergs, we sailed to one at a little distance, and filled our water-casks. The berg crumbled and fell while we were doing so, but nobody was hurt; and in two days more, after a closing skirmish with the ice-pack, we headed homeward. On the twentieth we made our last salutation to the Devil's Thumb; and on the twenty-third, in the evening, we were near enough to Uppernavik for a little boating party of us to make it a visit.

With the exception of Kangiartsoak, this is the most northern of the Danish settlements. Its latitude is 72° 47′, three hundred and seventy miles within the Arctic circle. But reaching it, we felt as if we had renewed our communication with the world; for here, once in every year, comes the solitary trader from Copenhagen. We had become so familiar with the dreariness of Greenland, that the glaring red gables of the three houses, and the white curiosity, which stood for a steeple above the church, were absolutely cheering; and we landed, poor souls! after our twelve miles' row, with hearts as elate as ever frolicked among the orange-groves of Brazil or the cocoa-palms of the Eastern Pacific.

Disappointment once more! The governor had gone to Pröven; the Danish ship had gone to Pröven; the priest had gone to Pröven. But the gentler sex remained. The governor's lady gave us a kindly welcome, and extended to us all the hospitalities of his mansion.

The mansion was far from picturesque. It was a square block of heavy timber, running into a high-peak gable. The roof was of tarred canvas, laid over boards; the wooden walls coated with tar, and painted a glowing red. A little paling, white and garden-like, inclosed about ten feet of prepared soil, covered with heavy glass frames; under which, in spite of the hoar-frost that gathered on them, we could detect a few bunches of crucifers, green radishes, and turnip-tops. It was *the* garden, the distinctive appendage of the governor's residence.

Inside the house—it is the type of those at Disco and Pröven—you pass by a narrow-boarded vestibule to a parlor. This parlor, a room of dignified consideration, is twelve feet long by eleven: beyond it, a door opens to display the suite, a second room, the state chamber, of the same size.

The most striking article of furniture is the stove, a

tall, black cylinder, such as I have seen in the Baltic cities, standing like a column in the corner: the next, a platoon of tobacco-pipes paraded against the wall: the next—let me be honest, it was the first—a table, with a clean white cloth, and plates, knives, and forks, all equally clean. Overhead hang beams as heavy as the carlines of a ship's cabin: below is an uncovered floor of scrupulous polish: the windows are recessed, glazed in small squares, and opening, door-like, behind muslin curtains: the walls canvas, painted, and decorated with a few prints altogether remarkable for intensity of color. The looking-glass; I reserve it for more special mention. It was not very large, but it was the first we had encountered since we came into the regions of ice. "To see ourselves as others see us" is not always the prayer of an intelligent self-love. Sharp-visaged, staring, weather-beaten old men, wrinkle-marked, tawny-bearded, haggard-looking: the boys of Uppernavik are better bred than the New Yorkers, or they would have mobbed us.

The ladies—they were ladies, they knew no superiors; they were self-possessed, hospitable; they wore frocks, and they did not laugh at us—the ladies spread the meal, coffee, loons' eggs, brown bread, and a welcome. We ate like jail-birds. At last came the crowning act of hospitality; on the bottom of a blue saucer, radiating like the spokes of a wheel or the sticks of a Delaware's camp-fire, crisp, pale, yet blushing at their tips, and crowned each with its little verdant tuft—*ten radishes!* Talk of the mango of Luzon and the mangostine of Borneo, the cherimoya of Peru, the pine of Sumatra, the seckel-pear of Schuylkill meadows; but the palate must cease to have a memory before I yield a place to any of them alongside the ten radishes of Uppernavik.

On the twenty-fifth we reached the Whale-fish Islands, and at six in the evening were near enough to be towed in by our boats and anchor off Kronprinsen. Flocks of kayacks hung about our vessel, like birds about a floating spar. We thought them more

sprightly and active than the Esquimaux we had been among; but perhaps it is as unfair to judge of the Esquimaux without his kayack as of a sloth off his tree. There was a bright boy among them, under ten years of age, who could manage a little craft they had built for him admirably. He called to us that his name was Paul. Next him was our old friend, Jans, of the overturners—whose portrait I have given in the margin of the following page—and under our bow, Zacharias, the quarter-breed; and Paul, senior, the pilot of my fur expedition to Lievely.

I promised, in an early part of my book, to say something more about the kayack and its occupant. I return for a few minutes to the subject now.

The common length of the kayack is about eighteen feet, its breadth on deck some twenty-one inches,

and its depth ten inches in the middle, just such as to allow its occupant to sit with his feet extended on the bottom and his hips below the deck. It is always built with a nice adaptation to his weight.

Its frame is light enough to startle all our notions of naval construction, and it is covered with nothing but tanned sealhide. Yet in this egg-shell fabric the Esquimaux navigator habitually, and fearlessly, and successfully too, encounters risks which his more civilized rivals in the seal-hunt, the men of New Bedford

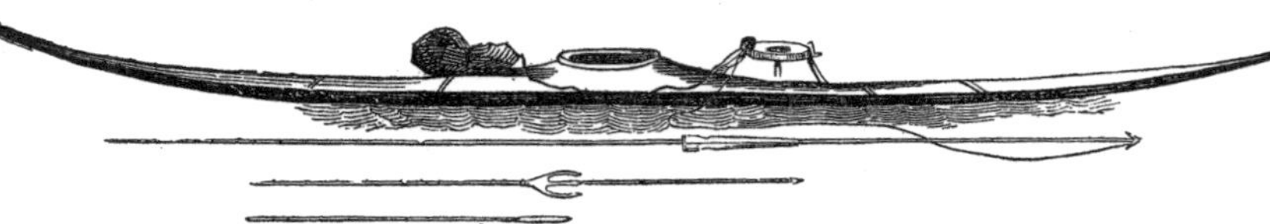

and Stonington, would rightfully shrink from. I am not sure that I can make such a description of its proportions and structure as a ship-builder would understand; but the drawings I annex have been made carefully from one of the best models, and may be relied on for all the information that can be gathered from them.

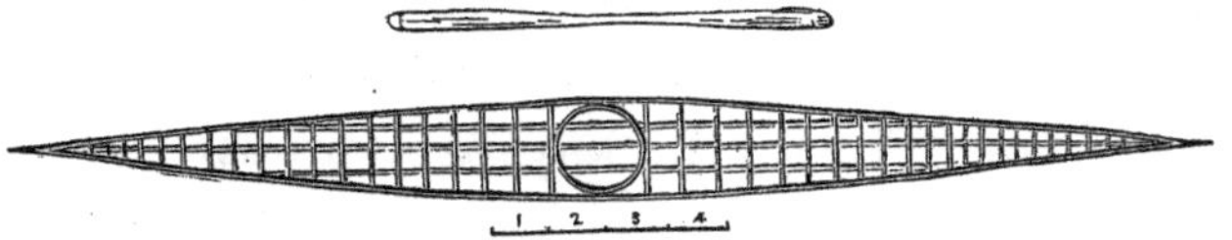

The skeleton consists of three longitudinal strips of wood on each side—it would be wrong to call them timbers, for they are rarely thicker than a common plastering lath — stretching from end to end, and shielded at the stem and stern by cutwaters of bone. The upper of these, the gunwale, if I may call it so, is

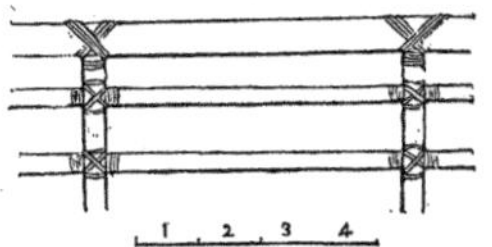

somewhat stouter than the others. The bottom is framed by three similar longitudinal strips. These are crossed by other strips or hoops, which perform the office of knees and ribs: they are placed at a distance of not more than eight to ten inches from one another. Wherever the parts of this frame-work meet or cross, they are bound together with reindeer tendon very artistically. The general outline is, I think, given accurately in the sketch on the opposite page.

Over this little basket-work of wood is stretched the coating of seal hides, which also covers the deck, very neatly sewed with tendon, and firmly glued at the edges by a composition of reindeer horn scraped and liquefied in oil. A varnish made of the same materials is used to protect the whole exterior.

The *pah*, or man-hole, as we would term it, is very

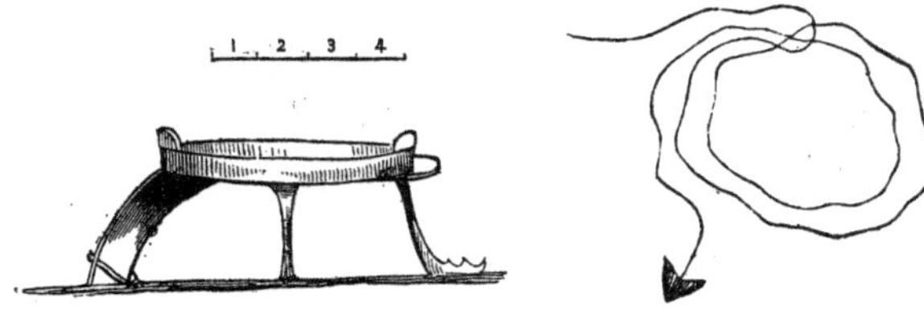

nearly in the centre of the little vessel, sometimes a few inches toward the stern. It is circular or nearly so, wide enough to let the kayacker squeeze his hips through it, and no more. It has a rim or lip, secured upon the gunwale, and rising a couple of inches above the deck, so as to permit the navigator to bind it water-tight around his person. Immediately in front of him is his *as-say-leut*, or line stand, surmounted by a reel, with the sealing-line snugly coiled about it, and revolving on its centre with the slightest touch. He has his harpoon and his lances strapped at his side; his rifle, if he owns one, stowed away securely between decks.

Just behind the kayacker rests his bladder-float or air-bag, an air-tight sack of seal-skin, always kept inflated, and fastened to the sealing-line. It performs the double office of a buoy, and a break or drag to retard the motion of the prey after it is struck.

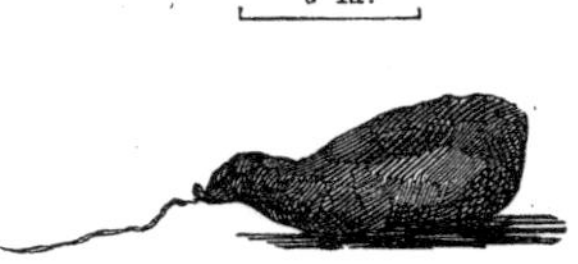

The harpoon, or principal lance (*unahk*), is also attached to the sealing-line. It is a most ingenious device. The rod or staff is divided at right angles in two pieces, which are neatly jointed or hinged with tendon strips, but so braced by the manner in which the tendon is made to cross and bind in the lashing, that, except when the two parts are severed by lateral pressure, they form but a single shaft. The point, gener-

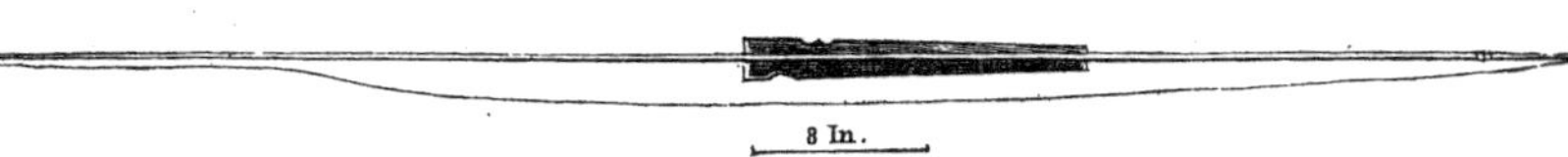

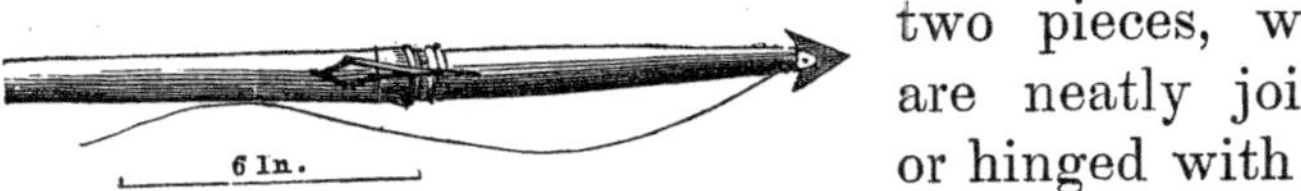

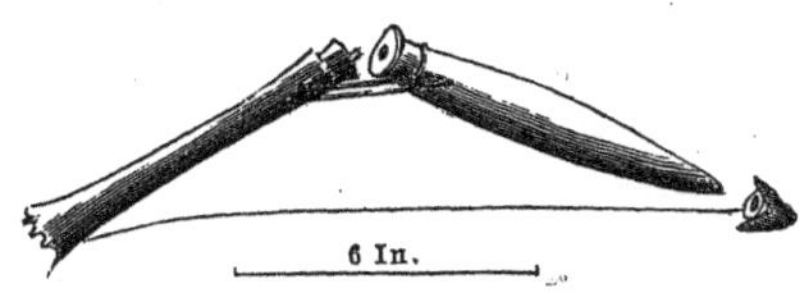

6 In.

ally an arrow-head of bone, has a socket to receive the end of the shaft: it disengages itself readily from its place, but still remains fast to the end of the line. Thus, when the kayacker has struck his prey, the shaft escapes the risk of breaking from a pull against the grain by bending at the joint, and the point is carried free by the animal as he dives.

At the right centre of gravity of the harpoon, that point, I mean, at which a cudgel-player would grasp his staff, a neatly-arranged *cestus* or holder (*noon-sok*)

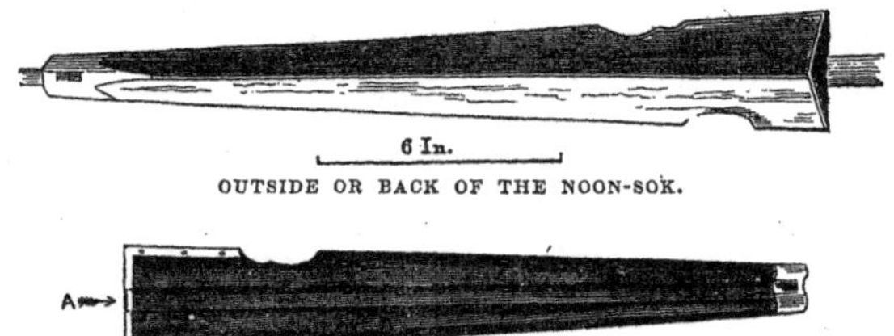

6 In.

OUTSIDE OR BACK OF THE NOON-SOK.

8 In.

INSIDE OR SECTION OF THE NOON-SOK.

fits itself on the shaft. It serves to give the kayacker a good grip when casting his weapon, but slides off from it, and is left in the hand, at the moment of drawing back his arm. The bird javelin (*neu-ve-ak*),

8 In.

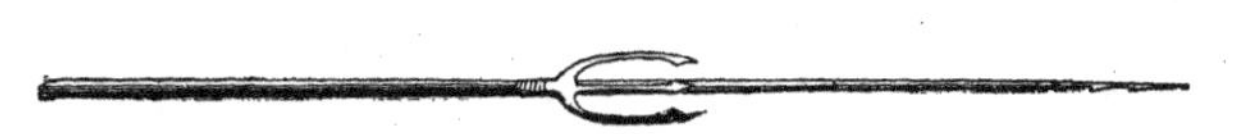

the seal lance (*ah-gnu-ve-to*), and the rude hunting-knife

8 In.

(*ka-poot*), will be easily understood from my sketches.

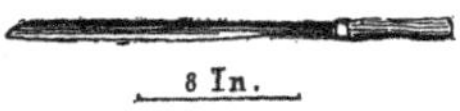

8 In.

The paddle (*pa-uh-teet*), about which a knowing Esquimaux will waste as many words as a sporting gentleman upon a double-barreled Manton or a bridle-bit of peculiar fancy, is in every respect a beautifully considered instrument. It never exceeds seven feet in length. It is double-bladed, and its central portion, which receives the hands, presents an ellipsoid face, well adapted to a secure grasp. The blades are four inches in width, and some two feet in length, forming very nearly sections of a cone. Their edges and tips are carefully guarded from the cutting action of the ice by the ivory of the walrus or narwhal.

Thus constructed and furnished, its seal-skin covering renewed every year, the kayack is the life, and pastime, and pride of its owner. He carries it on his shoulder into the surf, clad in his water-proof seal-skin dress, belted close round the neck, his hood firmly set above; wedges himself into the man-hole, unites himself by a lashing to its rim, and paddles off for a frolic outside the breakers, or it may be a seal-hunt, or to throw his javelin at the eider, or perhaps to carry dispatches to some distant settlement, or to take part in a crusade against the reindeer.

In their long excursions in search of deer, the kayackers paddle their way to the nearest portage along the coast, and shoulder their little skiff till they reach the interior lakes. Their dexterity is admirable in the use of their weapons. I have seen them spear the eider on the wing and the loon as he was diving. Scudding along at a rate equal to that of a five-oared whale-boat, they fling their tiny javelin far ahead, and, without interrupting their progress, seize it as they pass.

The authorities of Greenland communicate constantly with their different posts by means of the kayack. On these occasions the express consists of two, traveling together for assistance and fellowship. They are expeditious, and proverbially reliable. They travel only during the day. At night they land upon some well-remembered solitude; the kayack is carried up, and laid beside the leeward face of some protecting rock, and, after a scanty meal, the Hosky seats himself once more in its closely-fitting hole; then, drawing over him his water-tight hood, he leans for support against the naked stone, and sleeps. One of these messengers arrived at Holsteinberg while we were there from Fredericshaab, three hundred and sixty miles in ten days; traveling along a tempestuous coast, with varying winds and currents, at a mean rate of thirty-six miles a day.

It is said the expertness of the kayacker increases as you proceed south. If the natives of Julianshaab and Lichtenfels surpass those of Egedesminde and Holsteinberg, their feats are unnecessarily wonderful. Here are some of them, not performed as such, but illustrating the accomplishments of a well-trained man.

Extending out from an offsetting mountain-ridge to the north of Holsteinberg, is a rocky reef or ledge, over which the sea breaks heavily, and the currents run with perplexing caprice and force. In almost all sorts of weather, if there be only light enough to see, the kayacks may be met playing about these surf-beaten passages, regardless of wind, swell, or tides. When our vessel was entering port, we were boarded by a kayack pilot. In spite of the heavy seaway, he approached fearlessly to the side of the brig, then, poising himself on the slope of the waves, he avoided the trough, and, passing a running bowline fore and aft over his little craft, man and boat were lifted bodily on board.

Going out to seaward, with a heavy inshore surf rolling, is no trifle, even to well-manned whale-boats The kayacker paddles quietly out toward the breakers. The roaring lip of green water bends roof-like over him. Down cowers the pliant man, his right shoulder buried in the water, and his hooded head bowed upon his breast. An instant and he emerges on the outer side with a jutting impulse, shaking the water from his mane, and preparing for a fresh encounter.

The somerset, the "cantrum," as the whalers term it, may be seen any hour of the day for a plug of tobacco or a glass of rum. I have seen it with different degrees of address; but one, that Mr. Müller, the governor of Holsteinberg, told me of, is the perfection of dextrous overturning. The kayacker takes a stone, as large as he can grasp in his hand, holding the paddle by the imperfect grip of the thumbs. He whirls his hands over his head, upsets his little bark, buries it bottom up, and rights himself on the other side, still holding the stone.

But after all, the crowning feat is the every-day one of catching the seal. For this the kayack is constructed, and it is here that its wonderful adaptation of purpose is best displayed. Without describing the admirable astuteness with which he finds and approaches his prey, let us suppose the kayacker close upon a seal. The line-stand is carefully examined, the coil adjusted, the attachments to the body of the boat so fixed that the slightest strain will separate them. The bladder-float is disengaged, and the harpoon tipped with its barb, which forms the extremity of the coil.

In an instant the kayacker has thrown his body back and sent his weapon home. Whirr! goes the little coil, and the float is bobbing over the water—not far, however, for the barb has entered the lungs, and the seal must rise for breath. Now the harpoon is picked up, its head remaining in the victim; and the kayack comes along. Here is required discretion as well as address. The hunter has probably but two weapons, a lance and a knife. The latter he can not part with, and even the lance brings him to closer quarters than the safety of his craft would invite; for the contortions of a large seal thus wounded may tear it at some of the seams, and the merest crevice is certain destruction. If he has with him the light javelin which he uses for spearing birds, he may be tempted to employ it now; but this, I believe, is not altogether sportsmanlike. The lance generally gives the *coup-de-grace.*

And now, from the greasy and somewhat odoriferous recesses of the kayack, you see him taking a dirty little coil of walrus hide, bearing several queer little toggles of bone. With a knowing gash of his knife, he makes a hole in the under jaw of the seal: the bone is passed through; and the seal, towed alongside, comes in to rejoice the expectant wife and children.

Small and frail as the kayack is, its perfect adaptation and beautiful management make it nearly independent of the mere danger of the sea. What, then, makes the kayacker's pursuit one of constant excitement, and often of fatal peril?

It is the risk of perforation. The Greenland seas abound with ice and drift-wood. The kayacker is firmly wedged—as one with his vessel; and the kayack itself is a mere diaphragm of skin, stretched on a wooden frame. Even by the friction of use, it becomes as attenuated as parchment, and sometimes parts by the mere contraction of changing temperatures. I have seen them at the brig's quarter so transparent that the wash of the waves, and even the floating actinia, were visible through their sides. The seams, too, however carefully secured at first, will nevertheless warp in the sunshine. Constant scrutiny and skill can hardly insure them against hazard.

This proves itself sadly. About three kayacks a year are missing from Holsteinberg, and the other settlements have a nearly similar ratio of mortality. The kayack is sometimes the coffin of its owner, and the two skeletons have more than once been found together on the lonely beaches of this bleak coast.

In quiet weather, however, by much address, two may save one; or by towing, if the distance be not great from shore, even one may save another. The first of these modes of rescue consists in lashing the two kayacks at the sides of the wreck, or by running the paddle that belonged to it through the strong cross-lines of walrus hide which stretch across the tops of the other two. The unfortunate man is then extricated from the *pah* or hole, and sits very comfortably behind with a knee on each boat. I have seen Esquimaux carried ashore from our brig in this manner. In the other case, the unfortunate, with his inflated float, may grasp the stern of his friendly helper, and be towed to shore; but in these icy waters nature sustains herself with difficulty against the cold.

It has happened sometimes, but so very rarely as to be chronicled always for a wonder, that a strong and determined fellow, with the aid of bladder-float, and superhuman exertion besides, has managed to reach the shore. The last who did so was found frozen stiff on the beach, his float attached to his person. It was to the north of Uppernavik.

I had heard stories of the voluntary expatriation of some of these poor people. It was said that men who had been missing for years were found afterward in the neighborhood of Cape Walsingham, having made the transit of the bay on the ice in midwinter. But I believe it to be a libel, and that Home is home even to a Greenlander. Mr. Zimmel, the inspector for the time at Egedesminde, told me that the ice between Cape Walsingham and Holsteinberg, and above, is never absolutely fast. Sometimes, he said, it was so impacted against the coast as to appear continuous, and upon a change of wind afterward would drive across the bay, so as to open on the one shore and close on the other.

This occasional tendency of the ice-raft to float across the bay has given rise to some fearful accidents. It would be difficult for fiction to exceed some of the stories that are well authenticated of these poor nomads.

Esquimaux who have gone out with kayack or sledge have been mourned as dead. Years afterward messages have come by the whalers of their safety in the unknown regions of the West, and of their adoption there; but after trials too fearful to be recounted. Some years ago—the year was mentioned, but I have forgot it—a couple of Esquimaux, relatives, set out on a sledge in quest of seal. The great ice-plain formed one continuous sheet from the Greenland shore as far as the eye could reach. During the night, one of them, awaking from a heavy sleep, found that the wind had shifted to the eastward. It was blowing gently, and could hardly have been blowing long. They harnessed in their dogs, urged them to their utmost speed, and made for the land they had left. Too late! a yawning chasm of open water lay already between. A day was lost in frantic despair. It blew a gale, an offshore southeaster. The fog rose, the wind still from the east: the shore was gone.

The story is a wild one. They reharnessed the dogs, and turned to the west, one hundred and thirty trackless miles of ice before them. On the third day the dogs gave out: one of the lost men killed his fellow, and revived the animals with his flesh. The wretched survivor at last reached the North American shore about Merchant's Bay. Years afterward, this account came over by a circuitous channel to the Greenland settlement. He had married a new wife, had a new family, a new home, a new country, from which, had he desired it never so much, there could be for him no return.

The traditions of all the settlements have tales of similar disaster. Yet the Esquimaux are a happy race of people, happy so far as content and an elastic temperament go to make up happiness.

I should like to dilate for a while on some of their superstitions, which crop out now and then through their adopted faith, as if to show the Scandinavian mythology it overlays. I have the materials by me, too, for some passages about their seemingly innate fondness for music, their roundelays and hymns, the little organ at Holsteinberg, which has come back from Denmark repaired since Sir John Ross's visit, the violins of the church orchestra, and the abominably iterated accordions, with their kindred Jews-harps. I should have been excused, perhaps, for adding a chapter also on the probabilities of Sir John Franklin's company being yet alive, and the duty of adventurous Christendom to persist in the effort for their rescue.

But the story of our cruise is told; and my readers will be almost as willing as I was to hurry onwards to our own shores. Before these pages can pass through the press, I shall have given such assurance as it is in my power to give of my convictions that the missing party may be found, and should be sought for. If God shall favor me, I may be able to speak hereafter, from a renewed and more intimate personal knowledge, of the habits and feelings of the Greenland people.

We left the settlements of Baffin's Bay on the 6th of September, 1851, grateful exceedingly to the kind-hearted officers of the Danish posts; and after a run of some twenty-four days, unmarked by incident, touched our native soil again at New York. Our noble friend, Henry Grinnell, was the first to welcome us on the pier-head.

APPENDIX.

A. Instructions of the Secretary of the Navy to Lieut. De Haven, commanding the U. S. Grinnell Expedition.

B. Lieut. De Haven's Report on the Return of the Expedition.

C. Current Chart, and Half-monthly Meteorological Abstracts of the Log-book of the U. S. Brig Advance during the Cruise, prepared by Charles A. Schott, Esq., of the U. S. Coast Survey.

D. Half-monthly Abstract of the mean Force of the Wind, the mean Temperature of the Air and Water, and the mean Height of the Barometer at the Level of the Sea during the Cruise, prepared by Charles A. Schott, Esq., U. S. Coast Survey.

E. Table of the relative Frequency of the Winds in each month from June, 1850, to August, 1850, and from January, 1851, to August, 1851 (all inclusive), on the meridian of Baffin's Bay, and from September, 1851, to December, 1851, (both inclusive), on more western Meridians, prepared by Charles A. Schott, Esq., U. S. Coast Survey.

F. Lecture on the Access to an Open Polar Sea in connection with the Search after Sir John Franklin and his Companions, read before the American Geographical and Statistical Society at its regular monthly meeting, by Dr. Kane, December 14, 1852.

APPENDIX.

A.

INSTRUCTIONS OF THE SECRETARY OF THE NAVY TO LIEUT DE HAVEN, COMMANDING THE U. S. GRINNELL EXPEDITION.

United States Navy Department,
Washington, Wednesday, May 15, 1850.

SIR,—Having been selected to command the expedition in search of Sir John Franklin and his companions, you will take charge of the brigantines, the Advance and Rescue, that have been fitted out for that service, and as soon as you are ready, proceed with them to sea, and make the best of your way to Lancaster Sound.

These vessels have been furnished to the government for this service by the munificence of a private citizen, Mr. Henry Grinnell, of New York. You will, therefore, be careful of them, that they may be returned to their owner in good condition. They have been provisioned for three years.

Passed Midshipman S. P. Griffin has been selected to command one of the vessels. You will, therefore, consider him as your second in command. Confer with him, and treat him accordingly.

The chief object of this expedition is to search for, and, if found, afford relief to Sir John Franklin, of the Royal Navy, and his companions.

You will, therefore, use all diligence and make every exertion to this end, paying attention as you go to subjects of scientific inquiry only so far as they may not interfere with the main object of the expedition.

Having passed Barrow's Straits, you will turn your attention northward to Wellington Channel, and westward to Cape Walker, and be governed by circumstances as to the course you will then take.

Accordingly, you will exercise your own discretion, after seeing the condition of the ice, sea, and weather, whether the two vessels shall here separate—one for Cape Walker, and the other for Wellington Straits; or whether they shall both proceed together for the one place or the other.

Should you find it impossible, on account of the ice, to get through to Barrow's Straits, you will then turn your attention to Jones's Sound and Smith's Sound. Finding these closed or impracticable, and failing of all traces of the missing expedition, the season will probably then be too far advanced for any other attempts. If so, you will return to New York.

Acquaint Passed Midshipman Griffin before sailing, and from time to time during the voyage, fully with all your plans and intentions, and before sailing appoint a place of rendezvous; change it as often as circumstances may render a change desirable, but always have a place of rendezvous fixed upon, so that in case the two vessels of the expedition may at any time become separated, each may know where to look for the other.

Nearly the entire Arctic front of the continent has been scoured without finding any traces of the missing ships. It is useless for you to go there, or to re-examine any other place where search has already been made. You will, therefore, confine your attention to the routes already indicated.

The point of maximum cold is said to be in the vicinity of Parry Islands. To the north and west of these there is probably a comparative open sea in summer, and therefore a milder climate.

This opinion seems to be sustained by the fact that beasts and fowls are seen migrating over the ice from the mouth of Mackenzie River and its neighboring shores to the north. These dumb creatures are probably led by their wise instincts to seek a more genial climate in that direction, and upon the borders of the supposed more open sea.

There are other facts elicited by Lieutenant Maury, in the course of his investigations touching the winds and currents of the ocean, which go also to confirm the opinion, that beyond the icy barrier that is generally met with in the Arctic Ocean, there is a Polina, or sea free from ice.

You have assisted in these investigations at the National Observatory, and are doubtless aware of the circumstances which authorize this conclusion; it is therefore needless to repeat them.

This supposed open sea and warmer region to the north and west of Parry Islands are unexplored. Should you succeed in finding any opening there, either after having cleared Wellington Straits, or after having cleared Parry Islands by a northwardly course from Cape Walker, enter as far as in your judgment it may be prudent to enter, and search every headland, promontory, and conspicuous point for signs and records of the missing party. Take particular care to avail yourself of every opportunity for leaving as you go records and signs to tell of your welfare, progress, and intentions.

For this purpose you will erect flag-staffs, make piles of stone, or other marks in conspicuous places, with a bottle or barrica buried at the base containing your letters.

Should the two vessels be separated, you will direct Passed Midshipman Griffin to do likewise.

Avail yourself of every opportunity, either by the Esquimaux or otherwise, to let the Department hear from you; and in every communication be full and particular as to your future plans and intended route.

If by any chance you should penetrate so far beyond the icy barrier as to make it, in your judgment, more prudent to push on than to turn back, you will do so, and put yourself in communication with any of the United States naval forces or officers of the government serving in the waters of the Pacific or in China, according to your necessities and opportunities. Those officers will be instructed to afford you every facility possible to enable you to reach the western coast of the United States in safety.

In the event of your falling in with any of the British searching parties, you will offer them any assistance of which they may stand in need, and which it may be in your power to give. Offer, also, to make them acquainted with your intended route and plans, and be ready to afford them every information of which you may have become possessed concerning the object of your search.

In case your country should be involved in war during your absence on this service, you will on no account commit, or suffer any one of the expedition to commit, the least act of hostility against the enemy, of whatever nation he may be.

Notwithstanding the directions in which you have been recommended to carry your examinations, you may, on arriving out upon the field of operation, find that by departing from them your search would probably be more effectual.

The Department has every confidence in your judgment, and relies implicitly upon your discretion; and should it appear during the voyage that, by directing your attention to points not named in this letter, traces of the absent expedition would probably be found, you will not fail to examine such points. But you will on no account uselessly hazard the safety of the vessels under your command, or unnecessarily expose to danger the officers and men committed to your charge.

Unless circumstances should favor you, by enabling you to penetrate, before the young ice begins to make in the fall, far into the unexplored regions, or to discover recent traces of the missing ships and their gallant crews, or unless you should gain a position from which you could commence operations in the season of 1851 with decided advantage, you will endeavor not to be caught in the ice during the ensuing winter, but, after having completed your examinations for the season, make your escape, and return to New York in the fall.

You are especially enjoined not to spend, if it can be avoided, more than one winter in the Arctic regions.

Wishing you and your gallant companions all success in your noble enterprise, and with the trust in God that He will take you and them in his holy keeping, I am, very respectfully, your obedient servant,

WILLIAM BALLARD PRESTON.

To Edwin J. De Haven, Lieutenant commanding the American Arctic Expedition, &c., New York.

B.

LIEUT. DE HAVEN'S OFFICIAL REPORT OF THE AMERICAN ARCTIC EXPEDITION.

U. S. Brig Advance,
New York, October 4, 1851.

SIR,—I have the honor to submit the following as the proceedings of the squadron under my command subsequent to the 22d of August, 1850, up to which time the Department is already advised of its movements.

On the 23d of August we approached Port Leopold; but the necessity of a detention here to search for information was precluded by our falling in with the English yacht Prince Albert, Commander Forsyth, R. N. He informed us that the harbor was still filled with ice, so as to render it inaccessible to vessels. A boat, however, had been sent in, but no traces of the missing expedition were found.

We now stood over for the north shore, passing to the eastward of Leopold Island, threading our way through much heavy stream-ice. Barrow's Straits to the westward presented one mass of heavy and closely-packed ice, extending close into the coast of North Somerset. On the north shore we found open water, reaching to the westward as far as Beechy Island.

At noon on the 25th we were off Cape Riley, where the vessel was hove to, and a boat sent ashore to examine a cairn erected in a conspicuous position. It was found to contain a record of H. B. M.'s ship Assistance, deposited the day before. Another record informed us that our consort had visited the cape at the same time with the Assistance.

Fragments of painted wood and preserved meat tins were picked up on the low point of the cape; there were also other indications that it had been the camping ground of some civilized traveling or hunting party. Our speculations at once connected them with the object of our search.

While making our researches on shore, the vessel was set by a strong current near the point, where, becoming hampered by some masses of ice, she took the ground. Every effort was made to get her off, but the falling tide soon left her hard and fast. We now lightened her of all weighty articles about deck, and prepared to renew our efforts when the tide should rise. This took place about midnight, when she was hauled off without apparent injury.

The Prince Albert approached us while aground, and Commander Forsyth tendered his assistance; it was not, however, required. Soon after, the Rescue came in sight from around Beechy Island, and making us out in our awkward predicament, hove to in the offing, and sent a boat in. She had been up Wellington Channel as far as Point Innes. The condition of the ice prevented her from reaching Cape Hotham (the appointed place of rendezvous), so she had returned in search of us.

On the 26th, with a light breeze, we passed Beechy Island, and run through a narrow lead to the north. Immediately above Point Innes the ice of Wellington Channel was fixed and unbroken from shore to shore, and had every indication of having so remained for at least three years. It was generally about eight feet thick, and the sharp, angular hummocks, peculiar to recently-formed ice, had been rounded down to gentle hillocks by the action of the weather for several seasons. Further progress to the north was out of the question. To the west, however, along the edge of the fixed ice, a lead presented itself, with a freshening wind from the southeast. We ran into it, but at half way across the channel our headway was arrested by the closing ice. A few miles beyond this, two of the English vessels (one a steamer) were dangerously beset. I deemed it prudent to return to Point Innes, under the lee of which the vessels might hold on in security until a favorable change should take place.

On Point Innes distinct traces of an encampment were found, together with many relics similar to those found at Cape Riley. Captain Penny (whose squadron we met here) picked up a piece of paper containing the name of one of the officers of Franklin's Expedition, written in pencil, thus proving beyond a doubt that some of his party had encamped here; but when, or under what circumstances, it was difficult to say. The preserved-meat cans, moreover, bore the name of the person who had supplied his ships with that article.

On Point Innes we also found the remains of an Esquimaux's hut; but it had evidently been abandoned for many years. No recent traces of this people were found on any of the shores of Lancaster Sound that we visited.

The weather becoming more favorable, we retraced our steps as far as Beechy Island, in order to make more minute investigations in that quarter. The vessels were made fast to the land-ice on the northwest side of the island on the 27th of August. The schooner Felix, Captain Sir John Ross, R. N., and the squadron under Captain Penny, joined us at this point. Consulting with these gentlemen, a joint search was instituted along the adjacent shores in all directions. In a short time one of Captain Penny's men returned and reported that he had discovered *several graves*. On examination, his report proved to be correct. Three well-made graves were found, with painted head-boards of wood, the inscriptions on which were as follows:

1st.

"Sacred to the memory of W. Braine, R. M., H. M. S. 'Erebus.' Died April 3d, 1846, aged 32 years. 'Choose ye this day whom you will serve.'"

2d.

"Sacred to the memory of Jno. Hartwell, A. B., H. M. S. 'Erebus,' aged 23 years. 'Thus saith the Lord of hosts, consider your ways.'"

3d.

"Sacred to the memory of Jno. Torrington, who departed this life January 1st, A.D. 1846, on board H. M. S. 'Terror,' aged 20."

Near the graves were also other unmistakable evidences of the missing expedition having passed its first winter here. They consisted of innumerable scraps of old rope and canvas; the blocks on which stood the armorer's anvil, with many pieces of coal and iron around it; the outlines of several tents or houses, supposed to have been the site of the Observatory and erections for sheltering the mechanics. The chips and shavings of the carpenter still remained. A short distance from this was found a large number of preserved-meat tins, all having the same label as those found at Point Innes.

From all these indications the inference could not fail to be arrived at that the Erebus and Terror had made this their first winter quarters after leaving England. The spot was admirably chosen for the security of the ships, as well as for their early escape the following season. Every thing, too, went to prove, up to this point, that the expedition was well organized, and that the vessels had not received any material injury.

Early on the morning of the 28th of August, H. B. M. ship Resolute (Captain Austin), with her steam-tender, arrived from the eastward. Renewed efforts were made by all parties to discover some written notice, which, according to his instructions, Sir J. Franklin ought to have deposited at this place in some conspicuous position. A cairn of stones, erected on the highest part of the island, was discovered. A most thorough search with crows and picks was instituted at and about it, in the presence of all hands. This search was continued for several days, but not the slightest vestige of a record could be found. The graves were not opened or disturbed.

Captain Sir John Ross had towed out from England a small vessel of about twelve tons. He proposed leaving her at this point, to fall back upon in case of disaster to any of the searching vessels. Our contribution to supply her was three barrels of provisions.

From the most elevated part of Beechy Island (about eight hundred feet high) an extensive view was had, both to the north and west. No open water could be seen in either direction.

On the 27th of August we cast off from Beechy Island, and joined our consort at the edge of the fixed ice, near Point Innes. Acting Master S. P. Griffin, commander of the Rescue, had just returned from a searching excursion along the shore, on which he had been dispatched forty-eight hours before. Midshipman Lovell and four men composed his party. He reports that, pursuing carefully his route to the northward, he came upon a partially-overturned cairn, of large dimensions, on the beach a few miles south of Cape Bowden. Upon strict examination, it appeared to have been erected as a place of depôt of provisions. No clew could be found within it or around as to the persons who built it, neither could its age be arrived at.

At two P.M. of the 28th, reached Cape Bowden without further discovery. Erecting a cairn, containing the information that would prove useful to a distressed party, he commenced his journey back.

Until the 3d day of September, we were detained at this point by the closing in of the ice from the southward, occasioned by strong northeast winds, accompanied with thick weather and snow. On this day the packed ice moved off from the edge of the fixed ice, leaving a practicable lead to the westward, into which we at once stood. At midnight, when about two thirds the way across the channel, the closing ice arrested our progress. We were in some danger from heavy masses coming against us, but both vessels passed the night uninjured. In the evening of the 4th we were able to make a few more miles westing, and the following day we reached Barlow's Inlet. The ice being impracticable to the southward, we secured the vessels at its entrance. The Assistance and her steam-tender were seen off Cape Hotham, behind which they disappeared in the course of the day.

Barlow's Inlet would afford good shelter for vessels in case of necessity, but it would require some cutting to get in or out. The ice of last winter still remained unbroken.

A fresh breeze from the north on the 8th caused the ice in the channel to set to the southward. It still remained, however, closely packed on Cape Hotham. On the 9th, in the morning, the wind shifted to the westward, an opening appeared, and we at once got under way. Passing Cape Hotham, a lead was seen along the south side of Cornwallis Island, into which, with a head wind, we worked slowly, our progress being much impeded by bay ice; indeed, it brought us to a dead stand more than once. The following day we reached Griffith's Island, passing the southern point of which the English searching vessels were descried made fast to the ice at a few miles distant. The western lead closing at this point, we were compelled to make fast also.

The ice was here so very unfavorable for making further progress, and the season was so far advanced, that it became necessary to take future movements into serious consideration. A consultation was had with Mr. Griffin, and after reviewing carefully all the circumstances attending our position, it was judged that we had not gained a point from which we could commence operations in the season of 1851 with decided advantages. Therefore, agreeably to my instructions, I felt it an imperative duty to extricate the vessels from the ice, and return to the United States.

The state of the weather prevented our acting immediately upon this decision.

September 11th, wind from the eastward, with fog and snow; we were kept stationary. Much bay ice forming. Thermometer 26°. Early in the morning of the 12th the wind changed to the northwest, and increased rapidly to a heavy gale, which coming off, the ice brought with it clouds of drift snow.

The Rescue was blown from her ice anchors, and went adrift so suddenly that a boat and two of her men were left behind. She got under sail, but the wind was too strong for her to regain the ice. The driving snow soon hid her from us. The Advance came near meeting the same fate. The edge of the floe kept breaking away, and it was with much difficulty that other ice anchors could be planted further in to hold on by. The thermometer fell to 8°; mean for the twenty-four hours, 14°.

On the morning of the 13th, the wind having moderated sufficiently, we got under way, and working our way through some streams of ice, arrived in a few hours at Griffith's Island, under the lee of which we found our consort, made fast to the shore, where she had taken shelter in the gale, her crew having suffered a good deal from the inclemency of the weather. In bringing to under the lee of the island, she had the misfortune to spring her rudder, so that on joining us it was with much difficulty she could steer. To insure her safety and more rapid progress, she was taken in tow by the Advance, when she bore up with a fine breeze from the westward. Off Cape Martyr, we left the English squadron under Captain Austin. About ten miles further to the east, the two vessels under Captain Penny, and that under Sir John Ross, were seen secured near the land. At 8 P.M. we had advanced as far as Cape Hotham. Thence, as far as the increasing darkness of the night enabled us to see, there was nothing to obstruct our progress, except the bay ice. This, with a good breeze, would not have impeded us much; but unfortunately, the wind, when it was most required, failed us. The snow with which the surface of the water was covered rapidly cemented, and formed a tenacious coat, through which it was impossible, with all our appliances, to force the vessels. At 8 P.M. they came to a dead stand, some ten miles to the east of Barlow's Inlet.

The following day the wind hauled to the southward, from which quarter it lasted till the 19th. During this period the young ice was broken, its edges squeezed up into hummocks, and one floe overrun by another until it all assumed the appearance of heavy ice.

The vessels received some heavy nips from it, but they withstood them without injury. Whenever a pool of water made its appearance, every effort was made to reach it, in hopes it would lead us into Beechy Island, or some other place where the vessel might be placed in security; for the winter set in unusually early, and the severity with which it commenced forbade all hopes of our being able to return this season. I now became anxious to attain a point in the neighborhood from whence, by means of land parties, in the spring, a goodly extent of Wellington Channel might be examined.

In the mean time, under the influence of the south wind, we were being set up the channel. On the 18th we were above Cape Bowden, the most northern point seen on this shore by Parry.

The land on both shores was seen much further, and trended considerably to the west of north. To account for this drift, the fixed ice of Wellington Channel, which we had observed in passing to the westward, must have been broken up and driven to the southward by the heavy gale of the 12th.

On the 19th the wind veered to the north, which gave us a southerly set, forcing us at the same time with the western shore. This did not last long, for the next day the wind hauled again to the south, and blew fresh, bringing the ice in upon us with much pressure. At midnight it broke up all around us, so that we had work to maintain the Advance in a safe position, and keep her from being separated from her consort, which was immovably fixed in the centre of a large floe.

We continued to drift slowly to the N.N.W. until the 22d, when our progress appeared to be arrested by a small low island, which was discovered in that direction, about seven miles distant. A channel of three or four miles in width separated it from Cornwallis Island. This latter island, trending northwest from our position, terminated abruptly in an elevated cape, to which I have given the name of Manning, after a warm personal friend and ardent supporter of the expedition. Between Cornwallis Island and some distant high land visible in the north, appeared a wide channel leading to the westward. A dark, misty-looking cloud which hung over it (technically termed frost smoke), was indicative of much open water in that direction.

This was the direction to which my instructions, referring to the investigations at the National Observatory concerning the winds and currents of the ocean, directed me to look for open water.

Nor was the open water the only indication that presented itself in confirmation of this theoretical conjecture as to a milder climate in that direction. As we entered Wellington Channel, the signs of animal life became more abundant, and Captain Penny, commander of one of the English expeditions, who afterward penetrated on sledges much toward the region of the frost smoke, much further than it was possible for us to do in our vessels, reported that he actually arrived on the borders of this open sea.

Thus these admirably drawn instructions, deriving arguments from the enlarged and comprehensive system of physical research, not only pointed with emphasis to an unknown open sea into which Franklin had probably found his way, but directed me to search for traces of his expedition in the very chan nel at the entrance of which it is now ascertained he had passed his first winter.

The direction in which search with most chances of success is now to be made for the missing expedition, or for traces of it, is no doubt in the direction which is so clearly pointed out in my instructions.

To the channel which appeared to lead into the open sea over which the cloud of frost smoke hung as a sign, I have given the name of *Maury*, after the distinguished gentleman at the head of our National Observatory, whose theory with regard to an open sea to the north is likely to be realized through this channel. To the large mass of land visible between N.W. to N.N.E., I gave the name of *Grinnell*, in honor of the head and heart of the man in whose philanthropic mind originated the idea of this expedition, and to whose munificence it owes its existence.

To a remarkable peak bearing N.N.E. from us, distant about forty miles, was given the name of *Mount Franklin*. An inlet or harbor immediately to the north of Cape Bowden was discovered by Mr. Griffin in his land excursion from Point Innes on the 27th of August, and has received the name of *Griffin Inlet*.

The small island mentioned before was called Murdaugh's Island, after the acting master of the Advance.

The eastern shore of Wellington Channel appeared to run parallel with the western, but it became quite low, and being covered with snow, could not be distinguished with certainty, so that its continuity with the high land to the north was not ascertained.

Some small pools of open water appearing near us, an attempt was made about fifty yards, but our combined efforts were of no avail in extricating the Rescue from her icy cradle. A change of wind not only closed the ice up again, but threatened to give us a severe nip. We unshipped her rudder and placed it out of harm's way.

September 23d was an uncomfortable day. The wind was from northeast, with snow. From an early hour in the morning the floes began to be pressed together with so much force that their edges were thrown up in immense ridges of rugged hummocks. The Advance was heavily nipped between two floes, and the ice was piled up so high above the rail on the starboard side as to threaten to come on board and sink us with its weight. All hands were occupied in keeping it out. The pressure and commotion did not cease till near midnight, when we were very glad to have a respite from our labors and fears. The next day we were threatened with a similar scene, but it fortunately ceased in a short time.

For the remainder of September and until the 4th of October, the vessels drifted but little. The winds were very light, the thermometer fell to minus 12, and ice formed over the pools in sight sufficiently strong to travel upon.

We were now strongly impressed with the belief that the ice had become fixed for the winter, and that we should be able to send out traveling parties from the advanced position for the examination of the lands to the northward. Stimulated by this fair prospect, another attempt was made to reach the shore, in order to establish a depôt of provisions at or near Cape Manning, which would materially facilitate the progress of our parties in the spring; but the ice was still found to be detached from the shore, and a narrow lane of water cut us from it.

During the interval of comparative quiet, preliminary measures were taken for heating the Advance, and increasing her quarters, so as to accommodate the officers and crews of both vessels. No stoves had as yet been used in either vessel; indeed, they could not well be put up without placing a large quantity of stores and fuel upon the ice. The attempt was made to do this, but a sudden crack in the floe where it appeared strongest, causing the loss of several tons of coal, convinced us that it was not yet safe to do so. It was not until the 20th of October we got fires below. Ten days later, the housing cloth was put over, and the officers and crew of the Rescue ordered on board the Advance for the winter. Room was found on the deck of the Rescue for many of the provisions removed from the hold of this vessel. Still, a large quantity had to be placed on the ice.

The absence of fires below had caused much discomfort to all hands ever since the beginning of September, not so much from the low temperature, as from the accumulation of moisture by condensation, which congealed as the temperature decreased, and covered the wood-work of our apartments with ice. This state of things soon began to work its effect upon the health of the crews. Several cases of scurvy appeared among them, and, notwithstanding the indefatigable attention and active treatment resorted to by the medical officers, it could not be eradicated; its progress, however, was checked.

All through October and November we were drifted to and fro by the changing wind, but never passing out of Wellington Channel. On the 1st of No vember, the new ice had attained the thickness of thirty-seven inches. Still, frequent breaks would occur in it, often in fearful proximity to the vessels. Hummocks, consisting of massive, granite-like blocks, would be thrown up to the height of twenty, and even thirty feet. This action in the ice was accompanied with a variety of sounds impossible to be described, but when heard never failed to carry a feeling of awe into the stoutest hearts. In the stillness of an Arctic night, they could be heard several miles, and often was the rest of all hands disturbed by them.

To guard against the worst that could happen to us—the destruction of the vessels—the boats were prepared and sledges built. Thirty days' provisions were placed in for all hands, together with tents and blanket bags for sleeping in. Besides this, each man and officer had his knapsack containing an extra suit of clothes. These were all kept in readiness for use at a moment's notice.

For the sake of wholesome exercise, as well as to inure the people to ice-traveling, frequent excursions were made with our laden sledges. The officers usually took the lead at the drag ropes; and they, as well as the men, underwent the labor of surmounting the rugged hummocks with great cheerfulness and zeal. Notwithstanding the low temperature, all hands usually returned in a profuse perspiration. We had also other sources of exercise and amusements, such as foot-ball, skating, sliding, racing, with theatrical representations on holidays and national anniversaries. These amusements were continued throughout the winter, and contributed very materially to the cheerfulness and general good health of all hands.

The drift had set us gradually to the southeast, until we were about five miles to the southwest of Beechy Island In this position we remained comparatively stationary about a week. We once more began to entertain a hope that we had become fixed for the winter; but it proved a vain one, for on the last day of November a strong wind from the westward set in, with thick, snowy weather. This wind created an immediate movement in the ice. Several fractures took place near us, and many heavy hummocks were thrown up. The floe in which our vessels were imbedded was being rapidly encroached upon, so that we were in momentary fear of the ice breaking from around them. and that they would be once more broken out and left to the tender mercies of the crashing floes.

On the following day (the 1st of December) the weather cleared off, and the few hours of twilight which we had about noon enabled us to get a glimpse of the land. As well as we could make it out, we appeared to be off Gascoigne Inlet.

We were now clear of Wellington Channel, and in the fair way of Lancaster Sound, to be set either up or down, at the mercy of the prevailing winds and currents. We were not long left in doubt as to the direction we had to pursue. The winds prevailed from the westward, and our drift was steady and rapid toward the mouth of the sound.

The prospect before us was now any thing but cheering. We were deprived of our last fond hope, that of becoming fixed in some position whence operations could be carried on by means of traveling parties in the spring. The vessels were fast being set out of the region of search.

Nor was this our only source of uneasiness. The line of our drift was from two to five miles from the north shore, and whenever the moving ice met with any of the capes or projecting points of land, the obstruction would cause fractures in it, extending off to and far beyond us.

Cape Hurd was the first and most prominent point; we were but two miles from it on the 3d of December. Nearly all day the ice was both seen and heard to be in constant motion at no great distance from us. In the evening a crack in our floe took place not more than twenty-five yards ahead of the Advance. It opened in the course of the evening to the width of one hundred yards.

No further disturbance took place until noon of the 5th, when we were somewhat startled by the familiar and unmistakable sound of the ice grinding against the side of the ship. Going on deck, I perceived that another crack had taken place, passing along the length of the vessel.

It did not open more than a foot: this, however, was sufficient to liberate the vessel, and she rose several inches bodily, having become more buoyant since she froze in. The following day, in the evening, the crack opened several yards, leaving the sides of the Advance entirely free; and she was once more supported by and rode in her own element. We were not, though, by any means, in a pleasant situation. The floes were considerably broken in all directions around us, and one crack had taken place between the two vessels. The Rescue was not disturbed in her bed of ice.

December 7th, at 8 A.M., the crack in which we were had opened and formed a lane of water fifty-six feet wide, communicating ahead at the distance of sixty feet with ice of about one foot in thickness, which had formed since the 3d. The vessel was secured to the largest floe near us (that on which our spare stores were deposited). At noon the ice was again in motion, and began to close, affording us the pleasant prospect of an inevitable "nip" between two floes of the heaviest kind. In a short time the prominent points took our side, on the starboard just about the main-rigging, and on the port under the counter and at the fore-rigging; thus bringing three points of pressure in such a position that it must have proved fatal to a larger or less strengthened vessel.

The Advance, however, stood it bravely. After trembling and groaning in every joint, the ice passed under and raised her about two and a half feet. She was let down again for a moment, and then her stern was raised about five feet. Her bows being unsupported, were depressed almost as much. In this uncomfortable position we remained. The wind blew a gale from the eastward, and the ice all around was in dreadful commotion, excepting, fortunately, that in immediate contact with us. The commotion in the ice continued all through the night, and we were in momentary expectation of witnessing the destruction of both vessels. The easterly gale had set us some two or three miles to the west.

As soon as it was light enough to see on the 9th, it was discovered that the heavy ice in which the Rescue had been imbedded for so long a time was entirely broken up, and piled up around her in massive hummocks. On her pumps being sounded, I was gratified to learn that she remained tight, notwithstanding the immense straining and pressure she must have endured.

During this period of trial, as well as in all former and subsequent ones, I could not avoid being struck with the calmness and decision of the officers, as well as the subordination and good conduct of the men, without an exception. Each one knew the imminence of the peril that surrounded us, and was prepared to abide it with a stout heart. There was no noise, no confusion. I did not detect, even in the moment when the destruction of the vessels seemed inevitable, a single desponding look among the whole crew; on the contrary, each one seemed resolved to do his whole duty, and every thing went on cheerily and bravely.

For my own part, I had become quite an invalid, so much so as to prevent my taking an active part in the duties of the vessel, as I always had done, or even from incurring the exposure necessary to proper exercise. However, I felt no apprehension that the vessel would not be properly taken care of, for I had perfect confidence in one and all by whom I was surrounded. I knew them to be equal to any emergency; but I felt under special obligations to the gallant commander of the Rescue for the efficient aid he rendered me. With the kindest consideration and most cheerful alacrity, he volunteered to perform the executive duties during the winter, and relieve me from every thing that might tend in the least to retard my recovery.

During the remainder of December the ice remained quiet immediately around us, and breaks were all strongly cemented by new ice. In our neighborhood, however, cracks were daily visible. Our drift to the eastward averaged nearly six miles per day, so that on the last of the month we were at the entrance of the sound, Cape Osborn bearing north from us.

January, 1851. On passing out of the sound, and opening Baffin's Bay, to the north was seen a dark horizon, indicating much open water in that direction.

On the 11th a crack took place between us and the Rescue, passing close under our stern. It opened, and formed a lane of water eighty feet wide. In the afternoon the floes began to move, the lane was closed up, and the edges of the ice coming in contact with so much pressure, threatened the demolition of the narrow space which separated us from the line of fracture. Fortunately the floes again separated, and assumed a motion by which the Rescue passed from our stern to the port bow, and increased her distance from us 700 yards, where she came to a stand. Our stores that were on the ice were on the same side of the cracks as the Rescue, and of course were carried with her.

The following day the ice remained quiet; but soon after midnight on the 13th, a gale having sprung up from the westward, it once more got into violent motion. The young ice in the crack near our stern was soon broken up, the edges of the thick ice came in contact, and fearful pressures took place, forcing up a line of hummocks which approached within ten feet of our stern. The vessel trembled and complained a great deal.

At last the floe broke up around us into many pieces, and became detached from the sides of the vessel. The scene of frightful commotion lasted until 4 A.M. Every moment I expected the vessel would be crushed or overwhelmed by the massive ice forced up far above our bulwarks. The Rescue being further removed on the other side of the crack from the line of crushing, and being firmly imbedded in heavy ice, I was in hopes would remain undisturbed. This was not the case; for, on sending to her as soon as it was light enough to see, the floe was found to be broken away entirely up to her bows, and there formed into such high hummocks that her bowsprit was broken off, together with her head, and all the light wood-work about it. Had the action of the ice continued much longer she must have been destroyed.

We had the misfortune to find sad havoc had been made among the stores and provisions left on the ice; and few barrels were recovered, but a large portion were crushed and had disappeared.

On the morning of the 14th there was again some motion in the floes. That on the port side moved off from the vessel two or three feet, and there became stationary. This left the vessel entirely detached from the ice round the water-line, and it was expected she would once more resume an upright position. In this, however, we were disappointed, for she remained with her stern elevated, and a considerable list to starboard; being held in this uncomfortable position by the heavy masses which had been forced under her bottom. She retained this position until she finally broke out in the spring.

We were now fully launched into Baffin's Bay, and our line of drift began to be more southerly, assuming a direction nearly parallel with the western shore of the bay at a distance of from forty to seventy miles from it.

After an absence of eighty-seven days, the sun, on the 29th of January, rose his whole diameter above the southern horizon, and remained visible more than an hour. All hands gave vent to delight, on seeing an old friend again, in three hearty cheers.

The length of the days now went on increasing rapidly, but no warmth was yet experienced from the sun's rays; on the contrary, the cold became more intense. Mercury became congealed in February, also in March, which did not occur at any other period during the winter.

A very low temperature was invariably accompanied with clear and calm weather, so that our coldest days were perhaps the most pleasant. In the absence of wind, we could take exercise in the open air without feeling any inconvenience from the cold. But with a strong wind blowing, it was dangerous to be exposed to its chilling blasts for any length of time, even when the thermometer indicated a comparatively moderate degree of temperature.

The ice around the vessels soon became again cemented and fixed, and no other rupture was experienced until it finally broke up in the spring and allowed us to escape. Still we kept driving to the southward along with the whole mass. Open lanes of water were visible at all times from aloft; sometimes they would be formed within a mile or two of us. Narwhals, seals, and dovekies were seen in them. Our sportsmen were not expert enough to procure any, except a few of the latter, although they were indefatigable in their exertions to do so. Bears would frequently be seen prowling about; only two were killed during the winter; others were wounded, but made their escape. A few of us thought their flesh very palatable and wholesome; but the majority utterly rejected it. The flesh of the seal, when it could be obtained, was received with more favor.

As the season advanced, the cases of scurvy became more numerous, yet they were all kept under control by the unwearied attention and skillful treatment of the medical officers. My thanks are due to them, especially to Passed Assistant Surgeon Kane, the senior medical officer of the expedition. I often had occasion to consult him concerning the hygiene of the crew; and it is in a great measure owing to the advice which he gave and the expedients which he recommended, that the expedition was enabled to return without the loss of one man. By the latter end of February the ice had become sufficiently thick to enable us to build a trench around the stern of the Rescue, sufficiently deep to ascertain the extent of the injury she had received in the gale at Griffith's Island.

It was not found to be material; the upper gudgeon alone had been wrenched from the stern post. It was adjusted, and the rudder repaired in readiness for shipping when it should be required. A new bowsprit was also made for her out of the few spare spars we had left, and every thing made seaworthy in both vessels before the breaking up of the ice.

On the 1st of April a hole was cut in some ice that had been forming since our first besetment in September; it was found to have attained the thickness of seven feet two inches.

In this month (April) the amelioration of the temperature became quite sensible. All hands were kept at work, cutting and sawing the ice around the vessels, in order to allow them to float once more. With the Rescue they succeeded, after much labor, in attaining this object; but around the stern of the Advance the ice was so thick that our thirteen-feet saw was too short to pass through it. Her bows and sides, as far aft as the gangway, were liberated.

After making some alteration in the Rescue for the better accommodation of her crew, and fires being lighted on board of her several days previous, to remove the ice and dampness which had accumulated during the winter, both officers and crew were transferred to her on the 24th of April. The stores of this vessel, which had been taken out, were restored, the housing cloth taken off, and the vessel made in every respect ready for sea. There was little prospect, however, of our being able to reach the desired element very soon. The nearest water was a narrow lane more than two miles distant. To cut through the ice which intervened would have been next to impossible. Beyond this lane, from the mast-head, nothing but interminable floes could be seen. It was thought best to wait in patience, and allow nature to work for us.

In May the noon-day sun began to take effect upon the snow which covered the ice; the surface of the floes became watery, and difficult to walk over. Still, the dissolution was so slow in comparison with the mass to be dissolved, that it must have taken us a long period to become liberated from this cause alone. More was expected from our southerly drift, which still continued, and must soon carry us into a milder climate and open sea.

On the 19th of May the land about Cape Searle was made out, the first that we had seen since passing Cape Walter Bathurst, about the 20th of January A few days later we were off Cape Walsingham, and on the 27th passed ou of the Arctic Zone.

June 6th, a moderate breeze from southeast, with pleasant weather; ther mometer up to 40° at noon, and altogether quite a warm and melting day. During the morning a peculiar crackling sound was heard on the floe. I was inclined to impute it to the settling of the snow drifts as they were acted upon by the sun; but in the afternoon, about five o'clock, the puzzle was solved very lucidly, and to the exceeding satisfaction of all hands. A crack in the floe took place between us and the Rescue, and in a few minutes thereafter the whole immense field in which we had been imbedded for so many months was rent in all directions, leaving not a piece exceeding one hundred yards in diameter. This rupture was not accompanied with any noise. The Rescue was entirely liberated, the Advance only partially. The ice in which her after-part was imbedded still adhered to her from the main chains aft, keeping her stern elevated in its unsightly position. The pack (as it may now be called) became quite loose, and but for our pertinacious friend acting as an immense drag upon us, we might have made some headway in any desired direction. All our efforts were now turned to getting rid of it. With saws, axes, and crowbars the people went to work with a right good will, and after hard labor for forty-eight hours, succeeded. The vessel was again afloat, and she righted. The joy of all hands vented itself spontaneously in three hearty cheers. The after part of the false keel was gone, being carried away by the ice. The loss of it, however, I was glad to perceive, did not materially affect the sailing or working qualities of the vessel. The rudders were shipped, and were once more ready to move, as efficient as on the day we left New York.

Steering to the southeast, and working slowly through the loose but heavy pack, on the 9th we parted from the Rescue in a dense fog, she taking a different lead from the one the Advance was pursuing.

On the morning of the 10th, with a fresh breeze from the north, under a press of sail, we forced away into an open and clear sea, in latitude 65° 30′, about thirty-five miles from the spot in which we were liberated.

The wind, which in the ice was merely fresh, proved to be in clear water a gale, with a heavy sea running. Through this we labored until the next morning. When it moderated, the coast of Greenland was in sight.

Our course was now directed for the Whale-fish Islands (the place of rendezvous appointed for our consort), which we reached on the 16th, not, however, without having some difficulty in getting through the unusual number of bergs which lined the coast. In an encounter with one, we lost a studding-sail boom.

I had two objects in visiting these islands, that of verifying our chronometers and to recruit our somewhat debilitated crews. The latter object I learned, on arriving, could be much better obtained, and the former quite as well, at Lievely, on Disco Island, for which place I bore up, leaving orders for the Rescue to follow us. We arrived on the 17th, and the Rescue joined us the day after.

The crews were indulged with a run on shore every day that we remained, which they enjoyed exceedingly after their tedious winter confinement. This recreation, together with a few vegetables of an antiscorbutic character which were obtained, was of much benefit to them. There were no fresh provisions to be had here at this season of the year. Fortunately, one of the Danish company's vessels arrived from Copenhagen while we remained, and from her we obtained a few articles that we stood much in need of. The company's store was nearly exhausted, but what remained was kindly placed at our disposal.

On the 22d, our crews being much invigorated by their exercise on *terra firma*, and the few still affected with the scurvy being in a state of convalescence, we got under way, with the intention of prosecuting the object of the expedition for one season more, at least.

From the statement made to us at Lievely, the last winter had been an extraordinary one. The winds had prevailed to an unusual degree from the northwest, and the ice was not at any time fixed. The whaling fleet had passed to the northward previous to our arrival.

On the 24th we met with some obstruction from the ice off Hare Island, and on the following day our progress was completely arrested by it at Storoe Island. In seeking for a passage we got beset in a pack near the lee shore, near to which we were carried by the drifting ice, and narrowly escaped being driven on the rocks. After getting out of this difficulty, we availed ourselves of every opening in the ice, and worked slowly to the northward, near the shore.

On the 1st of July we were off the Danish port and settlement of Pröven, and as the condition of the ice rendered further progress at present impossible, we went in and anchored to wait for a change.

Here, again, some scurvy grass was collected, and the men allowed to run on shore.

On the 3d we got under way, and ran out to look at the ice; but finding it still closely packed, returned to our anchorage.

On the 6th the accounts from our look-out on the hill near us were more favorable. Again we got under way, and finding the pack somewhat loose, succeeded in making some headway through it. The following day we got into clear water, and fell in with two English whaling vessels, the Pacific and Jane. To their gentlemanly and considerate commanders we are much indebted for the supplies furnished us, consisting of potatoes, turnips, and other articles, most acceptable to people in our condition. Much interesting news was also gained from them respecting important events which had occurred since we left home.

Their statements as to the condition of the ice to the northward was any thing but flattering to our prospects. They had considered it so very unfavorable as to abandon the attempt to push through Melville Bay, and were now on their way to the southward.

On the 8th we communicated with the settlement of Uppernavik. The next day two more English whaling vessels passed on their way to the southward. At the same time, the M'Lellan, of New London, the only American whaler in Baffin's Bay, was descried, also standing south. On communicating with her, we were rejoiced to find letters and papers from home, transmitted by the kindness of Mr. Grinnell.

We remained by the M'Lellan several hours, in order to close our letters and dispatch them by her. Several articles that we stood much in need of were purchased from her.

On the 10th, the Baffin's Islands being in sight to the north, we met the remainder of the whaling fleet returning. They confirmed the accounts given us by the Pacific and Jane in regard to the unfavorable condition of the ice for an early passage through Melville Bay.

The following are the names of the vessels communicated with, viz.: Joseph Green, of Peterhead; Alexander, of Dundee; Advice, of do.; Princess Charlotte, of do.; Horn, of do.; Ann, of Hull; Regalia, of Kirkaldy; Chieftain, of do.; and Lord Gambier, of ——. My notes are unfortunately at fault as to the names of their enterprising and warm-hearted commanders, each of whom vied with the other in showering upon us such articles as they knew we must be in want of, consisting of potatoes, turnips, fresh beef, &c. My proposition to compensate them they would not entertain for a moment, and I take this occasion of making public acknowledgment of the valuable aid rendered us, to which no doubt much of our subsequent good health is owing.

On the 11th, in attempting to run between the Baffin's Islands, the Advance grounded on a rocky shoal. The Rescue barely escaped the same fate, by hauling by the wind on discovering our mishap. Fortunately, there was a large grounded berg near, to which our hawsers could be taken for hauling off, which we succeeded in doing after twenty-four hours' hard work. The vessel had not, apparently, received any injury; but a few days later another piece of her false keel came off, supposed to have been loosened on this occasion.

The ice to the north of the islands was too closely packed to be penetrated, and the prevalence of southerly winds afforded but little prospect of a speedy opening.

On the 16th, the searching yacht Prince Albert succeeded in reaching near to our position, after having been in sight for several days. Mr. Kennedy, her commander, came on board and brought us letters.

The berth in which our vessels were made fast in this place was alongside of a low tongue of an immense berg, which by accurate measurement towered up to the height of two hundred and forty-five feet above the water level. It was aground in ninety-six fathoms water, thus making the whole distance from top to bottom eight hundred and twenty-one feet. We saw many bergs equally as large as this, and some much larger; but this was the only one we had so good an opportunity of measuring with accuracy.

On the 17th the ice opened a little, and we got under way. Hence till the 27th, with almost incessant work, by watching every opening, we continued to make a few miles each day, the Prince Albert keeping company with us. On this day, while running through a narrow lead, the ice closed suddenly. The Advance was caught in a tight place, and pretty severely nipped. We managed to unship her rudder, but before it could be secured the crashing ice carried it under. We had lines fast to it, however, and after the action of the ice ceased, it was extricated without injury. The Rescue and Prince Albert, although near us, were in better berths, and escaped the severe nip the Advance received.

We were closely beset in this position, and utterly unable to move until the

4th of August, when the ice slacking a little, we succeeded in getting hold of the land ice one mile further to the north. The Prince Albert was still in the pack, a mile or two to the southward of us. Mr. Kennedy informed me that it was his intention to abandon this route and return to the southward, as soon as his vessel could be extricated from her present position, in hopes of finding the ice more practicable in that direction. Some letters and papers that he had brought out for the other English searching vessels, he placed on board of us; unfortunately, we were unable to deliver them.

We lost sight of the Prince Albert on the 13th. For our own part, there was no possibility of moving in any direction. The berth we had taken up, under the impression that it was a good and safe one, proved a regular trap; for the drift pack not only set in upon us, but innumerable bergs came drifting along from the southward, and stopped near our position, forming a perfect wall around us at not more than from two hundred to four hundred yards distance. Many unsuccessful attempts were made to get out. The winds were light, and all motion in the ice had apparently ceased. The young ice, too, began to form rapidly, and was only prevented from cementing permanently together the broken masses around us by the frequent undulations occasioned by the overturning or falling to pieces of the neighboring bergs.

My anxiety daily increased at the prospect of being obliged to spend another winter in a similar, if not worse situation, than was that of the last.

On the 18th the ice was somewhat looser. We immediately took advantage of it, and managed to find an opening between the large bergs sufficiently wide to admit the passage of the vessels. Outside the bergs we had open water enough to work in.

We stood to the northwest, but the lead closing at the distance of a few miles, and the ice appearing as unfavorable as ever, I did not deem it prudent to run the risk of besetment again at this late period of the season, and considering that even if successful in crossing the pack, it would be too late to hope to attain a point on the route of search as far as we had been last year, therefore, in obedience to that clause in my instructions which says, "You are especially enjoined not to spend, if it can be avoided, more than one winter in the Arctic regions;" accordingly, with sad hearts that our labors had served to throw so little light upon the object of our search, it was resolved to give it up and return to the United States.

We therefore retraced our steps to the southward. The ice that had so much impeded our progress had entirely disappeared. We touched for refreshment by the way at some of the settlements on the coast of Greenland, where we were most kindly and hospitably received by the Danish authorities.

Leaving Holsteinberg on the 6th of September for New York, the two vessels were separated in a gale to the southward of Cape Farewell. The Advance arrived on the 30th ultimo, and the Rescue on the 7th instant, with grateful hearts from all on board to a kind and superintending Providence for our safe deliverance from danger, shipwreck, and disaster during so perilous a voyage.

I have the honor to be, sir, your obedient servant,

(Signed) Edwin J. De Haven, Lieut. commanding Arctic Expedition.

To the Honorable William A. Graham, Secretary of the Navy, Washington.

C.

METEOROLOGICAL ABSTRACT.

The meteorological abstract was prepared from the private journal of Dr Kane and the notes in the log-book of the Advance.

The latitude and longitude, ocean currents, directions, and force of winds, are given as in the "log."

The following abbreviations, adopted by Lieutenant Maury from those of Captain Beechy, are used to denote the state of the weather:

STATE OF WEATHER.

b for blue sky.
c " clouds.
d " drizzling rain.
f " thick fog.
g " dark stormy weather.
h " hail.
l " lightning.
m " misty or hazy.
o " cloudy.
p for passing showers.
q " squally.
r " continuous rain.
s " snow.
t " thunder.
u " ugly threatening weather.
w " wet dew.
A star * under any letter denotes an extraordinary degree.

The force of the wind is marked as follows:

0 for calm.
1 " light airs
2 " light breeze.
3 " gentle.
4 " moderate.
5 " fresh.
6 " stormy.
7 for moderate gale.
8 " fresh gale.
9 " stormy gale.
10 " heavy gale.
11 " storm.
12 " hurricane.

The state of the weather, and the direction and force of the wind, were noted hourly; the daily mean and the *true* direction have been given in the abstract. Three hourly observations (with some exceptions) were made for the temperature of air, and water, and atmospheric pressure, of which the daily mean readings are given in the abstract. The readings of the aneroids are given uncorrected, as mere approximations. For all of this labor I am indebted to the intelligence and zeal of my friend, Mr. Schott, of the United States Coast Survey.

E. K. K

HALF-MONTHLY ABSTRACTS OF THE LOG-BOOK OF THE UNITED STATES BRIG ADVANCE.

MONTH OF MAY. — ATLANTIC OCEAN.

Date. 1850.	Latitude in at Noon.	Longitude in at Noon.	Variation observed.	Current, true Direction.	Drift in 24 Hours.	Mean true Direction of the Wind.	Force of the Wind.	Mean Temp. of the Air.	Mean Temp. of Surface of the Water.	Mean Height of the Barometer.	Sky and Weather.	Remarks.
	° ′ ″	° ′ ″	° ′									
24	....	....	(5 54 W.)	....	..	E. ½ N.	4	..	..	..	cloudy.	Passed Sandy Hook.
25	40 17 45 N.	72 50 40 W.	....	W. ¾ S.	11	E. by N.	..	+49.7	+51.3	30.333	cloudy.	Moderate breezes.
26	39 28 28	72 04 15	....	W. ¾ S.	22	E. by S. ½ S.	..	56.3	55.8	30.165	foggy.	Moderate breezes.
27	39 40 00	70 04 00	....	....	..	W. by S.	..	53.0	53.6	29.85	clear day.	Moderate breezes.
28	40 17 35	67 30 15	....	....	..	N. by W. ½ W.	..	50.3	58.2	29.76	clear.	Fresh breezes.
29	40 30 45	65 13 48	....	N.E. ¼ E.*	35*	N.W.	..	48.9	52.8	29.93	pleasant.	* Since the 26th. Fresh breezes.
30	41 44 08	63 08 00	....	E.S.E. ¼ E.	12	N.	..	45.2	46.0	30.01	clear.	Moderate breezes.
31	42 03 13	61 39 12	....	S.S.E. ¾ E.	19	E. by N. ½ N.	..	43.1	42.0	30.08	rainy.	Moderate breezes.
								+49.5	+51.3	30.01		Means.

JUNE, 1850. — ATLANTIC OCEAN.

Date. 1850.	Latitude in at Noon.	Longitude in at Noon.	Variation observed.	Current, true Direction.	Drift in 24 Hours.	Mean true Direction of the Wind.	Force of the Wind.	Mean Temp. of the Air.	Mean Temp. of Surface of the Water.	Mean Height of the Barometer.	Sky and Weather.	Remarks.
	° ′ ″	° ′ ″	° ′									
1	43 38 33 N.	61 03 02 W.	....	....	..	E. by N.	5	+39.5	+39.3	30.06	o. f. r.	8 o'clock, 50 fathoms water, coarse sand; at 6 o'clock, no bottom with 100 fathoms.
2	44 19 27	60 34 17	....	....	..	N. by E.	5	38.7	38.6	29.75	o. f. r.	40 fathoms water, yellow and black sand.
3	44 57 57	59 11 17	....	E. ½ N.*	29*	W.	5	40.4	38.4	30.03	b. c.	* Since the 31st. Sandy bottom in 70 fathoms; 35 fathoms water in the evening.
4	45 53 45	56 31 44	....	N.N.E. ¾ E.	10	N.W. by W.	3	39.9	39.3	30.30	b.	30 fathoms water, rocky bottom.
5	46 12 25	55 06 57	24 17 W.	....	..	S.W. by S.	1	42.0	39.2	30.42	b. c.	78 fathoms water, rocky bottom. Temperature in 50 fathoms, 37°; surface, 42°.
6	46 27 59	53 49 40	....	N.E. ½ E.	20	S.W. by S.	3	42.1	38.9	30.36	b. c.	Land in sight, bearing N.E. by N. Icebergs in sight. Bearing of Cape Race, N.E. by E. ½ E. 40 fathoms water, rocky bottom.
7	47 15 05	52 34 01	....	E. ¼ S.	10	S. by W.	3	42.3	39.2	30.15	b. c.	At 100 fathoms no bottom. Temperature at this depth, 30°; surface, 39°. Bearing of Cape Spear light, N. by E. Several icebergs in sight.
8	48 19 00	52 27 05	....	....	..	S.S.W. ½ W.	4	42.1	36.3	29.86	o. f. d.	Land and icebergs in sight.
9	49 53 30	52 08 32	....	N. by E.*	24*	S. by E.	2	40.7	36.3	29.74	o. f.	* Since the 7th. Many icebergs in sight.
10	50 30 48	51 25 37	....	S. ¾ W.	6	N.N.W.	4	38.4	35.1	29.88	o. b. c.	Water of a light greenish hue.
11	50 52 43	50 46 57	....	....	..	N.E. by N.	3	35.6	35.0	30.04	f. r. c.	Several icebergs in sight.
12	53 02 11	50 59 17	....	....	..	S.E. by S.	5	39.7	37.8	29.56	o. f.	
13	55 21 01	51 18 15	....	N.W.*	7*	W.	4	44.1	41.4	29.64	b. c.	* Since the 10th. Heavy squall.
14	56 29 01	51 07 07	....	N.N.W. ¾ W.	10	....	1	48.5	42.6	29.88	b. c.	Heavy squall from the E.
15	58 06 56	51 49 35	....	....	..	E.S.E.	6	42.8	41.0	29.66	c. r.	
							4	+41.1	+40.6	29.95		Means

HALF-MONTHLY ABSTRACTS OF THE LOG-BOOK OF THE UNITED STATES BRIG ADVANCE.

June, 1850. Davis's Straits.

Date.	Latitude in at Noon.	Longitude in at Noon.	Variation observed.	Current, true Direction.	Drift in 24 Hours.	Mean true Direction of the Wind.	Force of the Wind.	Mean Temp. of the Air.	Mean Temp. of Surface of the Water.	Mean Height of the Barometer.	Sky and Weather.	Remarks.
1850.	° ′ ″	° ′ ″	° ′									
16	60 56 00 N.	53 14 00 W.	....	N.W. ¾ W.*	60*	E. by N.	5	+41.2	+38.1	29.55	o. r.	* Since the 14th. Water of a light green. Several icebergs in sight.
17	62 22 26	54 22 45	....	N.N.W. ¼ W.	23	S.E. by E.	3	42.7	39.0	29.70	b. c. f.	One iceberg in sight.
18	63 06 51	54 42 55	53 34 W.	N.W. ¼ N.	21	N.N.E.	1	41.5	38.5	29.75	o. f.	Temperature of the water: surface, 39°; 10 fathoms, 37°.7; 20 fathoms, 37°.0; 50 fathoms, 37°.0; 100 fathoms, 37°.3. No bottom at 270 fathoms, temperature, 38°. Var. in lat. 63° 4′, long. 54° 44′.
19	63 58 00	54 12 08	....	N.E.	5	N.W. by W.	2	..	..	..	o. f.	Passed icebergs.
20	64 37 17	53 11 59	57 12 W.	E.N.E. ½ E.	11	N.W.	2	38.4	38.0	29.85	b. c. f.	Var. in lat. 64° 47′, long. 53° 1′. Two icebergs in sight.
21	65 21 55	53 07 20	....	N.E.	6	N.N.W.	4	36.3	37.6	29.70	b. c.	Northern extreme of island bears N.E. ½ E. Saw a flag-staff or beacon.
22	65 29 46	54 20 10	....	S. ½ W.	11	S.W. by W.	3	37.9	37.1	29.75	o. b. c.	Land in sight.
23	67 03 07	54 24 52	67 05 W.	N.	17	S.E. by S.	3	41.7	36.3	29.77	b. c.	Var. in lat. 67° 12′, long. 54° 23′. Land supposed to be Holsteinberg. Sounded in 25 fathoms water. Passed several large icebergs.
24	....	....	....	....	..	S. ½ W.	7	38.7	35.5	29.80	o. r.	Whale-fish Island, at anchor, 12 fathoms water.
25	....	....	....	....	..	W. by S.	4	36.9	..	29.86	b. c.	Whale-fish Island, at anchor.
26	....	....	....	....	..	S.S.W. ½ W.	3	39.0	..	30.12	o. b. c. r.	Whale-fish Island, at anchor.
27	....	....	....	....	..	E.	..	..	..	..	..	Whale-fish Island, at anchor.
28	....	...	....	....	..	E. ½ N.	1	..	..	..	b. c.	Whale-fish Island, at anchor.
29	....	....	....	....	..	E.S.E. ½ E.	2	38.5	35.5	29.83	b. c.	Whale-fish Island, got under way at noon.
30	69 27 32	55 26 42	....	E. ¾ N.	15	S.E. by S.	3	38.2	33.2	29.67	b. c. o. d.	Many icebergs in sight. Off Disco Bay.
							3	+39.2	+36.9	29.77		Means.

HALF-MONTHLY ABSTRACTS OF THE LOG-BOOK OF THE UNITED STATES BRIG ADVANCE.

JULY, 1850. BAFFIN'S BAY.

Date. 1850.	Latitude in at Noon. ° ′ ″	Longitude in at Noon. ° ′ ″	Variation observed. ° ′	Current, true Direction.	Drift in 24 Hours.	Mean true Direction of the Wind.	Force of the Wind.	Mean Temp. of the Air.	Mean Temp. of Surface of the Water.	Mean Height of the Barometer.	Sky and Weather.	Remarks.
1	70 44 18 N.	56 28 48 W.	....	N.E. by N.	7	S.E. by S.	2	+36.6	+32.4	29.76	b. c. f.	Drift ice, pack ice, and many icebergs in sight.
2	71 24 21	55 52 27	....	S. ¾ E.	3½	N.	2	39.2	34.7	29.77	b. c.	Off Cranstown. Many icebergs in sight.
3	72 01 09	57 08 27	....	Northerly.	4	N. ½ W.	4	35.5	33.3	29.89	b. c. o. f.	Pack and floe ice.
4	72 23 44	57 19 48	....	....	..	Variable.	1	34.4	34.0	30.04	b. c. f.	Sailing through loose floe ice.
5	72 38 11	57 17 35	....	Northerly.	..	E.N.E.	2	36.0	35.4	29.90	b.	Refracted detortion very great. Sailing through ice.
6	72 54 51	....	....	....	..	N. by W.	1	41.6	35.9	29.77	b. c.	Off Uppernavik. Compass very sluggish. Terrestrial refraction too great to obtain sight for longitude. Many icebergs in sight.
7	73 46 02	57 15 15	....	....	..	S.E. by S.	3	43.6	32.5	29.78	b.	Sailing through the pack. At 11 P.M. got jammed in the ice. Long., by bearing of Cape Shackleton, 57° 45′ 00″.
8	....	....	....	....	..	S. by W.	3	32.6	29.9	29.81	c.	In the pack.
9	74 08 19	....	....	....	..	S.W. by W.	2	33.5	29.2	29.65	o. f. c.	In the pack. Ice too thick to force through.
10	74 08 20	59 05 15	....	....	..	S. by E.	3	32.6	29.3	29.72	b. c. o.	In the pack. Observed dip of magnetic needle, 77° 10′.
11	74 13 47	59 04 15	84 54 W.	N.*	3¾	N.W. by N.	3	33.1	29.1	29.42	b. c.	* Drift of the pack.
12	....	....	....	....	..	S.S.W.	5	35.0	29.7	29.26	c.	Ice opened, got under way.
13	74 22 18	59 12 14	83 58	N.*	8½	N.E. by. E.	2	36.5	29.6	29.75	b. c.	* Drift of pack in two days. Floes too closely packed to move.
14	74 22 16	....	....	....	..	E.N.E.	1	37.5	30.5	29.88	c. o.	In the pack. Ice loosening a little.
15	74 20 45	59 16 09	....	S.W. by S.*	2	N.N.E.	2	35.7	30.6	30.03	b. c. f.	* Drift of pack.
							2	+36.2	+31.7	29.76		Means.
						Correction		+ 0.				

HALF-MONTHLY ABSTRACTS OF THE LOG-BOOK OF THE UNITED STATES BRIG ADVANCE.

JULY, 1850. BAFFIN'S BAY.

Date. 1850.	Latitude in at Noon.	Longitude in at Noon.	Variation observed.	Current, true Direction.	Drift in 24 Hours.	Mean true Direction of the Wind.	Force of the Wind.	Mean Temp. of the Air.	Mean Temp. of Surface of the Water.	Mean Height of the Barometer.	Sky and Weather.	Remarks.
	° ′ ″	° ′ ″	° ′									
16	74 19 03 N.	59 21 35 W.	85 12 W.	S.W.	2¼	N. by W.	2	+34.3	+30.7	29.93	b. c.	In the pack. Observed dip, 77° 50′.
17	74 13 36	59 20 51	85 10 W.	S.	5½	N.W. by N.	2	35.6	29.5	29.75	b.	In the pack.
18	....	....	....	....	..	N.W. by N.	1	33.8	29.3	30.02	o. s.	In the pack. Ice three feet thick, loosening a little.
19	....	....	....	....	..	E. by S.	1	35.8	29.8	30.17	o. f.	In the pack. Cutting through ice.
20	....	....	....	....	..	S. by E.	3	35.5	30.4	30.21	o. r.	In the pack. Ice very tough every where.
21	....	....	....	....	..	S.	3	34.0	29.8	30.06	o. r. b. c.	In the pack. Ice opening.
22	74 14 00	59 36 00	....	W.*	4	N.N.W.	4	32.4	29.6	29.94	o. b. f.	In the pack. * Drift in five days. Ice very tough.
23	74 09 18	59 38 40	....	S. ¼ E.	5	N.N.W.	2	34.7	29.6	29.98	b. c.	In the pack. Ice tight around us.
24	74 05 16	59 38 59	....	S.	3½	N.W.	3	35.8	30.1	29.88	b. c.	In the pack. Moved three ship's lengths.
25	74 04 59	59 45 02	....	....	..	N.W.	1	38.9	30.4	30.02	b.	In the pack.
26	74 03 28	59 52 03	....	....	..	N.W.	3	36.6	30.1	30.03	b.	In the pack. Drift supposed northerly. Ice tightening.
27	73 57 35	59 56 00	....	S.	6	N.W. by N.	3	36.9	30.0	29.82	b.	In the pack.
28	73 54 26	60 06 27	....	S.W. ½ S.	4	W. by N.	3	37.3	30.2	29.32	b. c.	Escaped from the pack ice after a close confinement since the evening of the 7th.
29	74 53 00	59 53 56	....	....	..	E. by N.	5	38.8	32.0	29.44	b. c. f.	Many icebergs in sight. Much floe ice drifting past us rapidly.
30	....	....	....	....	..	E. by N.	2	36.7	30.0	29.68	o. c.	Heaving ahead between an iceberg and a heavy field of ice.
31	75 02 27	59 50 42	....	....	..	N.W. by N.	3	34.6	30.6	29.68	b. c. f.	Ice closing.
							3	+35.7	+30.1	29.88		Means.
						Correction		− 0.3				

HALF-MONTHLY ABSTRACTS OF THE LOG-BOOK OF THE UNITED STATES BRIG ADVANCE.

August, 1850. Baffin's Bay.

Date. 1850.	Latitude in at Noon.	Longitude in at Noon.	Variation observed.	Current, true Direction.	Drift in 24 Hours.	Mean true Direction of the Wind.	Force of the Wind.	Mean Temp. of the Air.	Mean Temp. of Surface of the Water.	Mean Height of the Barometer.	Sky and Weather.	Remarks.
	° ′ ″	° ′ ″	° ′									
1	75 03 27 N.	59 50 22 W.	....	....	..	Variable.	1	+32.8	+30.4	29.90	o. f. b.	Made fast to the land floe. Thick fog.
2	75 05 08	59 51 12	89 56 W.	....	..	S.W.	1	35.4	31.5	29.89	b.	Warped about ¾ths of a mile to the eastward.
3	75 08 47	59 59 22	....	No drift.	..	S.E.	2	34.3	30.8	29.96	b. f.	Much obstructed by the bay ice. Open water to the S. and E. Water sky.
4	75 09 33	60 01 19	....	....	..	N.N.W.	2	35.5	31.7	29.94	b.	Refraction very great. Ice opening to the N.E. Warped ⅓d of a mile.
5	75 09 27	60 01 25	....	S.	1	N.N.W.	1	37.0	32.0	29.94	b.	Measured height of a berg near us, by triangulation, 107 feet. Warping toward Browne's Islands.
6	75 11 05	60 03 05	....	....	..	E.N.E.	1	35.8	32.2	29.93	b. c.	Still in pack.
7	75 12 46	59 59 12	....	....	..	N.E.	1	38.3	32.1	29.96	b. c.	Fast with ice.
8	75 17 08	....	....	....	..	N.E.	1	38.5	32.1	30.00	b. c.	Young ice, in some places thick enough to bear a man.
9	75 22 19	....	....	....	..	E.N.E.	2	33.8	33.3	29.87	b. c. f.	Ice drifting to the leeward. Glaciers.
10	75 28 28	....	....	....	..	N.E. by N.	1	34.8	34.7	30.00	b. f. o.	Thermometer 53° in the sun. Fog sometimes so thick as not to see a ship's length.
11	....	....	....	....	..	E. by N.	3	35.0	32.0	30.07	o. f.	Ice opening a little.
12	75 33 37	61 13 37	....	....	..	N.E by N.	1	34.5	32.2	30.05	o. f.	Difficulty in steering the vessel on account of the currents.
13	75 49 47	....	....	....	..	N. by E.	2	34.1	34.1	30.14	b. c.	Beating to the eastward through bay ice.
14	....	....	....	....	..	N.	2	37.0	32.1	30.02	b. c.	Open water. Melville Bay.
15	75 58 28	....	....	....	.	Variable.	2	39.2	34.4	30.13	b. c.	Rocky bottom at 32 fathoms. Off Cape York.
							2	+35.8	+32.4	29.99		Means.
						Correction		-- 0.1				

HALF-MONTHLY ABSTRACTS OF THE LOG-BOOK OF THE UNITED STATES BRIG ADVANCE.

AUGUST, 1850. BAFFIN'S BAY, LANCASTER SOUND, ETC.

Date. 1850.	Latitude in at Noon.	Longitude in at Noon.	Variation observed.	Current, true Direction.	Drift in 24 Hours.	Mean true Direction of the Wind.	Force of the Wind.	Mean Temp. of the Air.	Mean Temp. of Surface of the Water.	Mean Height of the Barometer.	Sky and Weather.	Remarks.
	° ′ ″	° ′ ″	° ′									
16	76 03 00 N.*	68 06 18 W.*	....	....	..	W. by S.	1	+38.6	+35.1	30.17	b. c.	* At 7 P.M. on shore. Off Crimson Cliffs. An island and bore, by compass, N. 9° W. Cape York, S. 29° W.
17	76 03 41	....	....	....	..	N.N.W.	2	37.3	33.8	30.18	b.	Off Cape Dudley Diggs. Ran to the north 17 miles and landed on the shore. This is the most northern point of terra firma reached by the expedition. Lat. 76° 20′ 41″.
18	76 06 11	71 49 03	....	....	..	E.S.E.	4	35.2	32.9	30.29	b. c. f.	Crossing the bay for Lancaster Sound. Passed a good deal of floe ice.
19	....	....	....	....	..	E.S.E.	5	36.2	35.0	30.32	o. f.	Many bergs in sight, lining the shore.
20	....	....	....	....	..	E. by N.	7	35.6	32.2	29.91	o. f.	Lancaster Sound. Very little ice seen. No bottom at 110 fathoms. Water of a light appearance.
21	....	....	....	....	..	E. by S.	3	34.6	30.6	29.86	o.	Lancaster Sound.
22	....	....	....	....	..	S. by W.	1	34.8	31.8	29.98	o. f.	Barrow's Strait.
23	....	....	....	....	..	N.W.	3	33.8	31.5	30.10	b. f.	Barrow's Strait.
24	....	....	....	....	..	N.W. by W.	4	36.3	33.2	30.09	b. c. f.	A good deal of stream ice off shore. Barrow's Strait.
25	74 39 26	....	....	....	..	N.W. by N.	4	..	..	..	o. f.	Off Cape Riley. Stream ice off shore.
26	....	....	....	....	..	Variable.	2	30.8	30.0	29.98	o. s.	Wellington Channel. Warping clear of icebergs. Heavy pack ice to the westward (true).
27	....	....	....	....	..	Variable.	3	34.2	29.7	29.87	o. c.	Union Bay. Vessels in the land ice.
28	....	....	....	....	..	Variable.	3	31.5	29.0	29.62	b. o.	Union Bay.
29	....	....	....	....	..	S. by W.	3	30.6	29.1	29.68	o.	Wellington Channel. No change in the ice.
30	....	....	....	....	..	S.S.E.	4	30.7	30.0	29.75	o. s.	Off Point Innes. No change in the ice.
31	....	....	....	....	..	S.E. by S.	7	34.0	30.4	29.85	o. f.	Off Point Innes. Ice slowly closing with the land.
							4	+34.2	+31.6	29.97		Means.
						Correction		+ 0.3				

HALF-MONTHLY ABSTRACTS OF THE LOG-BOOK OF THE UNITED STATES BRIG ADVANCE.

SEPTEMBER, 1850. WELLINGTON CHANNEL.

Date. 1850.	Latitude in at Noon.	Longitude in at Noon.	Variation observed.	Current, true Direction.	Drift in 24 Hours.	Mean true Direction of the Wind.	Force of the Wind.	Mean Temp. of the Air.	Mean Temp. of Surface of the Water.	Mean Height of the Barometer.	Sky and Weather.	Remarks.
	° ′ ″	° ′ ″	° ′									
1	....	....	....	....	..	S.E. by S.	7	+34.9	+30.4	29.84	o. f. b. c.	Sounded in 30 fathoms water, ¾ths of a mile from shore. Off Point Innes.
2	....	....	....	....	..	Variable.	2	35.5	30.8	30.03	o. f.	Off Point Innes. The tide changed and set to the south (true). The floe we are fast to seems to drift in the same direction.
3	....	....	....	....	..	N.	2	33.1	30.4	30.23	o. f.	Loose ice drifting to the N. and W. (compass).
4	74 47 27 N.	92 35 45 W.	140 12 W.	....	..	N.	1	27.5	29.1	30.32	o. b. c.	True bearing of Cape Riley, S. 62° 42′ E. Ice closing in upon us.
5	....	....	140 52 W.	....	..	N. by W.	2	28.7	30.3	30.36	b. c.	Sounded in 38 fathoms water, soft mud. True bearing of Barlow's Inlet, S. 84° 52′ W. Ice opening.
6	....	....	....	....	..	Variable.	1	32.3	31.6	30.38	b. c. o. f.	Barlow's Inlet. Ice opening and closing.
7	....	....	....	....	..	E.	2	31.4	30.5	30.54	c. f. b.	Off Barlow's Inlet.
8	....	....	....	....	..	N.N.E.	3	25.2	30.6	30.71	o. s. f.	Off Barlow's Inlet. No change in the ice.
9	....	....	...	....	..	W.	3	27.6	29.9	30.46	c. o. f.	Open water in sight to the westward (true). Barrow's Strait.
10	....	....	....	....	..	N.W.	4	34.3	29.8	30.27	o. f.	A great deal of bay ice about us. Barrow's Strait.
11	....	....	....	....	..	S.W.	2	28.1	29.0	29.87	o. s.	No change in the ice. Barrow's Strait.
12	....	....	....	....	..	N.W.	6	14.6	..	29.72	o. b. c.	Floe ice drifting to the northward. Barrow's Strait. A feeble aurora at midnight.
13	....	....	....	....	..	N.W. by W.	5	13.4	..	29.99	b. c. o. s.	Pancake ice very thick. Barrow's Strait.
14	....	....	....	....	..	S.S.E.	3	21.5	..	30.12	o. s. b. c.	Got into a lead of open water. Barrow's Strait.
15	....	....	....	....	..	S.W. by S.	4	19.0	..	30.03	c. s. o.	Entrance of Wellington Channel. A feeble aurora.
							3	+27.1	+30.2	30.18		Means.
						Correction		+ 0.1				

HALF-MONTHLY ABSTRACTS OF THE LOG-BOOK OF THE UNITED STATES BRIG ADVANCE.

SEPTEMBER, 1850. WELLINGTON CHANNEL.

Date.	Latitude in at Noon.	Longitude in at Noon.	Variation observed.	Current, true Direction.	Drift in 24 Hours.	Mean true Direction of the Wind.	Force of the Wind.	Mean Temp. of the Air.	Mean Temp. of Surface of the Water.	Mean Height of the Barometer.	Sky and Weather.	Remarks.
1850.	° ′ ″	° ′ ″	° ′									
16	....	....	....	....	..	S.	5	+22.5	..	29.92	o. s.	Ice opening and in motion. Wellington Channel.
17	....	....	....	....	..	S.	4	23.7	..	29.77	o. s.	Muddy bottom in 110 fathoms. Little motion in the ice.
18	....	....	....	....	..	S.S.W.	2	23.0	..	29.72	o.	The ice bears the appearance of the fixed ice of the channel. Thick, heavy ice all round us.
19	75 20 11 N.	....	....	....	..	N.	5	19.5	..	29.52	o. s.	True bearing of Advance Bluff, S. 28° 34′ W. Ice opening in the leads.
20	....	....	....	....	..	N.E.	4	27.8	..	29.18	o.	Western shore of Wellington Channel. Ice broke up around us.
21	75 20 38	....	....	....	..	S. by W.	4	20.6	..	29.64	o. c. b.	No change in the ice.
22	75 24 21	....	....	....	..	S.E.	3	20.1	..	29.88	o. c.	True bearing of Advance Bluff, S. 1° 16′ W. Rough magnetic bearing, N. 13° W. Ice in motion.
23	....	....	....	....	..	N.E. by E.	3	22.0	..	29.74	o. s.	Western shore of Wellington Channel. Ice piling up and giving us heavy rips.
24	75 23 28	....	....	....	..	N.N.W.	2	12.4	..	29.60	b. c.	Ice breaking and piling up.
25	....	....	....	....	..	W.S.W.	2	15.3	..	29.74	o.	Several leads of open water in sight
26	75 24 52	....	....	....	..	S.W.	2	11.0	..	29.83	c. b.	No motion in the ice.
27	....	....	....	....	..	N.N.W.	2	8.8	..	29.92	o. s.	No motion in the ice.
28	....	....	....	....	..	N.W. by W.	2	5.0	..	30.00	b. c.	
29	....	....	....	....	..	S.	2	9.7	..	30.10	b. c. s.	
30	....	....	....	....	..	W.	2	6.4	..	30.08	o. s.	
							3	+16.5	..	29.77		Means.
						Correction		+ 0.1				

HALF-MONTHLY ABSTRACTS OF THE LOG-BOOK OF THE UNITED STATES BRIG ADVANCE.

OCTOBER, 1850 — WELLINGTON CHANNEL.

Date. 1850.	Latitude in at Noon. ° ′ ″	Longitude in at Noon. ° ′ ″	Variation observed. ° ′	Current, true Direction.	Drift in 24 Hours.	Mean true Direction of the Wind.	Force of the Wind.	Mean Temp. of the Air.	Mean Temp. of Surface of the Water.	Mean Height of the Barometer.	Sky and Weather.	Remarks.
1	....	....	....	....	..	W.S.W.	3	+10.5	..	29.97	o. s.	Little motion in the ice.
2	75 24 52 N.	93 31 10 W.	....	N. 31° W.*	48*	N.W.	2	10.8	..	29.85	o. m. s.	* Drift since the 14th ult.
3	....	....	....	....	.	....	0	3.4	..	30.02	b. c. f.	
4	....	....	....	....	..	N.	2	− 1.6	..	30.17	b. c. m.	Ice opening to the southward.
5	....	....	....	....	..	N.	5	+ 2.1	..	30.11	b. o. m.	
6	....	....	....	....	..	N.	7	+ 4.9	..	29.88	o. s.	
7	74 54 07	93 09 52	....	S. 11° E.*	30	N.	5	+ 8.1	..	29.89	b. m.	* Drift since the 2d.
8	....	....	....	....	..	N. by W.	3	+ 8.0	..	30.07	b.	
9	....	....	....	....	..	N.	1	+14.1	..	30.20	o. m.	
10	....	....	....	....	..	N.W. by W.	5	+ 8.9	..	29.87	o.	
11	74 44 17	92 48 17	135 40 W.	S. 28° E.*	12	S.S.W.	4	+ 4.0	..	29.98	b. c.	* Drift since the 7th. Observations taken at 7 P.M.
12	74 54 32	92 54 14	....	N. 9° W.	10	S.	5	+10.2	..	30.11	o. m. s.	
13	....	...	....	....	..	S.	2	+16.0	..	30.50	o. s.	
14	....	....	....	....	..	E.	1	+ 6.0	..	30.73	b. c.	
15	....	....	....	....	..	N.	1	− 1.2	..	30.73	b.	
							3	+ 6.9	..	30.13		Means.
						Correction....		+ 0.1				

HALF-MONTHLY ABSTRACTS OF THE LOG-BOOK OF THE UNITED STATES BRIG ADVANCE.

OCTOBER, 1850. WELLINGTON CHANNEL.

Date.	Latitude in at Noon.	Longitude in at Noon.	Variation observed.	Current, true Direction.	Drift in 24 Hours.	Mean true Direction of the Wind.	Force of the Wind.	Mean Temp. of the Air.	Mean Temp. of Surface of the Water.	Mean Height of the Barometer.	Sky and Weather.	Remarks.
1850.	° ′ ″	° ′ ″	° ′									
16	....	....	....	....	..	N.	4	+ 0.0	..	30.45	b.	
17	....	....	....	....	..	N.N.E.	4	+ 2.9	..	30.17	b.	A faint aurora to the southward (true) at 1 A.M.
18	....	....	....	....	..	N.E. by N.	3	+ 4.8	..	30.08	b. c.	
19	....	....	....	....	..	N.N.E.	2	+ 3.3	.	29.99	b. c.	
20	....	....	....	....	..	N.E. by N.	4	+ 3.0	..	29.90	b. c.	
21	....	....	....	....	..	N.E. by N.	2	+ 2.0	..	29.89	b. m.	A faint aurora, 8° E. of magnetic north.
22	....	....	....	....	..	S.W.	1	— 0.6	..	30.15	o. s. b. m.	A faint aurora, more bright with segment.
23	....	...	....	....	..	N.	1	+ 3.3	..	30.05	b. c. s.	
24	....	....	....	....	..	N. by W.	3	— 0.1	..	29.96	o. s.	Drifting to the southward (true).
25	....	....	....	....	..	N.N.W.	2	— 6.8	..	30.12	b. c. o.	Drifting to the southward (true).
26	....	....	....	....	..	N. by E.	2	— 1.0	..	30.22	b. m. c.	Very faint aurora.
27	....	....	....	....	..	N.	2	— 5.9	..	30.30	o. m. b.	Bistre-colored auroral segment, 20° E. of magnetic axis.
28	....	....	....	....	..	E.S.E.	1	—13.3	..	30.25	b.	
29	....	....	....	....	..	....	0	—14.8	..	30.15	b. m.	Faint nebulous aurora.
30	....	....	....	....	..	N.N.E.	1	— 7.4	..	..	b. o. m.	Officers and crew of the Rescue moved on board.
31	....	....	....	....	..	N.	2	—13.5	..	29.99	b. c. m.	Observed a small aurora to the northward (by compass), 1 A.M.
							2	— 2.8	..	30.18		Means.
						Correction		— 0.1				

HALF-MONTHLY ABSTRACTS OF THE LOG-BOOK OF THE UNITED STATES BRIG ADVANCE.

November, 1850. Wellington Channel.

Date. 1850.	Latitude in at Noon. ° ′ ″	Longitude in at Noon. ° ′ ″	Variation observed. ° ′	Current, true Direction.	Drift in 24 Hours.	Mean true Direction of the Wind.	Force of the Wind.	Mean Temp. of the Air.	Mean Temp. of Surface of the Water.	Mean Height of the Barometer.	Sky and Weather.	Remarks.
1	....	....	....	....	..	N.N.W.	5	—12.2	..	29.97	b. m.	A parhelion visible.
2	....	....	....	....	..	N.W.	2	—10.6	..	30.03	o. s.	Ice three feet thick. Off Beechy Island.
3	....	....	....	....	..	S.E. by E.	5	—12.8	..	30.03	b. m.	Two parhelia, visible from 10 to 12 A.M. Off Beechy Island.
4	....	....	....	....	..	S.E. by E.	3	— 8.1	..	30.06	b. o. m.	Off Beechy Island.
5	....	....	....	....	..	S.E. by S.	4	— 4.0	..	30.18	o. s.	Off Beechy Island.
6	....	....	....	....	..	S.E.	7	— 2.2	..	29.93	o. b. m.	Off Beechy Island.
7	....	....	....	....	..	E. by N.	3	— 3.0	..	29.85	b. o. m.	Off Beechy Island.
8	....	....	....	....	..	N. by W.	3	—10.9	..	30.04	b.	Aurora to the southward and westward, 5 A.M. (true). Drifting slowly to the northward and westward.
9	....	....	....	....	..	E.N.E.	4	— 9.8	..	29.98	b. m.	Off Beechy Island. Very little drift since yesterday.
10	....	....	....	....	..	E.S.E.	9	+ 6.6	..	29.50	b. o. m.	Off Beechy Island. Heavy snow-drift.
11	...	....	....	....	..	N.E. by N.	4	+10.7	..	29.65	o. m.	Ice much broken near the vessel.
12	....	...	....	...	..	N. by E.	6	— 7.4	..	30.08	o. m.	Off Beechy Island.
13	....	....	....	....	..	N. by E.	4	—15.3	..	30.32	b. m.	Off Beechy Island.
14	....	....	....	....	..	N.W. by W.	2	—15.4	..	30.32	b. m.	Off Beechy Island
15	....	....	....	....	..	E. by S.	2	— 6.8	..	30.16	o. m.	Off Beechy Island.
							4	— 6.7	..	30.01		Ten auroras observed during the month.
						Correction		+ 0.2				

HALF-MONTHLY ABSTRACTS OF THE LOG-BOOK OF THE UNITED STATES BRIG ADVANCE.

November, 1850. Entrance of Wellington Channel and Barrow's Strait.

Date. 1850.	Latitude in at Noon. ° ′ ″	Longitude in at Noon. ° ′ ″	Variation observed. ° ′	Current, true Direction.	Drift in 24 Hours.	Mean true Direction of the Wind.	Force of the Wind.	Mean Temp. of the Air.	Mean Temp. of Surface of the Water.	Mean Height of the Barometer.	Sky and Weather.	Remarks
16	....	....	....	....	..	E.	1	— 7.2	..	30.25	b. c. o.	Off Beechy Island.
17	....	....	....	....	..	....	0	—10.2	..	30.43	b. c.	Off Beechy Island.
18	74 36 53 N.	91 45 45 W.	....	S. 46° E.*	25	S.E. by E.	1	—19.1	..	30.59	b.	* Drift since the 12th ult.
19	....	....	....	....	..	S.E.	7	—10.3	..	30.40	b. m.	A circle round the moon, and two paraselenæ visible. Heavy snow-drift.
20	....	....	....	....	..	S.E. by E.	5	— 1.6	..	30.05	o. m.	Off Beechy Island. Heavy snow drift.
21	....	...	....	....	..	N. by E.	2	— 9.6	..	30.20	b. c.	Off Beechy Island.
22	....	...	....	....	..	N.	2	— 6.3	..	30.32	b. c.	Off Beechy Island.
23	....	....	....	....	.	N.	2	— 4.8	..	30.33	b. c.	Off Beechy Island.
24	....	....	....	....	..	N.N.W.	3	— 9.1	..	30.40	b. c. m.	Beechy Island bearing by compass, S. by E. Cape Riley, S.S.W. ¾ W. Drift to the eastward (true).
25	....	....	....	....	..	S.E.	4	— 6.7	..	30.62	b. o. m.	Off Beechy Island.
26	....	....	....	....	..	S.S.E.	2	—13.0	..	30.68	b. m.	Off Beechy Island.
27	....	....	....	....	..	W. by N.	1	— 7.3	..	30.46	o. m.	Off Beechy Island.
28	....	....	....	....	..	N.W. by N.	1	—11.5	..	30.34	b. m.	Barrow's Strait. Drifted a little to the eastward (true). Frost smoke to the eastward.
29	....	....	....	....	..	W.N.W.	2	— 3.5	..	30.25	o. m.	Barrow's Strait. Cape Riley bears S. by E. ½ E. Beechy Island, S.E. ½ S.
30	....	....	....	....	..	N.W. by W.	2	— 8.6	..	30.29	o. s.	Barrow's Strait.
							2	— 8.6	..	30.37		Means.

HALF-MONTHLY ABSTRACTS OF THE LOG-BOOK OF THE UNITED STATES BRIG ADVANCE

DECEMBER, 1850. BARROW'S STRAIT.

Date. 1850.	Latitude in at Noon. ° ′ ″	Longitude in at Noon. ° ′ ″	Variation observed. ° ′	Current, true Direction.	Drift in 24 Hours.	Mean true Direction of the Wind.	Force of the Wind.	Mean Temp. of the Air.	Mean Temp. of Surface of the Water.	Mean Height of the Barometer.	Sky and Weather.	Remarks.
1	....	....	....	....	..	N.W. by W.	4	—28.9	..	30.36	b. m.	A bright aurora, in the form of a band, extending from the zenith to the horizon, in a N.W. and S.E. direction (true), 4 P.M. The aurora reappeared at 9h. 10m., but lasted only 15 minutes.
2	....	....	....	....	..	N.W. by W.	5	—27.3	..	30.33	b. m.	
3	....	....	....	....	..	N.W.	2	—23.9	..	30.15	b. m.	Faint aurora visible for a short time. Cape Hurd bears, by compass, S. by W. ¼ W. West Bluff of Rigsby's Inlet, S.E. ¼ S. Table Hill, S.E. by E. ½ E. Cape Ricketts, E. by N.
4	....	....	....	....	..	W. by N.	2	—19.1	..	30.05	b. m.	Leopold Island bears, by compass, N.W.
5	....	....	....	....	..	N.E. by E.	3	—13.0	..	30.05	b. m.	A transit aurora, ending with luminous bands, to the S.E. Compass bearing of Leopold Island, east point, N.W. ½ N. Cape Fellfoot, S.W. by W. ½ W. Cape Herschel, a remarkable perpendicular bluff, S.S.E. Cape Hurd, E.N.E.
6	....	....	....	...	..	E.S.E.	3	—15.5	..	30.23	b. m.	Faint aurora, 4 A.M., to the W. (true). Comp. bearings: Eastern point of Leopold Island, N.W. by N.; western, N.N.W.; Bluff on north shore, S.E. by S. Eastern shore of Prince Regent's Inlet in sight.
7	....	....	....	....	..	E. by N.	4	—14.5	..	30.38	b. m.	Ice in an uproar. Counted eleven shooting stars at 11h. 10m. to S.W., five at one time, the rest within a few minutes.
8	....	....	....	....	..	E.N.E.	6	—12.7	..	30.40	b. m.	Faint aurora, 3 A.M., to the southward and eastward (true); another, 10 A.M., to the N.W. (true). Ice squeezing up. Compass bearings: Remarkable bluff, S.S.W. ½ W.; Cape Ricketts, E. ½ N.; east point of Leopold Island, N.W. ½ W.
9	....	....	....	....	..	....	0	—15.9	..	30.29	b.	Compass bearings: Cape Fellfoot, S.W. ¼ W.; Cape Herschel, S. by W.; Cape Hurd, E. by N.; west point of Leopold Island, N.W. ½ W.; Cape Clarence, N.W. by W.
10	....	....	....	....	..	N. by E.	3	—18.5	..	30.20	b. m.	Cape Hurd bears E.N.E.; Cape Fellfoot bore, by compass, S.W. by S.; Cape Herschel, S.E. by S. Drifting to the eastward (true).
11	....	....	....	....	..	N.	5	—19.1	..	30.00	b. m.	Cape Fellfoot 6¾ W. by compass, five miles distant. An aurora to the southward, 4 A.M.
12	....	....	....	....	..	N.W. by W.	6	—13.5	..	29.83	b. m.	Cape Fellfoot E. by compass; Hobhouse Inlet bears S. by E.
13	....	....	....	....	..	W.	2	— 8.9	..	29.86	b. m. o.	West cape of Croker's Bay bears S. ¼ W. by compass.
14	....	....	....	....	..	W.N.W.	1	— 7 6	..	29.91	b. c. m.	A paraselene visible for an hour, 3 P.M. Lancaster Sound.
15	74 20 06 N.	86 26 16 W.	....	S. 79° E.*	87*	N.W. by. N.	3	— 2.5	..	30.02	b. c.	* Drift since the 18th.
							3	—16.1	..	30 13		Means.

HALF-MONTHLY ABSTRACTS OF THE LOG-BOOK OF THE UNITED STATES BRIG ADVANCE

DECEMBER, 1850. LANCASTER SOUND.

Date.	Latitude in at Noon.	Longitude in at Noon.	Variation observed.	Current, true Direction.	Drift in 24 Hours.	Mean true Direction of the Wind.	Force of the Wind.	Mean Temp. of the Air.	Mean Temp. of Surface of the Water.	Mean Height of the Barometer.	Sky and Weather.	Remarks.
1850.	° ′ ″	° ′ ″	° ′									
16	....	....	....	....	..	W. by N.	4	—11.4	..	30.17	b. c.	Lancaster Sound.
17	....	....	....	....	..	S.W. by W.	2	—11.8	..	30.22	b. c. m.	Lancaster Sound. Two paraselenæ visible
18	74 20 32 N.	85 11 30 W.	....	S. 88° E.*	20	N.E. by E.	0	—11.8	..	30.23	b. c. m.	* Drift since the 15th. A paraselene visible. Compass bearings: Cape Crawfurd, (supposed) W.N.W. ½ W.; centre of Powell's Inlet, E.N.E.; Cape Bullen, S. by E.
19	....	....	....	....	..	Variable.	1	—13.3	..	30.02	b. m.	
20	....	....	....	....	..	W. by S.	6	—12.6	..	29.51	b. c. m.	Two very brilliant paraselenæ, circle almost entire.
21	....	....	....	....	..	S.W. by W.	2	—17.7	..	29.74	b. c.	A halo round the moon. The finest print may be read with facility at noon by turning it toward the south. An opening in the ice.
22	....	....	....	....	..	S.W. by W.	2	—11.5	..	30.00	b. c. m.	Ice squeezing and piling up.
23	....	....	....	....	..	....	0	— 7.5	..	30.12	b. c. m.	Lancaster Sound.
24	....	....	....	....	..	....	0	— 5.7	..	30.20	b. c. m.	A halo about the moon.
25	....	....	....	....	..	Variable.	1	—11.3	..	30.22	b. c. m.	
26	....	....	....	....	..	W. by S.	4	—11.8	..	29.84	b. m.	Two paraselenæ visible. Faint aurora at noon, to the southward. An aurora in form of a bow, passing through the zenith in a N.W. and S.E. direction. 11 P.M., another paraselene visible.
27	....	....	....	....	..	S.S.W.	1	—12.5	..	30.05	b. m.	An aurora visible at 5 A.M., at 6 A.M. another one. In the afternoon an aurora passing through the zenith in a N. and S. direction, 10 P.M.
28	74 18 08	82 10 18	....	S. 87° E.*	51	S.S.W.	1	—16.5	..	30.30	b. c. m.	* Drift since the 18th. Longitude at 7 P.M., 82° 10′ 18″. Auroras visible; one passing 30° from the zenith, in form of an arch, to the westward, 1 A.M. and 8 A.M.
29	....	....	....	....	..	W.S.W.	3	—11.3	..	29.94	b. c. m.	An aurora passing near the zenith in an E. and W. direction, 4 A.M.
30	....	....	....	....	..	W.S.W.	1	—22.2	..	29.64	b. m.	Lancaster Sound.
31	....	....	....	....	..	W. by S.	2	—26.8	..	29.47	b. m.	Compass bearings: Cape Warrender, E. ¼ N.; Cape Osborn, S.S.E. ½ E. Auroras visible: one appeared in the form of an arch extending to the horizon in N.N.E. and S.W. direction, passing 15° from the zenith, 10 P.M.
							2	—13.5	..	29.98		Means.

HALF-MONTHLY ABSTRACTS OF THE LOG-BOOK OF THE UNITED STATES BRIG ADVANCE.

JANUARY, 1851. LANCASTER SOUND.

Date. 1851.	Latitude in at Noon.	Longitude in at Noon.	Variation observed.	Current, true Direction.	Drift in 24 Hours.	Mean true Direction of the Wind.	Force of the Wind.	Mean Temp. of the Air.	Mean Temp. of Surface of the Water.	Mean Height of the Barometer.	Sky and Weather.	Remarks.
	° ′ ″	° ′ ″	° ′									
1	....	....	....	....	..	W.S.W.	1	—26.5	..	29.36	b. m.	A faint aurora visible to the southward, 11 P.M.
2	....	....	....	....	..	W.	3	—25.7	..	29.37	b. m.	An aurora passing near the zenith, in an E. and W. direction, 1 A.M. Two auroras visible (7 A.M.), one passing through the zenith in an E. and W. direction, the other in faint beams radiating from the southward.
3	....	....	....	....	..	....	0	—26.1	..	29.62	b. m.	An aurora to the southward, 4 A.M. Cape Warrender bears N.E. ½ E.; Cape Castlereagh, W.N.W., by compass.
4	....	....	....	....	..	W.	3	—21.3	.	29.53	b. c. m.	5 A.M., an aurora visible to the southward and westward. Cape Warrender bears N.E. Cape Osborn, E. by S., by compass.
5	....	....	....	....	..	W. by N.	3	— 3.9	..	29.59	b. m. o.	
6	....	....	....	....	..	W. by S.	2	— 0.8	..	29.67	o. m. s.	
7	....	....	....	....	..	W.	3	—14.4	..	29.96	b. c. m.	Depth of the water, 144 fathoms.
8	....	....	....	....	..	W.S.W.	1	—21.2	..	30.14	b. m.	Cape Warrender bears, N.E. ¾ N.; Cape Castlereagh, N.N.W.; Cape Liverpool, W. ½ N., by compass.
9	....	....	....	....	..	W by S.	2	—13.9	..	30.02	b. m.	
10	....	....	....	....	..	W.	3	—17.3	..	29.83	b.	Compass bearing of Cape Castlereagh, N. by W. ¾ W.
11	....	....	....	....	..	W.	4	— 9.5	..	29.73	b. o. m.	A paraselene, very bright, 3 A.M. A crack in the ice. A halo about the moon.
12	....	....	....	....	..	W.	4	— 8.1	..	29.82	b. c. o. m	Crack closing slowly.
13	....	....	....	....	..	W.	5	—15.3	..	29.83	o. m. b. c.	The ice much broken about the vessel. Compass bearings: Cape Walter Bathurst, W.N.W. ½ W.; Cape Hay, N. by W.
14	....	....	....	....	..	W.N.W.	5	—24.8	..	29.98	b. c. m.	
15	....	....	....	....	..	W.N.W.	4	—22.1	..	30.08	b. m.	3 A.M., a faint aurora to the southward. Ice squeezing to the northward.
							3	—16.6	..	29.76		Means.

HALF-MONTHLY ABSTRACTS OF THE LOG-BOOK OF THE UNITED STATES BRIG ADVANCE.

LANCASTER SOUND AND BAFFIN'S BAY.

JANUARY, 1851.

Date.	Latitude in at Noon.	Longitude in at Noon.	Variation observed.	Current, true Direction.	Drift in 24 Hours.	Mean true Direction of the Wind.	Force of the Wind.	Mean Temp. of the Air.	Mean Temp. of Surface of the Water.	Mean Height of the Barometer.	Sky and Weather.	Remarks.
1851.	° ′ ″	° ′ ″	° ′									
16	....	....	....	....	..	N.W. by N.	3	—18.2	..	30.14	c. m.	A partial eclipse of the moon was visible until 1h. 30m. A halo about the moon. Ice squeezing to the southward and eastward (true).
17	....	....	....	....	..	N. by E.	1	—27.2	..	30.10	b.	
18	73 46 49 N.	75 03 24 W.	....	S. 76° E.	118*	N.W. by N.	2	—25.3	..	29.84	b. m.	* Drift since Dec. 28th. A halo about the moon.
19	....	....	....	....	..	N.W. by W.	6	—20.5	..	29.61	b. m.	Heavy snow-drift. Paraselenæ visible, 11 P.M.
20	....	....	....	....	..	W.N.W.	5	—19.5	..	29.69	b. m.	Paraselenæ visible, 6 A.M.
21	....	....	....	....	..	N.W. by W.	5	—20.7	..	29.85	b. m.	Paraselenæ visible, 5 A.M. and 8 P.M.
22	....	....	....	....	..	N.W. by W.	5	—19.1	..	29.76	b. m.	Heavy snow-drift.
23	73 16 00*	....	....	....	..	W.N.W.	4	—17.6	..	29.58	b. m.	* At 10 P.M. A faint aurora visible, 10 P.M.
24	....	....	....	....	..	S.E. by S.	1	—24.9	..	29.81	b. c. m.	
25	....	....	....	....	..	N.E. by E.	2	—16.1	..	30.16	b. m.	
26	73 09 13	72 02 21*	....	S. 53° E.	62**	N. by W	2	— 9.7	..	30.33	o. m.	* At 9 P.M. ** Drift since the 18th. Aurora visible to the northward, 9 P.M.
27	....	....	....	....	..	N.W.	4	—11.3	..	30.17	b. m.	Auroras to the southward and westward, near the horizon, 2 A.M. and 8 A.M. A heavy snow-drift.
28	72 52 45	71 15 35*	....	S. 39° E.	21**	N.W. by W.	3	—11.0	..	30.00	b. m.	* 8h. 30m. P.M. ** Since the 26th. About two thirds of the sun's disk visible from the top-gallant yard.*
29	72 49 15	70 59 15	94 2 W.	S. 53° E.	6	W.N.W.	1	—18 9	..	30.19	b.	6 A.M., faint aurora near the horizon. One third of the sun's disk visible from the deck. 11 P.M., faint aurora near the horizon, to the S.W. and N.
30	....	....	....	....	..	N.W. by W.	1	—13.5	..	30.17	o. m.	Sound of ice breaking up.
31	....	....	....	....	..	N.W. by W.	3	— 4.4	.	29.35	o. s.	
							3	—17.3	..	29.92		Means.

* Auroras on the 28th 1 A.M., light aurora from W. to S W., two arcs of light, the southern being about 10°, the western 20° from the horizon at the middle point.

HALF-MONTHLY ABSTRACTS OF THE LOG-BOOK OF THE UNITED STATES BRIG ADVANCE

FEBRUARY, 1851. BAFFIN'S BAY.

Date. 1851.	Latitude in at Noon. ° ′ ″	Longitude in at Noon. ° ′ ″	Variation observed. ° ′	Current, true Direction.	Drift in 24 Hours.	Mean true Direction of the Wind.	Force of the Wind.	Mean Temp. of the Air.	Mean Temp. of Surface of the Water.	Mean Height of the Barometer.	Sky and Weather.	Remarks.
1	....	....	....	....	..	W.	2	—11.7	..	29.26	c. o. b. m.	
2	....	....	....	....	..	W.	2	—25.1	..	29.62	b. c. m.	1 A.M., aurora visible to the southward and eastward (true), beams of light covering the whole of the eastern half of the heavens, most of them parallel to the plane of the meridian. Aurora extending to within 30° of the horizon, to the N.W. 7 P.M., an aurora visible, the beams radiating from the zenith. A noise sounding like the cracking of the ice.
3	....	....	....	....	..	W.N.W.	2	—27.0	..	29.65	b. c. m.	
4	....	....	....	....	..	W.N.W.	4	—18.1	..	29.43	b. m. o.	
5	....	....	....	....	..	N.W. by W.	2	—24.7	..	29.55	b. m.	Faint aurora seen to the southward and eastward.
6	....	....	....	....	..	N.W.	1	—37.3	..	29.80	b.	7 A.M., a faint aurora to the southward, near the horizon. The thermometer used since stood at 39° when the mercury in the artificial horizon was freezing.
7	....	....	....	....	..	Variable.	1	—38.0	..	29.88	b. m.	2 A.M., faint aurora seen to N.N.E. and S.S.W. 7 A.M., aurora to the S.E. and E. (true). The ice formed since the 13th of January was 27 inches thick.
8	72 19 40 N.	....	....	....	..	E.N.E.	1	—34.0	..	29.95	b. c. m.	1 A.M., very fine snow. At 5 P.M., a bright paraselene visible.
9	72 19 40*	68 56 22 W.	....	S. 52° E.**	48	S.W.	2	—31.4	..	30.01	b. m.	* At 7 P.M. ** Drift since the 29th ult.
10	....	....	....	....	..	E.S.E.	3	—20.6	..	30.32	o. m.	Ice formed in fire hole since yesterday, 4½ inches thick.
11	....	....	....	....	..	N.N.E.	3	—19.5	..	30.05	o. m.	
12	....	....	....	....	..	N.N.W.	2	—22.8	..	29.87	o. m.	7 P.M., a halo about the moon.
13	....	....	....	....	..	N.W. by W.	1	—34.3	..	30.01	b. m.	Three icebergs in sight. A fine, pleasant day. 7 P.M., faint aurora visible to the southward (true).
14	72 15 09	68 40 22	....	S. 45° E.*	7	Variable.	1	—33.4	..	30.08	b. c.	* Drift since the 9th. Sounding 200 fathoms of line, no bottom; line tended to the westward. Horizon much elevated by refraction into a wall-like appearance.
							2	—26.9	..	29.82		Means.

HALF-MONTHLY ABSTRACTS OF THE LOG-BOOK OF THE UNITED STATES BRIG ADVANCE.

FEBRUARY, 1851. BAFFIN'S BAY.

Date.	Latitude in at Noon.	Longitude in at Noon.	Variation observed.	Current, true Direction.	Drift in 24 Hours.	Mean true Direction of the Wind.	Force of the Wind.	Mean Temp. of the Air.	Mean Temp. of Surface of the Water.	Mean Height of the Barometer.	Sky and Weather.	Remarks.
1851.	° ′ ″	° ′ ″	° ′									
15	....	....	....	....	..	E. by S.	1	—38.4	..	30.11	b. m.	Two icebergs in sight to the eastward. Horizon much elevated by refraction. Land to the northward and westward (compass).
16	....	....	....	....	..	E.S.E.	1	—36.8	..	30.06	b.	
17	....	....	....	....	..	S.S.W.	1	—29.6	..	30.03	b. c. m.	Horizon much elevated by refraction.
18	....	....	....	....	..	W.	1	—37.0	..	30.12	b.	5 A.M., an aurora visible, passing near the zenith, in a N.N.W. and S.S.E. direction. A parhelion having three images of the sun.
19	....	...	....	....	..	W. by S.	1	—33.1	..	30.18	b. c. m.	A halo about the moon.
20	72 10 11 N.	68 36 40 W.	....	....	..	Variable.	1	—33.2	..	30.14	b. m.	Land in sight to the northward and westward. 1 A.M., a faint aurora to the E. 4 P.M., an aurora passing through the zenith, and extending to the horizon in a N.W. and S.E. direction (true).
21	....	...	....	....	.	W.	1	—37.8	..	30.21	b. m.	
22	....	....	....	....	..	W.N.W.	1	—41.0	..	30.52	b.	
23	....	....	....	....	..	N.E.	1	—29.0	..	30.62	o. m.	6 A.M., faint aurora seen about the zenith in a southward and westward direction. No bottom at 200 fathoms.
24	....	....	....	....	..	E.N.E.	2	—28.9	..	30.70	b. m.	
25	....	....	....	....	..	E. by S.	2	—18.5	..	30.54	o. m.	3 P.M., faint aurora visible, passing through the zenith in a N.W. and S.E. direction. At 10 P.M., several auroras seen to the northward and westward.
26	....	....	....	....	..	S.E.	1	—33.8	..	30.66	b.	1 A.M., an aurora to the southward and eastward. 9 P.M., several auroras visible in different parts of the heavens.
27	....	....	....	....	..	E.	2	—32.3	..	31.00	b. m.	3 A.M., aurora passing through the zenith in an E. and W. direction.
28	....	....	....	....	..	N.W. by N.	5	—22.1	..	30.40	b. m.	A heavy snow-drift.
							2	—32.2	..	30.38		Means.

HALF-MONTHLY ABSTRACTS OF THE LOG-BOOK OF THE UNITED STATES BRIG ADVANCE.

MARCH, 1851 BAFFIN'S BAY.

Date. 1851.	Latitude in at Noon.	Longitude in at Noon.	Variation observed.	Current, true Direction.	Drift in 24 Hours.	Mean true Direction of the Wind.	Force of the Wind.	Mean Temp. of the Air.	Mean Temp. of Surface of the Water.	Mean Height of the Barometer.	Sky and Weather.	Remarks.
	° ′ ″	° ′ ″	° ′									
1	71 55 40 N.	....	....	....	..	N.W.	2	—10.6	..	29.92	o. m.	Ice found to be three feet thick.
2	....	....	....	....	..	W. by S.	4	— 1.2	..	29.42	o. m. s.	A heavy snow-drift.
3	....	....	....	....	..	S. by E.	4	—13.1	..	29.83	b. c. m.	A heavy snow-drift. Could feel ice through a hole cut to the depth of 11 feet.
4	71 54 57	66 55 48 W.	....	S. 66° E.*	35	S.	2	—30.0	..	29.98	b. m.	* Drift since the 20th ult. Position at 9 P.M. No bottom at 330 fathoms.
5	71 53 02	....	....	....	..	N.W.	2	—37.9	..	29.75	b. m.	
6	71 51 18	....	....	....	..	S. by E.	2	—33.8	..	29.83	b. m.	
7	71 50 32	....	....	....	..	N.W. by N.	1	—34.7	..	29.91	b.	
8	....	....	....	....	..	W. by S.	1	—33.0	..	29.87	b. m.	11 A.M., a parhelion visible. 10 P.M., a halo about the moon.
9	71 48 20	....	....	....	..	E.S.E.	2	—30.1	..	29.96	b. m.	1 A.M., a faint aurora to the southward and eastward.
10	....	....	....	....	..	N.N.E.	3	—21.9	..	29.89	b. m.	7 P.M., a halo about the moon.
11	....	....	....	....	..	E.	5	—12.8	..	29.87	o. m.	3 A.M., heavy snow-drift. No bottom at 264 fathoms Line drifted southward.
12	71 41 27	....	....	....	..	W.	2	—27.0	..	30.28	b. m.	
13	71 37 20	....	....	....	..	N.W.	3	—27.3	..	30.42	b. m.	1 A.M., a bright paraselene visible for an hour. At noon, a bright parhelion, atmosphere filled with minute particles of snow. 2 P.M., heavy snow-drift.
14	....	....	....	....	..	N. by W.	5	—15.5	..	30.32	b. c. m.	A faint parhelion visible.
15	71 27 59	65 44 30	....	S. 38° E.*	36	N.W.	2	—12.5	..	30.20	b. c. m.	* Drift since the 4th. Position at 8½ P.M.
							3	—22.7	..	29.98		Means.

HALF-MONTHLY ABSTRACTS OF THE LOG-BOOK OF THE UNITED STATES BRIG ADVANCE.

BAFFIN'S BAY.

MARCH, 1851.

Date.	Latitude in at Noon.	Longitude in at Noon.	Variation observed.	Current, true Direction.	Drift in 24 Hours.	Mean true Direction of the Wind.	Force of the Wind.	Mean Temp. of the Air.	Mean Temp. of Surface of the Water.	Mean Height of the Barometer.	Sky and Weather.	Remarks.
1851.	° ′ ″	° ′ ″	° ′					+	+			
16	71 26 22 N.	....	....	....	..	N.W. by W.	3	— 7.4	..	30.24	b. m.	
17	71 20 36	....	....	....	..	N.W. by W.	4	—11.5	28	30.46	b. c. m.	No bottom at 310 fathoms.
18	....	....	....	....	..	W.N.W.	4	—14.2	..	30.61	b. m.	
19	71 09 25	....	....	....	..	S.W.	3	—14.4	..	30.28	b. m.	Opening in the ice 100 yards wide, extending from N.W. to S.E.
20	....	....	....	....	..	S.E. by S.	7	+ 3.5	..	30.06	m.	A heavy bank of vapor in the south.
21	71 17 52	....	....	....	..	N.W. by N.	5	— 7.0	..	29.71	b. c. m.	
22	71 09 11	....	....	....	..	N.W. by N.	4	—16.7	..	29.82	b. m.	
23	71 02 35	....	....	....	..	N.	4	—12.1	..	29.62	b. m.	1 A.M., an aurora passed through the zenith to the northward and westward. 8 P.M., a parhelion visible. 9 P.M., faint aurora visible to northward and westward (true).
24	70 55 09	64 04 00 W.	....	S. 45° E.*	46	N.N.W.	4	—16.8	..	29.79	b. m.	* Drift since the 15th. 1 A.M., an aurora visible passing near the zenith, from N. to S. 7 A.M., a parhelion; at noon with two circles. No bottom at 310 fathoms. Frost-smoke rising to the S.E. 10 P.M., aurora to the southward (true). 1 A.M., faint aurora to the southward and eastward.
25	70 46 33	....	....	....	..	N.W.	3	—19.7	..	29.97	b.	
26	70 43 56	63 44 33	....	S. 36° E.*	14	....	0	—19.5	..	30.03	b.	* Drift since the 24th. Position at 9 A.M. Cracking in the ice. 11 P.M., faint aurora to southward and eastward.
27	70 42 22	....	....	....	..	N.	1	—18.3	..	30.12	b. m.	1 A.M., frost-smoke. 6 P.M., frost-smoke.
28	70 40 43	....	....	....	..	S. by W.	3	—15.2	..	30.32	b. m.	2 P.M., frost-smoke on the horizon. To the S.W., N., and E. dense masses of vapor are hanging, as if over water. 11 P.M., aurora to the eastward (true).
29	70 43 56	....	....	...	..	S.E. by S.	4	— 8.2	..	30.32	b. m.	1 A.M., observed a long line of frost-smoke from mast-head to the southward (true).
30	70 46 34	....	....	....	..	S.E. by S.	2	— 3.0	..	30.07	b. m.	1 A.M., much frost-smoke seen to the S.E.
31	70 44 46	....	....	....	..	N. by E.	2	— 4.4	..	30.75	b. m.	
							4	—11.5	..	30.14		

HALF-MONTHLY ABSTRACTS OF THE LOG-BOOK OF THE UNITED STATES BRIG ADVANCE.

APRIL, 1851. BAFFIN'S BAY.

Date. 1851.	Latitude in at Noon.	Longitude in at Noon.	Variation observed	Current, true Direction.	Drift in 24 Hours.	Mean true Direction of the Wind.	Force of the Wind.	Mean Temp. of the Air.	Mean Temp. of Surface of the Water.	Mean Height of the Barometer.	Sky and Weather.	Remarks.
	° ′ ″	° ′ ″	° ′									
1	70 37 30 N.	63 42 00 W.	82 24 W.	S. 7° E.*	7	N.N.W.	3	— 6.3	..	30 03	b. m.	* Drift since the 26th ult. Observed a circle, except an arc cut off by the horizon, about the sun when his altitude was 8° 40′, its radius 21° 30; upon a line drawn horizontally through the sun were two luminous spots, while a third was seen vertically above it. At this last was the arc of a circle, apparently of the same radius and tangent to it. From the sun and each of the spots in its circle descended columns of light dazzling to the eye. No prismatic colors were visible at the time, although they were seen a short time before to the horizon. No bottom with 310 fathoms. 7 P.M., a bright parhelion visible. Cut a floe formed in September, and found it 7 ft. 2 inc. thick.
2	70 28 30	....	....	....	..	N.W. by N.	3	— 4.9	..	30.02	b. m.	For the description of the parhelion, see note at the bottom of the page.
3	70 19 09	....	....	....	..	N. by W.	4	— 4.2	..	29.96	b. c. m.	An appearance in the sky similar and equal in its parts to that described yesterday, but not as bright.
4	70 10 00	63 24 07	....	S. 13° E.*	28	W.S.W.	2	+ 0.8	..	30.07	o. m.	* Drift since the 1st inst.
5	....	....	....	....	..	N.N.E.	2	+ 1.9	..	30.20	o. m.	A lane of water to the southward, 1.5 miles.
6	70 03 33	....	....	....	..	S. by W.	1	— 5.5	..	30.41	b. m.	1 A.M., faint and fleeting aurora visible to the S.E. At 9 P.M., an aurora to the south (true).
7	....	....	....	....	..	S.E. by E.	2	+ 6.5	..	30.41	o. m.	No bottom with 310 fathoms. A small pool of water seen to the southward.
8	70 00 50	63 18 42	79 44 W.	S. 12° E.*	9	S.S.W.	2	+ 2.6	..	30.44	b. c.	* Drift since the 4th.
9	70 02 15	....	....	....	..	S.E. by S.	3	+11.8	..	30.34	o. m.	Put a mercurial thermometer in place of the spirit one used since the 6th of February, both agreeing at 11 and 12, but at times differing 3°, mercurial higher.
10	...	....	....	....	..	S.E. by E.	6	+25.5	..	29.71	o. m.	Heavy snow-drift. A crack opening, extending about one mile, N.W. and S.E.
11	....	....	....	....	..	S. by E.	4	+17.2	..	30.03	o. m.	Opening from N.N.E.
12	....	....	....	....	..	S.S.W.	3	+ 7.5	..	30.57	o. m. s.	Large pool of water to the southward (true). Ice much broken up; openings in every direction.
13	70 12 34	63 02 50	....	N. 25° E.*	13	S.S.W.	2	+10.6	..	30.89	b. c. o. m.	* Drift since the 8th.
14	....	....	....	....	..	Variable.	1	+14.6	..	31.01	o. m. s.	Pool of water in sight.
15	70 09 00	63 19 52	....	S. 26° W.*	7	....	0	+11.3	..	30 99	b. c. m.	* Drift since the 13th. Position at 4½ P.M. Water in sight.
							2	+ 6.0	..	30.34		Means.

Parhelion of the 2d of April.—Mist about the horizon: when the sun had attained the altitude of 4° 51′, observed the following: a circle, except the arc intercepted by the horizon, having the luminous spots upon it, one on each side of the sun, and at the same distance with it from the horizon, the third vertically above; a faint appearance of an arc tangential to the last point. The luminous columns noticed yesterday were seen, more dazzling, and toward the sun bordered with orange. Concentric with this circle, and outside of it, was another, similar in its parts, but much more faint; radius of inner circle measured from sun, 22° 00′; outer circle, 46° 30′. At 7h. 30m. the phenomena were more distinct, the outer circle being finely marked with the colors of the rainbow; the arc, tangent at the upper spot, was

HALF-MONTHLY ABSTRACTS OF THE LOG-BOOK OF THE UNITED STATES BRIG ADVANCE.

APRIL, 1851. BAFFIN'S BAY.

Date.	Latitude in at Noon.	Longitude in at Noon.	Variation observed.	Current, true Direction.	Drift in 24 Hours.	Mean true Direction of the Wind.	Force of the Wind.	Mean Temp. of the Air.	Mean Temp. of Surface of the Water.	Mean Height of the Barometer.	Sky and Weather.	Remarks.
1851.	° ′ ″	° ′ ″	° ′									
16	70 07 13 N.	63 00 03 W.	80 49 W.	S. 78° E.*	7	....	0	+ 7.0	..	30.91	b. c.	No water in sight. Thermometer in the sun stood at 76° at 10½ A.M.
17	70 04 01	....	....	....	..	N.	2	10.0	..	30.83	b. c.	Water in sight.
18	69 57 51	....	....	....	..	N.N.W.	2	4.5	..	30.71	b. m.	A small pool of water to the northward.
19	69 52 50	63 03 22	....	S. 3° W.*	14	S.W. by W.	3	11.4	..	30.57	b. m.	* Drift since the 16th. Position at 8 A.M.
20	69 51 43	....	....	....	..	S. by E.	3	5.2	..	30.40	b. c.	
21	....	....	....	....	..	S.S.E.	2	14.0	..	30.17	b. c. m.	
22	....	....	....	....	..	S.E.	3	24.2	..	29.93	o. s.	* Position at 3.45 P.M.
23	69 52 01*	63 02 06	....	....	..	Variable.	3	18.0	..	30.12	b. m.	Ship's head altered to the eastward.
24	....	....	....	....	..	S. by W.	1	27.0	..	30.22	o. m. s.	Several openings in the ice.
25	69 46 50	....	....	....	..	N.W. by W.	2	19.2	..	30.55	o. m.	* Drift since the 23d. Position at 4.20 P.M.
26	69 39 42	63 08 46	....	S. 9° W.*	13	N. by W.	2	1.0	..	30.68	b.	
27	69 35 50	....	....	....	..	N. by W.	2	3.7	..	30.32	b. c.	No open water in sight. No bottom with 310 fathoms. The line tended to the northward and westward (true).
28	....	....	....	....	..	W. by N.	3	0.8	..	30.27	o. m. b. c.	
29	69 24 40	63 04 26	....	S. 6° E.*	15	S.E.	1	0.0	..	30.64	b.	* Drift since the 26th. Position at 4.20 P.M.
30	69 23 16	....	....	....	..	N.E. by N.	1	3.2	..	30.78	b.	Found the ice 5 feet 5 inches thick.
							2	+ 9.9	..	30.47		Means.

HALF-MONTHLY ABSTRACTS OF THE LOG-BOOK OF THE UNITED STATES BRIG ADVANCE.

May, 1851. Baffin's Bay.

Date. 1851.	Latitude in at Noon.	Longitude in at Noon.	Variation observed.	Current, true Direction.	Drift in 24 Hours.	Mean true Direction of the Wind.	Force of the Wind.	Mean Temp. of the Air.	Mean Temp. of Surface of the Water.	Mean Height of the Barometer.	Sky and Weather.	Remarks.
	° ′ ″	° ′ ″	° ′									
1	69 20 48 N.	....	....	....	..	....	0	+10.7	..	30.56	b. f.	
2	69 18 17	....	....	....	..	N. by W.	3	16.0	..	30.56	b. f. o.	3 A.M., fog falling in large flakes on the deck.
3	69 09 00	63 01 50 W.	80 13 W.	S. 4° E.*	16	N.	3	9.3	..	30.60	b. c.	* Drift since the 29th.
4	69 05 00	....	....	....	..	N.N.W.	3	9.5	..	30.25	c. m. s.	
5	69 01 24	....	....	....	..	S.W. by W.	1	19.4	..	30.00	o. b.	
6	68 59 14	....	....	....	..	S.W. by W.	2	22.5	..	29.94	o. b. c.	
7	68 59 31	....	....	....	..	S.W.	5	22.4	..	29.74	b. c.	Heavy snow-drift. Water in sight in all directions.
8	....	....	....	....	..	W.N.W.	6	11.8	..	30.46	b. c.	Heavy snow-drift.
9	68 41 40	62 01 55	....	S. 38° E.*	35	S.W. by W.	2	14.7	..	30.82	b. c.	* Drift since the 3d.
10	68 40 52	....	....	....	..	S.W. by W.	2	20.8	..	30.67	b. c.	
11	68 37 33	....	....	....	..	N.E. by N.	2	19.5	..	30.65	b. c. o.	
12	68 34 18	....	....	....	..	N. by E.	4	13.6	..	30.50	b. c. o. m.	Open water in sight.
13	68 28 05	....	....	....	..	N.N.W.	4	13.7	..	30.33	o. s.	Open water in sight.
14	68 22 45	....	....	....	..	N.W. by N.	4	18.0	..	30.21	o. s.	
15	68 12 45	61 42 53	...	S. 14° E.*	30	N.W. by W.	5	17.9	..	30.15	b. c.	* Drift since the 9th
							3	+16.0	..	30.36		Means.

HALF-MONTHLY ABSTRACTS OF THE LOG-BOOK OF THE UNITED STATES BRIG ADVANCE.

May, 1851. Baffin's Bay.

Date.	Latitude in at Noon.	Longitude in at Noon.	Variation observed.	Current, true Direction.	Drift in 24 Hours.	Mean true Direction of the Wind.	Force of the Wind.	Mean Temp. of the Air.	Mean Temp. of Surface of the Water.	Mean Height of the Barometer.	Sky and Weather.	Remarks.
1851.	° ′ ″	° ′ ″	° ′									
16	68 04 24 N.	61 14 02 W.	73 13 W.	S. 51° E.*	13	N.W.	4	+18.3	..	30.15	b. c.	* Drift since the 15th.
17	....	....	....	....	..	N.W. by N.	3	21.9	..	30.12	o. m. c. s.	Open water in sight all round us.
18	67 50 31	....	....	....	..	N.W. by N.	5	17.7	..	30.07	o. s. b. c.	No bottom with 230 fathoms. Land discerned to the S.W. (true).
19	....	....	....	....	..	N.W.	4	16.3	..	29.97	o. c.	
20	....	....	....	....	..	W.N.W.	3	23.3	..	29.96	o. c. s.	Land plain in sight to the southward and westward, 20 miles distant (estimated). Supposed to be Cape Searle.
21	67 10 42	60 25 00	....	S. 19° E.*	57	N.E. by E.	1	28.7	..	30.09	o. s.	* Drift since the 16th.
22	67 06 01	....	....	....	..	N.E. by E.	1	27.9	..	30.13	o. m. c.	
23	67 00 00	60 37 06	....	S. 23° W.*	12	W. by S.	2	23.7	..	30.02	o. m. b. c.	* Drift since the 21st.
24	....	....	....	....	..	S.E. by E.	4	27.9	..	30.13	b. c. s.	
25	....	....	....	....	..	N.W.	7	23.2	..	29.66	c. m. s.	
26	66 40 42	60 54 49	74 50 W.	S. 24° W.*	17	Variable.	2	27.8	..	29.92	c. b. s.	* Drift since the 23d. Two parhelia visible. True bearing of Cape Walsingham, E. 63° 22′ W.
27	66 41 40	60 54 45*	....	S.	3	Variable.	2	24.9	..	29.99	b. c. m.	* At 5¾ P.M. With 230 fathoms line got bottom, fine sand. Bearing of Cape Walsingham, S. 74° 30′ W. (true).
28	66 33 41	60 52 25*	72 03 W.	S. 6° E.	8	Variable.	2	25.8	..	30.08	b. c.	* At 5¼ P.M. Cape Walsingham, 10 or 12 miles distant, bears, by compass, N. ¼ W. Sounded in 190 fathoms, sandy bottom.
29	66 32 15	....	....	....	..	N.W.	2	25.5	..	30.27	b. c. m.	No bottom with 165 fathoms. Cape Walsingham bears N. ¼ E. (by compass).
30	66 28 00	60 28 20*	71 56 W.	S. 60° E.**	11	N.E. by E.	2	25.9	..	30.53	b. c.	* At 5½ P.M. ** Drift since the 28th. Cape Walsingham bore N. 10° E. True bearing of hummock, N. 25° 26′ W.; Saddle Island, N. 79° 26′ W.
31	66 29 04	60 11 42*	72 10 W.	N. 82° E.	7	S.	3	28.2	..	30.61	b. c.	* At 5½ P.M. A great deal of water in sight from aloft. Cape Walsingham bearing, by compass, N. ¼ E.; Mount Raleigh, N. by W.
							3	+24.2	..	30.11		Means.

HALF-MONTHLY ABSTRACTS OF THE LOG-BOOK OF THE UNITED STATES BRIG ADVANCE

JUNE, 1851 — DAVIS'S STRAIT.

Date. 1851.	Latitude in at Noon.	Longitude in at Noon.	Variation observed.	Current, true Direction.	Drift in 24 Hours.	Mean true Direction of the Wind.	Force of the Wind.	Mean Temp. of the Air.	Mean Temp. of Surface of the Water.	Mean Height of the Barometer.	Sky and Weather.	Remarks.
	° ′ ″	° ′ ″	° ′									
1	66 32 39 N.	59 50 46 W.	69 22 W.	N. 67° E.	9	E.	3	+30.1	..	30.50	b. c.	
2	....	....	....	....	..	E. by S.	3	34.1	..	30.45	o. m. s.	No land in sight.
3	66 30 50	59 34 38	70 06 W.	S. 75° E.*	7	E. by S.	3	31.7	..	30.64	b. c. m.	* Drift since the 1st. Position at 5¼ P.M. No land in sight. The surf breaking on the ice to the northward and eastward.
4	66 31 22	59 19 25	....	N. 85° E.	6	E. by S.	3	33.5	.	30.55	b. c. m.	Mount Raleigh bears N. ¾ W. Cape Walsingham, N. by compass.
5	66 32 53	59 06 17	71 10 W.	N. 75° E.	6	S.E.	3	35.6	..	30.62	b. c.	On this day occurred the great disruption of the ice. The floes immediately around us had remained in process of freezing since January 13th without disturbance. Heard the sea breaking on the ice to the northward. Ice cracking and opening in all directions, making floes large and small, which were rising and falling as if acted on by a heavy sea.
6	....	....	....	....	..	W. by S.	4	32.9	..	30.53	b. o. f.	
7	66 20 18	....	....	....	..	N. by W.	4	32.4	..	30.47	b. c.	
8	....	....	....	....	..	W. by S.	2	33.2	..	30.58	c. m. f.	A great deal of heavy ice drifted past us during the first part of the watch.
9	65 56 01	....	....	....	..	N.W. by N.	3	32.5	+30.0	30.55	f. b. c. m.	The ice very slack; thick fog, land and six icebergs in sight. Sailing through floe ice.
10	65 38 47	....	....	....	..	N.	7	32.3	32.4	30.38	c. m. b. c.	Very little drift ice, many bergs. A short, heavy swell.
11	....	....	....	....	..	N.N.E.	5	34.2	32.8	30.28	o. f.	Land in sight.
12	66 09 48	54 41 47	....	....	..	N.N.W.	3	33.5	33.3	30.31	o. m. b.	Sounded in 30 fathoms water. Icebergs in sight. At noon sounded in 25 fathoms water, coral bottom.
13	67 07 13	....	....	...	..	W.	3	32.2	32.1	30.37	o. f. c.	Sounded in 25 fathoms; in 19 fathoms, shells and sand. Many pieces of drift ice. Two rocky islands in sight, bearing, by compass, S.E. by E. ½ E. A great number of icebergs in sight.
14	67 43 58	....	....	....	..	W.N.W.	2	32.2	31.7	30.25	c. m.	Heavy drift pieces. In 15 fathoms water found current setting W. (compass) one mile per hour, eight hours later it slackened. In 23 fathoms, no bottom.
15	67 58 30	....	....	....	..	N.N.E.	2	32.0	31.5	30.22	o. m. f. b.	Passed a great number of bergs, grounded bergs, and drift ice. Strong current setting to the S. Several islands in sight.
							3	+32.8	+32.0	30.45		Means.

HALF-MONTHLY ABSTRACTS OF THE LOG-BOOK OF THE UNITED STATES BRIG ADVANCE.

JUNE, 1851. BAFFIN'S BAY.

Date. 1851.	Latitude in at Noon. ° ′ ″	Longitude in at Noon. ° ′ ″	Variation observed. ° ′	Current, true Direction.	Drift in 24 Hours.	Mean true Direction of the Wind.	Force of the Wind.	Mean Temp. of the Air.	Mean Temp. of Surface of the Water.	Mean Height of the Barometer.	Sky and Weather.	Remarks.
16	68 46 55 N.	....	....	....	..	S.S.E.	2	+33.0	+34.7	30.26	f. b. c.	Standing in for Whale-fish Islands. Land in sight, supposed to be Vester Island. Disco Island in sight. Passed several icebergs.
17	....	....	....	....	..	E.	3	44.5	..	30.21	b. c.	Anchored in eight fathoms water. Upper part of Lievely harbor still filled with winter ice.
18	69 14 22	53 24 40 W.	....	....	..	Variable.	2	41.6	37.0	30.21	b. c.	At anchor, Lievely. Chronometer compared at Graah and Parry's observatory; loss in rate in 13 months, 23.8 seconds.
19	69 14 22	53 24 40	....	....	..	W.S.W.	2	41.5	..	30.12	b. c. f.	At anchor, Lievely.
20	69 14 22	53 24 40	....	....	..	S.W. by S.	3	37.1	..	30.16	o. r. f.	At anchor, Lievely.
21	69 14 22	53 24 40	....	....	..	W.S.W.	3	41.7	..	30.20	c. f.	At anchor, Lievely.
22	....	....	....	....	..	N.W.	3	36.0	35.5	30.14	b. c.	Many bergs in sight at 11 P.M., standing in.
23	69 24 09	....	....	....	..	S.W. by S.	3	35.1	33.8	30.14	b. c. s.	Many bergs in sight, land about 10 miles distant. Standing along the land.
24	....	....	....	....	..	S. by E.	5	34.7	32.8	29.98	o. s.	Passed many bergs and drift ice. Amid large bergs, weather dark and threatening. Made the N.W. Point of Kanarsuck Land. Passed through a group of 40 icebergs.
25	....	....	....	....	..	S. by E.	5	34.2	31.7	29.78	o. r. s.	Many bergs and light floe ice. Off Cape Lawson. At Storoë Islands the ice became impassable; had to turn back. Weather very thick. Passed a ledge of rocks not mentioned on the chart.
26	....	....	....	....	..	S.W.	3	32.4	30.2	30.05	o.m.s.b.c.	Sounded in 95 fathoms, muddy bottom.
27	....	....	....	....	..	S.S.W.	3	33.2	31.4	30.24	o. m. s.	Rocky bottom in 15 fathoms water. Sailing through loose ice. Dark Head in sight. Weather very thick.
28	72 24 32	....	....	....	..	W.N.W.	2	32.5	30.6	30.52	c. m. b. c.	Land in sight. Ice loose in direction of Haroë Island.
29	72 22 02	55 45 27	....	....	..	N.N.W.	2	33.2	30.0	30.55	b.	Good deal of loose ice about. True bearing of Dark Head, S. 7° 52′ W. Ice loose and driving about with the tides.
30	....	....	....	...	..	Variable.	1	38.8	32.4	30.50	c.	No change in the ice.
							3	+36.7	+32.7	30 20		Means.

HALF-MONTHLY ABSTRACTS OF THE LOG-BOOK OF THE UNITED STATES BRIG ADVANCE.

JULY, 1851. BAFFIN'S BAY.

Date. 1851.	Latitude in at Noon.	Longitude in at Noon.	Variation observed.	Current, true Direction.	Drift in 24 Hours.	Mean true Direction of the Wind.	Force of the Wind.	Mean Temp. of the Air.	Mean Temp. of Surface of the Water.	Mean Height of the Barometer.	Sky and Weather.	Remarks.
	° ′ ″	° ′ ″	° ′									
1	72 27 18 N.	....	....	....	..	S.	2	+44.3	..	30.48	c. r.	Three fathoms water. At anchor, Pröven.
2	72 27 18	....	....	....	..	S.W.	1	40.0	..	30.32	o. r.	At anchor, Pröven.
3	72 27 18	....	....	....	..	Variable.	1	37.6	+31.5	30.48	o. r.	At anchor, Pröven.
4	72 27 18	....	....	....	..	W.N.W.	2	35.6	31.0	30.41	o. f. r. m.	At anchor, Pröven.
5	72 27 18	....	....	....	..	W.	2	36.9	..	30.34	o. m.	At anchor, Pröven.
6	....	....	....	....	..	S.W. by W.	1	38.7	37.7	30.26	o. b. f.	
7	....	....	....	....	..	N.	3	38.9	32.3	30.26	b.	Ice loose. Beating through loose floe ice.
8	....	....	....	....	..	Variable.	2	39.7	33.8	30.24	b.	Heavy stream of ice. Off Sanderson's Hope. Latitude of Uppernavik by midnight altitude, 72° 55′ 30″ N. Many bergs in sight. Beating along the land.
9	....	....	....	....	..	N. by W.	1	40.0	36.2	30.00	b.	Working through numerous bergs. A good deal of ice in sight.
10	....	....	....	....	..	S. by E.	3	39.2	33.6	30.19	b. c. m.	Heavy bergs and loose ice. Land about five miles distant.
11	....	....	....	....	..	S. by W.	2	38.7	32.5	30.29	b. c.	Run aground.
12	....	....	....	....	..	S. by E.	3	39.8	30.8	30.12	b. c.	
13	....	....	....	....	..	S.	4	36.5	32.0	29.92	b. c.	Ice driving slowly to the northward on both sides of the island.
14	....	....	....	....	..	....	0	33.9	30.0	30.04	o. f.	
15	74 04 32	....	....	....	..	E. by N.	1	35.2	30.0	30.06	b. c. f.	Ice loose and setting to the south.
							2	+38.3	+32.6	30.22		Means.

HALF-MONTHLY ABSTRACTS OF THE LOG-BOOK OF THE UNITED STATES BRIG ADVANCE.

July, 1851. **Baffin's Bay.**

Date.	Latitude in at Noon.	Longitude in at Noon.	Variation observed.	Current, true Direction.	Drift in 24 Hours.	Mean true Direction of the Wind.	Force of the Wind.	Mean Temp. of the Air.	Mean Temp. of Surface of the Water.	Mean Height of the Barometer.	Sky and Weather.	Remarks.
1851.	° ′ ″	° ′ ″	° ′									
16	....	....	....	....	..	N. by E.	2	+35.3	+29.0	30.03	b. c.	Some open water appearing to the northward.
17	....	....	....	....	..	Variable.	2	34.3	30.0	29.93	b. c.	Ice closely packed.
18	....	....	....	....	..	N.	2	36.3	30.3	30.10	b. c.	Ice opening somewhat.
19	....	....	....	....	..	Variable.	3	36.3	30.0	30.34	b. c.	Devil's Thumb in sight. Ice closing.
20	74 19 29 N.	....	....	....	..	N. by W.	2	36.0	30.1	30.31	c.	Ice opening and closing.
21	....	....	....	....	..	Variable.	2	35.9	30.0	30.47	c. r.	A glacier in sight, very large bergs off it
22	....	....	....	....	..	N. by E.	2	35.7	35.2	30.51	b. c.	No change in the ice.
23	....	....	....	....	..	Variable.	2	37.8	33.7	30.50	c.	Great many bergs in sight.
24	74 34 54	....	....	....	..	N.E. by N.	1	39.7	33.0	30.38	b. c.	Ice closing and slackening.
25	....	....	....	....	..	S.E. by S.	3	36.9	33.3	30.35	o. r. c. f.	Ice closing and slackening.
26	....	....	....	....	..	S.E. by S.	3	35.8	31.0	30.30	c. f. b.	Ice squeezing and piling up. Many heavy bergs near us. Ice opening.
27	....	....	....	....	..	N.E. by E.	2	37.2	32.5	30.28	o. r.	The ice occasionally in motion.
28	....	....	....	....	..	S. by E.	5	33.8	..	30.18	o. r.	Ice quiet.
29	74 40 26	....	....	....	..	S. by E.	3	38.0	..	30.05	b.	Signs of opening.
30	....	....	....	....	..	S.E. by E.	4	38.2	..	29.81	b. c.	Ice slackening and closing.
31	....	....	....	....	..	S.E.	3	34.8	..	29.77	b. c. m.	
							3	+36.4	+31.5	30.22		Means

HALF-MONTHLY ABSTRACTS OF THE LOG-BOOK OF THE UNITED STATES BRIG ADVANCE.

AUGUST, 1851. BAFFIN'S BAY.

Date. 1851.	Latitude in at Noon.	Longitude in at Noon.	Variation observed.	Current, true Direction.	Drift in 24 Hours.	Mean true Direction of the Wind.	Force of the Wind.	Mean Temp. of the Air.	Mean Temp. of Surface of the Water.	Mean Height of the Barometer.	Sky and Weather.	Remarks.
	° ′ ″	° ′ ″	° ′									
1	....	....	....	....	..	S. by E.	3	+32.7	..	30.06	o. f.	Ice still closely packed.
2	74 40 23 N.	....	....	....	..	N.N.W.	2	32.5	..	29.89	c. b.	Ice opened a little.
3	....	....	....	....	..	S. by E.	2	32.1	+30.3	29.71	b. c. f.	Ice loose and drifting to the southward. Several bergs in sight. At midnight ice closed.
4	....	....	....	....	..	N.E. by E.	2	33.1	32.0	29.75	c. s. b.	Ice loose round us. Many bergs. Land distant 10 miles. An immense glacier in sight. Loose blue bottom at 440 fathoms.
5	74 41 39	58 30 07 W.	....	....	..	S.E. by S.	3	35.5	..	29.88	b. c.	Devil's Thumb seen. Young ice ¾ths of an inch thick. Ice loose and broken.
6	....	....	....	....	..	E. by S.	2	35.1	..	30.21	o. m.	Ice closing.
7	....	....	....	....	..	W. by N.	1	36.2	..	30.50	o. f.	No change in the ice.
8	74 41 38	....	....	....	..	N.N.W.	2	34.4	..	30.70	b. f. c.	No change in the ice.
9	....	....	....	....	..	Variable.	1	34.9	..	30.75	o. f.	Ice loose and much broken.
10	....	....	....	....	..	N. by W.	1	37.3	..	30.79	o.	No change.
11	....	....	....	....	..	N.W. by N.	1	37.7	..	30.60	b.	No change.
12	....	....	....	....	..	N.E.	1	37.1	..	30.55	b.	Slight motion of the ice. Young ice ½ an inch thick.
13	74 42 04	....	....	....	..	Variable.	2	34.4	..	30.53	b. c.	Some icebergs ahead. Ice more closely packed.
14	....	....	....	....	..	S.	1	30.9	..	30.43	f.	No change in the ice.
15	....	....	....	....	..	S.	2	32.5	..	30.25	o. m.	Ice squeezing and breaking up.
							2	+34.4	..	30.31		Means.

HALF-MONTHLY ABSTRACTS OF THE LOG-BOOK OF THE UNITED STATES BRIG ADVANCE.

AUGUST, 1851. BAFFIN'S BAY.

Date.	Latitude in at Noon.	Longitude in at Noon.	Variation observed.	Current, true Direction.	Drift in 24 Hours.	Mean true Direction of the Wind.	Force of the Wind.	Mean Temp. of the Air.	Mean Temp. of Surface of the Water.	Mean Height of the Barometer.	Sky and Weather.	Remarks.
1851.	° ′ ″	° ′ ″	° ′									
16	....	....	....	....	..	N.W. by N.	1	+35.7	..	30.17	o. f.	Ice squeezing up. A large berg half a mile from us capsized, and then righted again.
17	....	....	....	....	..	N. by E.	1	34.9	+34.0	30.16	b.	Ice loosening.
18	....	....	....	....	..	E. by N.	2	33.7	..	30.02	b. f.	Icebergs very numerous; floe ice and thick fog.
19	74 41 30 N.	....	....	....	..	W. by N.	2	30.1	..	29.98	f.	Many bergs and a good deal of berg ice in sight. The fog lifted enough to show that we were nearly surrounded by icebergs.
20	....	....	....	....	..	S.S.E.	3	35.0	34.5	30.25	o. f. d. s.	Passed a number of bergs. Devil's Thumb bore, by compass, S.E.; Wilcox Point, by compass, E.N.E. Off Duck Islands.
21	....	....	....	....	..	N.W. by W.	4	33.3	34.3	30.32	c. m. f.	The Duck Islands on the starboard bow. Sugar-loaf Hill in sight. Number of icebergs between.
22	73 20 26	....	....	....	..	Variable.	2	32.7	34.4	30.26	o. m. c.	Made the land. Passed a number of bergs.
23	72 57 52	....	....	....	..	N.E.	1	38.6	36.3	30.25	c. m. b.	Working for Uppernavik.
24	....	....	....	....	..	Variable.	2	37.0	37.8	30.04	o. c.	Uppernavik in sight. Off Sanderson's Hope. Off Pröven.
25	....	....	....	....	..	N.	4	35.6	36.8	30.02	b. c.	Off southern point of Lawson Island. Swartehuck bore, by compass, S. by N.; Cranstown, S.S.E. Many bergs. Off the Omenak's Fiord. Haroë Island about eight miles distant.
26	69 30 35	....	....	....	..	N.	2	38.9	38.2	30.22	c.	Off Disco Island. Kanarsuck Point bore S.S.E. ½ E., by compass.
27	....	...	....	....	..	N.W. by N.	1	40.0	39.9	30.26	b. c. m.	Made the Whale-fish Islands. 12 fathoms water, sandy bottom. Hunde Islands on the starboard.
28	....	....	....	....	..	E.S.E.	3	47.5	37.0	30.08	b.	Came up to Egedesmunde. Four fathoms water.
29	....	....	....	...	.	N	3	43.1	37.5	29.61	b. c.	At anchor, Bunkë Islands.
30	68 04 26	....	....	....	..	S.	3	40.1	38.2	29.75	o. r. d.	A heavy swell from the W. (compass). Omanassuk bearing S.E. (mag.).
31	67 46 57	54 18 47 W.	....	....	..	W.S.W.	2	40.7	38.7	29.87	o. r. m.	Land in sight.
							2	+37.3	+36.7	30.08		Means.

HALF-MONTHLY ABSTRACTS OF THE LOG-BOOK OF THE UNITED STATES BRIG ADVANCE.

SEPTEMBER, 1851. BAFFIN'S BAY.

Date. 1851.	Latitude in at Noon.	Longitude in at Noon.	Variation observed.	Current, true Direction.	Drift in 24 Hours.	Mean true Direction of the Wind.	Force of the Wind.	Mean Temp. of the Air.	Mean Temp. of Surface of the Water.	Mean Height of the Barometer.	Sky and Weather.	Remarks.
	° ′ ″	° ′ ″	° ′									
1	67 00 06 N.	....	....	....	..	W.S.W.	2	+39.0	+38.6	29.96	b. m. c. r.	Made a low chain of islands. A heavy, irregular sea running. Standing in for anchorage at Holsteinberg.
2	66 56 00	53 30 43 W.	....	....	..	S. by E.	2	40.0	..	30.23	b. c.	At anchor, Holsteinberg. Several small auroras visible to the southward and eastward (true). Latitude of governor's house, 66° 55′ 55″.
3	66 56 00	53 30 43	....	....	..	Variable.	1	44.6	..	30.04	b. c.	At anchor, Holsteinberg.
4	66 56 00	53 30 43	....	....	..	W.	1	45.5	..	29.99	c.	At anchor, Holsteinberg.
5	66 56 00	53 30 43	....	....	..	W.	2	.	..	..	b. c.	At anchor, Holsteinberg.
6	....	....	....	....	..	N.N.E.	2	40.7	40.4	30.12	b.	At 3 P.M., Holsteinberg bore S.E. by E. $\frac{3}{4}$ E. by compass, distant about 16 miles. 11 P.M., aurora visible.
7	66 18 42	54 23 43	....	....	..	S.S.E.	2	37.8	39.5	29.97	c. o. r. s.	Land in sight.
8	66 03 21	53 47 00	....	Nd. and Ed.	..	W. by S.	1	39.5	39.4	29.99	b. c.	Land in sight. Cast of the lead, 45 fathoms. Before midnight several fine auroras visible; one, in the form of an arc, was constant; at times it contained all the colors of the rainbow.
9	65 16 48	53 44 00	....	Nd.	..	N. by W.	4	38.3	38.6	30.01	b. c. r.	1 A.M., auroras visible in different parts of the heavens. Nye Sukkertoppen distant 21 miles.
10	62 39 47	52 40 45	....	Nd. and Wd.	..	N. by W.	5	37.3	42.1	30.10	c. g. s.	Passed icebergs.
11	60 48 30	50 55 42	....	Nd. and. Ed.	..	N.W. by N.	4	39.1	41.7	30.22	c. s. g.	Large iceberg.
12	58 32 13	49 46 43	....	Sd. and Nd.	..	N.W. by W.	4	42.0	43.8	30.36	b. c. r.	Irregular tumbling sea. Entered the Atlantic homeward bound
							3	+40.3	+40.5	30.09		Means.

D.

HALF-MONTHLY ABSTRACT

of the mean Force of the Wind, the mean Temperature of the Air and Water, and the mean Height of the Barometer at the Level of the Sea.

Mean Latitude.	Month.	Force of the Wind.	Temperature of the Air.	Temp. of Surface of the Water.	Height of Barometer.
°	1850.				
49.4 N.	June.	4	+41.1	+40.6	29.95
65.8	"	3	39.2	36.9	29.77
73.1	July.	2	36.2	31.7	29.76
74.4	"	3	35.7	30.1	29.88
75.4	August.	2	35.8	32.4	29.99
75.2	"	4	34.2	31.6	29.97
74.8	September.	3	27.1	30.2	30.18
75.4	"	3	16.5	--	29.77
74.9	October.	3	6.9	--	30.13
74.8	"	2	— 2.8	--	30.18
74.7	November.	4	— 6.7	--	30.01
74.6	"	2	— 8.6	--	30.37
74.3	December.	3	—16.1	--	30.13
74.3	"	2	—13.5	--	29.98
	1851.				
73.8	January.	3	—16.6	--	29.76
73.3	"	3	—17.3	--	29.92
72.5	February.	2	—26.9	--	29.82
72.1	"	2	—32.2	--	30.38
71.7	March.	3	—22.7	--	29.98
71.0	"	4	—11.5	--	30.14
70.3	April.	2	+ 6.0	--	30.34
69.8	"	2	9.9	--	30.47
68.7	May.	3	16.0	--	30.36
67.2	"	3	24.2	--	30.11
66.8	June.	3	32.8	32.0	30.45
70.2	"	3	36.7	32.7	30.20
73.3	July.	2	38.3	32.6	30.22
73.8	"	3	36.4	31.5	30.22
74.7	August.	2	34.4	--	30.31
71.8	"	2	37.3	36.7	30.08
64.4	September.	3	40.3	40.5	30.09

E.

TABLE OF THE RELATIVE FREQUENCY OF THE WINDS

in each Month, on the Meridian of Baffin's Bay (during the Months of September, October, November, and December, on a more Western Meridian), showing the Number of Days on which each of the eight Winds blow.

Mean Latitude.	Mean Longitude.	Month.	Calm.	Variable.	N.	N.E.	E.	S.E.	S.	S.W.	W.	N.W.
°	°											
57 N.	54 W.	June, 1850.	1	..	3	1	6	3	4	5	3	4
74	58	July.	..	1	7	1	4	2	5	1	1	9
75	70	August.	..	5	4	5	5	3	3	1	1	4
75	93	September.	..	2	5	2	1	2	5	5	2	6
75	93	October.	2	..	14	5	2	..	2	3	..	3
75	93	November.	1	..	7	2	3	10	..	..	1	6
74	85	December.	3	3	2	2	1	1	1	5	8	5
73	75	Jan., 1851.	1	..	3	1	..	1	..	1	12	12
72	70	February.	..	3	2	3	3	3	..	2	6	6
71	66	March.	1	..	6	..	2	1	4	3	3	11
70	63	April.	2	2	4	2	..	6	5	4	1	4
68	62	May.	1	3	4	4	..	1	1	4	2	11
68	57	June.	..	2	4	2	5	2	2	5	4	4
73	56	July.	1	6	6	2	1	4	7	2	1	1
74	56	August.	..	4	5	3	3	2	5	..	3	6
For the fall months . . .		Sept. October Nov.	3	2	26	9	6	12	7	8	3	15
For the winter months .		Dec. Jan. Feb.	4	6	7	6	4	5	1	8	26	23
For the spring months .		March April May	4	5	14	6	2	8	10	11	6	26
For the summer months (mean of 1850 and '51)		June July August	1	9	16	8	11	7	12	7	7	14
For the year			12	22	63	29	23	32	30	34	42	78

From which it appears that N. and N.W. winds blow during five months of the year. During the other seven months the winds are equally frequent from each of the other quarters.

F.

Lecture on the Access to an Open Polar Sea in connection with the Search after Sir John Franklin and his Companions, read before the American Geographical and Statistical Society at its regular monthly meeting, by Dr. Kane, December 14, 1852.

The north pole, the remote northern extremity of our earth's axis of rotation, is regarded, even by geographers, with that mysterious awe which envelops the inaccessible and unknown.

It is shut out from us by an investing zone of ice ; and this barrier is so permanent, that successive explorers have traced its outline, like that of an ordinary sea-coast.

The early settlements of Iceland, and their extension to Greenland, as far back as 900 A.D., indicated a protruding tongue of ice from the unknown north, along the coast of Greenland. I must express a doubt if the early voyages of Cabot, and Frobisher, and the Cortereals did more than establish detached points of this line. The voyages, however, of the Basque and Biscayan fishermen, about 1575, to Cape Breton, made us aware of a similar ice-raft along the coasts of Labrador to the north ; and the commercial routes of the old Muscovy company, aided by the Dutch and English whalers, extended this across to Spitzbergen, and thence to the regions north of Archangel, in the Arctic Seas. The English navigators of the days of Elizabeth, the " notable worthys of the Northe Weste Passage," spoke of a similar ice-raft up Baffin's and Hudson's Bays, and the Russo-Siberians gave us vaguely a girding-line of ice, which protruded irregularly from the Asiatic and European coasts into the Polar Ocean. Lastly, Cook proved that the same barrier continued across Behring's Straits as high as 70° 44′ north.

From all this it appeared that the approaches to the pole were barricaded with solid ice. We owe to the march of modern discovery, especially stimulated by the search after its great pioneer, Sir John Franklin, our ability accurately to define nearly all the coasts of a great polar sea, if not to lay down the no less interesting coast of a grand continuous ice-border that encircles it.

It is worthy of remark, that this ice, although influenced by winds, currents, and deflecting land masses, retains through the corresponding period of each successive year a strikingly uniform outline.

During the winter and spring, from October to May, or eight months of the year, it may be found traveling down the coast of Labrador almost to Newfoundland, blockading the approaches into Hudson's Bay, and cementing into one great mass the numberless outlets which extend from it and Baffin's Bay to the unknown coasts of the north.

Influenced by the earth's rotation, this ice accumulates toward the westward, leaving an uncertain passage along the eastern waters of Baffin's Bay ; after which it resumes its march along the eastern coast of Greenland, shutting in that extensive region appropriated to the interesting legend, or that meteorological myth, as it has been designated by Humboldt, of " Lost Greenland." Its next course is to the northeast, sometimes enveloping Iceland ; and thence, extending to the east by Jan Meyen's Land and Spitzbergen, it crosses the meridian of Greenwich at some point between the latitudes of 70° and 73°.

I now call your attention to a remarkable feature in this great ice coast line. Upon reaching a longitude of about 70° east, it suddenly turns toward the north, forming a marked indentation as high as latitude 80° ; then, coming again to the southeast until it reaches Cherie Island, it continues on with a varying line to the unexplored regions north of Nova Zembla.

This indentation or sinuosity, best known as the old "Fishing Bight" of the Greenland Seas, is undoubtedly due to the thermal influences of the Gulf Stream. We know that the coasts of Nova Zembla feel the influences of its waters ; and Petermann, and many others, guided by the projected curves of Dove, suppose that its heated current is deflected by that peninsula, so as to impress the polar ice to a greater degree of northing than on any other part of our globe.

It would be important to the objects of my communication, that I should trace this ice throughout its entire extent ; but I have not the means of doing so with exactness. Barentz, in 1596, was arrested by ice in latitude 77° 25′, upon the meridian of 70° east. Pront-schitscheff met the same rebuff at the same height thirty degrees further west (100° east). Anjou, Matieuschin, and Wrangell found it in a varying belt along the Asiatic coast, at furthest but fifty miles in width.

The enterprise of our American whalers has also traced this ice across Behring's Straits, as high as latitude 72° 40′ ; and it is probable that Herald Island, in latitude 71° 17′, is a part of a great island chain, continued from Cape Yacan to Banks' Land and the Parry Islands ; an archipelago whose northern faces are yet unexplored, but which undoubtedly serves as a cluster of points of ice-cementation, and abounds more or less with polar ice at all seasons of the year.

We have now followed, throughout its entire circuit, this immense investing body. The circumpolar ice, as I will venture to name it, may be said to bound an imperfect circle of 6000 miles in circumference with a rude diameter of 2000 miles, and an area, if we admit its continuity to the pole, one third larger than the continent of Europe.

But theory has determined that this great surface is not continuous. It is an annulus, a ring surrounding an area of open water—the Polynya, or Iceless Sea.

Polynya is a Russian word, signifying an open space ; and it is used by the Siberians to indicate the occasional vacancies which occur in a frozen water surface. Although such a vacancy as applied to a polar sea is generally recognized to exist, it is right for me to state that this opinion is not based upon the results of exploration. It it due rather to the well-elaborated inductions of Sabine and Berghaus, and especially of our accomplished American hydrographer, Lieutenant Maury. The observations of Wrangell and Penny, and still more lately of Captain Inglefield, although strongly confirmatory, were limited to a range of vision in no instance exceeding fifty miles, and were subject to all the deceptions of distance. As, however, the arguments in favor of the existence of such a sea are of the highest interest to future geographical research, and, so far as I am aware, have never yet been grouped together, I shall take the liberty of presenting them to the society.

The North Polar Ocean is a great mediterranean, draining the northern slopes of three continents, and receiving the waters of an area of 3,751,270 square miles. Indeed, the river systems of the Arctic Sea exceed those of the Atlantic.

The influences of congelation too, aided by the diminished intensity and the withdrawal of the solar ray, increase the atmospheric precipitation, and probably diminish the compensating evaporation. Yet this position calls for further investigation to establish it absolutely; for recent experiments show that even in the dark hours of winter, and at temperatures of fifty degrees below zero, evaporation goes on at a rapid rate. That it holds, however, in general terms, is evident from the inferior specific gravity of the Arctic waters. They are less salt than those of more equatorial regions. Their average specific gravity (1.0265) indicates about 3.60 per cent. of saline matter.

The atmospheric precipitation extending to the adjacent land slopes, the melting of the snows and accumulated glacial material, and the floods of the great Siberian rivers, are sufficient to account for this.

With such sources of supply, it is evident that this surcharged basin must have an outlet, and its contents a movement independent of the laws of currents generally operative, which would determine them toward the equator.

The avenues of entrance to and egress from the polar basin are but three; Behring's Straits, the estuaries of Hudson's and Baffin's Bays, and the interval between Greenland and Norway, upon the Atlantic Ocean, known as the Greenland Sea. In Behring's Straits, it is probable, from imperfect observations, that the surface current sets during a large portion of the year from the Pacific into the Arctic Sea, with a velocity varying from one to two and a half knots an hour. Neither the soundings nor the diameter of this strait indicate any very large deep-sea discharge in the other direction.

The Gulf Stream, after dividing the Labrador current, has been traced by Professor Dove to the upper regions of Nova Zembla; so that Baffin's Bay, and the Hudson, and Greenland Seas, constitute the only uniform outlet to the polar basin.

It is by these avenues, then, that the enormous masses of floating ice, with the deeply-immersed bergs, and the still deeper belt of colder water, are conveyed outward. Underlying the Gulf Stream, whose waters it is estimated at least to equal in volume, the vast submerged icy river flows southward to the regions of the Caribbean. The recent labors of the United States Coast Survey and Nautical Observatory have, as the society is aware, developed and confirmed the previously-broached idea of a compensating system of polar and tropical currents; and we are prepared to consider these colder streams as equalizers to the heated areas of the tropical latitudes, and analogous in cause and effect to the recognized course of the atmospheric currents.

In fact, Dove, Berghaus, and Petermann, three authorities entitled to the highest respect, recognize for the Arctic Ocean a system of revolving currents, whose direction during summer is from north to south, and during winter the reverse, or from the south to the north. The isotherms of Lieutenant Maury (projected by Professor Flye) point clearly to the same interesting result. Contrasting these great movements of discharge and supply with the surface actions, we find during the summer months a movement along the northern coasts of Russia, clearly from east to west, from Nova Zembla westwardly and southwestwardly to Spitzbergen, where, after an obscure bifurcation, it is met by a great drift from the north, and carried along the coast of Greenland, in a large body known as the East Greenland current. The observations collected by Lieutenant Commanding De Haven show that this stream is deflected around

Cape Farewell, passing up the Greenland coast to latitude 74° 76′; where, after coming to the western side of the bay, it passes along the eastern coast of America, even to the Capes of Florida. During the winter, when the great rivers of Siberia and America lose their volume by the action of the frost, a current has been noted from the Faroe Islands, north and east, along the Asiatic coast, toward Behring's Straits. And then it is that the great surface ice, formed upon the coasts of Asia, gives place to a warmer stream, and the heated waters of the Gulf current bathe and temper the line of the Siberian coast.

All these facts go to prove that the polar basin is not only the seat of an active supply and discharge, but of an intestine circulation independent of either; while the intercommunication of the whales (*B. mysticetus*), between the Atlantic and Pacific, as shown by Maury, proves directly that the two oceans are united.

Admitting the important fact of a moving, open sea, the recognized equalization of temperatures attending upon large water masses follows of course. But is the Arctic Sea, in fact, an unvaried expanse of water? For if it be not, the excessive radiation and other disturbing influences of land upon general temperature are well known. It is, I think, an open sea. And an argument may be deduced for this belief from the icebergs. The iceberg is an offcast from the polar glacier, and needs land as an essential element in its production —as much so as a ship the dock-yard on which she is built, and from which she is launched. From the excessive submergence of these great detached masses, they may be taken as reliable indices of the deep-sea currents, while their size is such that they often reach the latitudes of the temperate zone before their dissolution. Now it is a remarkable fact that these huge ice hulks are confined to the Greenland, Spitzbergen, and Baffin Seas. Throughout the entire circuit of the Polar Ocean, almost seven thousand miles of circumscribing coast we have but forty degrees which is ever seen to abound in them.

A second argument, bearing upon this, is found in the fact that a large area of open water exists, between the months of June and October, in the upper parts of Baffin's Bay. This mediterranean Polynya is called by the whalers the North Water. After working through the clogging ice of the intermediate drift, you pass suddenly into an open sea, washing the most northern known shores of our continent, and covering an area of 90,000 square miles.

The iceless interval is evidently caused by the drift having traveled to the south without being re-enforced by fresh supplies of ice; and the latest explorations from the upper waters of this bay speak of avenues thirty-six miles wide extending to the north and east, and free.

The temperature of this water is sometimes 12° above the freezing point; and the open bays or sinuosities, which often indent the Spitzbergen ice as high as 81° north latitude, have been observed to give a sea-water temperature as high as 38° and 40°, while the atmosphere indicates but 16° above zero.

But, besides these, we have arguments growing out of the received theories of the distribution of temperature upon the surface of the earth.

The actual distribution of heat in this shut-out region can only be inferred.

The system of isothermals, projected by Humboldt upon positive data, ceased at 32°; and the views of Sir John Leslie (based upon Mayer's theorem), that the north pole was the coldest point in the Arctic regions, have, as the members are aware, since been disproved.

Sir David Brewster, by a combination of the observations of Scoresby, Gieseke, and Parry, determined the existence of two poles of cold, one for either hemisphere, and both holding a fixed relation to the magnetic poles. These two seats of maximum cold are situated respectively in Asia and America, in longitudes 100° west and 95° east, and *on the parallel* of 80°. They differ about five degrees in their mean annual temperature; the American, which is the lower, giving three degrees and a half below zero. The isothermals surround these two points, in a system of returning curves yet to be confirmed by observation; but the inference which I present to you, without comment or opinion, is, that to the north of 80°, and at any points intermediate between these American and Siberian centres of intensity, the climate must be milder, or, more properly speaking, the mean annual temperature must be more elevated.

Petermann, taking as a basis the data of Professor Dove, deduces a movable pole of cold, which in January is found in a line from Melville Island to the River Lena, and, gradually advancing with the season into the Atlantic Ocean, recedes with the fall and winter to its former position. Such a movement is clearly referable to the summer land currents with their freight of polar ice.

With the consolidation of winter, the ice recedes, and the Gulf Stream enters more perceptibly into the far north. The mean temperature of the northeast coast of Siberia is forty or fifty degrees colder than that of the western shores of Nova Zembla, while in July it is twenty degrees higher.

But if any point between 75° and 80° north latitude, a range sufficiently wide to include all the theories, be regarded as the seat of the greatest intensity of cold, we may, perhaps, infer the state of the Polar Sea from the known temperatures of other regions, equally distant with it from this supposed centre; though, as the lines of latitude do not correspond with those of temperature, this must be done with caution.

I have been interested for some time in examining this class of deflections; and I find that they point to some interesting conclusions as to the fluidity of the region about the pole, and its attendant mildness of weather.

Thus, for instance, at Cherie Island, surrounded by moving waters, but in a higher latitude than Melville Island, the seat of the greatest observed mean annual cold, the temperature was found so mild throughout the entire Arctic winter, that rain fell there upon Christmas-day.

Barentz, a most honest and reliable authority, speaks of the increasing warmth as he left the land to the north of 77°. The whalers north of Spitzbergen confirm the saying of the early Dutch, that the "Fisherman's Bight" is as pleasant as the sea of Amsterdam.

Egedesminde and Rittenback, two little Danish and Esquimaux settlements on the west coast of Greenland, in latitude 70°, with a climate influenced by adjacent land masses, but nevertheless not completely ice-bound, are in the isothermal curve (summer curve) of 50°, giving us a vegetation of coarse grasses, and a few crucifers.

In West Lapland, as high as 70°, barley has been, and I believe is still grown; though here is its highest northern limit. If 80° be our centre of maximum cold, the pole, at 90°, is at the same distance from it as this West Lapland limit of the growth of barley!

But there are other arguments based upon known facts, and facts popularly recognized, bearing upon the theory of an open sea:

THE MIGRATIONS OF ANIMAL LIFE. At the utmost limits of northern travel attained by man, hordes of animals of various kinds have been observed to be traveling still further.

The Arctic zone, though not rich in species, is teeming with individual life, and is the home of some of the most numerous families known to the naturalist. Among birds, the swimmers, drawing their subsistence from open water, are predominant; the great families of ducks, *Auks*, and procellarine birds (*Anatinæ*, *Alcinæ*, and *Procellarinæ*), throng the seas and passages of the far north, and even incubate in regions of unknown northernness. The eider duck has been traced to breeding grounds as high as 78° in Baffin's Bay, and in conjunction with the brent goose, seen by us in Wellington Channel, and the loon and little auk, pass in great flights to the northern waters beyond. The mammals of the sea—the huge cetacea, in the three great families, *Belinidæ*, *Delphinidæ*, and *Phocidæ*, represented by the whales, the narwhal and the seal, as well as that strange marine pachyderm, the tusky walrus, all pass in *schools* toward the northern waters. I have seen the white whale (*Delphinopterus beluga*) passing up Wellington Channel to the north for nearly four successive days, and that too while all around us was a sea of broken ice.

So with the quadrupeds of this region. The equatorial range of the polar bear (*U. maritimus*) is misconceived by our geographical zoologists. It is further to the north than we have yet reached; and this powerful beast informs us of the character of the accompanying life, upon which he preys.

The ruminating animals, whose food must be a vegetation, obey the same impulse or instinct of far northern travel. The reindeer (*Cervus tarandus*), although proved by my friend, Lieutenant M'Clintock, to winter sometimes in the Parry group, outside of the zone of woods, comes down from the north in herds as startling as those described by the Siberian travelers, a "moving forest of antlers."

The whalers of North Baffin's Bay, as high as 75°, shoot them in numbers, and the Esquimaux of Whale Sound, 77°, are clothed with their furs. Five thousand skins are sent to Denmark from Egedesminde and Holsteinberg alone.

Before passing from this branch of my subject, I must mention, also, that the POLAR DRIFT-ICE comes first from the north. The breaking up, the thaw of the ice-plain, does not commence in our so-called warmer south, but in regions to the north of those yet attained. Wrangell speaks of this on the Asiatic Seas, Parry above Spitzbergen; and my friend, Captain Penny, shrewd, bold, and adventurous, confirms it in his experience of Wellington Sound.

In addition to all this, we have the OBSERVATIONS OF ACTUAL TRAVEL; although this, confirmatory as it is, must, like the theoretical views, be received with caution. Barentz saw an opening water beyond the northernmost point of Europe; Anjou the same beyond the Siberian Bear Islands; and Wrangell, in a sledge journey from the mouth of the Kolyma, speaks of a "vast illimitable ocean," illimitable to mortal vision.

To penetrate this icy annulus, to make the "northwest passage" the northeast passage to reach the pole, have been favored dreams since the early days of ocean navigation. Yet up to this moment complete failure has attended every attempt. One voyager, William Scoresby, known to the scientific world for the range and exactness of his observation, passed beyond the latitude of 81° 30′. But after discarding the apocryphal voyages of the early Dutch, whose imperfect nautical observation rendered entirely unreliable their assertions of latitudes, we have the names of but two who may be said to have attained the parallel of 82°; Heindrich Hudson in 1607, and Edward Parry in our own times.

This latter navigator felt that the sea, ice-clogged with its floating masses, was not the element for successful travel, and with a daring unequaled, I think, in the history of personal enterprise, determined to cross the ice upon sledges. The spot he selected was north of Spitzbergen, a group of rocks called the Seven Islands, the most northern known land upon our globe. With indomitable resolution he gained within four hundred and thirty-five miles of his mysterious goal, and then, unable to stem the rapid drift to the southward, was forced to return.

But the question of access to the Arctic pole—the penetration to this open sea—is now brought again before us, not as in the days of Hudson, and Scoresby, and Parry, a curious problem for scientific inquiry, but as an object claiming philanthropic effort, and appealing thus to the sympathies of the whole civilized world—the rescue of Sir John Franklin and his followers.

The recent discoveries by the united squadrons of De Haven and Penny, of Franklin's first winter quarters at the mouth of Wellington Channel, aided by the complete proofs since obtained that he did not proceed to the east or west, render it beyond conjecture certain that he passed up Wellington Channel to the north.

Here we have lost him; and, save the lonely records upon the tomb-stones of his dead, for seven years he has been lost to the world. To assign his exact position is impossible: we only know that he has traveled up this land-locked channel, seeking the objects of his enterprise to the north and west. That some of his party are yet in existence, this is not the place to argue. Let the question rest upon the opinions of those who, having visited this region, are at least better qualified to judge of its resources than those who have formed their opinions by the fireside.

The journeys of Penny, Goodsir, Manson, and Sutherland have shown this tract to be a tortuous estuary, a highway for the polar ice-drift, and interspersed with islands as high as latitude 77°; beyond which they could not see. It is up this channel that the searching squadron of Sir Edward Belcher has now disappeared, followed by the anxious wishes of those who look to it as the final hope of rescue. I regret to say, that after considering carefully the prospects of this squadron, I have to confess that I am far from sanguine as to its success. It must be remembered that Wellington Channel is all that has just been stated, tortuous, studded with islands, and a thoroughfare for the northern ice; and the open water sighted by Captain Penny is not to be relied on, either as extending very far, or as more than temporarily unobstructed. If we look up from the highlands of Beechy Head, fifty miles of apparently open navigation is all that we can assert certainly to have been attained by the searching vessels, and to reach the present known limits of the sound would require a progress in a direct line on their part of at least one hundred and thirty miles.

They left, moreover, on the fifth of August; and early as this is there considered, and open as was the season, they have but forty days before winter cements the sea, or renders navigation impossible by clogging the running gear. By a fortunate concurrence of circumstances, the squadron of Sir Edward

Belcher may do every thing; but I must repeat that I am far from sanguine as to their success. The chances are against their reaching the open sea.

It is to announce, then, another plan of search that I am now before you; and as the access to the open sea forms its characteristic feature, I have given you the preceding outline of the physical characteristics of the region, in order to enable you to weigh properly its merits and demerits.

It is in recognition of the important office which American geographers may perform toward promoting its utility and success, that I have made the society the first recipient of the details and outlines of my plan.

Henry Grinnell, the first president and now a vice-president of this society, has done me the honor of placing his vessel, the Advance, at my disposition; and the Secretary of the Navy has assigned me to "special duty" for the conduct of the expedition.

My plan of search is based upon the probable extension of the land masses of Greenland to the far north—a view yet to be verified by travel, but sustained by the analogies of physical geography. Greenland, though looked upon by Giéseke as a congeries of islands cemented by interior glaciers, is, in fact, a peninsula, and follows in its formation the general laws which have been recognized since the days of Forster as belonging to peninsulas with a southern trend. Its abrupt, truncated termination at Staaten-Hook is as marked as that which is found at the Capes Good Hope and Horn of the two great continents, the Comorin of Peninsular India, Cape South East of Australia, or the Gibraltar of Southern Spain.

Analogies of general contour, which also liken it to southern peninsulas, are even more striking. The island groups, for instance, seen to the east of these southern points, answering to the Falkland Islands, Madagascar, Ceylon, New Zealand, the Bahamas of Florida, and the Balearics of the coast of Spain, are represented by Iceland off the coast of Greenland. It has been observed that all great peninsulas, too, have an excavation or bend inward on their western side, a "concave inflection" toward the interior. Thus, South America between Lima and Valdavia, Africa in the Gulf of Guinea, India in Cambaye, and Australia in the Bay of Nuyts, are followed by Greenland in the great excavation of Disco. Analogies of the same sort may offer when we consider those more important features of relief so popularly yet so profoundly treated by Professor Guyot.

Greenland is lined by a couple of lateral ranges, metamorphic in structure, and expanding in a double axis to the N.N.W. and N.N.E. They present striking resemblances to the Ghauts of India, being broken by the same great injections of green-stone, and walling in a plateau region where glacial accumulations correspond to those of the Hindostan plains.

The culmination of these peaks in series indicates strongly their extension to a region far to the north. Thus from the South Cape of Greenland to Disco Bay, in lat. 70°, the peaks vary in height from 800 to 3200 feet. Those of Pröven, lat. 71°, are 2300, and those observed by me in lat. 76° 10′, gave sextant altitudes of 1380 feet, with interior summits at least one third higher.

The same continued elevation is observed by the whalers as high as 77°, and Scoresby noted nearly corresponding elevations on the eastern coasts, in lat 73°. The coast seen by Inglefield, to the north of 78°, was high and commanding.

From these alternating altitudes, continued throughout a meridian line of nearly eleven hundred geographical miles, I infer that this chain follows the nearly universal law of a gradual subsidence, and that Greenland is continued further to the north than any other known land. In the old continents the land slopes toward the Arctic Sea; but although in the New World the descent of the land generally is to the east, the law of the gradual decline of meridional chains is universal.

Believing, then, in such an extension of Greenland, and feeling that the search for Sir John Franklin is best promoted by a course which will lead directly to the open sea—feeling, too, that the approximation of the meridians would make access to the west as easy from Northern Greenland as from Wellington Channel, and access to the east far more easy—feeling, too, that the highest protruding headland will be most likely to afford some trace of the lost party, I am led to propose and attempt this line of search.

Admitting such an extension of the land masses of Greenland to the north, we have the following inducements for exploration and research:

1. Terra firma as the basis of our operations, obviating the capricious character of ice travel.

2. A due northern line, which, throwing aside the influences of terrestrial radiation, would lead soonest to the open sea, should such exist.

3. The benefit of the fan-like abutment of land, on the north face of Greenland, to check the ice in the course of its southern or equatorial drift, thus obviating the great drawback of Parry in his attempts to reach the pole by the Spitzbergen Sea.

4. Animal life to sustain traveling parties.

5. The co-operation of the Esquimaux; settlements of these people having been found as high as Whale Sound, and probably extending still further along the coast.

The point I would endeavor to attain would be the highest attainable seats of Baffin's Bay, from the sound known as Smith's Sound, and advocated by Baron Wrangell as the most eligible site for reaching the north pole.

As a point of departure it is two hundred and twenty miles to the north of Beechy Island, the starting-point of Sir Edward Belcher, and seventy miles north of the utmost limits seen or recorded in Wellington Channel.

The party should consist of some thirty men, with a couple of launches, sledges, dogs, and gutta percha boats. The provisions to be pemmican, a preparation of dried meat, packed in cases impregnable to the assaults of the Polar bear.

We shall leave the United States in time to reach the bay at the earliest season of navigation. The brig furnished by Mr. Grinnell for this purpose is admirably strengthened and fully equipped to meet the peculiar trials of the service. After reaching the settlement of Uppernavik, we take in a supply of Esquimaux dogs, and a few picked men to take charge of the sledges.

We then enter the ice of Melville Bay, and, if successful in penetrating it, hasten to Smith's Sound, forcing our vessel to the utmost navigable point, and there securing her for the winter. The operations of search, however, are not to be suspended. Active exercise is the best safeguard against the scurvy; and although the darkness of winter will not be in our favor, I am convinced that, with the exception, perhaps, of the solstitial period of maximum obscurity, we can push forward our provision depôts by sledge and launch, and thus prepare for the final efforts of our search.

In this I am strengthened by the valuable opinion of my friend, Mr. Murdaugh, late the sailing-master of the Advance. He has advocated this very sound as a basis of land operations. And the recent journey of Mr. William Kennedy, commanding Lady Franklin's last expedition, shows that the fall and winter should no longer be regarded as lost months.

The sledges, which constitute so important a feature of our expedition, and upon which not only our success but our safety will depend, are to be constructed with extreme care. Each sledge will carry the blanket, bags, and furs of six men, together with a measured allowance of pemmican; a light tent of India-rubber cloth, of a new pattern, will be added; but for our nightly halt the main dependence will be the snow-house of the Esquimaux. It is almost incredible, in the face of what obstacles, to what extent, a well-organized sledge party can advance. The relative importance of every ounce of weight can be calculated, and the system of advanced depôts of provisions organized admirably.

Alcohol or tallow is the only fuel; and the entire cooking apparatus, which is more for thawing the snow for tea-water than for heating food, can be carried in a little bag. Lieutenant M'Clintock, of Commander Austin's expedition, traveled thus eight hundred miles—the collective journeys of the expedition equaled several thousand; and Baron Wrangell made by dogs 1533 miles in seventy-four days, and this over a fast-frozen ocean.

But the greatest sledge journey upon record is that of my friend, Mr. Kennedy, who accomplished nearly 1400 miles, most of it in mid-winter, without returning upon his track to avail himself of deposited provisions. His only food—and we may here learn the practical lesson of the traveler, to avoid unnecessary baggage—was pemmican, and his only shelter the *snow-house.*

It is my intention to cover each sledge with a gutta percha boat, a contrivance which the experience of the English has shown to be perfectly portable. Thus equipped, we follow the trend of the coast, seeking the *open sea.*

Once there, if such a reward awaits us, we launch our little boats, and, bidding God speed us, embark upon its waters.

THE END.

www.ingramcontent.com/pod-product-compliance
Lightning Source LLC
LaVergne TN
LVHW021230110826
845150LV00002B/295